PROMOTING
HEALTH
THROUGH
PUBLIC
POLICY

PROMOTING HEALTH THROUGH PUBLIC POLICY

Nancy Milio, Ph.D., R.N.

Professor of Nursing
School of Nursing
Professor of Health Administration
School of Public Health
University of North Carolina at Chapel Hill
Chapel Hill, North Carolina

 F. A. DAVIS COMPANY • Philadelphia

Printed in the United States of America

Library of Congress Cataloging in Publication Data

Milio, Nancy.
 Promoting health through public policy.

 Includes bibliographical references and index.
 1. Medical policy—United States. 2. Public health—United States. I. Title. [DNLM: 1. Health promotion—United States. 2. Health policy—United States. 3. Public policy—United States. 4. Public health administration—United States. WA 540 AA1 M5p] RA395.A3M474   362.1'068   80-25275
 ISBN 0-8036-6177-0

To Sam and Filomena Milio,
my parents

". . . The human soul, it seems to me,
orientates itself afresh every now
and then. It is doing so now. No
one can see it whole, therefore.
The best of us catch a glimpse of
a nose, a shoulder, something turning
away, always in movement. Still, it
seems better to me to catch this
glimpse, than to sit down . . . and
make large oil paintings of fabulous
fleshy monsters complete from top
to toe . . . Life has to be sloughed:
has to be faced: to be rejected;
then accepted on new terms with rapture.
    ". . . Are we not always
hoping? and though we fail every
time, surely we do not fail so
completely as we should have
failed if we were not in the
beginning, prepared to attack
the whole. One must renounce
[success, after the task] is
finished; but not before it is
begun."

Virginia Woolf, Letters: 1912–1922.
(Harcourt Brace Jovanovich, New York, 1978)

PREFACE

In the November chill a dusty back road in the rural South led into tobacco country. The glare of a setting sun outlined the sheds and their fuel tanks, characteristic of flue-cured tobacco farming. The old road, increasingly burdening the car with potholes, finally led to the Bowe farmstead.

At least six dogs, all bony and some pregnant, roamed among battered cars and equipment. There were a few chickens and dairy cows among the small corn and vegetable plots. To one side was a wood two-by-four shack, the family's home only four or five years ago. The new house was brick, and small, and financed by a Federal low-income housing loan.

Inside, Sada Bowe, black-skinned, was busy at the table in her plywood kitchen; it adjoined an uncarpeted living room. She was engaged with a white county agent discussing her debts. He quickly left and said he'd call again.

Sada Bowe was on her own. Her husband, Ben, had died suddenly last year. It was left to her to learn to farm tobacco. She'd always left those things to him.

The job of providing for the family was, of course, just an addition to her normal tasks of rearing 10 children, one of whom was adopted and autistic. As always, but now more so, the older ones helped the younger. And Sada helped the 4-H Club and the church, trying not to stop too long to appease her gnawing, arthritic joints.

Pausing in her too-busy afternoon, Sada Bowe described how she managed her farmstead. In the background beat the relentless yet encouraging sounds from her teens' rock band in practice. She told how tobacco grew from tiny, almost invisible seed into large green plants with their high-grade upstalk leaves and low-grade, low-priced downstalk leaves, thriving in sandy soil. She talked of the economics of growing; how each year the "government tells you" how much acreage you can plant in tobacco, or allow a renter to plant, in order to become eligible to receive the guaranteed base price, supported by government loans. She did not know how acreage limits were decided, nor the price, nor how tobacco producer associations collectively decided to accept or reject Federal price proposals and other subsidies. Sada was just "told" by government bureaucrats or by the tobacco growers' group, mostly by mail.

On that same afternoon, some miles distant in the state capital, attractive women representatives of a large cigarette manufacturer were repeating their daily tour talk. They described new product lines as luxurious, sexy, or masterful, noting that some of the gases "are believed to be harmful." They then guided visitors through the plant's highly automated production process, which could turn out 3600 cigarettes per machine per minute, with sufficient noise to make normal conversation inaudible. With that, visitors were escorted to the street door without opportunity for questions. . . .

The health problems posed by cigarette smoking and the economics of tobacco represent just one of several major dilemmas of health policy which have not yet been confronted clearly, fully, or openly by the health field or by Federal policy-makers. This book will attempt to face these dilemmas. It will offer an interpretation of the problem of making health in the United States. It will develop a perspective on what the health problem is. It will present a view of health policy as public policy that affects health and not just health services. And it will put forward an approach to policy-making that takes into account the analytic and political issues, as well as the unintended effects of policy. What would happen to Sada Bowe, for example, if current farm policies were altered in order to promote the health of Americans? What could be done so that her health and well-being are protected in the short term as prospects for health—hers and others'—improve for the longer term?

I have tried to provide a plausible view of today's health problem and a useable approach to coming to grips with it. My view is drawn from a broad array of analytic literature in the basic, clinical, economic, and social sciences of the health professions and other disciplines; from government statistical, and oversight reports, and from interpretations derived from my experiences in community health and community organization, research, education, and public health advocacy.

Because this book is an effort to develop a comprehensive perspective, it does not purport to provide final answers to the scope of questions it addresses. Indeed, given current knowledge, it cannot—now or in the foreseeable future. Not surprisingly, this will present problems to some readers. For some in the service professions it may seem too impersonal and abstract; for academics, not precise and qualified enough. For policy-makers it may not be pragmatic enough; for activists, not radical enough. For some of the reading public it may seem too laden with jargon; for methodologists, too light in terms of their particular analytic methods.

For readers who want more detail, I have consistently cited the sources on which my interpretations rest. In later chapters there is discussion of data problems. For those who prefer a general sense of the whole, I have constructed diagrams to illustrate the flow of my thinking and basic concepts.

My hope is that, whatever its limitations, this book may provide a common framework for various readerships, people who often are isolated from each other and the public because of the specialized languages and concepts of their fields. Perhaps this broad framework will contribute to their focus on, discussion of, and working at the immensely difficult problem of making health in this country.

Nancy Milio

ACKNOWLEDGMENTS

Just to list my colleagues in the health professions and social sciences who generously took time to read parts or all of several drafts of the manuscript of this book cannot indicate my gratitude nor what I learned from them. Yet this is the only way I can publicly acknowledge my debt. Though they may not agree with all of my conclusions, I extend sincere thanks to Ellen Alkon, M.D.; Patricia Z. Barry, Dr.P.H.; Jeanne Quint Benoliel, D.N.Sc.; Ann A. Bliss, R.N., M.S.W.; Henrik Blum, M.D., M.P.H.; Elaine Bursic, M.P.H.; Leslie A. Falk, M.D., M.P.H.; Loretta C. Ford, R.N., Ed.D.; Gail Gordon, Dr.P.H.; Jeoffrey Gordon, M.D., M.P.H.; Catherine A. Gutmann, R.N., M.P.H.; Ruth Hubbard, Ph.D.; Bernice Kaplan, Ph.D.; Alfred Katz, D.S.W.; Mary Ann Lewis, M.S.N.; Arden Miller, M.D., M.P.H.; Phyllis Moore, D.N.Sc.; Hal Morgenstern, Ph.D.; Nell Murphy, M.S.N., M.P.H.; Maria C. Phaneuf, R.N., M.P.H.; Harry Phillips, M.D., M.P.H.; Doris Roberts, Ph.D.; Eva Salber, D.P.H., M.D.; Cecil Sheps, M.D., M.P.H.; Barbara Thomas, Ph.D.; Harriet Tolpin, Ph.D.; and Elizabeth Tornquist, M.A.

Several colleagues, in critiquing the manuscript, went beyond what I could reasonably hope or expect. For their uncommon efforts I am most grateful to Dr. Mary Costanza of the University of Massachusetts Medical School; Mr. William Himelhoch, author and therapist, New York; Dr. Pat Duffy Hutcheon, consultant sociologist, Vancouver, Canada; Mr. Mark Kleiman, Executive Director of the Consumer Coalition for Health, Washington, D.C.; Dr. Ingeborg Mauksch, Professor of Nursing, Vanderbilt University; Dr. George Pickett, Director of the West Virginia Department of Health; and Sir Geoffrey Vickers, general systems analyst and consultant, Reading, England.

Others who gave generous assistance in the preparation of the manuscript are Sally Bostley, David Strogatz, Angela Hayes, and Karen Bauman.

My thanks go also to Dorothy Gamble, M.S.W., who introduced me to "Sada Bowe."

N.M.

CONTENTS

INTRODUCTION

1

HEALTH AND HEALTH-MAKING

Prospects for the health of Americans will be determined by public policy, by those decisions which shape contemporary environments in communities, workplaces, homes, and schools. Public policy sets parameters for the mode and character of industrial and agricultural production, corporate management, and individual behavior. By laying out the range of options from which organizations and individuals make their choices, thus formulating modern patterns of living, public policy is not only an influence on environment: it is an inextricable and critical part of today's and tomorrow's environment. As such it is a crucial variable for affecting the health of the population. However elusive it may be, in principle, at least, public policy is more amenable to change than "acts of God," other less predictable shapers of environment, or the human genetic pool. Public policy is therefore of major importance to those who are concerned about the health of current and future generations.

Health is not a "state" to be captured and dealt with; nor is it some achievement to be attained with finality. It is rather the response of people to their environments. It is a response that allows them to go about their daily activities without personal restrictions that can be prevented. To make informed judgments about what can be prevented requires an understanding of what other modern, affluent societies have been able to accomplish, as well as some social groups in this country, and an historical view of humankind.

Illness exists when people's responses occur in ways that keep them from pursuing their usual round of life. The precise point at which human responses become incapacitating and defined as "illness" depends on the perspective of the definer. To the individual, illness occurs when he or she feels unable to engage fully in normal activities: this is in fact the definition of a day of restricted activity, measured among Americans in the ongoing Health Interview Survey. To the medical practitioner, specific physical or biochemical signs usually must exist, quite apart from a patient's subjective symptoms, before a person is considered medically ill under a diagnostic class. From the viewpoints of the employee, supervisor, or economist, illness means the degree of restricted capacity that results in a day lost from work. To a parent it often means changes in a child's activity that might lead to problems if he or she were allowed to attend school. For an epidemiologist, an increase in rates of physician-reported diagnoses or of illnesses discovered by community surveys might mean illness in excess of what is normally found within comparable but more healthy populations.

From a policy perspective, complete consensus on the point at which human responses become incapacitating—when "health" becomes "illness"—is not necessary. What is essential is an understanding of the degree of freedom from disability that other populations have achieved, as well as the differences in disability which exist among segments of the U.S. population. The meaning of health for policy purposes must also encompass the viewpoints of the general public and of medical practitioners, employers, and social scientists. It must be applicable to the total population and its various segments. It must be measurable by indicators that make sense within the framework of daily living.

The health problem that challenges policy in the United States today is the unnecessarily large amount of several forms of illness which threaten people's capacity to live productive lives, especially those who belong to less advantaged subgroups of Americans, but other subgroups as well. Measured in days of restricted activity, or in other ways, much of this disability can be prevented—but not mainly by attacking each expression of illness as it occurs in each individual.

When health is viewed as an enabling response by people to their environments, the task for public policy becomes one of creating environments—all of which have biotic and constructed socioeconomic and interpersonal facets—that are likely to elicit health responses from most people most of the time. To be health-making, policy must place emphasis on enhancing people's health-building activities, not simply on repairing the health damage they incur from workplace, home, or community environments.

The practical consequences of health-making policy would show up even in currently used indicators of health status, in which health is inferred by the absence of illness. It is plausible to expect that most people, relying on their own subjective definitions of health, would report fewer days of restricted activity due to illness and impairment. Employers would see fewer days of work missed because of illness. Most important, the need for restricted living that results from chronic diseases in the middle decades of life would decrease, as would a large share of the acute illness that is incurred by people with chronic diseases. More healthful environments would also mean that healthier women would have fewer low-birth-weight infants. These babies would be less likely to have the severe acute illnesses of infancy and childhood. With less chronic disability in midlife, people would enter their later decades with more vitality. Overall the vital period of life would be extended. The dying phase would be shortened and less encumbered by pain, and rates of death for both infants and adults under age 65 would decline.

Living in environments that could bring about these improvements in the conventional indicators of health* would also mean that individuals would be better able to develop and pursue their personal views of "health." They would be free to set new spiritual, intellectual, and physical goals while exploring new avenues for human development.

The obligation of health policy, if it is to serve the health interests of the public, does not extend to assuring every individual the attainment of personally defined "health." In a democratic society that seeks at least internal equanimity, if not humaneness and social justice, the responsibility of government is to establish environments that make possible an attainable level of health for the total population. This responsibility includes the assurance of environmental circumstances that do not impose more risks to health for some segments of the population than for others, for such inequality of risk would doom some groups of people—regardless of their choice—to a reduction in opportunities to develop their capacities.

This nation does not have a health policy. It has, at best, a limited program for providing health services to a large proportion of Americans, one which is not able to grant sufficient access to services for those in greatest need of them. There is no statutorily mandated focus of responsibility for developing a policy that can actually improve the health status of Americans. The Department of Health and Human Services does not serve that purpose. There is no publicly accountable means to estimate the impact of public policy on the health of the public, and therefore little basis for planning or proposing national policy options that are likely to improve the health of Americans.

---

*For a discussion of the problems involved in measuring health, see Chapters 10 and 11.

Several propositions are put forward in this book. Stripped to their barest, they maintain that people's health is primarily the result of the environments in which they live and the patterns of behavior they follow. Those patterns are shaped by environments, and environments are shaped by public policy. Finally, public policy is shaped by the information that is available to the policy-makers as well as by the material interests of those who are organized to assert their claims.

The evidence from which these propositions are derived will be discussed in detail. The reader can then judge their plausibility.

Taken together they suggest, in ways that will be explored, the form that health-making policy could take in the United States. The scope of such policy would extend beyond the provision of health services to environments. Its strategic goal would be to assure that individuals and organizations have useable opportunities for making choices between health-promoting and health-damaging alternatives. The instruments to deploy this strategy would be the same accepted array of tools now used, the same ones that implement current policies which are shaping the environments, lifestyles, and health status of all Americans.

Policy decisions are constantly being made that affect the health of Americans in direct or subtle ways, through the ecology and the economy, through farm and factory production, distribution, and consumption. This process continues whether or not the effects are known, or, if known, are made explicit to policy-makers and the public. The health interests of Americans will be better served if the impacts of policies affecting health-important aspects of environments and patterns of living were assessed, and if health-making policy options were put forward for open consideration in the policy-making process.

The prospects for effectively meeting the problems involved in developing health-making policy depend ultimately upon the degree to which the public becomes involved in the process. Effective participation by the public depends on the extent to which people have better opportunities for organized action and access to other policy-influencing resources, such as the mass media. To effectively develop health-making policy, public policies must foster public interest advocacy to the same extent that they do for those groups who share an interest in the status quo.

The most important force that can help to shift the balance in policy-making in favor of the public and its health interests is the historic fact of this era: the scarcity and rising costs of many basic resources. This reality will require significant changes in American ways of thinking, and it can be a watershed that will cause Americans, through collective efforts, to move in a more health-making direction.

PART 1
THE ORIGINS OF HEALTH
AND ILLNESS

2

THE NATURE OF MODERN ILLNESS

Making health, as a policy goal, requires an interpretation of the nature of today's health problem. The typical approach, summarized below, focuses on quantifiable aspects of illness, including tabulations of the various forms of illness, implying that they are separate entities.

Another view of the health problem will be developed afterward. Its focus is on the interconnection between "causes" and illnesses and the ways they affect each other, as well as on the linkages among "causes" and among illnesses. All these ties suggest the plausibility of viewing today's health problem as a response to modern environments, and one therefore amenable to improvement through public policy measures.

CONVENTIONAL PARAMETERS

One way to portray the nature of the modern health problem is to describe it in numerical terms. It becomes a profile of acute and chronic conditions which typically occur in the course of a year and represent the total amount of known illness. Taking them together, it is possible to get a general sense of the overall burden of illness on Americans.

The incidence of acute conditions and the prevalence of chronic conditions occur within an average U.S. community population at a rate of about 3000 conditions for each 1000 persons. This includes illnesses for which people *do not* seek medical care. Two-thirds are acute conditions, more than half of which are common respiratory illnesses such as colds and influenza (Fig. 1).*

Just over 10 percent of all annually recorded illnesses are acute injuries, mainly cuts and bruises, sprains and strains. Another 10 percent are acute infections, among them the common childhood diseases; and the digestive disorders, which include dental caries. Childbearing and related conditions account for just over 0.5 percent of all health conditions reported annually.

All told, among every 1000 persons in an average community, two acute conditions per person and one chronic illness per person occur within a single year. As later discussion shows, however, health problems are never so evenly distributed.

Of the chronic conditions the most frequent are respiratory problems, primarily sinus trouble, asthma, and hay fever, followed by bronchitis. Next are the heart and circulatory illnesses, the most frequent of which are hypertension, rheumatic fever and other heart problems, hemorrhoids, and varicose veins. Coronary heart disease accounts for 0.5 percent of annual illness and represents less than a third of all forms of heart disease.

Another tenth of all illness consists of chronic muscle and bone problems, mainly arthritis and rheumatism, as well as skin problems such as corns, callouses, and eczema.

Chronic hormonal and nervous system problems make up about 5 percent of annual illness. These include diabetes, migraine headaches, paralyses, and hearing and vision disorders. If serious depressive disorders, schizophrenia, and alcohol and drug dependency are included, they add an estimated 1 percent to overall annual illness.

Still less common are chronic digestive problems, of which constipation and stomach ulcers are most frequent.

Finally, cancers account for 0.5 percent of yearly illness. The most common forms are breast, respiratory, colon, and uterine tumors.

Severity of Illness

Another dimension of the health problem is the seriousness of its impact on people's lives, measured in several ways. When death is the measure of severity, chronic illness takes on overwhelming prominence, with heart disease, cancer, and stroke accounting for more than 70 percent of annual deaths. Acute injuries and accidents, principally motor vehicle casualities, take another 5 percent of lives. Diabetes, chronic lung conditions, liver disorders, and perinatal illnesses each account for less than 2 percent of all deaths each year.

---

*For detail, see Tables 7 and 8 in the Appendix.

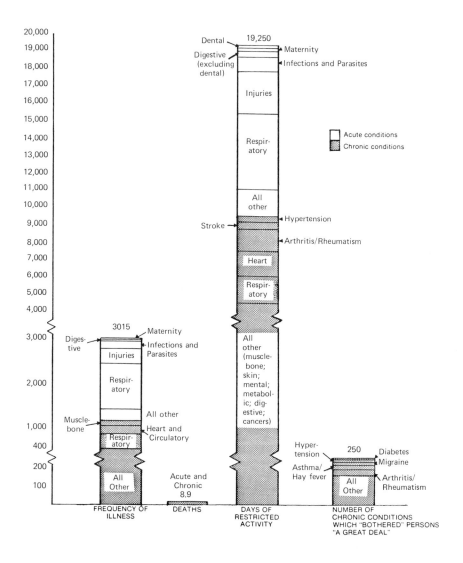

FIGURE 1. Profile of contemporary health and illness during one year, 1975. Rates of illness, death, disability, and bothersomeness are for each 1000 persons. (Adapted from data of the U.S. National Center for Health Statistics.)

11

Taken together, however, these deaths, while severe in their impact on specific individuals and their families, annually affect only eight or nine persons out of every 1000 in the "average" community. This is in stark contrast to the 3000 health problems just described, which affect the everyday lives of those 1000 people each year (see Fig. 1).

The picture of contemporary illness changes dramatically when the severity of health conditions is judged by how much they restrict people's activities. As a result of acute illnesses each year, a person experiences an average of 10 days of restricted activity, based on self-judgments of normal activity, and not necessarily implying loss of work or school. In addition, assuming that each person has one chronic condition, he or she will be restricted in performing usual tasks for almost 10 days per year.

The overall impact of the most common illnesses, spread across the population, is thus equivalent to about 19 days of restricted living for each person each year. This includes 5 days for each of two acute conditions and 9 days for one chronic condition, whether or not such illnesses are treated in a medical setting (see Fig. 1).

The most restricting types of conditions, quite in contrast to their frequency, are tuberculosis, cerebrovascular disease (stroke), chronic heart and lung disease, liver disorders, and arthritis, based on the average number of days that people are disabled for each condition. Among the least restricting are headaches, acute skin conditions, acute digestive problems, dental caries, acute bronchitis, common childhood infections, and maternity conditions. However, when all of these days of disability are taken together, the illnesses responsible for most of them—because they are so prevalent and disabling—are acute respiratory problems, injuries, and chronic lung and heart diseases (see Fig. 1).

Another measure of the seriousness of these disorders, beyond their impact on daily activity, is the way they are dealt with when brought into the medical care system. About two-thirds of the health problems experienced by an average person in an average year are brought to private physicians.[1] More than a fifth of these visits last 5 minutes or less, and half have no scheduled follow-up visit. Furthermore, physicians judge that over 80 percent of their office visits are either "not serious" or only "slightly serious."[2]

A final way to view health problems in numerical terms is to learn how sick people regard them. This information exists for the chronic illnesses. Again the picture which emerges is a striking contrast when compared with illness judged by the threat to life or by the opinions of medical practitioners.

More than 25 percent of chronic conditions "bother" Americans "a great deal," and one person in four experiences this degree of discomfort from chronic illness (see Fig. 1). The remaining 75 percent of chronic conditions are thought of as less bothersome or not troublesome at all. However, there is wide variation among specific conditions. The most bothersome are migraines, chronic lung conditions, stroke, and constipation. Least troublesome are hypertension, varicose veins, diabetes, and hernias. However, on an overall community basis, because the most bothersome conditions are not necessarily the most common, arthritis and asthma are the most prevalent of the very troubling illnesses (see Fig. 1).

All of these health problems, whether considered to be most or least bothersome, are among the more restricting chronic conditions. Yet the degree of personal concern that people express about them bears no relationship to whether they are life-threatening, as are asthma and diabetes, or susceptible of developing into a major disease, as is hypertension. In other words, the medical seriousness of an illness is not an indication of the degree of personal discomfort it may cause.

The composite numerical picture of modern illness which emerges here consists largely of relatively few conditions that are commonly recognizable. The impact of this overall profile on most people most of the time is far greater than that of illnesses which result in death among relatively few. It includes a good deal of restricted living and personal discomfort. However, when the health problem is viewed only through percentages, rates and ranks of commonness of occurrence, threat of death, and restrictions on activity, or by physician-judged seriousness or patient-judged bothersomeness, the results show quite different conditions taking first place. The shape of the problem is quite different when viewed through the survey data of planners, the impressions of practitioners, or the experiences of patients.

These contrasting, if not antithetical, perspectives alone do not offer much guidance in dealing with the problem of finding the ways that can bring greatest gains in contemporary health.[3] The use of such listings of illnesses and deaths encourages the use of traditional policy strategies which attack each condition separately, most often after the illness is manifest. A more comprehensive approach to the problem is necessary in order to provide policy guidance that can move beyond the often-repeated wish to promote health and prevent disease—one that recognizes the interconnections among health problems, their origins, and their consequences.

ANOTHER VIEW OF HEALTH

If disease-by-disease tabulations do not clearly point the way toward strategies for health improvement, there is another way of looking at the contemporary health problem. It encompasses the statistical picture just presented. Its focus, however, is on the *relationships* between the origins of

13

illness and the health of people. Recent evidence* has suggested the nature of these interconnections. *Different forms* of illness have *similar origins* in environments and patterns of personal behavior. Several *different sources* of origin may contribute to the *same form* of illness. *Environments,* as used here, include the biophysical, socioeconomic, and interpersonal dimensions experienced in the main contexts of living: at the workplace, in the home and community, and, for the fetus, in the womb. *Patterns of personal behavior* encompass the habits of routine, everyday living. They are initially discussed here as though they were separate from their environmental contexts, as often occurs in the behavioral literature. The interconnections between environments and behavior patterns will be developed in this chapter and suggested in later ones.

The degree of risk of experiencing illness depends not only on the health-damaging characteristics of one's environment, but also on the extent of exposure and one's current health status. Both the likelihood and severity of illness may be further influenced by whether risky circumstances and activities each *add* to the odds for illness, or whether they interact in ways that actually *multiply* the risks of becoming disabled.

Once illness becomes a fact in people's lives, it may itself become an origin of more illness. It may force changes in environments and activities in ways that increase the risks of illness. It may aggravate underlying illness. It may become complicated or extend into a fulminating and more severe form of response within the individual. Illness amplifies throughout the contexts of human lives. It reverberates with people's capacity to respond in healthful ways, the ways which preserve or enhance their ability to live productively.

Environmental Origins

The modern health problem, with its characteristic numerical contours, is by no means inevitable. It may be interpreted as a set of responses by modern populations to historically new circumstances. Populations that have continued to function within the older, traditional environments of more isolated and nonindustrialized regions have a different profile from that of urban industrial peoples.[4-7] Studies of these populations suggest that preindustrial peoples may have had fewer disabilities, although their average life-spans were shorter.[8,9] There is also evidence to suggest that physiologically normal blood pressure may be 100/60 as a lifetime constant, and not the modern average of 120/80 which rises with age. Blood cholesterol may be 100 to 140 mg. percent over a lifetime, rather than the 200 mg. percent or

---

*These findings are summarized in Table 1 in the Appendix.

more which rises with age in most modern populations.[10] These findings call into question whether in fact humankind can healthfully tolerate its new environments.[11-14]

The litany of potential health damage from modern environments is long and familiar. Pollutants in the air, including particulate matter, hydrocarbons from industry and automobiles, carbon monoxide from cigarette smoke and exhaust fumes, and plutonium from the nuclear power and defense industries, contribute directly to the risk of developing various forms of acute and chronic lung disease and lung cancer.[15,16] Air-suspended particles also appear to increase the risk of stomach cancer.[17]

These contaminants are even more concentrated at certain worksites, as are other health-damaging agents such as asbestos, pesticides and radiations, tars and oils, plastics, chemicals and metals, as well as some viruses and bacteria. These present increased risks of illness in the occupational groups exposed to them. In addition to lung problems, such environments may induce or promote cancers of the genitourinary tract and the liver, and may induce inflammations of the skin. Contaminated environments threaten the reproductive capacity of both men and women, and predispose to an increased risk of congenital defects in the unborn.[18]

Industrial and other pollutants, by processes which are unplanned or unaccountable, may also enter the biophysical environment of communities and so raise the risk of health damage to their populations. This may occur through seepage of toxic agents or carcinogens, such as some hydrocarbons into the drinking water, or by contamination of the food supply from fallout, which contributes to such conditions as lead poisoning in children.[19,20]

In addition, certain job-related activities create greater than average risks for accident and injury. These account for well over a third of all accidental injuries.[21] More subtle internal injuries can occur in the workplace from whole-body vibrations, and industrial noise can impair hearing.[22,23]

Rotating workshifts, when they occur more often than about once every 3 weeks, increase potential health-damaging responses as body rhythms become desynchronized in relation to daylight and darkness. This interferes with sleep and rest, and so impairs alertness and self-protection from accident. Abrupt alterations in working hours can upset hormonal and other balances, which can produce respiratory and digestive disorders, and alter the effectiveness of medically necessary drugs.

Another potential illness-inducing situation occurs when workload is increased, in amount, intensity, or responsibility, without compensating adjustments for the workers involved. In these circumstances coronary heart disease and heart attack become more likely.[25-28]

The biophysical environment of the home, its adequacy in space, water systems, temperature, and structure, can contribute to risks of accidental injury and some acute infections.[29] Moreover, interpersonal ties at home as well as in the workplace, if fraught with persistent conflict because of unsatisfying relationships, become implicated in illness, such as coronary heart problems and arthritis, and in serious accidents.[30]

Origins in Personal Behavior

People's sedentary work activities, on the job or at home, and their lack of vigorous exercise are also implicated in coronary heart disease.[31,32] Insufficient physical activity normally contributes to weight gain. Should individuals also overeat habitually, their chances for becoming obese (i.e., 20 percent beyond their statistically most healthful or "ideal" weight) inevitably increase. Obesity is basically the result of diets containing too many calories for one's size and activity.

OVERNUTRITION

High-caloric diets have become typical of Americans and contribute directly to several modern illnesses, including coronary heart disease, hypertension, stroke, arthritis and gout, and gallbladder disease. Overeating also contributes to toxemia of pregnancy and prolonged labor, with subsequent risks to both mother and infant.[33-36]

High-caloric diets usually are excessive in either fats or sugars, or both. Not only have Americans steadily increased their total dietary caloric intake, but they have also shifted their consumption of its component nutrients. The century-long trend, especially since 1960, has been to increase dietary beef and its fat, other cholesterol foods, sugars, and refined starches such as pastries and white breads. At the same time, Americans have eaten less whole grain and fibrous foods.[37,38] A half century ago, two thirds of people's carbohydrate came from starches, a large share of which were whole grains. By the mid-1970s, this pattern had reversed, and over half of carbohydrates now come from sugars.[39]

A related reversal, which has occurred only in the last two decades, is the shift from fresh to processed fruits and vegetables; over 55 percent are now eaten *after* processing. This further reduces dietary fiber and increases sodium content as well.[40] A serving of frozen or canned peas, for example, contains from 100 to 230 times the sodium of fresh peas.[41,42]

The list of other health consequences of this overall eating pattern is a long one. Fats, particularly saturated fats and cholesterol from the increasing use of beef, are implicated in coronary heart disease and in cancers of the breast and colon.[43-47] Diets high in sugars are also associated with these conditions and with diabetes, thromboses, gastric ulcers, certain infec-

16

tions, and dental caries.[48-51] Low-fiber diets may contribute to colon cancer and to varicosities, hemorrhoids, and constipation.[52-54] A third or more of the new cases and of deaths from cancer may be related to diet and nutrition.[55]

UNDERNUTRITION

Undereating, although not nearly as widespread in this country as overeating, has clearly important health-damaging effects. It is especially prevalent in low-income families with young children, childbearing women, and elders.[56] Increased risks of gastrointestinal and respiratory infections, and of adverse drug reactions in adults, may occur as a result of underweight and undernutrition.[57-59] Chronic undernutrition also dims a person's prospects for recovery from existing illness.[60] Children are likely to have more than the usual amount of acute illness and to be delayed in physical and intellectual growth.[61-64] Among pregnant women the consequences of undereating are damaging not only to women, through prenatal toxemia and postpartum infection and hemorrhage, but also to fetuses and infants. The unborn are at risk for congenital defects, low birth weight, infections, and perinatal death.[65-69]

The diets of infants, even in an affluent society, may be damaging to health. Possible contaminants range from pesticides, which can flow through mothers' breast milk, to lead contained in canned milk formula and originating from cow forage. All may produce toxic or cancerous effects in babies.[70]

In addition to such dietary patterns, which are among the most pervasive forms of personal behavior, other culturally endemic practices are implicated in important ways in the contemporary health problem.

ALCOHOL

Moderate or heavy alcohol drinking, not necessarily to the addictive levels of alcoholism, is associated with mouth and throat cancers, liver cirrhosis, adverse drug reactions and drug poisoning, and serious injury or death from automobile accidents, as well as homicide and suicide.[71-74] Alcohol use may also induce digestive disorders, problems with sugar metabolism, heart muscle damage, cardiovascular illness, and malnutrition.[75-78] During pregnancy, consumption of two or more drinks a day by women in the later trimesters is likely to result in lower newborn birth weight or even stillbirth; six or more drinks daily can produce brain and other malformations known as the fetal alcohol syndrome.[79,80]

CIGARETTES

Among the most discussed habits in recent years is smoking. The evidence clearly relates cigarette smoking to the most frequent and most serious of contemporary illnesses in adults, including acute bronchitis and influenza, chronic lung conditions, coronary heart disease and heart attack, stroke and cancers of the lung (perhaps up to 80 to 90 percent of these) and of the mouth, larynx, esophagus, and bladder; it contributes to the development of gastric ulcers as well.[81-83]

Although changing to filter cigarettes may reduce the risk of death from lung cancer, it appears to increase the risk of coronary heart disease.[84] *Reducing* the number of cigarettes smoked is not likely to lower the risks of premature death.[85] However, *cessation* of smoking does diminish death risk from heart and lung disease and cancer, and certainly reduces symptoms.[86-87]

Smoking during pregnancy slows fetal growth, resulting in lower birth weights, and increases the risk of perinatal deaths, especially from respiratory disorders.[88,89] Parents who smoke produce, in effect, an environment for their children which increases their risk of acute respiratory illnesses, including influenza, bronchitis, and pneumonia.[90]

OTHER DRUG HABITS

A relatively new and increasing pattern of personal behavior which contributes to modern illness is the use of prescribed and over-the-counter drugs as well as street drugs. Barbiturates and sedatives, tranquilizers, antidepressants, hallucinogens, and marijuana contribute to automobile accident injury and death.[91-94] In pregnant women these and other medications may produce congenital defects in the newborn.[95] Estrogens increase the risk of heart attack and uterine cancer in women, and DES, the antimiscarriage pill, has produced a precancerous condition, vaginal adenosis, in the daughters of DES mothers.[96] Oral contraceptives increase women's risk of death from heart attack, as well as the likelihood of stroke, gallbladder disease, and cancers of the uterus, vagina, and liver.[98-103] The use of medication to induce labor and childbirth adds to the chances of respiratory distress and subsequent risks for the newborn.[104,105]

Summary

The foregoing overview has described major health-important aspects of environments and activities implicated in the modern health problem. It shows not only that each implicating factor may contribute to several forms of illness (e.g., that smoking increases people's risks of acute and chronic lung diseases, cancers, and heart disease), but also that each form of illness may be related to several of these factors: throat cancer, for example, is associated not only with smoking, but also with alcoholic drinks and worksite pollutants. A closer reading of the evidence which follows suggests more complex dimensions of modern illness—more than the simple association between risk factors and diseases. It reveals how the impact on people's health is related both to the extent of their exposure to risks and to the combinations of risks they face.

Dose-Related and Cumulative Risks

Many of the most frequent and serious health problems are dose-related. They are either initiated or made more severe according to people's exposure to different amounts of toxic agents (see Table 1 in the Appendix). The chronic lung diseases, for example, develop and progress according to the size of the offending dose of air pollution, or of cigarette smoke, or both.[106-108] Similarly, lung cancer is dose-related to cigarette smoking: the heavier the smoker, the higher the risk of cancer. Liver cirrhosis is likewise related to the amount of alcohol consumed, and dental caries to the quantity of sugars eaten, especially sucrose.[109,110]

The most common acute conditions, respiratory illnesses in both adults and children, are responses to levels of air pollution, among other things.[111-113] The physiology of healthy people is disrupted, without development of illness, depending upon the amount of cigarette smoke and other pollutants in their environment, indoor or outdoor. Coughing, headache, eye and throat irritation, and a reduced capacity for physical exercise may result.[114-116]

A level of poor air quality which is mildly disruptive to healthy people has more detrimental effects on the ill, including exacerbation of heart and lung diseases, and even death. As the air further deteriorates, their illnesses become worse.[117] The effects on the weight of the growing fetus because of maternal smoking or alcohol consumption are also dose-related.[118,119]

An additional characteristic of many illnesses is their cumulative quality, in response to even a low dose of a toxic agent sustained over a period of time. Chronic obstructive lung disease, lung cancer, certain heart conditions, and hypertension are such responses to low levels of cigarette smoke and some air pollutants, among other toxic agents.[120-125] Moderate drinking of alcohol over a number of years increases risks of cancer of the throat and liver cirrhosis.[126] Some emotional disorders are also cumulative in nature.[127-129] Acute respiratory conditions become more prevalent in populations, especially among children, that have been exposed to air pollution for 3 or more years.[130] Years of industrial noise bring a cumulative loss of hearing in workers.[131]

Undernutrition, malnutrition, and obesity also may be thought of as the cumulative effect of diets which are insufficient, in whole or part, or excessive in amount.[132-138] Undernutrition has a further cumulative impact during pregnancy, especially in the later months, resulting in increased risk of illness and death for both mother and child.[140,141]

Incremental Illness: Additive and Multiplied Risks

The modern health problem also has important, although not well understood, incremental characteristics, apart from its dose-related and cumulative nature. The risk of incurring some forms of illness at the outset, or of experiencing them more severely, is greater under some circumstances independent of the extent of people's exposure to their origins.

LINKS WITH BIOPHYSICAL RISKS

The enlarged risk may be additive, the simple addition of two risks. Two such health risks, for example, are cotton dust and cigarette smoking. Occupational exposure to cotton textile dust increases workers' risk of chronic lung disease. People who smoke are at risk of lung disease. When textile workers smoke, their risk becomes greater than the risk incurred if they worked at a nonpolluted site or if they did not smoke. In other words, their risk of chronic lung disease is the sum of the two risks, cotton textile dust and smoking, each of which independently contributes to lung disease.[142,143]

Similarly, the chances of children having acute respiratory conditions as a result of their parents' smoking is increased if they *also* live in poorly ventilated surroundings.[144] Again, where some occupations, such as trucking, impose certain risks of injury and accident, there are added risks when truckers must also be cargo-handlers or work at an increased pace.[145,146]

In these situations the incremental chances for developing certain forms of illness are additive. In other circumstances, however, two risks combined may equal *more than* their sum. The increment is multiplicative, or synergistic, in its potential to evoke illness.

For example, two risks that increase the likelihood of people to develop acute respiratory infections are air pollution, an environmental risk, and chronic lung disease, an underlying illness and biological risk. People with chronic lung disease have a greater susceptibility to acute lung infections than others do. When they live in air-polluted areas, however, their risk becomes greater than that associated with chronic lung disease added to the risk of infection associated with air pollution which exists for the total population. Their risk is multiplied.[147-149]

Similarly, using air pollution and smoking as risk factors for chronic lung disease, the risk for smokers who breathe polluted air is greater than the combined risks of people who smoke but otherwise breathe clean air and of nonsmokers who breathe polluted air. The smokers' risk increases synergistically.[150]

20

LINKS WITH SOCIOECONOMIC RISKS

For purposes of designing health policy, some of the most important contexts that may be regarded as raising the risks of illness, sometimes additively and in some situations synergistically, concern socioeconomic conditions, and especially those pertaining to people with low incomes. Poorer people are at higher risk of virtually all acute and chronic illnesses. Low income can mean the absolute low levels resulting from low-paying jobs and chronic underemployment or unemployment, or the relatively lower income resulting from reduced disposable income that occurs when prices increase.

This point is illustrated at the broadest level of the national economy. Recession and an increase in joblessness sustained over a number of years predispose to a rise in average death rates, especially from cardiovascular and liver disease, suicide, and homicide. These deaths occur between 1 and 4 years after the beginning of the economic downturn.[151,152] For particular social groups, however, the impact on health is even greater and more damaging. Pregnant women in families whose income has dropped, and especially those whose income has declined from a previous low, incur increased risks of illness and death for themselves and their infants.[153,154] When disposable income drops among young adults, there are increased risks of alcohol-related problems, suicide, or homicide.[155]

On the other side of the economic coin, inflation, with or without recession, reduces the purchasing power of certain groups, such as elders whose average income is already low and whose risk for illness is already high. When their food buying capacity drops, they become even more likely to succumb, for example, to influenza and death.[156-158] At the same time, among those for whom inflation or economic growth has rather quickly and artificially increased their disposable income, or when the relative price of certain goods, such as alcohol, has dropped, there have been significant increases in auto accidents and cases of liver cirrhosis.[159,160]

There is a measurable illness response in the overall population to shifts in the national economy, as certain groups *temporarily* enter a lowered-income situation. The impact on health, however, is even more severe on those groups who are already at greater health risk because of their *long-term* low-income circumstances.

In a comparable way, the hazards to women and babies associated with pregnancy and infancy are greater when they occur in situations of inadequate income. Risks of illness and death related to maternal illness, high fertility, age, obstetrical history, and availability of health services increase at least additively for low-income pregnant women.[161-172]

In some circumstances, however, the risks are multiplied. Risks for stillbirth and perinatal death increase synergistically among women who bear their second or later child before age 18.[173] Moreover, any of these hazards, when combined with a pattern of maternal undereating, whether in terms of calories or protein, will cause the risk of infant death to rise synergistically.

Infancy itself represents a relatively high risk to life, but in the context of poverty that risk is multiplied. Infants at age 1 week to 12 months who were born with low birth weights (and who therefore had a higher death risk than normal-birth-weight babies) were compared with babies born with normal birth weights. Those who lived in low-income environments had an additive risk of death due to their low birth weight and family income. Those of *normal* birth weight had a *synergistically* higher risk than that incurred if their families were not poor. In other words, if their socioeconomic status had matched in "normality" the normal or average physiological status with which they entered the world, their risk of death would be very low. Poverty raised their vulnerability to illness and death more than infancy itself does among normal newborns.[174-176]

Although a small but measurable chance for child abuse exists among young families, this risk rises when their income is low and child care services are not available; when educational and training opportunities for the wage-earner do not exist, especially when the sole breadwinner is a woman; or when telephone communication is not available, as in some rural or low-income areas.[177-179]

A final example of the additive health impact of economic circumstances concerns stomach cancer. Although the risks for this disease among the general population are low and, in fact, decreasing, they are far higher among those of low income, and may be increasing. This may result from the living and working conditions of the poor, who live in more highly polluted surroundings where they are exposed to the air-suspended particulates thought to be implicated in this form of cancer. People who must live in polluted areas and in poverty face added risks of stomach cancer.[180]

Other categories of social status, often related to income, confer added risks for a wide range of chronic and acute disease and disability. These include blacks and Hispanics, young children, elders, divorced or separated persons, single males, and women with a powerless role in the household (see Tables 1 and 7 in the Appendix).

LINKS WITH HABITS

Personal behavior patterns can also bring incremental risk of illness (see Table 1). As a stark example there is a given risk of homicide in populations in which the possession of handguns is widespread. That risk is even greater in the vast majority of states without strict gun control laws.[181]

22

When youth and adults use such drugs as sedatives, tranquilizers, and marijuana, they increase their likelihood of having fatal accidents, especially in automobiles. These risks are additively increased when alcohol is also used.[182-185]

People with sedentary occupations show a greater than average chance of coronary heart disease and heart attack. Those who also fail to engage in vigorous exercise outside of their worklife have even higher risks.[186]

High salt content in people's customary eating patterns is associated with hypertension, stroke, and heart disease. Those who combine a salty diet with a high caloric intake heighten their risks even more.[187] Similarly, those whose eating pattern includes both high-caloric and high-fat foods have higher risks of such health-damaging responses as coronary heart disease, diabetes, arthritis and gout, and gallbladder disorders.[188,189] If these habits include, as is likely, high saturated fat and cholesterol components, and/or sugars, or if other patterns include smoking, physical inactivity, or some combination of these, coronary heart risk increases additively at least.[190-192]

For smokers, cigarette-related risks are additively higher if they also live in an air-polluted environment, regardless of their personality type, whether the presumably more aggressive "A" type or the more accepting "B."[193] Smokers who are also beefeaters and live in air-polluted areas have increased risk for cancers of the lung, digestive and genitourinary systems, and breast.[194] The use of alcohol among people who also smoke, overeat, and are relatively sedentary adds again to their risks for cardiovascular illness.[195,196]

Smokers face, as well, a number of risks which increase synergistically in some combinations. Their risks are already higher than nonsmokers for coronary heart disease, heart attack, acute respiratory illness, and lung cancer. These risks are *multiplied* if they are exposed at the worksite to such environmental contaminants as carbon monoxide, mine dust, or asbestos, or, in the case of heart disease, if they have hypertension or elevated blood cholesterol, each of which carries its own risk to health.[197,198]

Habits of cigarette smoking and alcoholic drinking each increase the risk of cancer of the mouth and throat, 150 percent and 160 percent respectively, over nonsmokers who are nondrinkers. Those who both smoke and drink have a risk that is higher than the simple addition of the cancer risks for each activity. It is 440 percent more, or 4.4 times that of the nonsmoking nondrinker.[199,200]

For alcoholics, patterns of eating low-protein foods, or of exposure to environmental or occupational cancer-causing agents, or drug use, bring at least additive risks for cancer, heart disease, and other problems.[201,202]

Among pregnant women, a combination of two dose-related factors, in-

23

creased air pollution and smoking—each of which can result in low-birth-weight babies—acts at least additively in raising these risks.[203] Health risks *multiply* for women who smoke *and* who use oral contraceptives. For them, the likelihood of death from heart attack is *more than* the combined risks of women who *either* smoke *or* use the pill.[204,205]

In all these instances, each pattern of behavior carries a risk for health damage. Among those who engage in two or more such activities customarily, the chances of illness rise incrementally, at least beyond the risk incurred from any one pattern, often as the sum of several risks, and sometimes in multiplier fashion.

LINKS WITH UNDERLYING ILLNESS

Modern health problems are incremental in still another sense. The onset or severity of illness, or both, often can be affected by the presence of underlying illnesses. These may be past and cured or current, known or unknown, with or without symptoms, or still confined to their genetic potential. In other words, prior or inborn predisposition to illness potentiates the health-damaging impact of biophysical, social, and economic conditions, and the personal habits which in themselves raise the risks for disease and death.

Coronary heart disease and heart attack, for example, are a clear risk among groups who follow the dietary, smoking, drinking, exercise, residential, and occupational patterns discussed earlier. In those who *have already* developed hypertension or diabetes, elevated blood cholesterol, or low glucose tolerance, the coronary risks are higher still.[206-215] While the risk of chronic lung disease is higher among smokers and is related to the amount they smoke as well as how long they have smoked, their risk is increased further if they have heart disease, asthma, or pneumonia.[216-218] The likelihood and severity are enlarged further among those few who have a familial tendency for chronic lung disease, and among the far greater number of people who have low incomes.[219] Persistent environmental noise is likely to raise the normal blood pressure of all persons so exposed. However, among those who already have hypertension, their condition becomes worse.[220]

In a roughly comparable way, the socioeconomic circumstances of persons with cancer affect their chances for survival. The poor, even when they are at the same stage of illness as others, and even if they receive treatment of similar quality, are less likely to survive, *especially* when they have the most treatable forms of cancer. In other words, when their prognosis under medical treatment is theoretically best, the past circumstances of the sick poor allow them to respond less fully to medical support than

24

more advantaged people. The risks imposed by poverty become even greater than those imposed by cancer.[221,222]

These incremental risks pertain especially, but not exclusively, to men. There are others peculiar to women. Women who use oral contraceptives, for example, face low but measurable risks of heart attack, stroke, or gallbladder disease, but their risks rise at least additively when they have hypertension, diabetes, or elevated blood cholesterol.[223]

While pregnant women's risks for low-birth-weight babies and death, as well as for maternal cancers, increase when they smoke cigarettes, the chances increase further when they are *also* acutely or chronically ill, or have had previous obstetrical problems.[224,225] Occupational hazards which make cancers or fetal defects more likely become potentially *more* damaging among diabetic pregnant women.[226] Although undereating during pregnancy increases the likelihood of maternal illness and major birth defects for all women, the presence of hypertension, diabetes, or other major illness in such women brings added risk. Further increments occur among those who are also short in stature, who have had a low weight prior to pregnancy, who smoke, who are having their first child, or who are without health care.[227,228] Risks to the unborn from maternal drug or alcohol addiction are additive when pregnant women *also* have prenatal or previous obstetrical problems, cesarean section, or chronic or neuropsychiatric illnesses.[229]

Mutual-Causal Reverberations

While ordinary, everyday activities and environments are directly linked to the modern illness profile, their effects may often compound health damage through dose or intensity, and accumulate over time. They may act additively and sometimes synergistically with one or more habit or circumstance, or with people's underlying illness, in various combinations, raising the risks of illness among segments of the population. The net effect is to overpower people's capacity to continue their normal round of life.

LINKAGES AMONG ILLNESSES

Once having developed a degree of disability, the ill are more likely than others to become more ill. This can happen in several ways. Iatrogenic complications, those resulting from treatment itself, may occur. These include drug reactions, infections resulting from surgery or hospitalization, or delayed healing in response to a noisy hospital environment.[230-234]

Debilitating diseases may make patients vulnerable to otherwise relatively harmless microorganisms and subsequent infections, or may increase the severity of less serious problems.[235-238] Certain modern health problems appear to cluster in their occurrence when surveyed in populations. Those who have had a stroke, for example, are more likely than others to have ischemic heart disease or hypertension, peripheral vascular disease, diabetes, heart attack, gastric ulcer, and osteoarthritis.[239,240] People with hypertension are more likely to have coronary heart disease;[241-243] those with arteriosclerotic heart disease to have cancer of the colon;[244] and those with gastric ulcers are more likely to have diabetes and coronary thromboses. Again, persons with heart disease, diabetes, or stroke are more likely to have one of the other two conditions than persons who have none of them.[245] The chronically ill are not only more likely to have more than one chronic illness, but also to have almost 25 percent more acute illness than those who are free from chronic disease.[246,247]

Mental and physical forms of illness are linked with each other in several ways, further illustrating the interconnections among people's health problems. Those who have *either* emotional or physical illness are also more likely than others to have *both* kinds of problems.[248] When certain *similar* circumstances produce illness, the manifestations may be predominantly *either* emotional *or* physical.[249,250] Furthermore, the most pervasive characteristic—common to all forms of illness and regardless of culture or region—is anxiety, a normal, potentially beneficial emotional response to uncertainty.[251,252] Taken to an extreme, however, anxiety can bring health-damaging forms of behavior, and if prolonged, may result in physical disorders[253] (see Chapter 3).

ILLNESS AND ITS ENVIRONMENTAL EFFECTS

These reverberating ties among forms of illness suggest that they are linked through common processes, both physiological and socioenvironmental. The entire interacting network affects people's health, the capacity which increases or decreases their chances for living unnecessarily restricted lives.

Poor health, for example, is the major reason for middle-aged men and women to permanently leave the labor force, and for women it is also a deterrent from ever entering the work force. As a result, their incomes become significantly lowered, with up to one in five of these people spending less than they need to maintain a minimally adequate diet. This is especially so for blacks and women.[254-256] Other adults, regardless of age, who have a long-term disability resulting from impairment or other illness, are not only in poorer health and have lower incomes, but these very circumstances place strains on their family and social life, and result in higher rates of separation and divorce.[257-259]

In addition to the pain from broken personal ties, the disabled face dimmer prospects for health. Lower income, less adequate food, and loss of

26

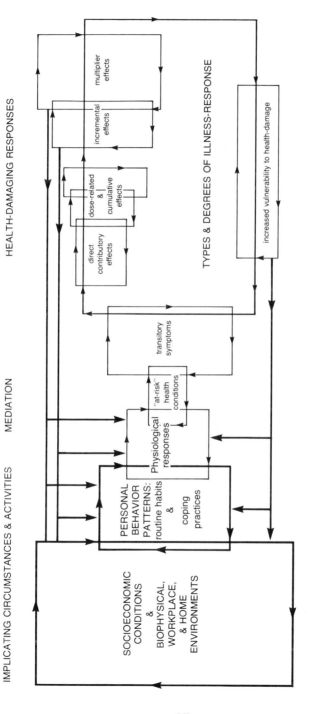

IMPLICATING CIRCUMSTANCES & ACTIVITIES   MEDIATION   HEALTH-DAMAGING RESPONSES

FIGURE 2. Mutual-causal interconnections in contemporary health and illness.

physical and psychological support from family raise their risks for more chronic and acute illness. In effect, as their social and economic conditions change, and as a result, their patterns of personal behavior, their chances for developing new, or more severe, illness also increase (Fig. 2). Health problems have changed their circumstances, placing them in the category of low-income persons or others who are at higher risk of illness: those who must live in poor, hazardous areas, or who have limited food budgets and little discretionary income for recreational activities.

Illness reverberates through lives and livelihoods, affecting circumstances which may in turn make for more illness, if something does not intervene. In a more general sense, peoples' illnesses, as a response to their environments, interact or reverberate with the causal sources of illness, and so may feed back into still more risks to health and life (see Fig. 2). "Cause" and "effect" thus merge: the origins of people's capacity to respond to their world, either in health-building or in incapacitating ways, and the *responses* themselves (i.e., "health" or "illness") are mutually causal. Health and illness, as a spectrum of human response, have a mutually causal relationship with people's environments.

Before addressing the policy implications of this interpretation of modern illness, a fuller picture of the problem will be developed by exploring it next within the more intimate, interpersonal context of people's lives and within the human physiological medium.

REFERENCES

1. Milio, N.: *The team delivery of primary care: a comparative analysis of policy approaches to health improvement using available (National Center for Health Statistics) data,* in *Proceedings, Policy Issues in Primary Health Care.* DHEW Health Planners Region VII (University of Iowa Health Services Research Center, 1978).
2. National Center for Health Statistics: *National Ambulatory Medical Care Survey May 1973–April 1974.* Rockville, Md., 1975.
3. White, K.: *Contemporary epidemiology.* Am. J. Epidemiol. 3(4):295–303, 1974.
4. Vallin, J.: *World trends in infant mortality since 1950.* World Health Statistics Rep. 29:646–674, 1976.
5. Puffer, R. R., and Serrano, C. V.: *Patterns of Childhood Mortality Inter-American Investigation of Mortality in Childhood.* Pan American Health Organization, Washington, D.C., 1973.
6. Winikoff, B.: *Nutrition, population and health: some implications for policy.* Science 200:895–902, 1978.
7. Stein, Z., et al.: *Famine and human development: the Dutch hunger winter of 1944/45.* Oxford University Press, New York, 1975.
8. Powles, J.: *On the limitations of modern medicine.* Sci. Med. Man 1:1–30, 1973.
9. Vogel, V.: *American Indian Medicine.* Ballantine, New York, 1970.

10. National Center for Health Statistics: *A comparison of levels of serum cholesterol of adults 18–74 years of age in the United States in 1960–62 and 1971–74.* Adv. Data, vol. 5, February 22, 1977.
11. Wynder, E.: *Personal habits.* Bull. N.Y. Acad. Med. 54(4):397–412, 1978.
12. Eyer, J.: *Hypertension as a disease of modern society.* Int. J. Health Serv. 5:539–558, 1975.
13. Powles, op. cit.
14. Glueck, C. J., et al.: *Diet and coronary heart disease: another view.* N. Engl. J. Med. 298(26):1471–1474, 1978.
15. Environmental Protection Agency: *Health Consequences of Sulfur Oxides: A Report from CHESS (Community Health and Environmental Surveillance System), 1970–1971.* Research Triangle Park, N.C., 1974.
16. Gofman, J.: *The plutonium controversy.* J.A.M.A. 236:284–286, 1976.
17. Winkelstein, W.: *Contemporary perspectives on prevention.* Bull. N.Y. Acad. Med. 51(1):27–38, 1975.
18. National Heart, Lung and Blood Institute: *Respiratory Diseases, Task Force Report on Prevention, Control, and Education.* Washington, D.C., March 1977.
19. Kraybill, H.: *Carcinogenesis induced by trace contaminants in potable water.* Bull N.Y. Acad. Med. 54(4): 413–427, 1978.
20. *Oversight of Biomedical and Behavioral Research in the U.S., 1977.* Hearings before the Subcommittee on Health and Scientific Research of the Committee on Human Resources, U.S. Senate, 95th Congress, Part II, June 8, 10, 1977.
21. Krute, A., and Burdette, M.: *Disability survey.* Soc. Sec. Bull. 41(4):3–17, 1978.
22. Key, M., et al.: *Occupational Diseases: A Guide to Their Recognition.* National Institute for Occupational Safety and Health, Cincinnati, June 1977.
23. Jonsson, A., and Hansson, L.: *Prolonged exposure to a stressful stimulus (noise) as a cause of raised blood pressure in man.* Lancet, January 8, 1977, pp. 86–87.
24. Winget, C. M., Hughes, L., and LaDou, J.: *Physiological effects of rotational work shifting: a review.* J. Occup. Med. 20(3):204–210, 1978.
25. House, J.: *Occupational stress and coronary heart disease: a review and theoretical integration.* J. Health Soc. Behav. 15:12–27, 1974.
26. Theorell, T., and Floderus-Myrhed, B.: *Workload and risk of myocardial infarction—a prospective psychosocial analysis.* Int. J. Epidemiol. 6:17–21, 1977.
27. Cooper, C. L., and Crump, J.: *Prevention and coping with occupational stress.* J. Occup. Med. 20:420–426, 1978.
28. Haynes, S. G., et al.: *The relationship of psychosocial factors to coronary heart disease in the Framingham Study. Part II. Prevalence of coronary heart disease.* Am. J. Epidemiol. 197:384–400, 1978.
29. Loring, W., and Hinkle, L.: *The Effect of the Man-Made Environment on Health and Behavior.* Center for Disease Control, Atlanta, 1977.
30. Theorell and Floderus-Myrhed, op. cit.
31. Schettler, G.: *Risk factors of coronary heart disease: West German data.* Prev. Med. 5:216–225, 1976.
32. Morris, J.: *Primary prevention of heart attack. Bull. N.Y. Acad. Med.* 51(1):62–74, 1975.
33. Olefsky, J., et al.: *Effects of weight reduction on obesity.* Clin. Invest. 53:64–67, 1974.
34. Gordon, T., and Kannel, W.: *Effects of overweight on cardiovascular diseases.* Gerontology 28:80–88, 1973.

35. *Prevalence and natural history of obesity in the United Kingdom,* in *Research on Obesity.* Department of Health and Social Security, London, 1976.
36. U.S. Senate Select Committee on Nutrition and Human Needs: *Diet Related to Killer Diseases. Obesity Hearings II.* Washington, D.C., February 1,2, 1977.
37. Newberne, P.: *Diet and nutrition.* Bull. N.Y. Acad. Med. 54(4):385–396, 1978.
38. Economic Research Service: *Food Changes in the United States.* Washington, D.C., 1974.
39. Ibid.
40. Ibid.
41. Senate Select Committee, op. cit.
42. Smith, W.: *Epidemiology of hypertension.* Med. Clin. North Am. 61:467–486, 1977.
43. Stamler, J., et al.: *Risk factors and the etiopathogenesis of atherosclerotic diseases.* Am. Assoc. Pathol. Bacteriol. 62(2):A100–153, 1971.
44. U.S. Senate Select Committee on Nutrition and Human Needs: *Dietary Goals for the U.S.* Washington, D.C., 1977.
45. Kneese, A., and Schulze, W.: *Environmental problems: environment, health and economics—the case of cancer.* Am. Econ. Rev. 67(1):326–332, 1977.
46. Howell, M.: *Diet as an Etiological Factor in the Development of Cancers of Colon and Rectum.* J. Chron. Dis. 28:67–80, 1975.
47. Joosens, J.: *Patterns of food and mortality in Belgium.* Lancet 50:1069–1072, 1977.
48. Stamler, et al., op. cit.
49. Cleave, T.: *Over-consumption.* Public Health 91(3):127–131, 1977.
50. U.S. Senate Select Committee on Nutrition and Human Needs: *Nutrition and Diseases: 1973 Hearings, Part II.* Washington, D.C., April 30–May 2, 1973.
51. Hood, L. F., et al.: *Carbohydrates and Health.* AVI Publishing Company, Westport, Conn., 1976.
52. Senate Select Committee, 1/1977, op. cit.
53. Hood et al., op. cit.
54. Newberne, op. cit.
55. Ibid.
56. National Center for Health Statistics: *Dietary Intake of Persons 1–74 Years of Age in the United States.* Adv. Data, vol. 6, March 2, 1977.
57. *Clinical and Subclinical Malnutrition, Their Influence on the Capacity to Do Work.* Progress Report, 1971/75, Medical College of Wisconsin Research Service, Milwaukee, 1975.
58. Scrimshaw, N. S.: *Nutrition and the Health of Nations.* Occasional Papers Series, Vol. I, No. 11. Institute of Nutrition, University of North Carolina, Chapel Hill, February 1978.
59. Basu, T.: *Interaction of drugs and nutrition.* J. Hum. Nutrition 31:449–458, 1977.
60. Berg, J. W., et al.: *Economic status and survival of cancer patients.* Cancer 39:467–477, 1977.
61. Owen, G., and Lippman, G.: *Nutritional status of infants and young children: U.S.A.* Pediatr. Clin. North Am. 24:211–227, 1977.
62. Freeman, H., et al.: *Relations between nutrition and cognition in rural Guatemala.* Am. J. Public Health 67:233–239, 1977.
63. Dahlman, N., et al.: *Influences of environmental conditions during infancy on final body stature.* Pediatr. Res. 11:695–700, 1977.
64. International Union of Nutritional Sciences: *Report: guidelines on the atrisk*

concept and the health and nutrition of young children. Am. J. Clin. Nutrition 30:242–254, 1977.

65. Slocumb, J., and Junitz, S.: *Factors affecting maternal mortality and morbidity among American Indians.* Public Health Rep. 92:349–356, 1977.

66. Naeye, R., et al.: *Relation of poverty and race to birth weight and organ and cell structure in the newborn.* Pediatr. Res. 5:17–22, 1971.

67. Higgins, A.: *Nutrition status and the outcome of pregnancy.* J. Can. Diet Assoc. 37(1):17–35, 1976.

68. Sinclair, J., and Saigal, S.: *Nutritional influences in industrial societies.* Am. J. Dis. Child 129:549–553, 1975.

69. Brown, R.: *Interaction of nutrition and infection in clinical practice.* Pediatr. Clin. North Am. 24:241–251, 1977.

70. *Oversight of Biomedical and Behavioral Research in the U.S., 1977.* Hearings before the Subcommittee on Health and Scientific Research of the Committee on Human Resources, U.S. Senate, 95th Congress, Part II, June 8, 10, 1977.

71. Lieber, C. S.: *The metabolic basis of alcohol's toxicity.* Hosp. Prac., February 1977, pp. 73–80.

72. Alcohol, Drug Abuse and Mental Health Administration: *Alcohol and Health—June 1974.* National Institute on Alcohol Abuse and Alcoholism, Washington, D.C., 1974.

73. *Summary Proceedings: Tripartite Conference on Prevention.* Alcohol, Drug Abuse and Mental Health Administration, Washington, D.C., 1977.

74. Pradhan, S. N.: *Drug Abuse, Clinical and Basic Aspects.* C. V. Mosby, St. Louis, 1977, pp. 11–83.

75. Lieber, op. cit.

76. DeLint, J., and Schmidt, W.: *Alcoholism and Mortality.* Addiction Research Foundation, Toronto, 1974.

77. Turner, T., et al.: *Measurement of alcohol-related effects in man: chronic effects in relation to levels of alcohol consumption.* Johns Hopkins Med. J. 141:239, 1977.

78. Gyntelberg, F., and Meyer, J.: *Relationship Between Blood Pressure and Physical Fitness, Smoking and Alcohol Consumption.* Acta Med. Scand. 195(5):375–380, 1974.

79. Little, R.: *Moderate alcohol use during pregnancy and decreased infant birth weight.* Am. J. Public Health 67(12):1154–1156, 1977.

80. Clarren, S., and Smith, D.: *The fetal alcohol syndrome.* N. Engl. J. Med. 298(19):1063–1067, 1978.

81. *The effects of smoking on health.* Morbidity and Mortality Weekly Report 26(18), May 6, 1977.

82. National Heart, Lung and Blood Institute: *Respiratory Diseases, Task Force Report on Prevention, Control and Education.* Washington, D.C., March, 1977.

83. Wynder, op. cit.

84. Wald, N.: *Mortality for lung cancer and coronary heart disease in relation to changes in smoking habits.* Lancet, January 17, 1976, pp. 136–138.

85. Huhti, E., et al.: *Chronic respiratory disease, smoking and prognosis for life—an epidemiological study.* Scand. J. Resp. Dis. 58(3):170–180, 1977.

86. Center for Disease Control: *The Health Consequences of Smoking—A Reference Edition: Selected Chapters from 1971 through 1975; Reports with Cumulative Index for All Reports, 1964–1975.* Atlanta, 1976.

87. Leeder, S., et al.: *Change in respiratory symptom prevalence in adults who*

31

alter their smoking habits. Am. J. Epidemiol. 195:522–529, 1977.
88. Center for Disease Control, 1976, op. cit.
89. Holsclaw, D. S., Jr., and Topham, A. L.: *The effects of smoking on fetal, neonatal and childhood development.* Pediatr. Ann. 7(3):105–136, 1978.
90. Center for Disease Control: *Health Consequences of Smoking, 1975.* Atlanta, 1975.
91. Austin, G. A., et al. (eds.): *Drug Users and Driving Behaviors.* National Institute on Drug Abuse, Rockville, Md., 1977.
92. Sharma, S.: *Barbiturates and driving.* Accident Anal. Prev. 8:27–31, 1976.
93. Smart, R. G.: *The Problems of Drugs and Driving: An Overview of Current Research and Future Needs.* Substudy No. 685. Addiction Research Foundation, Toronto, 1975.
94. Sterling-Smith, R. S.: *Alcohol, marihuana and other drug patterns among operators involved in fatal motor vehicle accidents,* in Israelstam, S., and Lambert, S. (eds.): *Alcohol, Drugs and Traffic Safety. Proceedings of the Sixth International Conference on Alcohol, Drugs and Traffic Safety. Toronto, September 8–13, 1974.* Addiction Research Foundation, Toronto, 1975, pp. 93–105.
95. Ase, J.: *Environmental causes of birth defects.* Cont. Ed. Fam. Physicians 3:39–46, 1975.
96. Weiss, K.: *Vaginal cancer: an iatrogenic disease?* Int. J. Health Serv. 5:235–251, 1975.
97. *National Institutes of Health Consensus Development Conference on Estrogens and Postmenopausal Women.* PMA Newsletter, September 17, 1979.
98. Jick, H., et al.: *Oral contraceptives and nonfatal myocardial infarction.* J.A.M.A. 239(14):1403–1406, 1978.
99. Jick, H., et al.: *Noncontraceptive Estrogens and Nonfatal Myocardial Infarction.* J.A.M.A. 239(14):1407–1408, 1978.
100. Jain, A.: *Mortality risk associated with the use of oral contraceptives.* Studies Fam. Planning 8(3):50–54, 1977.
101. Doll, R.: *Epidemiology of cancer: current perspectives.* Am. J. Epidemiol. 104:396–404, 1976.
102. Sartwell, P.: *Oral contraceptives—another look.* Am. J. Public Health 68(4):323–326, 1978.
103. *Exposure of patients to ionizing radiations.* WHO Chron. 29:90, 1975.
104. National Institutes of Health, reported in *New York Times,* April 10, 1975.
105. Arms, S.: *Immaculate Deception.* Houghton-Mifflin, Boston, 1975.
106. Environmental Protection Agency, 1974, op. cit.
107. National Heart, Lung and Blood Institute, 1977, op. cit.
108. Lebowitz, M.: *Smoking habits and changes in smoking habits as they relate to chronic conditions and respiratory symptoms.* Am. J. Epidemiol. 105:534–543, 1977.
109. Lieber, op. cit.
110. Hood, op. cit.
111. Williams, L., et al.: *Implications of the observed effect of air pollution on birth weight.* Social Biol. 24:1–9, 1977.
112. Environmental Protection Agency, 1974, op. cit.
113. Holland, W.: *Effects of air pollution on children.* Pediatrics 53(5):839–840, 1974.
114. Hammer, D., et al.: *The Los Angeles Student Nurse Study.* Arch. Environ. Health 28:255–560, 1974.
115. Federal Interagency Task Force on Air Quality Indicators: *A Recommended Air*

Pollution Index. Council on Environmental Quality, Environmental Protection Agency, Washington, D.C., 1976.
116. Levy, D., et al.: *The relationship between acute respiratory illness and air pollution levels in an industrial city.* Am. Rev. Respir. Dis. 116:167–173, 1977.
117. Federal Interagency Task Force, op. cit.
118. Holsclaw, op. cit.
119. Center for Disease Control, 1976 op. cit.
120. Environmental Protection Agency, 1974, op. cit.
121. Lebowitz, op. cit.
122. Lebowitz, M.: *Occupational exposures in relation to symptomatology and lung function in a community population.* Environ. Res. 14:59–67, 1977.
123. Huhti, op. cit.
124. *The effects of smoking on health,* op. cit.
125. National Heart, Lung and Blood Institute, 1977, op. cit.
126. Alcohol, Drug Abuse and Mental Health Association, 1974, op. cit.
127. Brenner, M. H.: *Trends in alcohol consumption and associated illnesses.* Am. J. Public Health 65(12):1279–1292, 1975.
128. Brenner, M. H.: *Health Costs and Benefits of Economic Policy.* Int. J. Health Serv. 7:581–623, 1977.
129. Cobb, S., and Kasl, S.: *Termination: The Consequence of Job Loss.* National Institute of Occupational Safety and Health, Cincinnati, 1977.
130. Environmental Protection Agency, 1974 op. cit.
131. Jonsson, op. cit.
132. Scrimshaw, op. cit.
133. Vallin, J.: *World trends in infant mortality since 1950.* World Health Statistics Rep. 29:646–674, 1976.
134. Cleave, op. cit.
135. Olefsky, op. cit.
136. *Prevalence and natural history,* op. cit.
137. Senate Select Committee, February 1977, op. cit.
138. Senate Select Committee, 1973, op. cit.
139. Gordon, op. cit.
140. Slocumb, op. cit.
141. Sinclair, op. cit.
142. National Heart, Lung and Blood Institute, 1977, op. cit.
143. Lenowitz, op. cit.
144. Center for Disease Control, 1975, op. cit.
145. Gruber, G.: *Relationships Between Wholebody Vibration and Morbidity Among Interstate Truck Drivers.* National Institute of Occupational Safety and Health, Cincinnati, 1976.
146. Key, op. cit.
147. Hammer, op. cit.
148. Lave, L., and Seskin, E.: *Air pollution and human health.* Science 169:723–733, 1970.
149. Williams, op. cit.
150. Environmental Protection Agency, 1974, op. cit.
151. Brenner, 1975, op. cit.
152. Brenner, 1977, op. cit.
153. Brenner, M. H.: *Fetal, infant and maternal mortality during periods of economic instability.* Int. J. Health Serv. 3(2):245–55, 1973.
154. Brenner, 1977, op. cit.

155. Wald, op. cit.
156. U.S. Senate Select Committee on Nutrition and Human Needs: *Food Price Changes 1973–74 and Nutritional Status.* Washington, D.C., February 1974.
157. Eyer, J.: *Prosperity as a cause of death.* Int. J. Health Serv. 7(1):125–150, 1977.
158. Eyer, J.: *Does unemployment cause the death rate peak in each business cycle? A multifactor model of death rate change.* Int. J. Health Serv. 7:625–663, 1977.
159. Brenner, 1977, op. cit.
160. Eyer, op. cit.
161. National Center for Health Statistics: *Infant Mortality Rates: Socioeconomic Factors, U.S.* Washington, D.C., March 1972.
162. Slocumb, op. cit.
163. Brown, op. cit.
164. Dahlmann, op. cit.
165. Owen, op. cit.
166. Chase, H. C.: *Infant mortality and its concomitants, 1960–1972.* Med. Care 15:8:662–674, 1977.
167. Senate Select Committee, June 1973, op. cit.
168. *The Decomposition of Effects of Sociodemographic Variables on Area Infant Mortality Rates: A Path-Analytic Solution.* Paper presented before the Statistics Section, American Public Health Association, 105th Annual Meeting, Washington, D.C., October 31, 1977.
169. Low, J. A., et al.: *Intrauterine growth retardation: a preliminary report of long-term morbidity.* Am. J. Obstet. Gynecol. 130:534–543, 1978.
170. Antonovsky, A., and Bernstein, J.: *Social class and infant mortality.* Sci. Med. 11:453–470, 1977.
171. Eisner, N., et al.: *Improvement in infant and perinatal mortality in the United States, 1965–1973. Priorities for intervention.* Am. J. Public Health 68(4):359–366, 1978.
172. Vallin, op. cit.
173. Muller, C.: *Methodological issues in health economics research relevant to women.* Women and Health 1:1, January–February, 1976.
174. Gortmaker, S.: *Poverty and infant mortality in the U.S.* Am. Sociol. Rev. 44:280–97, 1979.
175. Stein, Z., et al.: *Famine and Human Development: The Dutch Hunger Winter of 1944/45.* Oxford University Press, New York, 1975.
176. Puffer, R. R., and Serrano, C. V.: *Patterns of Childhood Mortality Inter-American Investigation of Mortality in Childhood.* Pan American Health Organization, Washington, D.C., 1973.
177. Hunter, R., et al.: *Antecedents of child abuse and neglect in premature infants: a prospective study in a newborn intensive care unit.* Pediatrics 61:629–635, 1978.
178. Newberger, E., et al.: *Pediatric social illness: toward an etiologic classification.* Pediatrics 60:178–185, 1977.
179. Garbarino, J.: *A preliminary study of some ecological correlates of child abuse: the impact of socioeconomic stress on mothers.* Child Dev. 47:178–185, 1976.
180. Winkelstein, op. cit.
181. *GAO report recommends new law to control guns.* Nation's Health April 1, 1978, p. 3.
182. Austin, G. A., et al. (eds.): *Drug Users and Driving Behaviors.* National Institute on Drug Abuse, Rockville, Md., June 1977.
183. Sharma, op. cit.

184. Smart, op. cit.
185. Sterling-Smith, op. cit.
186. Morris, J.: *Primary prevention of heart attack.* Bull. N.Y. Acad. Med. 51(1):62–74, 1975.
187. Smith, W.: *Epidemiology of hypertension.* Med. Clin. North Am. 61:467–486, 1977.
188. *Prevalence and natural history,* op. cit.
189. Senate Select Committee, February 1977, op. cit.
190. Gordon, op. cit.
191. Stamler, op. cit.
192. Schettler, op. cit.
193. Center for Disease Control, 1976, op. cit.
194. Kneese, op. cit.
195. Logan, R., et al.: *Risk factors for ischemic heart disease in normal men aged 40—Edinburgh-Stockholm Study.* Lancet, May 6, 1978, pp. 949–954.
196. Gyntelberg, op. cit.
197. Center for Disease Control, 1976, op. cit.
198. *Effects of smoking on health,* 1977, op. cit.
199. Alcohol, Drug Abuse and Mental Health Association, 1974, op. cit.
200. McMichael, A. J.: *Increases in laryngeal cancer in Britain and Australia in relation to alcohol and tobacco consumption trends.* Lancet, June 10, 1978, pp. 1244–1247.
201. Lieber, op. cit.
202. Fisher, E., et al.: *Alcoholism and other concomitants of mitochondrial inclusions in skeletal muscle.* Am. J. Med. Sci. 261(2):85–89, 1971.
203. Kneese and Schultz, op. cit.
204. Jain, op. cit.
205. Arntzenius, A., et al.: *Reduced high density lipoprotein in women aged 40–41 using oral contraceptives.* Lancet, June 10, 1978, pp. 1221–1223.
206. Stamler, op. cit.
207. Schettler, op. cit.
208. *Prevalence and natural history,* 1976, op. cit.
209. Senate Select Committee, February 1977, op. cit.
210. Gordon, 1973, op. cit.
211. Logan, op. cit.
212. Center for Disease Control, 1976, op. cit.
213. *The effects of smoking on health,* 1977, op. cit.
214. Wilhelmsen, L., et al.: *Primary Risk Factors in Patients with Myocardial Infarction.* Am. Heart J. 91:412–419, 1976.
215. Gyntelberg, op. cit.
216. Center for Disease Control, 1975, op. cit.
217. Huhti, op. cit.
218. National Heart, Lung and Blood Institute, 1977, op. cit.
219. Cohen, B. H., et al.: *Risk factors in chronic obstructive pulmonary disease (COPD).* Am. J. Epidemiol. 105:223–232, 1977.
220. Jonsson, op. cit.
221. Berg, J. W., et al.: *Economic status and survival of cancer patients.* Cancer 39:467:477, 1977.
222. Yerascaris, C. A., and Kim, J. H.: *Socioeconomic differentials in selected causes of death.* Am. J. Public Health 68:342–351, 1978.
223. *Oral contraceptives and heart risk.* Fam. Plann. Perspect. 7:145–147, 1975.

224. *The effect of smoking on health,* 1977, op. cit.
225. Center for Disease Control, 1976, op. cit.
226. Hunt, V.: *Occupational Health Problems of Pregnant Women: Report and Recommendations for the Office of the Secretary DHEW.* Washington, D.C., April 30, 1975.
227. Sinclair, op. cit.
228. Slocumb, op. cit.
229. Gordon, 1978, op. cit.
230. Waldron, I.: *Increased prescribing of valium, librium and other drugs—an example of the influence of economic and social factors on the practice of medicine.* Int. J. Health Serv. 7(1), 1977.
231. Center for Disease Control: *National Nosocomial Infections Study—U.S., 1975–76.* Morbidity and Mortality Weekly Report 26(46), November 18, 1977.
232. Caransos, G., et al.: *Drug-induced illness leading to hospitalization.* J.A.M.A. 228:713–717, 1974.
233. Fife, D.: *Noise and hospital stay.* Am. J. Public Health 66:680–681, 1976.
234. Hadley, S., and Strupp, H.: *Contemporary views of the negative effects in psychotherapy.* Arch. Gen. Psychiatry 33:1291–1302, 1976.
235. Slocumb, op. cit.
236. International Union of Nutritional Sciences, op. cit.
237. Higgins, op. cit.
238. Sinclair, op. cit.
239. Pell, S.: *The identification of risk factors in employed populations.* Trans. N.Y. Acad. Sci. 36(4):341–356 (Series II), 1974.
240. Kuller, L.: *Epidemiology of cardiovascular diseases: current perspectives.* Am. J. Epidemiol. 104:425–456, 1976.
241. Kuller, op. cit.
242. Benditt, E.: *The origin of atherosclerosis.* Sci. Am. 236(2):74–85, 1977.
243. Stamler, op. cit.
244. Doll, op. cit.
245. Senate Select Committee, 1973, op. cit.
246. Berki, S., and Kobashigawa, B.: *Socioeconomic and need determinants of ambulatory care use: path-analysis of the 1970 Health Interview Survey data.* Med. Care 14:5, 1976.
247. National Center for Health Statistics, 1974, op. cit.
248. Andrews, G., et al.: *The relationship between physical, psychological and social morbidity in a suburban community.* Am. J. Epidemiol. 105:324–329, 1977.
249. Hinkle, L.: *Ecological observations of the relation of physical illness, mental illness and the social environment.* Psychosom. Med. 23:289–297, 1961.
250. Hinkle, L.: *The concept of 'stress' in the biological and social sciences.* Sci. Med. Man 1:31–48, 1973.
251. Kalimo, E., and Rabin, B.: *Relationships among indicators of morbidity: cross-national comparisons.* J. Chron. Dis. 29:1–14, 1976.
252. Haynes, 1/1978, op. cit.
253. Moss, G.: *Illness, Immunity and Society.* Wiley Interscience, New York, 1974.
254. Irelan, L., et al.: *Almost 65: Baseline Data from the Retirement History Study.* Social Security Administration, Office of Research and Statistics, Washington, D.C., 1976.
255. Quinn, J.: *The Early Retirement Decision: Evidence from the 1969 Retirement History Study.* Staff Paper No. 29. Social Security Administration, Washington, D.C., 1977.

36

256. Burdette, M., and Frohlich, P.: *The Effect of Disability in Unit Income—1972 Survey of Disabled and Nondisabled Adults.* Report No. 9. Social Security Administration, Office of Research and Statistics, Washington, D.C., 1977.
257. Franklin, P.: *Impact of disability on the family structure.* Soc. Sec. Bull., May 1977.
258. Nagi, S.: *An epidemiology of disability among adults in the United States.* Millbank Memorial Fund Quarterly/Health and Society, Fall 1976, pp. 439–465.
259. McManus, L. A.: *The Effects of Disability on Lifetime Earnings.* Staff Paper No. 30. Social Security Administration, Washington, D.C., 1978.

3

THE PICTURE OF HEALTH

IN INTERPERSONAL AND

BIOLOGICAL FRAMES

The ways individuals deal with changes in their personal lives—changes brought on by illness or otherwise related to their work, home, or community situations—are sometimes called "coping." Used here, coping refers to the behavior that people adopt to protect themselves psychologically from their personal problems.[1] The question now is not *whether* environments and personal activities affect health. It is through what paths they affect health and through what kinds of environment–personal behavior interrelationships at the one-to-one level where people meet face-to-face.

The almost forbidding complexity of these issues has been only recently and cautiously approached in the studies of the numerous fields of knowledge which are concerned with one or more of their aspects. The following discussion nevertheless attempts to show how these studies may fit together to help form the picture of modern health and illness.

Coping practices may be thought of as one connecting pathway between people's environments and their physiological response to their world. The issue of importance here is how these coping practices may affect people's health. The review of recent studies that follows will show that some coping practices are more effective than others for achieving their purpose of protecting persons from distressful feelings about their problems. People in some social groups cope more effectively than others. This is basically because they have more resources at their disposal to help them. Within a situation of limited economic resources, however, the support of other people makes a degree of difference that is beneficial. Even these assisted efforts to cope, however, soon find their limits in the wider world, which *individuals* can do little to change.

39

The types of coping practices people use may affect their health through several indirect and interconnected paths which will be explored. The effects on health that may occur depend on the nature of the problem. Such questions as how individuals perceive their problem, how distressful it seems to them, how helpful others may be, and whether or not they solve their problem appear to have no simple and direct connection with the impact the problem has on their health. Emotional distress is not equivalent to physiological stress.

The potential which both coping practices and everyday habits have for placing people at risk of illness, through their effects on the same kinds of physiological and biochemical processes, is also reviewed. These are then placed in societal and historical perspective.

This will complete the picture of the health-important linkages between environments and people's behavior, visualized in societal, interindividual, and physiological contexts. It begins to suggest the most effective focus for health-making policy in addressing the complex modern health problem. A working exploratory hypothesis of these linkages, useable for purposes of policy design, is developed in Part 2.

PERSONAL BEHAVIOR: COPING PRACTICES AND EVERYDAY HABITS

Forms and varieties of coping are among the repertoire of personal behavior patterns. Coping patterns are similar in several ways to the daily habits of physical activity, eating, drinking, smoking, and drug use discussed thus far. Both coping patterns and habits are part of lifelong learning. They are woven into the socialization processes of children and adults, importantly interpreted and taught by family and peer groups at school, work, and elsewhere. These primary groups themselves transmit the influences of ethnicity and social class, as well as occupational and cultural practices.

Once learned, both coping and habit patterns are quickly removed from consciousness and remain so, as long as they seem to be effective. Should they become ineffective when major changes occur in people's lives, such as marriage, illness, or job loss, individuals will often consciously attempt to change their ways of coping or other behavior patterns. In general, however, such patterns change only slowly over lifetimes and without much conscious intent. This is quite understandable because intentional changes, either in patterns of coping or personal habits, require considerable time and energy, which in turn must be drawn away from other, usually more central, concerns and activities.

The major difference, for purposes of this discussion, between patterns of coping and other personal habits is the way in which they are most likely to affect health. Eating and other habits used in the routines of life are more likely to affect health directly, through excesses or deficits. Coping patterns, used in times of uncertainty and change, are likely to affect health in more subtle and complex ways. Both of these aspects of personal behavior may have short- and long-term consequences for people's health.

THE INTERPERSONAL CONTEXT

People use three basic forms of coping to protect themselves. They may try to change the problematic situation which poses potential harm. They may try to alter their perception of the situation so that it no longer appears harmful or threatening. Or they may attempt to control the psychological or emotional distress which comes from the experience.[2,3] Neither the types of problems that people face, nor the means to cope with them effectively exist equally in men and women or among various income groups. Each social group tends to use variations of the basic coping strategies.[4-11]

In general, people cope most effectively in situations where the problems involve intimate relationships, as in home life, marriage, and child-rearing.[12] They are least successful in the larger-scale, impersonal circumstances of work and community life. This is readily understandable since the potentially harmful situations in the wider world are outside the control of any individual who might be hurt by them; and coping patterns, by definition, are part of an *individual's* means to deal with problem situations. It is easy to see how a person may more feasibly alter relations with spouse, lover, child, or parent, than with employer, teacher, or patron. If changing the problematic situation is not readily possible, as is most often the case, then altering one's perception of one's spouse, for example, is more likely to be effective, in the long term, than changing one's perception of a problem in the workplace. Still, one may conceivably alter a perception of employer or job; but to learn to believe that "money isn't important," when raises and promotions are granted to others, may be increasingly difficult as the years go by and one gets relatively poorer.

Perhaps this is why, in situations outside the control of individuals, the most common form of coping is neither to try to change the situation, nor to alter one's perception of it. Rather it is simply to accept the circumstances and then to try to manage the emotional distress which follows: to "live with it," "grin and bear it," or perhaps to escape from awareness of the distress through use of alcohol, drugs, food, sleep, accelerated living, or other means.[13,14]

The *coping responses* themselves—the changing of situations and of perceptions, or the managing of feelings—are important for protecting individuals psychologically. The salient feature is not "personality" or "innate characteristics" such as self-esteem. For example, individuals who respect themselves highly may indeed sometimes cope better in marriage situations than those who have little self-respect. However, persons with high self-esteem have not been found to cope better with distressful problems of childrearing, household economics, or the workplace.[15] People's experiences shape their personal characteristics, and these qualities, such as self-esteem, show up differently in different kinds of situations.

Bases for Variations in Coping

Women are less likely than men to use effective patterns of coping. They are more likely to ignore distress-creating problems and often thereby make them worse. The affluent are more likely than others to use effective coping patterns.[16-18] The reasons for these tendencies are suggested when coping behavior is viewed in a somewhat broader context, beyond the interpersonal relations between individuals, as the following discussion shows.

AVAILABLE RESOURCES AND THE NATURE OF DISTRESS

If coping patterns are one set of ways for individuals to deal with the world, any explanation of differences in abilities to cope must look at the "world" as it exists for people in various social groups. Some events, such as the loss of a job, are seen as distressful by most people, regardless of their social group.[19] However, this is likely to be far less emotionally troubling to the relative few who have independent incomes than to others, especially those with few job opportunities, such as teens, older people, the poor, and women.[20,21] Other events may bring distress only to some groups, such as failure to achieve a doctoral degree or to win in the stock market. In other words, the perception that men or women, affluent or poor, may have of a distressful event partly depends on the consequences of that event for their lives. Their own experiences and those of family and friends influence their perception of the event and its dangers or promise.[22] These experiences have been, and continue to be, influenced by their socioeconomic circumstances and by family and other resources available to them, resources that can help them to deal with their distress or with the problem that created their distress.

These resources include their *psychological* supports, their coping repertoire. People's responses depend on how much of a repertoire they have built up in the course of living, how "new" the situation is for them, and whether they have had experience in effectively coping with similar events.[23,24]

Coping patterns, however, depend more importantly upon available *social* and *economic* resources. This is especially true if people are to be able to use the more effective types of coping—those which involve the ability to change problematic situations or perceptions of them. Distressful events can become resolvable experiences when people have access to sufficient information and contacts to pursue alternatives. Social ties to intimate or trusted others may provide these opportunities and may also help in reinterpreting events, so as to foster new perceptions, or in supplying material aid.

Individuals without such social resources and support, but with economic resources, can often buy comparable assistance.[25,26] Disabled but affluent people can renovate their homes to suit their needs and hire personal staff to do what they are less able to do. Persons with emotional disturbances and financial means can hire psychiatrists and companions, and they can arrange long and comfortable periods of travel to take them away from distress-causing situations. This ability to "buy help" tends to influence their perceptions of what is "distressful" or unsatisfactory. It also affects the degree of distress they may feel, as well as the actions they may take, and therefore how well they cope with a given problem (Fig. 3).[27]

This relationship between material circumstances and perceptions of life's goodness is reflected generally in the views of Americans, and in particular of those over age 60. Individuals with poor health, low income, and little social contact consistently express dissatisfaction with life. In contrast, those who express feelings of well-being most often are the healthy with sufficient income and social ties.[28] The evidence clearly shows that those persons who have had adequate resources during their lives are most

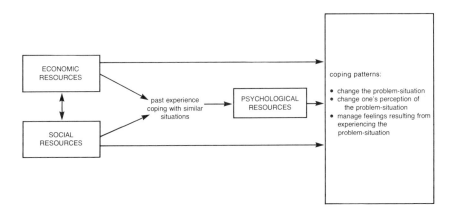

FIGURE 3. Individuals' capacity for meeting problems: sources and forms of coping patterns.

likely to be the most healthy and least ill (Fig. 4).* Those who are poor and less healthy accurately see themselves that way.[29-31]

The importance of having adequate material resources in order to feel content is brought out further in several surveys. One concerns the views expressed by high- and low-income people who became widowed. The loss of a spouse changed the opportunities for social relations among all of them. This, however, was more distressful to the poor than to the affluent who had resources to deploy in new ways. To the affluent, the loss was relatively less "costly." In another group of low-income people, improved housing increased their sense of well-being, even when it reduced their prospects for social contact.[32] A third study showed that, although elderly or disabled low-income people had widely different attitudes, living arrangements, and other circumstances, they all shared a desire for a larger and adequate income.[33] Among American workers who were asked what their priorities were, the higher-paid professionals wanted interesting work and the opportunity to develop themselves. The lower-paid blue-collar workers wanted good pay and the means to do the job. The professionals were clearly more satisfied. Whatever discontent they felt related to their wanting more opportunities for self-development. The manual workers were notably more dissatisfied, especially with their pay, fringe benefits, and job security.[34,35] It becomes apparent that material resources, of necessity, are paramount until they are relatively assured.[36]

All of this is consistent with other evidence which shows that among those with least, material resources are more important to feelings of well-being than among those who already enjoy adequate material circumstances and therefore do *not* have to worry about basic needs. Tangible resources, when lost by poorer people, produce more distress. In this way loss of income, of kin or friends, or of health is viewed predictably as a more distressful problem among the poor than among those at higher income levels. This relatively greater loss increases the likelihood that the poor will perceive similar events in the future with greater emotional pain.[37,38]

In addition to differences in the ways people perceive the distressfulness of events, the very nature of those events or changes themselves may differ. Some changes may be "happy" ones which have potential benefits, perhaps marriage or a new job, but are also distressful or anxiety-producing simply because of the inevitable uncertainty that is part of any newness. However, the degree of distress experienced from these situations seems less compared with the "unhappy" events of loss of intimates, or of failure or disability.[39-42] Affluent people are probably more likely to experience "happy" changes than are poorer people.[43]

---

*See also Table 2 in the Appendix.

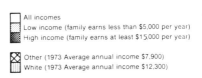

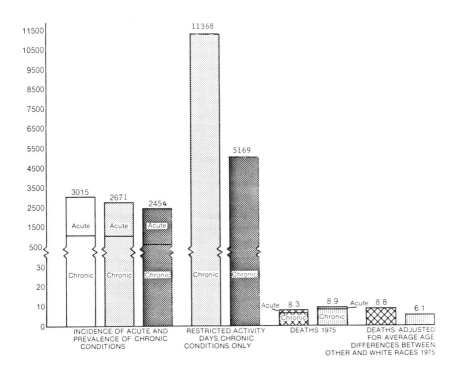

FIGURE 4. Differences in illness, disability, and death between low- and high-income groups, 1968–1975. Rates are for each 1000 persons in each specified group. (Adapted from data of the U.S. National Center for Health Statistics.)

It is plausible to conclude that economically advantaged people, because of their resources, are more likely to be both less distressed by situational problems and to use more effective coping patterns. What, however, makes for the differences in coping among people whose income is roughly the same?

COPING WITHIN ECONOMIC LIMITS

A study was done to compare the coping patterns of men who were in the same socioeconomic group and whose financial resources were similar.[44] All of the men's jobs were terminated because of a plant shutdown. Thus any differences that occurred in the ways they effectively handled the distress of job loss could reasonably be attributed to differences in their social, or interpersonal, resources.

Over a two-year period after job loss, those with the most weeks of unemployment during that time, and with fewest social resources of family and friends, expressed the most distress. Those workers who had support from kin and friends expressed feelings of resentment and lowered self-esteem but noted less anxiety and depression. After they became re-employed, their distress left them. However, for the men without such social support, finding a new job did not allay their distress. They continued to feel anxious and deprived.[44,45]

The central fact affecting all of these workers was the economic impact of job loss which close social contact could not change. Interpersonal support seemed to moderate, but not eliminate, their accompanying feelings of distress; only in special situations, among aged and disabled workers, were these feelings fully allayed. When the crisis period was over and the men were re-employed, social support seemed to speed the return of their normal, pre-crisis feelings. Such support did not prevent distress in an absolute sense, but it did *lessen* its severity and deter its prolongation, providing a kind of *secondary* prevention.[46,47]

Viewed within their economic group, people are able to face their problems more successfully when social resources are close by, rather than attempting to resolve them alone.[48] This view is further supported by observations which show that even among people who experience relatively few problems, those who are more isolated—the single, divorced, or separated, and the hospitalized—express more intense feelings of distress.[49]

Summary

People's feelings of distress and their ability to use effective coping patterns to handle their problems depend partly on the problem at hand, viewed within the context of their lives, and partly on the resources which their life situation affords. Thus their ability to employ coping patterns which are effective depends on both the distressfulness of a problem, relative to their experience, and on the psychological, social, and economic resources inherent in their past and current situations, all of which they may bring to bear on the problem (see Fig. 3).

The likelihood that problematic events will occur and their frequency of occurrence are different among the poor and the affluent. Poorer people tend to experience more uncertainties and serious threats to the absolute loss of their material and social resources, as do their friends and the communities in which they live. The multiplier effects of income loss for any social group, but especially for the already disadvantaged, bring not only distress, but also a reduction in social contacts as a direct result of lowered income. This brings more concomitant distress as it further diminishes social ties. The result is not only more problems, but also fewer means to cope with them effectively.[50,51]

This mushrooming quality of human experiences suggests that "crises," "life-changes," and "life-events" are more realistically viewed as merely short-term manifestations, the telescoping of processes which underlie and compose everyday living.[52,53] The factor which seems to affect people's distress about problems most significantly is their long-term nature, the *duration* of exposure to a problem. The chronicity of the situation seems more important in its impact than its crisis aspect. Thus among those social groups whose circumstances are relatively more uncertain and otherwise more problematic than those of other groups—the poor, ethnic minorities, elders, women—it is likely that a greater share of individuals will feel distressed and that they will also bear the consequences of illness that flow both from their circumstances and from their distress.

Uncertainty and threat surely flow through the experience of the affluent, the majority population groups, and the young. Relatively speaking, however, these groups have more resources with which to cope with the peaks of crisis and with the underlying processes, as well as with the concomitant distress.

HEALTH WITHIN THE PHYSIOLOGICAL MEDIUM

When the customary ebb and flow of living alters for persons, because of changes in economics or intimacies, and brings a period of uncertainty, they are likely to respond not only with emotional distress, however fully articulated or well-expressed. They are also likely to experience a physiological response of which they may or may not be aware. This response, expressed through the autonomic neuroendocrine system, includes the familiar changes in heartbeat, blood pressure, digestive secretions, and blood sugar, all parts of the "flight-fight" response to immediate threats or otherwise sensed unknowns.[54]

To develop more fully the picture of health and illness, forging the final link between environments and health, it will now be looked at and interpreted through the prism or medium of human physiology, where the impacts of living are brought together in each individual life. Two central questions emerge: First, in what ways do people's perceptions of their world put them at risk of illness, whether such perceptions concern what is appropriate in the routines of life, or what is adequate for coping with change, uncertainty, ambiguity, and wanted or unwanted developments? Secondly, what effects do people's feelings and actions, as a result of their perceptions, have on their health?

Health and illness, viewed as reverberating responses to the multiplicities of human experience, derive from both direct and indirect relationships between people and the world outside their physiological medium. The most important relationships between human experience and illness are perhaps the *indirect* ones, those resulting from people's perceptions of their biophysical, socioeconomic, and interpersonal environments and of what constitutes appropriate and effective action, thinking, and feeling in both the routines and changes of human life. The *direct* impact of experience on health results from those situations, whether or not people perceive them accurately or are aware of them at all, which will unequivocally affect their well-being and survival. These range from long-term changes in the ecology and economy, through natural and man-made upheavals, to the increase of pathogens and carcinogens, or to conspiracies to do violence among groups or individuals.

The "flight-fight" response occurs to immediate short-term threats. However, in circumstances where uncertainties persist, where persons do not have enough information or other resources to end uncertainty or threat, whatever its form, further physiological adaptation occurs that can lower resistance to infections and physical or chemical agents. This may eventually produce an exaggerated inflammatory response, such as joint swelling or allergies; blood cholesterol and related components may also rise through neuroendocrine-hormonal paths, as the body acts as if in a sustained state of preparedness for threats that may emerge from the unknown (see Table 1 in the Appendix).[55,56]

Links Between Problems and Personal Responses

Physiological responses were found in the two-year study, discussed earlier, of workers who experienced job loss because of a plant closing. In anticipation of, and during unemployment, these men experienced the

48

"flight-fight" physiological response, including increases in their blood cholesterol, glucose, uric acid, and gastric enzymes, as well as illness symptoms. Such changes occurred among men who were promptly guaranteed employment elsewhere prior to the plant shutdown, *whether or not* they had much or little social support from family or friends. Among the others, those who did *not* find reemployment until several months after the plant closing, there was a difference between the ones who had social support and those without such resources. The workers *without* support had significantly *more* illness symptoms during the periods of anticipating job loss and during unemployment. Moreover, for these workers, higher cholesterol levels *persisted* even after everyone had found reemployment. Thus, after the problem was resolved, the blood cholesterol of the supported men returned to lower levels, but not so for the workers lacking social support. It was this latter group that also continued to express feelings of distress over the changes which had occurred in their job situation. Nevertheless, all of the workers, supported and unsupported, with short and with prolonged unemployment, showed an autonomic nervous system response, namely, blood levels of cholesterol and uric acid that were higher at the beginning of the two-year period encompassing their job problems than at its end.[57,58]

As was noted earlier, the perceptions of the workers, their feelings of economic deprivation (not their actual income loss), were modified in those who had social support. Their expressed sense of emotional upset was in some respects less intense and less prolonged. However, feelings of deprivation persisted among the unsupported men and were associated with depression even after they returned to employment. Nevertheless, none of these aspects of psychological distress was directly related to the physiological changes or symptoms of illness which occurred in these men.[59,60]

When the problem of job loss itself had a relatively small impact—among those men who were guaranteed jobs elsewhere before plant shutdown—the existence or lack of social support did not affect the men's reports of distress, nor did it lessen their physiological responses (the raised cholesterol and slightly increased illness symptoms which occurred). However, among the workers whose job problem was prolonged, those who had supportive ties with family and friends apparently experienced less distress and fewer illness symptoms; their blood cholesterol rose and then dropped after reemployment. During prolonged unemployment the unsupported men, in contrast, expressed more distress, had more illness symptoms, and sustained elevated blood cholesterol even after reemployment. Thus, when a problem persists, among men of similar economic resources, those who have social support as an additional resource may experience less emotional distress and avoid more severe physiological and illness responses than would otherwise occur.

These conclusions are in line with observations of other populations. In groups of people who have adequate economic resources, social isolation is not associated with symptoms of illness; but when problems occur, social support moderates adverse effects on health.[61] Among lower-income people who face persistent problems, social isolation is associated with symptoms of illness even in the absence of additional crisis events.[62,63]

EMOTIONAL DISTRESS AND PHYSIOLOGICAL STRESS

Once people perceive a situation, within interpersonal or other larger environmental contexts, as a problem engendering some degree of emotional distress, their distress is visible in the physiological medium. It is detectable as measurable physiological stress. As used here, *stress* refers to general physiological responses expressed through the autonomic neuroendocrine system, to distinguish it from emotional *distress* or feelings and from *problem-situations* which may be perceived as distressful and, whether or not perceived, may evoke physiological stress.

The degree of distress as *verbally* expressed by an individual is not necessarily related to the degree of measurable physiological stress, although the intensity *felt* by the person is. Nor can the *kind* of emotion, whether "happy" or "unhappy," be determined by simply observing the concomitant physiological changes.[64,65] This is consistent with findings which show increases in people's symptoms of illness and anxiety in times of desirable changes; their symptoms, however, are somewhat less marked than in times of undesired changes.[66,67]

The types of variables which seem most important in linking people's "worlds" with their health include, first of all, the *problem-situation* itself, which can be observed by others and may include experiences as diverse as job loss, a new personal relationship, or environmental pollution. The problem may or may not be *perceived* by the affected individual, which in turn influences that person's feelings of *distress* concerning the problem. These feelings may be verbally expressed to others or kept to oneself, and may be felt in different intensities. Another variant is the person's physiological medium, which may register *stress* responses to both the problem *and* the feelings of distress. Finally, *signs and symptoms* of illness may occur, which are visible in physical or psychological forms or in some combination of these. The health problems arrive through paths which originate at the problem-situation. Their extent and severity depend upon the nature of the problem itself, the individual's perception of the problem and related feelings of distress, and the degree of physiological stress in response. All of these factors are embedded in and affected by an individual's personal history and current living conditions (Fig. 5). Just how important each of these influences is for determining health status has yet to

50

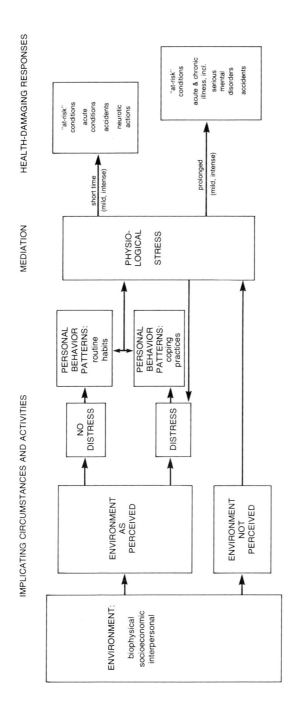

FIGURE 5. Environmental impacts on health: direct and indirect pathways.

51

be studied. Their relative importance probably differs somewhat within different segments of the population and is very likely to be related to the resources available to people, which they can bring to bear on the problem (see Table 3 in the Appendix).

Coping Practices and Their Health Effects

If perceived uncertainties are reflected in the human physiological medium, and such responses, when intense or prolonged, are associated with illness, how may people's coping patterns affect their physiology and risks of illness?

CHANGING THE PROBLEM-SITUATION

Conceivably, those who cope by attempting to change, rather than accept, their problem, without compensating adjustments in time, money, or other aids, may have to intensify their living patterns in order to give more time and effort to the problem. This in itself may increase physiological stress, whether or not the problem-solving efforts are eventually successful. This coping tactic has the effect of placing new demands on people. If these demands exceed their energies, then their very effort to solve the problem may contribute to prolonging their physiological stress, even though it may allay the emotional distress resulting from the problem.

Prolonged stress not only tends to increase people's susceptibility to acute illnesses, but, more significantly, it also places them at risk of chronic cardiovascular, digestive, and metabolic disorders, among others. Intense attention to resolving a problem may distract some people sufficiently to place them at risk of accidental injury.[68] For example, when a person with a job-related problem manages to change the situation with effort over a period of time, he or she may do so with sufficiently intense or prolonged physiological stress to experience an incipient chronic illness or exacerbate a prior one. Occupations which involve recurrent problems, such as administrative positions dealing with the uncertainties of interorganizational bargaining, as well as heavy workloads, interpersonal pressures, and environmental hazards tend to trigger the autonomic-neuroendocrine response. Reports cited previously of elevated blood cholesterol and higher risk of cardiovascular disease for certain occupations support this view.[69-71]

Those who may be said to create their own problems—to set career goals or seek to change programs and policies, or produce a work of art, and then mobilize their energies to resolve the problem—may be at higher risk of illness from concomitant physiological stress. Stress seems unavoidable in order for most people to achieve such goals when compensating resources are not at hand. This may be especially true in American work environments.[72] Such may be the case with "type A" persons and "workaholics."[73-75]

Others who live under stress-evoking circumstances include the poor person who must hold two or more jobs to make ends meet,[76] or the typical working women who must use part of her leisure time to accomplish nonpaid household tasks.[77] These are people who, while trying to change their problem-situations, face potential physiological and emotional distress. They are potentially at greater risk of illness than their more advantaged counterparts. The actual high risk of chronic illness among lower-income black men is well known (see Fig. 4 and Table 2).[78,79] There is also evidence that rates of chronic illness, traditionally associated with men, are increasing among women, especially those who are leading "male" work lives or are performing dual career and household roles.[80-85]

People may indeed solve their economic or personal problems and so quell their distress, but they also may develop, as a consequence, some form of illness. Others, who fail to solve their problems, may face even greater health risks. For example, those who fail, despite their efforts, to acquire an adequate income are likely to experience ongoing emotional distress, which for some becomes mental illness, along with prolonged physiological stress. Their risks of more illness increase as well because their food-buying and other purchasing power is reduced. The greater prevalence of all manifestations of illness, whether predominantly emotional or physical, among the poor suggests this conclusion.[86-90]

CHANGING PERCEPTIONS OF THE PROBLEM

For those who cope with their distressful situation by the alternative tactic of finding less distress-producing ways to perceive it, perhaps with the help of friends or hired aid, the stress response may subside, so long as their reinterpretation of the problem is reasonably in line with reality. In those for whom these new perceptions take the form of loose rationalizations, their distress may lessen, but the physiological stress may continue. The workers discussed earlier, whose feelings of distress diminished, still had signs of physiological stress until their unemployment problem was solved. Another possibility exists in which people's reinterpretations of their problems take an extreme form, divorced from reality, and result in bizarre behavior. This is one way to interpret acute neurotic behavior and, when prolonged, chronic psychoneurotic disorders or schizophrenia: they may be means of re-perceiving one's world in a way that makes ordinary relationships almost impossible.

LIVING WITH THE PROBLEM

A third possible way to cope, for those who can neither change their problem-situation nor effectively alter their perceptions of it, is to live with it and manage the distress—the feelings of anxiety, anger, frustration, or other variants—that it engenders. Depending upon the nature of the problem and the intensity of distress it produces, the resulting degree of sustained physiological stress may lead to health damage.

Risks of illness increase even more when people try to manage their feelings by turning to distress-numbing activities such as the use of intoxicants: alcohol, cigarettes, and other drugs. Other activities may run the gamut from routine to extraordinary, from eating to sky-diving, talking to frequent procreation. Such activities, although they may lessen distress temporarily, take on an addictive character when they become so engrossing as to diminish people's capacity to deal adequately with other aspects of their lives.[91-94] The very high risk for all forms of illness among addictive drinkers is a dramatic example.[95-97] Heavy smoking and obesity represent other presumably escapist coping patterns which increase people's risk of illness.[98-102]

These activities, such as eating, that may be used to numb distress, obviously are also part of everyday living and are not necessarily distress-managing devices for most people. They serve essential purposes of sustenance and pleasure. Their use is not necessarily governed by addictive needs, but rather by availability, economic access, and what people perceive as acceptable uses of time and money as learned from their sociocultural groups (see Chapters 7 and 8).[103-105]

It is important to note that whether or not coping patterns effectively reduce people's distress from their problems, their problem-solving efforts have no simple or direct relationship to what happens to their health.

The Biochemical Medium

Whether specific personal behavior patterns mark routine activity or are used as ways to manage emotional distress for some people in some contexts, the associated biochemical consequences are of the same type. This illustrates further the interconnections among the origins of illness and among illnesses themselves. Whether, for example, a high-caloric dietary pattern is the result of increased individual affluence and associated expectations, or the result of emotional distress, the consequences for health are similar: obesity and the increased risk of illness associated with elevated blood lipids and glucose. There may, however, be additional variations because of the different meanings attributed to the same pattern of behavior, depending on one's social group.

COMMON RESPONSES FROM DIVERSE ORIGINS

People's habits—whether enacted for purposes of sustenance, pleasure, conspicuous consumption, distress-management, or distress-numbing—elicit similar associated biochemical responses. If continued, they produce predictable, sustained biochemical changes that place people at increased risk of a variety of illnesses. Such "at-risk" conditions, in addition to obesity, include rises in blood lipids, especially cholesterol and the lipoproteins which carry it (the low-density lipoproteins, LDL); rises in blood sugar and triglycerides and the lipoproteins which carry them (the very low-density lipoproteins, VLDL), all associated with atherosclerotic cardiovascular disease; increased blood pressure and heart rate; reduced lung ventilation or clearance capacity, even when within normal ranges; undernutrition and nutritional deficiences, and an associated lowered capacity to detoxify toxic substances; fatigue and reduced alertness, coordination, or timely response; and low birth weight or slow intellectual or physical development, among others (see Table 1, Appendix).

Not only do different meanings or purposes for the *same* habits bring similar biochemical responses, but *different* habits do so as well. For example, diets high in cholesterol, sugars, or calories, certain birth control pills, alcohol, and cigarette smoking may all lead to increases in the various types of blood lipids; both smoking and alcohol may increase gastric acidity and irritation as well as interfere with the buffering processes of the pancreas and its insulin functions; diets high in sugars and calories may do so as well. Alcohol and other drugs may activate or potentiate toxic chemicals or carcinogens, or, like undernutrition, may diminish the capacity to detoxify drugs or other hazardous substances. Environmental pollutants, cigarette smoking, alcohol, undernutrition, desynchronization of body rhythms as in extreme changes of workshifts, as well as emotional distress and coping patterns may elicit the generalized autonomic neuroendocrine response to some degree. That spectrum of responses includes constriction of vessel walls; increased clotting time; increases in free fatty acids, blood sugar, catecholamines (epinephrine and norepinephrine), gastric enzymes, and adrenal steroids; reduced white cell defenses and changes in the immune response. All of these changes, when part of the maternal environment, may bring adverse responses in the growing fetus.[106-124]

In sum, within the physiological medium, similar and interrelated biochemical processes respond to the many interlinked environments and patterns of behavior which compose human experience, whether or not fully perceived or verbalized by individuals. When these responses, and the experiences which generate them, are intense or prolonged, sustained biochemical changes occur, often regardless of the specific sources of origin, which place persons at additional risk for illness. Such impacts on health may occur through decreased resistance to health-damaging agents, through direct damage from prolonged physiological stress, or through accidental injury because of reduced alertness.

COMMON PROCESSES IN HEART DISEASE AND CANCER

An intriguing though as yet speculative example of the ties among environments, behavior patterns, and health problems is the suggested common origins of the two most life-threatening and increasingly prevalent forms of illness, cardiovascular disease and cancer.[125-127]

The idea is that a single smooth-muscle cell in the wall of an artery may mutate in response to a mutagen, or tumor-initiator. This agent may derive from environmental sources and may take the form of ionizing radiation, an industrial chemical or metal, or a virus; it may be carbon monoxide or tars from ambient air or cigarette smoke, other air and water contaminants, pesticides, or additives to animal feed and human food.

Such agents are then carried by blood serum lipids—cholesterol, triglycerides, or their lipoprotein-bound fractions (VLDL,LDL). Presumably this carrying capacity is increased with any increase in serum lipids, whatever the source of that increase, whether by ingestion, production, reabsorption, or retention. As described earlier, these physiological responses are affected by diets high in cholesterol and sugars, and low in fiber; by alcohol and certain drugs; and by autonomic neuroendocrine responses to nicotine and distress-producing situations (Fig. 6).

The arterial muscle cell once mutated may simply remain with its changed potential dormant. Should other injurious agents—tumor-promoters—from the environment come in contact with it, again carried by serum lipids, the cell may be damaged and in need of repair. The injury and repair by cellular overgrowth, rather than by normal repair, reduce the capacity of the arterial wall to help clear the blood of serum lipids, especially VLDL and LDL. Thus overgrowth and fatty accumulation result in an atheroma, the fatty deposit which may eventually block the artery partially or completely. Ulceration may occur and blood clots may also form, dislodge, and block other vessels. These pathological processes are manifested in a number of familiar cardiovascular conditions, including heart attacks, strokes, and thromboses.

The severity and extent of the damage, as well as complications, will, of course, depend on the state of nutriment of the tissues and other protective mechanisms of the body; in other words, its state of physiological stress from other deficits or excesses.[128-133]

Cancers may develop in ways that are comparable to the development of cardiovascular conditions. Again, a single cell in lung, colon, breast, skin,

56

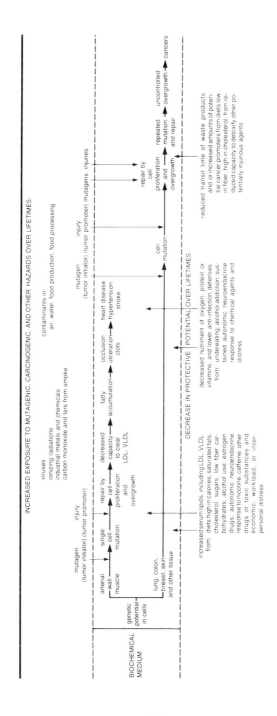

FIGURE 6. Some possible interrelationships between the biochemical medium and environmental circumstances and personal behavior in the development of cardiovascular disease and cancer.

57

or other tissue may be exposed to an environmental mutagen which is transmitted by serum lipids. Once mutated, the cell's potential may remain dormant; however, it may later be injured by any number of environmental tumor-promoters. Subsequent repair of the mutated cell produces a replication and proliferation of its changed growth potential. Over a person's fetal and adult lifetime, these cells may in turn be exposed to other tumor-initators or mutagens, and other injurious agents or tumor-promoters. This repeated sequence of mutation, injury, and repair with overgrowth may eventuate in uncontrolled overgrowth, or cancer.

Other circumstances increase or decrease the likelihood that these steps will reach a cancerous state. These include exposures to environmental mutagens and carcinogens; patterns of living which bring about high serum lipids and other reductions in the protective state of the physiological medium; and such time-related factors as chronological age, and duration or intensity of exposure to the hazardous agent.[134-136]

The pattern of physiological response suggested for both heart disease and cancer is a staged sequence, each step of which is necessary but not sufficient to bring about an illness-response of cardiovascular disease or cancer. Over a period of years all of the necessary steps may occur, given the typical long life expectancy of modern populations. Even so, the likelihood that tumor initiators and promoters will evoke responses depends not only on chronologically available time, but also on the numbers of tumor-causing agents in the environment, the patterns which bring certain persons into contact with them, and the other circumstances and activities of those persons' lives which increase the chances that their physiological media will intensify rather than reduce interaction with the hazardous agent (see Fig. 6).

Viewed in this way, it may seem remote that all of the necessary and sufficient conditions would be met to eventuate in coronary disease or cancer. And yet, viewed in historical perspective, never before have those necessary circumstances been so prevalent among human populations. The essentials characterize modern affluent societies: environmental substances and behavior patterns which set up the physiological medium to increasingly intense and sustained exposure to mutagens and to non-mutagenic tumor-promoting agents, over a lengthening lifespan.

THE SOCIETAL UMBRELLA FOR INTERPERSONAL CONTEXTS AND PHYSIOLOGICAL PROCESSES

Looking beyond the individual's interpersonal sphere and physiological medium to the wider world—however remote it is from the conscious distress or contentment of individuals—ecology and economy tap into the flow of everyday living for rich and poor, young and old, majority and minority. Earlier discussion showed that recession and inflation cause problems for some groups more than for others. Individuals must cope with them, whether effectively or not. In all-encompassing ways, upturns and downturns in the national economy, and increasingly in the international economy, shifting income and wealth from one part of the population to another, result in changes in habits such as eating, drinking, and the use of discretionary income.

Typical personal behavior among Americans, even as variations occur, is closely linked to a growth-oriented, industrial economy. It is a reflection at the personal level of directions taken on the national scale. The lavish use of energy for production brings more sedentary jobs and modes of transportation which reduce physical exercise and caloric expenditure. In order to obtain and retain what this affluent society makes available only to some, Americans have embraced a system of competition which requires time-oriented activity, calculation, and fast pace, which in turn contribute to accidents and generate distress. The ensuing desire to seek relief quickly makes for greater use of such readily available "solutions" as cigarettes, alcohol, and tranquilizers. Production for commercial consumption, valuing saleability first, inevitably contributes to a reduction in the quality and safety of ambient air and water, of workplaces, and of foods and other goods.[137]

At the same time that economic fluctuations change personal economic resources and modify consumption patterns, the web of social ties is itself changed. This stems from economy-based distress in families, resulting in more separations and divorce, and from intensity of workpace, loss of job security, consequent worker alienation, and diminishing labor organizational ties.[138-140] All affect the pervasiveness of distress and the capacity of large portions of the population to use effective coping patterns.

Likewise, changes in the ecology are producing changes in personal activities, increasingly perceptible in the kinds and amounts of available foods, drinking water, wood and pulp, and energy. Agriculture, for example, becomes more intensive, using more petroleum-based fertilizers and pesticides, and turning more toward artificial animal production. These practices, along with increases in processed foods, bring new ingredients into the human diet and burden the ecology at the same time. Increasing demands on the land exhaust its natural growing capacity and in turn require more intensive production methods, just to maintain farm output. New agricultural strains, developed to raise crop yields, become increasingly vulnerable to insects, temperature shifts, or other ecological changes which are themselves changing at a rate faster than in earlier human history.[141,142] New strains actually diminish food variety. Viewed in the perspective of human evolution, available types of fruits and grains have actually been

59

reduced by half.[143-145] The net effect on food habits is to change the type, quality, and amount of modern diets.

As ecology and economy alter with greater speed and increasingly affect patterns of personal behavior, individual consciousness of their impact on everyday living is likely to grow. With this awareness may come greater public concern about ecology and economy, and about the policy decisions which affect them. Those decisions are the ones that set the parameters for what people can do in the routines of everyday life and how they may cope with the uncertainties of living.

SUMMARY

Contemporary health and illness have many interrelated origins, not only in people's observable environments, but also in their perceptions of their biophysical, socioeconomic, and interpersonal circumstances and in their patterns of behavior as they interact with those environments. These patterns encompass situations that are both routine and predictable, and that are uncertain and changing in either desired or unwanted ways. The net consequences of these environments and behaviors, through responses within the human physiological medium, may be a heightened human effectiveness in some respects, such as solving certain perceived problems. They may also mean diminished effectiveness, such as transitory or chronic illness or injury, bringing predominantly physiological damage or primarily psychological incapacity.

Viewed in this way, distinctions between "mental" and "physical" illness become unnecessary and artificial. Health problems are, more realistically, the responses of overburdened persons. For some, illness is predominantly manifested in their social-psychological responses; for others, mainly in their physiological responses. For many, if not most, it is manifest in both the interpersonal and biochemical spheres, inseparable, except perhaps in the language and career lines of the helping professions. Illness is itself very often a problem that engenders uncertainty and distress. Insoluble problems of any origin may foster addictive behaviors, which have their consequences for health and interpersonal relationships. To attempt to separate "mental" and "physical" human experience, as problems of emotional illness or of physical illness, does not contribute to dealing effectively with today's health problem.

Placing the microscopic level of human physiology within its socioenvironmental and historical context points to the overall importance that the "outer" world has for what occurs within people. Whatever their genetic and congenital potential, people's environments set the limitations and possibilities for what becomes manifest in health. This suggests that reli-

60

ance on biochemical means to improve health would have only limited benefits.[146,147]

Likewise, the efforts of individuals to cope with their problems—whether or not they are helped by family, friends, or professionals—have inherent limits: the interpersonal context is constrained by the resources that are available in the community and society. This suggests that policy which predominantly emphasizes methods that will support individuals who have problems can have only limited impact on the modern health problem. The personal worlds represented by worksite, home, and community determine, for practical purposes, the parameters of what most people can do. To the extent that biochemical and personal support strategies can promote people's health and limit their illness-response, they will be more effective if greater emphasis is placed on changing the health-important aspects of environments and if policy is directed toward the creation of health-making opportunities to which individuals and groups of people can respond.

REFERENCES

1. Pearlin, L., and Schooler, C.: *The structure of coping.* J. Health Social Behav. 19(1):2–21, 1978.
2. Moss, G.: *Illness, Immunity, and Society.* Wiley Interscience, New York, 1974.
3. Pearlin and Schooler, op. cit.
4. Liem, R., and Liem, J.: *Social class and mental illness revisited: the role of economic stress and social support."* J. Health Social Behav. 19:139–156, 1978.
5. Askenasy, A., et al.: *Some effects of social class and ethnic group membership on judgments of the magnitude of stressful life events: a research note.* J. Health Social Behav. 18:432–439, 1977.
6. Pearlin and Schooler, op. cit.
7. Gersten, J., et al.: *An evaluation of the etiologic role of stressful life change events in psychological disorders.* J. Health Social Behav. 18:228–244, 1977.
8. Larson, R.: *Thirty years of research on the subjective well-being of older Americans.* J. Gerontol. 33(1):190–225, 1978.
9. Micklin, M., and Leon, C.: *Life change and psychiatric disturbance in a South American city: the effects of geographic and social mobility.* J. Health Social Behav. 19:92–107, 1978.
10. Myers, J., et al.: *Life events, social integration and psychiatric symptomatology.* J. Health Social Behav. 16:121–127, 1975.
11. Bureau of Labor Statistics: *The criteria for job satisfaction: Is interesting work most important?* Month. Labor Rev., May 1977.
12. Pearlin and Schooler, op. cit.
13. Ibid.
14. Peele, S.: *Redefining addiction: making addiction a scientifically and socially useful concept.* Int. J. Health Serv. 7(1), 1977.
15. Pearlin and Schooler, op. cit.

16. Ibid.
17. Myers et al., op. cit.
18. Liem and Liem, op. cit.
19. Ibid.
20. Askenasy et al., op. cit.
21. Pearlin and Schooler, op. cit.
22. Liem and Liem, op. cit.
23. Eaton, W.: *Life events, social supports and psychiatric symptoms: a re-analysis of the New Haven data.* J. Health Social Behav. 19:230–234, 1978.
24. Moss, op. cit.
25. Kaplan, B., et al.: *Social support and health.* Med. Care 15:47–58, 1977.
26. Moss, op. cit.
27. Larson, op. cit.
28. Ibid.
29. Johnston, S., and Ware, J.: *Income group differences in relationships among survey measures of physical and mental health.* Health Serv. Res. 11(4):416–429, 1976.
30. National Heart and Lung Institute: *The Public and High Blood Pressure: Survey Report, June 1973.* Washington, D.C., 1975.
31. Maddox, G., Douglass: *Self-assessment of health,* in Palmore, E. (ed.): *Normal Aging, II.* Duke University, Durham, N.C., 1974.
32. Larson, op. cit.
33. Tissue, T.: *Survey of Low Income Aged and Disabled.* Report No. 3. Social Security Administration, Office of Research and Statistics, Washington, D.C., 1978.
34. Bureau of Labor Statistics, op. cit.
35. House, J.: *Occupational stress and coronary heart disease: a review and theoretical integration.* J. Health Social Behav. 15:12–27, 1974.
36. Toney, M. B.: *The stimultaneous examination of economic and social factors in destination selection: employing objective and subjective measures.* Demography 15(2), 1978.
37. Larson, op. cit.
38. Pearlin and Schooler, op. cit.
39. Liem and Liem, op. cit.
40. Gersten et al., op. cit.
41. Hinkle, L.: *Ecological observations of the relation of physical illness, mental illness and the social environment.* Psychosom. Med. 23:289–297, 1961.
42. Moss, op. cit.
43. Myers et al., op. cit.
44. Cobb, S., and Kasl S.: *Termination: The Consequence of Job Loss.* National Institute of Occupational Safety and Health, Cincinnati, 1977.
45. Gore, S.: *The effect of social support in moderating the health consequences of unemployment.* J. Health Social Behav. 19:157–165, 1978.
46. Ibid.
47. Melick, M. E.: *Life change and illness: illness behavior of males in the recovery period of a natural disaster.* J. Health Social Behav. 19:335–342, 1978.
48. Andrews, G., et al.: *The relationship between physical, psychological and social morbidity in a suburban community.* Am. J. Epidemiol. 105:324–329, 1977.
49. Myers et al., op. cit.
50. Liem and Liem, op. cit.

51. Kessler, R.: *Stress, social status, and psychological distress.* J. Health Social Behav. 20:259–272, 1979.
52. Gersten et al., op. cit.
53. Hinkle, L.: *The concept of 'stress' in the biological and social sciences.* Sci. Med. Man 1:31–48, 1973.
54. Moss, op. cit.
55. Hinkle, op. cit.
56. Loring, W.: *Environmental health education: a different orientation.* Int. J. Health Ed. 20:1:51–56, 1977.
57. Cobb and Kasl, op. cit.
58. Gore, op. cit.
59. Ibid.
60. Tessler, R., and Mechanic, D.: *Psychological distress and perceived health status.* J. Health Social Behav. 19:254–262, 1978.
61. Andrews et al., op. cit.
62. Myers et al., op. cit.
63. Micklin and Leon, op. cit.
64. Moss, op. cit.
65. Selye, H.: *Stress without Distress.* J. B. Lippincott, New York, 1974.
66. Hinkle, op. cit.
67. Liem and Liem, op. cit.
68. Moss, op. cit.
69. House, op. cit.
70. Theorell, R., and Floderus-Myrhed, B.: *Workload and risk of myocardial infarction—a prospective psychosocial analysis."* Int. J. Epidemiol. 6:17–21, 1977.
71. Dodge, D., and Martin, W.: *Social Stress and Chronic Illness: Mortality Patterns in Industrial Society.* University of Notre Dame Press, South Bend, Ind., 1970.
72. Haynes, S. G., et al.: *The relationship of psychosocial factors to coronary heart disease in the Framingham Study. Part II. Prevalence of coronary heart disease.* Am. J. Epidemiol. 107:384–400, 1978.
73. House, op. cit.
74. Shimkin, D. B.: *Man, ecology and health.* Arch. Environ. Health 20:115, 1970.
75. *Bibliography on occupational health and safety.* Am. J. Public Health 65:609–619, 1975.
76. Brown, S.: *Moonlighting increased sharply in 1977, particularly among women.* Month. Labor Rev., January 1977, p. 27.
77. Owen, G., and Lippman, G.: *Nutritional status of infants and young children: U.S.A.* Pediatr. Clin. North Am. 24:211–227, 1977.
78. Tyroler, H.: *The Detroit Project Studies of Blood Pressure: a prologue and review of related studies and epidemiological issues.* J. Chron. Dis. 30:613–624, 1977.
79. Keil, J. E., et al.: *Hypertension: effects of social class and racial admixture: the results of a cohort study in the black population of Charleston, S.C.* Am. J. Public Health 67:634–639, 1977.
80. Nathanson, C. A.: *Sex, illness and medical care.* Soc. Sci. Med. 11:13–25, 1977.
81. Waldron, I.: *Why do women live longer than men?* Soc. Sci. Med. 10:349–62, 1976.
82. Lewis, C. E., and Lewis, M. A.: *The potential impact of sexual equality on*

health. N. Engl. J. Med. 297:863–869, 1977.
83. Rethersford, R.: *The Changing Sex Differential in Mortality.* Greenwood, Westport, Conn., 1975.
84. Holtzman, N.: *The goal of preventing early death,* in Papers on the National Health Guidelines. *Conditions for Change in the Health Care System, September 1977.* Health Resources Administration, Washington, D.C., 1977.
85. Milio, N.: *Health policy and women's health.* Health Care Mngmt. Rev. 2:21–36, 1977.
86. Gersten et al., op. cit.
87. Yeracaris, C. A., and Kim, J. H.: *Socioeconomic differentials in selected causes of death.* Am. J. Public Health 68:342–351, 1978.
88. Liem and Liem, op. cit.
89. Lerner, M., and Stutz, R. N.: *Have we narrowed the gaps between the poor and the nonpoor? Part II. Narrowing the gaps, 1959–1961 to 1969–1971: mortality.* Med. Care 15:8, 1977.
90. Kitagawa, E., and Hauser, P.: *Differential Mortality in the U.S.: A Study in Socioeconomic Epidemiology.* Harvard University Press, Cambridge, Mass., 1973.
91. Peele, op. cit.
92. Cooper, C. L., and Crump, J.: *Prevention and coping with occupational stress.* J. Occup. Med. 20:420–426, 1978.
93. Dicken, C.: *Sex roles, smoking and smoking cessation.* J. Health Social Behav. 19:324–334, 1978.
94. Haynes, S. G., et al.: *The relationship of psychosocial factors to coronary heart disease in the Framingham Study. Part I. Methods and risk factors.* Am. J. Epidemiol. 107:362–380, 1978.
95. Alcohol, Drug Abuse and Mental Health Administration: *Alcohol and Health— June, 1974.* National Institute on Alcohol Abuse and Alcoholism, Washington, D.C., 1974.
96. *Summary Proceedings, Tripartite Conference on Prevention.* Alcohol, Drug Abuse and Mental Health Administration, Washington, D.C., 1977.
97. Bell, R., and Thomas, D.: *Mortality experience of alcoholics and drug addicts under SSI, January 1974–April 1975,* in Research and Statistics Notes, No. 1. Office of Research and Statistics, Washington, D.C., 1977.
98. Center for Disease Control: *The Health Consequences of Smoking—A Reference Edition: Selected Chapters from 1971 through 1975. Reports with Cumulative Index for All Reports, 1964–1975.* Atlanta, 1976.
99. *The effects of smoking on health.* Morbidity and Mortality Weekly Report 26(18), 1977.
100. Gordon, T., and Kannel, W.: *Effects of overweight on cardiovascular diseases.* Gerontology 28:80–88, 1973.
101. *Prevalence and natural history of obesity in the United Kingdom,* in Research on Obesity. Department of Health and Social Security, London, 1976.
102. U.S. Senate Select Committee on Nutrition and Human Needs: *Diet Related to Killer Diseases, Obesity Hearings II.* Washington, D.C., February 1, 2, 1977.
103. Moss, op. cit.
104. Warner, K.: *The effects of the anti-smoking campaign on cigarette consumption.* Am. J. Public Health 67:645–650, 1977.
105. Economic Research Service: *Food Changes in the United States.* Washington, D.C., 1974.
106. Gordon, op. cit.

107. Olefsky, J., et al.: *Effects of weight reduction on obesity.* Clin. Invest. 53:64–67, 1974.
108. *Research on Obesity,* op. cit.
109. Stamler, J., et al.: *Risk factors and the etiopathogenesis of atherosclerotic diseases.* Am. Assoc. Pathol. Bacteriol. 62(2):A100–153, 1971.
110. Logan, R., et al.: *Risk factors for ischemic heart disease in normal men aged 40—Edinburgh-Stockholm Study.* Lancet, May 6, 1978, pp. 949–954.
111. Lieber, C. S.: *The metabolic basis of alcohol's toxicity.* Hosp. Prac., February 1977, pp. 73–80.
112. Fisher, E., et al.: *Alcoholism and other concomitants of mitochondrial inclusions in skeletal muscle.* Am. J. Med. Sci. 261(2):85–99, 1971.
113. Wapnick, S., and Jones, J. J.: *Alcohol and glucose tolerance.* Lancet 11(7769):180, 1972.
114. U.S. Senate Select Committee on Nutrition and Human Needs: *Nutrition and Diseases. 1973 Hearings, Part II.* Washington, D.C., April 30–May 2, 1973.
115. Scrimshaw, N. S.: *Nutrition and the health of nations,* in *Occasional Papers,* Vol. I, No. 11. Institute of Nutrition, University of North Carolina, Chapel Hill, 1978.
116. Muller, D., et al.: *The effect of pregnancy and two different contraceptive pills on serum lipids and lipoproteins in a women with a type III hyperlipoproteinemia pattern.* Br. J. Obstet. Gynaecol. 85:127–133, 1978.
117. Jonsson, A., and Hansson, L.: *Prolonged exposure to a stressful stimulus (noise) as a cause of raised blood pressure in man.* Lancet, January 8, 1977 pp. 86–87.
118. Winget, C. M., Hughes, L., and LaDou, J.: *Physiological effects of rotational work shifting: a review."* J. Occup. Med. 20(3):204–210, 1978.
119. Cobb and Kasl, op. cit.
120. House, op. cit.
121. Fraumeni, J.: *Chemicals in human teratogenesis and transplacental carcinogenesis.* Pediatrics 53 (5)(Suppl.):807–812, 1974.
122. Klatsky, A., et al.: *Alcohol consumption and blood pressure: Kaiser Permanente Multiphasic Health Examination data.* N. Engl. J. Med. 296(2):1194–1200, 1977.
123. Haynes, Part II, op. cit.
124. Glueck, C. J., et al.: *Diet and coronary heart disease: another view.* N. Engl. J. Med. 298(26):1471–1474, 1978.
125. Benditt, E.: *The origin of atherosclerosis.* Sci. Am. 236(2):74–85, 1977.
126. Cairns, J.: *The cancer problem.* Sci. Am. 234:64–78, 1975.
127. Weinstein, I.: *Current concepts on mechanisms of chemical carcinogenesis.* Bull. N.Y. Acad. Med. 54(4):366–383, 1978.
128. Wynder, E.: *Personal habits.* Bull. N.Y. Acad. Med. 54(4):397–412, 1978.
129. Berg, J. W., et al.: *Economic status and survival of cancer patients.* Cancer 39:467–477, 1977.
130. Tyroler, op. cit.
131. Muller, op. cit.
132. Moss, op. cit.
133. Hinkle, op. cit.
134. Weinstein, op. cit.
135. Cairns, op. cit.
136. Fraumeni, op. cit.
137. Milio, N.: *An ecological approach to the prevention of modern illness.* Am. J.

Public Health 2:7–11, 1977.
138. Eyer, J.: *Prosperity as a cause of death.* Int. J. Health Serv. 7(1):125–150, 1977.
139. Eyer, J.: *Does unemployment cause the death rate peak in each business cycle? A multifactor model of death rate change.* Int. J. Health Serv. 7:625–663, 1977.
140. Brenner, M. H.: *Health costs and benefits of economic policy.* Int. J. Health Serv. 7:581–623, 1977.
141. Brown, L.: *The 29th Day.* World Watch Institute, Washington, D.C., 1978.
142. Fernando, V., and Thomas, M.: *The role of technology in agriculture.* Int. J. Environ. Studies 11:35–38, 1977.
143. Robson, J.: *Fruit in the human diet: fruit in the diet of prehistoric man and of the hunter-gatherer.* J. Hum. Nutrition 32:19–26, 1978.
144. Wynder, op. cit.
145. Eyer, J.: *Hypertension as a disease of modern society.* Int. J. Health Serv. 5:539–558, 1975.
146. Eisenberg, L.: *The perils of prevention: a cautionary note.* N. Engl. J. Med. 297(22):1230–32, 1977.
147. Marmot, M.: *Epidemiological basis for the prevention of coronary heart disease.* Bull. WHO 57(3):331–347, 1979.

PART 2
A WORKING PROPOSITION
FOR MAKING HEALTH

4

THE HEALTH PROBLEM: PERSPECTIVE FOR POLICY

One way to approach the policy issue of how to deal effectively with the modern health problem is to ask: What environmental and other changes need to be made to measurably improve the health of Americans (see Chapters 1 and 10), and what strategies will make decisions by organizations and individuals in those new directions most likely?

Environments evoke health or illness depending upon how well they supply people with a balanced flow of the things that promote health. People deal with their environments in observable, patterned ways. This view suggests that a strategy for developing effective health-making policy must encompass the major origins of health and illness for the population: the health-important aspects of environments and behavior. It also requires a plausible and useable view of why people develop their typical patterns of choice, and, as importantly, why organizations—both governmental and corporate—make the policy choices they do (see Chapters 6 and 12). In other words, a working hypothesis is necessary about how people's environments affect their behavior. This would help in designing a health-making policy that can change some of the relationships of people to their environments and the ways of living that derive from them.

This chapter suggests the aims and scope for public policy that would be in the health interests of the public. Based on previous chapters, it proposes a strategic principle for designing health policy options. It asserts that less than healthful lifestyles are not a matter of "free" choice, but rather the result of opportunities available to people, and that policy affects those opportunities. It gives an overview and brief assessment of the health-improvement potential of major strategies for health-making policy: health education, interpersonal support, environmental change, and personal health services. Also discussed are the importance and usefulness of linking these strategies conceptually, within an ecological health framework, and organizationally, within a publicly accountable national entity. Later chapters take up a detailed analysis of current policies (Chapters 6 through 9) and the problems involved in designing and instituting new health-making policy (Chapters 10, 11, and 12).

HEALTH-MAKING POLICY: GOAL, OBJECTIVES, AND SCOPE

The health interests of Americans will be best served when the goal of health policy becomes the prevention of illness in the primary sense, before its onset. This is the way to achieve the largest improvement in freedom from restricted living in the prime decades of life, a burden that weighs on Americans needlessly and derives mostly from chronic illness. This thrust would have further healthful effects through associated declines in a significant share of acute illness and premature deaths (see Chapters 1 and 10). It would, as well, reverse or temper the other reverberating effects of illness in people's lives. *Primary* prevention would have priority over *secondary* prevention—the customary emphasis of the medical care system—which tries to detect illness and limit its extension after it begins (see Chapter 9).

Modern environments, as in the past, consist inevitably of both health-promoting and health-damaging circumstances. A major difference between modern and preindustrial environments is that health-promoting conditions exist in excess—a deleterious excess—for a large proportion of today's population. These include overabundant food and energy-intensive production, in which more energy is required to produce a commodity than is gained from its use. This is the case with a number of crops and modes of transportation. Other excesses include labor-saving devices, such as the many disposable items that cause waste removal and environmental problems, as well as automobiles and elevators that reduce even modest physical activity. More people have longer lifetimes of exposure to these living conditions which, when not excessive, are clearly essential for promoting health: food and ways to make human energy productive and creative. These excesses and others now contribute to health-damaging circumstances which are unprecedented, including air and water pollution and other ecological imbalances.

At the same time, in affluent countries, and the United States in particular, significant numbers of people still have a *deficit* of health-promoting circumstances and, often, an *excess* of some that are health-damaging.[1] These people are likely to be the poor who may lack food and health care,

70

and who live in polluted central cities. The poor who live in less urbanized areas are likely to be in somewhat better health. The well-fed, well-housed suburbanites, who are less exposed to health-damaging physical surroundings, are likely to be in better health than their middle-class counterparts who live in a "pollution-controlled," fast-paced urban setting (see Table 3, Appendix).[2]

Primarily because people have unequal exposure to environments and their resources, the burden of incapacitating responses to environments is not equally shared by all groups in the population. Thus the poor have *more* illness, especially of the seriously disabling forms, and more *severe* illness of all forms, including those that can be readily prevented. Because more of their young die, the poor have a shorter average lifespan. Most groups of poor children have smaller body size and greater problems with vision and hearing than do middle-class children. Their health potential is often not realized (see Figure 4, p. 45, and Table 7, Appendix).

Most, if not all, of the variations in the modern illness profiles of men and women, blacks and whites, and urban and rural residents can be understood as responses to the differing environments which they, as members of subgroups, typically experience. A crucial part of that experience is linked to their economic circumstances.[3-16]

Taking these realities into account, health policy could be developed from a viewpoint of human equity—equity among the *risks* of health and illness. All groups of people would be exposed to the *same* excesses and deficits of *both* health-promoting and health-damaging circumstances. This range includes the excess availability of animal fats, sugars, intoxicants, cars, and environmental contaminants, and the deficits of those same resources (Fig. 7). If this were so, the illness profile of the American poor would become more like that of the affluent, who are much healthier—although not as healthy as their counterparts in some other western countries. Policy might alternatively be developed with a view of some attainable optimum in health, for instance, the level achieved by some groups of Americans or by certain other nations.[17] Not only would all people be equally exposed to the pluses and minuses of environment, but the policy objectives would center on *minimizing health-damaging circumstances* and on *minimizing or eliminating both excesses and deficits* of health-promoting resources, such as selected food and energy supplies (see Fig. 7).

This implies a broad scope for health policy. It cuts across other types of policy that are almost never examined by government, or other health bodies, for their impact on Americans' health. These range from economics and energy to agriculture.*

---

*The health effects of a broad range of public policies are discussed in Chapters 6, 7, and 9.

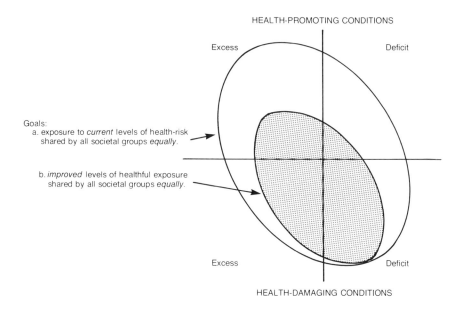

FIGURE 7. Alternative policy goals which could measurably improve the contemporary health profile.

This is not to suggest that the health effects of policy ought to *determine* policy decisions, or that such policies come under the jurisdiction of health authorities. Rather, the health interests of Americans will be better served if the health impacts of policy are known, and if, as a result, health-making policy options are recommended both to policy-makers and the public. Such recommendations could be channeled through a national, publicly accountable body. In this way, health-promoting alternatives would enter the decision-making forum. The profound effects of policy on people's lives would be displayed in full public view. It is, after all, the public who will finally pay for the policies that are chosen, with their money and with health or illness.

In the real world, it is difficult to say which of the two policy objectives—equity of health-risk exposure or optimum healthful exposure with equity—would be the more difficult to accomplish politically (see Table 6, Appendix).[18] However, prior to facing the political issues that have to do with the actual adoption of policy objectives and the making of policy choices (see Chapter 12), options for policy-makers must be developed (see Chapters 10 and 11). In order to propose credible options, a strategy is re-

72

quired that will produce sound estimates of the impacts of a range of health-making policies, ones that are convincingly applicable to American methods of governance and social expectations. The strategy outlined here speaks to the design of policy and how it affects the *choices*—the *decisions to act*—that are made by individuals and organizations.

A POLICY DESIGN STRATEGY

"Free" Choice and Lifestyle

Environments—embodying communities, workplaces, and households, and their biophysical, socioeconomic, and interpersonal facets—set the parameters, the limitations and possibilities, for human experience. Translated into a proposition about people's actions and activities, this means that patterns of behavior derive from the choices people make among the options available to them. People indeed make choices, but those choices are limited to what is immediately before them. Their *options*, or *opportunities for choice*, may be few or many, costly or almost costless. Their *costs*, although most often counted in dollars, also include time, effort, convenience, anxiety, and personal dignity, weighed against other priorities which claim their attention at any point in time. Their choices may be conscious or long since removed from consciousness and transformed into habit. Certain options may be open to all; others to only certain groups.

PUBLIC CHANGE AND PRIVATE OPTIONS

Inflation and recession in the national economic environment have the effect of changing the options for jobs and income, and for purchases, savings, and investment, for the overall population. This nation's experience of the mid-1970s showed how people's choices for consumption changed when their disposable incomes declined, causing their options for spending to narrow.[19] When purchasing power dropped, greater portions of family budgets went for sustenance items—food, housing, and transportation—with little remaining for leisure and distress-relieving pleasures. Food choices became less nutritive among low-income people as they cut down on costly fresh fruits and vegetables. Food for higher-income families sometimes became more nutritive as they substituted vegetable protein for high-fat meat protein.[20,21] Declines in family income can also mean that the potentially more health-promoting uses of discretionary income, such as vacations, may find cheaper substitutes in more drinking, smoking, or sedentary pastimes.[22]

Although personal behavior patterns change in response to changing opportunities for choice, people presumably try to maintain their custom-

73

ary routines, the ones familiar to family and friends. To do so, however, as options narrow, often requires the sacrifice of other things. The effort is costly, and such costs are clearly greater for those whose options were few to begin with.

When economic options narrow, strains are also placed on family relationships that might result in breakups. These troubles at the same time lessen the opportunities for social support available to each family member when they need it more as they face financial distress.

PERSONAL CHOICES AND PERSONAL INCOME

To say that people belong to a certain socioeconomic group is to say that they are likely to have a certain number of opportunities available from which they can choose where to work or be educated, where to live, how to get about, what to buy, and how to relax. Not only are the *number* of options and the range or spectrum for each kind of decision similar within a given social group, but the *relative cost* of each potential choice—how easy it is to choose one option over another—is also similar.[23]

In principle, for example, a poor family has the option to buy fresh fruit every day. But the cost, beyond the stated price, is the cost of other essentials that they must do without. A middle-income family has the same option of available foods but can exercise that option at lesser relative cost, that is, without giving up other essentials.

On the other hand, a higher-income family seeking a more healthful diet may, for example, have to pay a higher relative price for lower-fat, grass-fed beef if they must travel to a special shop, rather than to their local market, which may have only high-fat, corn-fed beef. Such a family, if it also wishes to be less sedentary, may have no option other than auto transportation if job and home are at great distance, or if reliable alternate forms of transportation are not available or convenient.

New choices, in diet, exercise, or any new patterns of personal behavior, may be either not possible at all, or possible only at great cost to the individual when new opportunities for choice are not readily at hand. In such circumstances only *small* proportions of people are likely to undertake and *sustain* changes in their everyday activities.

To bring earlier discussion into the present choice-making frame of reference, people with low incomes were found not as likely to use effective coping patterns because of their limited economic and social resources. In other words, the options available to them for choosing an effective repertoire of coping patterns are of a somewhat different spectrum than for more affluent people. If addictive activities, for example, are ways to erase the distress generated by an insoluble problem, and therefore ineffective forms of coping, then one might expect to find proportionately more of the read-

74

ily purchasable addictions among low-income groups, whose limited resources render more of their problems insoluble. This seems so, statistically, for problem drinking, smoking, and obesity.

In their use of alcohol, lower-income groups have *lower* proportions of drinkers but higher proportions of *addictive*, problem drinkers.[24] They also have higher proportions of *heavy* smokers (except for the *very* poorest who smoke somewhat less than higher-income groups). Among women, however, fewer of the poor and unemployed smoke than do more affluent and employed women.[25] A plausible explanation for the difference in smoking patterns between poor women and poor men is that the women are poorer than the men. Low-income women may therefore turn to high-caloric foods as a lower-cost substitute. People in lower economic brackets are proportionately more *obese* as a group, particularly the women. At the same time, the *average weight* of poorer people is lower than that of the affluent, probably because more of their children and childbearing women are underweight.[26,27]

In other words, income limitations prevent a large share of low-income people from engaging in drinking, smoking, or overeating to the extent that is possible among higher-income groups. However, compared to the more affluent, who have additional options for solving their problems or relieving their distress, people with lesser incomes are forced to choose among fewer alternatives for coping. Thus a greater share of them turn to what is at hand—alcohol, cigarettes, food—all economically accessible in an affluent society if substituted for other things. And they turn most to the least costly (cigarettes) or most available (excess calories).

Conversely, when families have growing personal incomes and more discretionary funds, they acquire new opportunities for purchases. They then add to their buying habits from among what is available and what they see as commensurate with their new status. Their new choices include more beef and alcohol, especially the higher-priced wines and liquors.[28]

The relationship between the pervasiveness of problem drinking and the costs of obtaining alcoholic beverages is further borne out when countries are compared. Whether or not a society approves of drinking as indicated in national surveys, the overall level of consumption (and a host of other problems related to abusive drinking) depends on the price of alcohol relative to the economy of the country.[29,30]

Finally, of the people who use drugs to cope with their distress, affluent employed persons are more likely to use prescribed drugs (barbiturates and tranquilizers) than are nonemployed persons, including housewives.[31] These drugs are the relatively easier choices for white-collar personnel to make, both for economic reasons and because they have easier access to medical services than do the nonemployed.[32]

The Strategic Principle

The general principle here, supported by a wide array of social research, is that most people most of the time will make *decisions* to act—*choices*— from among the *options*—the *opportunities* for making choices—available to them. They will most often choose those that are least costly in money, time, or inconvenience *in relation to* the benefits they gain, regardless of how they define benefits, value, or worth.[33,34]

This is a kind of personal calculus, although not a conscious one for most persons. It tries to get most of what one values in return for what one has available to expend. The degree of "cost" to the individual is always based on the size of the gap between "what you pay" and "what you get." It is a gain-for-cost calculation that is a very personal weighing of tangibles and intangibles, yet it is echoed in clear patterns among people of similar social groups and within whole populations.

From this perspective, personal behavior patterns are not simply "free" choices about "lifestyle," isolated from their social and economic context. Lifestyles are, rather, patterns of choices made from the alternatives that are available to people according to their socioeconomic circumstances and to the ease with which they are able to choose certain ones over others.

Policy as Option-Setting

The options available to the total population and to various social groups do not simply happen. Rather they are themselves the result of policy choices—governmental and corporate decisions concerning energy, technology, pollution, employment, income maintenance, taxation, pricing, food and agriculture, transportation, housing, health care, and other services. These policies represent the scope of health-making policy. Governments, especially at the Federal level, and corporations, especially the largest, and their interactions, set the range of alternatives available to people—how many, how varied, how costly or convenient—from which individuals make the choices that constitute their lifestyle, and, in turn, their profile of health and illness.

To bring about the largest improvement in health requires the development of policy that will change the options that organizations and individuals face today. A health-making policy strategy would eliminate or increase the cost of those options that now result in health-damaging situations. It would provide new, easier opportunities, or reduce the cost of current options, in areas that now lack health-promoting resources. It would increase the cost of opportunities where health-promoting resources exist in deleterious excess (see Chapters 8, 9, and 11, and Table 6, Appendix).

This approach assumes that governmental and corporate policies set the range of opportunities for choices about environments and activities—the number, type, and cost—for individuals directly and for organizations, whether public or private, commercial or nonprofit. Organizations, through their production and program policies, in turn, set options for individuals (Fig. 8). This approach emphasizes neither prohibition nor prescription, but rather new opportunities for choice-making. It implies a focus on changing the *circumstances* and *organizational decisions* which set out opportunities for individuals, rather than seeking to change the *individuals*. Furthermore, it permits shifts in policy that would bring greater equality among social groups in the extent to which they are exposed to health-damaging and health-promoting circumstances.

Individuals and organizations that want to continue to choose health-damaging options would be able to do so. However, they would pay a higher cost than if they made other choices. This would reverse the present situation in which individuals and organizations often face a higher cost for making health-promoting choices. Today, for example, an organization such as an ambulatory care center would have great difficulty surviving financially if it were to provide community-oriented, full-range, in-home services that have greater preventive capability than solely home health services. Nor could a farmers' cooperative survive very readily if it wished to alter production from tobacco to a vegetable protein commodity.

WEIGHING COMPONENT POLICY STRATEGIES

An Ecological Health Framework

Having a goal, objectives, and a basic strategic principle for the design of health-making policy, subsequent developmental issues concern which combinations of policy would provide the largest gains in health. This problem requires a framework in which to compare various policy thrusts. Encompassing the broad scope of health-related policies, it would include those that affect the health-important aspects of environments and personal behavior, including the provision of health services.

An "ecological" health framework would be built around the environments and behavior patterns that are most important for promoting health. It would not, as is implicit in current health services policy, be made up of classifications of diseases and symptoms, which are responses to environments. An ecological framework would set out the major environmental *settings*, including the national (and its now inseparable international counterpart), regional, and local communities; worksites; home arrangements; and the maternal environment of the unborn.

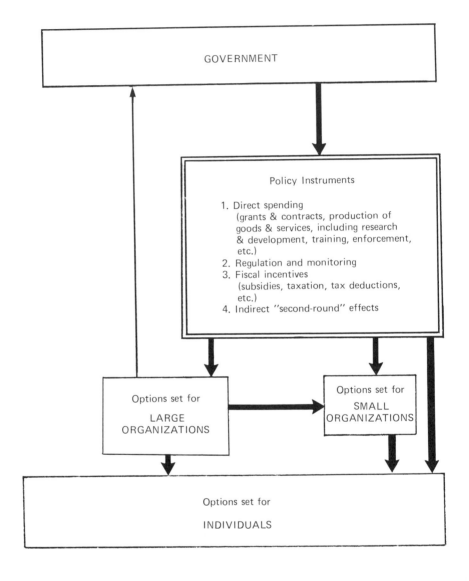

GOVERNMENT

Policy Instruments

1. Direct spending
   (grants & contracts, production of
   goods & services, including research
   & development, training, enforcement,
   etc.)
2. Regulation and monitoring
3. Fiscal incentives
   (subsidies, taxation, tax deductions,
   etc.)
4. Indirect "second-round" effects

Options set for

LARGE
ORGANIZATIONS

Options set for
SMALL
ORGANIZATIONS

Options set for

INDIVIDUALS

FIGURE 8. Public policy effects on organizations and individuals: the main paths and means by which policy sets options for the American people.

Each of these environments has a number of cross-cutting *dimensions*. The biophysical dimension includes biotic elements, such as air and microorganisms, and constructed elements, such as housing, roads, and production facilities. A second, socioeconomic, dimension includes the types and amounts of health-important resources available, such as money, energy, and food; how they are distributed, and by whom they are consumed. A third dimension of these environments is their interorganizational and interpersonal aspects. These include both the patterns of relationships between groups and those between individuals: whether, for example, they are fairly egalitarian, or one-sidedly dominating, as decisions are made; as well as how people perceive them and how they cope with them, whether as individuals or through collective efforts. Finally, a fourth, physiological and biochemical, dimension concerns the internal level of human response within various environmental settings. This facet would include, for example, measures of weight and serum cholesterol, as well as measures of disability, illness, and death at the workplace and in other settings.

In addition to the settings and their health-important dimensions, an ecological health policy framework would include the policy initiatives that impact on people's environments. These concern such *policy areas* as environmental protection and safety, energy and transportation, economic and income maintenance policy, farm and food policy, and human services. These would be further defined according to their *design*. Are they primarily individualistic, relying on giving individuals information, personal support, or other personal services? Or do they focus on environmental strategies, through regulation, or through accomplishing basic changes from past and current patterns in the control and distribution of basic resources?

This kind of framework makes possible the analysis of the nature of the health-important aspects of environments, the ways of living that flow from them, and the types of impacts that current policies have on them. It also provides a basis for developing health-making policy options.

An ecological framework would help in weighing the potential health improvement benefits and costs of component policy thrusts. The result may be that some of the traditional and more recent health proposals would merit a different emphasis than their proponents advocate.

Health Education

Health or lifestyle education, in an ecological health policy framework, would be a component policy, but one in a supportive rather than a primary role. As later discussion will show (see Chapter 5), its potential for primary prevention is highly questionable when alternatives are not available from which people can choose new patterns of living. Health education usually focuses on personal behavior, which is just one of the origins of illness. It emphasizes individual "risk factors" such as smoking or exercise, often without taking into account their inextricable links to socioeconomic and environmental circumstances.[35-37] The focus is then on ways of getting *individuals*, rather than organizational policies to change. As such, it carries a relatively low cost to policy-makers, both in program funds and politically. This is perhaps why it has had increasing visibility in recent years.[38,39]

Health education, within an ecological policy framework, might best be used when individuals (or organizations) have a wider range of options than they realize, or have low-cost options of which they are not aware. However, if people's opportunities for choice are narrow or costly, knowledge of this is only of limited help without some offer of material assistance beyond the giving of information. When people are aware of their options and of the costs involved, such as the economic, social, and health costs of smoking 15 cigarettes a day, additional information is not necessary (see Table 4, Appendix).

Social Support

Another supportive but selectively used component in an ecological policy framework consists of social support methods. These attempt to go beyond or strengthen the provision of information by offering a group context to support individuals who wish to make new choices, whether concerning personal habits, such as smoking or weight loss, or coping with problems, such as divorce or chronic illness. As an educational approach, social support groups encompass some aspects of health education but add elements of personal counseling in a group setting. They may help people to deal with the distress from their problems or to reinterpret their situations by suggesting more comfortable perceptions.[40]

The conceptual basis of social support tactics is broader than that of purely health education. The concept gives greater emphasis to environmental sources of illness and other problems. Mainly, however, it focuses on the interpersonal facet of environments, and on helping individuals to survive in, or change, their environments. Ideally, it is intended to prevent problems, to guide persons before emotional and physical crises occur.[41,42] In practice, social support groups are more likely to help in ameliorating or containing problems; for example, the citizen-led self-help groups, such as Alcoholics Anonymous, or groups designed to reduce the risk factors for various diseases, led by health professionals (see Chapter 5).[43-45]

The preventive intent of social support methods is limited by at least two constraints. First, the types of people most likely to use these services are those who have already decided to change some habit, or who already have a crisis. Both types are able and willing to set aside the necessary time and money to use this supportive mechanism;[46-50] that is, the gain-for-cost to them is high.

A more important limitation concerns the scope and depth of health-related problems with which social support groups can deal. New information, new perceptions, and group support are not sufficient when problems require material changes in order to stop their health-damaging consequences. When the problems are tied to such health-hazardous conditions as poverty or dangerous worksites, then health improvement most requires changing those conditions. In practice, social support groups are not equipped philosophically or materially to do this. "Social support" usually means verbal support.

Social support methods might best be used, if programmed to accommodate the time and money constraints of the persons involved, when people's problems concern circumstances which are *interpretably* hazardous; that is, when much of the problem is the person's limited perception of his or her situation, not the observable situation itself. In effect, this would involve mainly interpersonal problems. A group might then usefully supply new interpretations and suggest means to deal with the situation. A second area of some usefulness might be when the problem is a clearly hazardous circumstance which an individual does not perceive to be hazardous, as may occur at a worksite. The group may then serve a kind of consciousness-raising purpose.

It is important to note that accurate perceptions by individuals do not solve their problems. Material assistance still would be needed in order to provide an individual with options to leave or change a health-hazardous situation (see Table 5, Appendix).[51] Like health education, then, social support groups, as an isolated health improvement tactic, even if widely implemented, would not be likely to measurably change the profile of modern health problems.

Environmental Change

Environmental policies should play an enlarged role as a component of health-making policy. This is, of course, because environments, particularly their biophysical and socioeconomic facets, are predominant in setting out the array of options from which people choose their patterns of behavior. And since a number of illnesses derive from similar environmental situations, changing those environments could produce synergistic health improvements (see Chapter 11).

81

Environmental health concepts take a broad view of the origins of illness and thus have potential for the primary prevention of disease. Their focus obviously is not on changing individuals. Instead, their success derives from the fact that individuals can remain "passive." People are not required to continuously make conscious choices or to be reminded or supported to continue to make healthful choices. They need not be "active."[52-54] Fluoridated water, for example, makes up for a good deal of undisciplined toothbrushing.[55]

Environmental tactics have the effect of providing new healthful opportunities to large numbers of people and spreading the costs across the entire population. Each person does not have to do a mental calculus of gain-for-cost before acting. When people must make choices *continuously,* those choices are likely, of necessity, to differ at different points in time for any given individual. The resulting erratic patterns may have health-damaging consequences, such as irregular toothbrushing, or failure, even among seatbelt users, to "buckle up" every single time they ride in a car.

Traditionally, environmental policies emphasized water and air, accident prevention, and more recently toxic substances in food, at workplaces, and elsewhere.[56-62] The proponents are people in the health fields and others who may not have human health as a primary objective. Until very recently the health consequences of socioeconomic environments were not put forward as a matter for health policy, and even then by people outside the health professions.[63-71] (The development of a major socioenvironmental policy related to the nation's agricultural supply is discussed in Chapters 8 and 11.)

Personal Health Services

This nation's principal, explicit efforts to improve health have, of course, been made through the delivery of personal health services. They focus on the individual and attempt to detect and treat, cure or contain illness, and can sometimes prevent it at the outset. The underlying concept in this disease-by-disease approach to health improvement is a fairly delimited cause-effect relationship between person and disease agent. Although physicians espouse this view, there is some evidence that they do not follow it literally in everyday medical practice. This is simply because it does not work very well when they confront the complex reality of health problems in the context of people's everyday lives.[72,73] The serious limitations of this approach for making a measurable improvement in health have been explored and critiqued increasingly in recent years, often by physicians.[74-85]

New emphases in personal health services have been brought forward in the 1970s. The impetus has come from politically necessary efforts to con-

82

tain inflationary health care costs, and, perhaps, to bring more equity into the distribution of services. These changes include accelerated development of basic, ambulatory, primary level services over more complex, intensive inpatient care; and emphasis on efficacious services over those of unknown or of no known health benefits.[86-89]

Not discounting the limitations, inefficiencies, and inequities of personal health services (see Chapters 5 and 9), they nevertheless are an essential component of a prevention-oriented health policy.[90] Their scope and emphasis would be evaluated in comparison with other health improvement efforts, as later discussion will illustrate (see Chapter 11).

The improvement both of individual preventive and of reparative services is, of course, an essential goal. Those for whom prevention policy comes too late require repair and illness-limitation, care and comfort, which must be available to an even greater extent than for others. These people are predominantly the poor, urban and rural, of all ages. Moreover, those fortunate enough to enter old age without illness-caused disability will eventually require far better personal attention than is currently available to most people.

Linking the Components

There are many different views of health and health behavior, and of what health policy ought to be, as this brief overview suggests. They are not necessarily mutually exclusive. Their advocates are more likely to disagree on emphasis and the relative importance of each. Nowhere in the policy-making apparatus are they linked in overall conception, in planning and analysis. Nor are they examined for consistency, relative health effectiveness, or relative cost, or for equity of impact, superfluities, or omissions. This fragmentation is amply criticized. Increasingly, policy-makers and people in the health field call for integrative mechanisms to link the parts—concepts, planning and implementation, delivery of services, and research and evaluation. Such hopes are closer to realization in other affluent countries than in this one.[91-103]

An ecological framework for the development of health policy is, in essence, an integrated approach. Focused on prevention, its component policies and strategic thrust aim toward developing opportunities for health-making choices by organizations and individuals. Its policy components would be designed to make the creation and maintenance of healthful environments and personal habits the easiest—the "cheapest" and most numerous—choices for selection by governmental units and corporations, producers and consumers, among all the options available to them. Policies would emphasize the aspects of environments and ways of living which have largest potential for promoting health.

83

The analysis of health policy should then concern national policies that affect the biophysical environment and the socioeconomic conditions related to community, workplace, and home, as well as their direct and indirect effects on everyday personal consumption patterns and individuals' resources for coping with problems. It would include the personal health care system and the behavior patterns of both consumers and providers. Comparisons could be made of the effects of policies on the profile of modern health problems, using measures of restricted living in particular (see Chapter 10). The costs of implementing component policies could also be compared (see Chapter 11). These findings would then be a potential guide for the development of more effective policy and for the flow of new funds for health improvement.

The formation of a national organizational unit is a necessary step toward the development of health-making policy for Americans. A national health board is one such possible mechanism. It would be mandated by Federal statute and charged with responsibility for promoting the health interests of the public, including its various population subgroups. It would have final responsibility for the conduct of studies on the health impacts of public policy; for the development and recommendation to policy-makers of health-making policy options; and for seeing that the public received this information in a variety of useable and understandable forms and formats.

This policy perspective is both a framework for research and a working approach to policy development. It offers direction for research because knowledge about the health consequences, not to say the relative effectiveness, of health-related policy is very limited. With concerted effort and political will, the necessary comparative policy analyses could be undertaken. Without such systematic information, policy issues are nevertheless decided continuously. For this reason, the strategy for designing health-making policy is also a working principle for current policy-making.

Research can contribute to policy development. It cannot, of course, determine policy choices. Research can compare the impacts of various policies. At best it can show which ones, singly or in combination, might improve health most, at the least relative cost over a period of time, and for whom. Research studies cannot determine which health-promoting or health-damaging options should be increased or decreased, nor can they identify those options which should be given a higher or lower cost, and those mixes of policy which should be chosen, and when.

These choices are political decisions. The answers come most often from those who are organized to protect their interests, not necessarily from all segments of the population who will be affected by the policies. The economic issues involved in deploying policy that would bring large gains in health are indeed impressive (see Chapters 10 and 11), yet they are less formidable than the political complexities that would be encountered (see Chapter 12).

SUMMARY

Public policy can best deal with the unnecessary disability and death that constitute the modern health problem. It can do so by focusing on primary prevention and providing organizations and individuals with opportunities for creating healthful environments and patterns of everyday living. Such policy can thus allow Americans at least as much freedom from restricted lives as other nations have achieved. The scope of health-making cuts across policies affecting economy, ecology, and other concerns, many of which are not looked on as health-related. These policies should be linked conceptually within an ecological health framework. A broad conceptual perspective would make possible the necessary research to be done, analyzing and comparing the potential of various approaches for the improvement of the health of Americans. This would facilitate the development and recommendation of health-promoting policy options. It would allow full, open, and credible entry of health issues into public policy debates. A publicly accountable national entity is a necessary step in linking fragmented analytic and planning efforts and in beginning to develop health-making policy that effectively deals with the environments and ways of living that are the origins of health and illness.

REFERENCES

1. Milio, N.: Low-Cost Health Care in Rural-Poor Countries. Working Paper, Abt Associates, Boston, May 1975.
2. Yeracaris, C. A., and Kim, J. H.: Socioeconomic differentials in selected causes of death. Am. J. Public Health 68:342–351, 1978.
3. Newberne, P.: Diet and nutrition. Bull. N.Y. Acad. Med. 54(4):385–396, 1978.
4. Holtzman, N.: The goal of preventing early death, in Papers on the National Health Guidelines. Conditions for Change in the Health Care System. September 1977. Health Resources Administration, Washington, D.C., 1977.
5. Nathanson, C. A.: Sex, illness and medical care. Soc. Sci. Med. 11:13–25, 1977.
6. Nathanson, C. A.: Sex roles as variables in preventive health behavior. J. Commun. Health 3(2):142–155, 1977.
7. Lewis, C. E., and Lewis, M. A.: The potential impact of sexual equality on health. N. Engl. J. Med. 297:863–869, 1977.
8. Waldron, I.: Why do women live longer than men? Soc. Sci. Med. 10:349–62, 1976.
9. Keil, J. E., et al.: Hypertension: effects of social class and racial admixture: the results of a cohort study in the black population of Charleston, South Carolina. Am. J. Public Health 67:634–639, 1977.

85

10. Yeracaris and Kim, op. cit.
11. Lerner, M., and Stutz, R. N.: *Have we narrowed the gaps between the poor and the nonpoor? Part II. Narrowing the gaps, 1959–1961 to 1969–1971: mortality.* Med. Care 15:8, 1977.
12. *Leading causes of death in Africa, Asia and Latin America.* WHO Chron. 29:30–32, 1975.
13. *Leading causes of death in North America, Europe and Oceania.* WHO Chron. 29:106–7, 1975.
14. Tyroler, H.: *The Detroit Project Studies of Blood Pressure: a prologue and review of related studies and epidemiological issues.* J. Chron. Dis. 30:613–624, 1977.
15. Henrikson-Zeiner, T.: *Six-year mortality related to cardiorespiratory symptoms and environmental risk factors in a sample of the Norwegian population.* J. Chron. Dis. 29:15–33, 1976.
16. Zdichnec, B., et al.: *Some risk factors in pathologic aging.* J. Am. Geriatr. Soc. 25:259–263, 1977.
17. Cochran, A.: *World health problems.* Can. J. Public Health 66:280–287, 1975.
18. Rogers, P., and Rostenkowski, D.: *The National Leadership Conference on America's Health Policy: Keynote.* National J., July 1976, pp. 20–21.
19. Joint Economic Committee: *Inflation and the Consumer, 1974.* Congressional Staff Study. Washington, D.C., February 16, 1975.
20. U.S. Senate Select Committee on Nutrition and Human Needs: *Food Price Changes 1973–74 and Nutritional Status.* Washington, D.C., February 1974.
21. Economic Research Service: *Food Changes in the United States.* U.S. Department of Agriculture, Washington, D.C., 1974.
22. Cobb, S., and Kasl, S.: *Termination: The Consequence of Job Loss.* National Institute of Occupational Safety and Health, Cincinnati, June 1977.
23. U.S. Senate Select Committee on Nutrition and Human Needs: *Studies in Human Need: Rural Housing.* Washington, D.C., June 1972.
24. National Cancer Institute: *Adult Use of Tobacco, 1975.* National Institutes of Health, Washington, D.C., June 1976.
25. Alcohol, Drug Abuse and Mental Health Administration: *Alcohol and Health—June 1974.* National Institute on Alcohol Abuse and Alcoholism, Washington, D.C., 1974.
26. Brown, R., and Knittle, J.: *Prevention of Disease Through Optimal Nutrition: A Symposium.* Mt. Sinai Medical Center, New York, April 1976.
27. Reed, D., and Stanley, F. (eds.): *The Epidemiology of Prematurity.* Urban and Schwarzenberg, Baltimore, 1977, p. 14.
28. Economic Research Service, op. cit.
29. Whitehead, P., and Harvey, C.: *Explaining alcoholism: an empirical test and reformulation.* J. Health Social Behav. 15:57–65, 1974.
30. *Alcohol: a growing danger.* WHO Chron. 29:102–105, 1975.
31. Pradhan, S. N.: *Drug Abuse, Clinical and Basic Aspects.* C. V. Mosby, St. Louis, 1977, pp. 11–83.
32. Smart, R.: *Social policy and the prevention of drug abuse: perspectives on the unimodal approach,* in Glatt, M. (ed.): *Drug Dependence.* University Park Press, Baltimore, 1977.
33. Milio, N.: *A framework for prevention: changing health-damaging to health-generating life patterns.* Am. J. Public Health 66:435–439, 1976.
34. Bredemeier, H.: *Survey review of social exchange theory.* Contemp. Sociol. 646–650, 1977.

35. Breslow, L.: *Risk factor intervention for health maintenance.* Science 200:908–912, May 26, 1978.
36. Somers, A., and Somers, H.: *A proposed framework for health and health care policies.* Inquiry 14:115–170, 1977.
37. Knowles, J. (ed.): *Doing better and feeling worse: health in the U.S.* Daedalus 5:106, Winter 1977.
38. Public Health Service: *Forward Plan for Health, FY 1978–82.* Washington, D.C., 1976.
39. Fogarty International Center: *Preventive Medicine USA.* Prodist, New York, 1976.
40. Kaplan, B., et al.: *Social support and health.* Med. Care 15:47–58, 1977.
41. Cowan, E.: *Primary Prevention Misunderstood.* Soc. Policy 20–27, 1977.
42. Cooper, C. L., and Crump, J.: *Prevention and Coping with Occupational Stress.* J. Occup. Med. 20:420–426, 1978.
43. Gartner, A., and Riessman, F.: *Self-Help in the Human Services.* Jossey-Bass, San Francisco, 1977.
44. Robinson, D., and Henry, S.: *Self-Help and Health: Mutual Aid for Modern Problems.* Addiction Research Unit, University of London, 1977.
45. Cooper and Crump, op. cit.
46. Cunningham, R. (ed.): *The Holistic Health Centers: A New Direction in Health Care.* W. K. Kellogg Foundation, Battle Creek, Michigan, 1977.
47. Leppink, H., and de Grassi, A.: *Changes in Risk Behavior: Two Year Followup Study.* Paper presented to the Society of Prospective Medicine, San Diego, October 2, 1977.
48. U.S. Senate Select Committee on Nutrition and Human Needs: *Dietary Goals for the U.S.* Washington, D.C., 1977.
49. Rodnick, J. E., and Bubb, K.: *Patient education and multiphasic screening: it can change behavior.* J. Fam. Pract. 6:599–607, 1978.
50. Schramm, C. W.: *Wellness in Wisconsin.* Am. J. Public Health 3:19–27, 1978.
51. *Preliminary Report to the President from the President's Commission on Mental Health.* Office of the President, Washington, D.C., September 1, 1977.
52. Wigglesworth, E.: *Injury control: a state of the art review.* Aust. N.Z. J. Surg. 47(2):248–251, 1977.
53. Hadden, W.: *Energy damage and the ten countermeasure strategies.* J. Trauma 13:321–327, 1973.
54. Robertson, L.: *Behavioral research and strategies in public health: a demur.* Soc. Sci. Med. 9:165–170, 1975.
55. Carlos, J. (ed.): *Prevention and Oral Health.* National Institutes of Health, Washington, D.C., 1973.
56. International Union of Nutritional Sciences: *Report: Guidelines on the at-risk concept and the health and nutrition of young children.* Am. J. Clin. Nutrition 30:242–254, 1977.
57. Blane, H.: *Issues in preventing alcohol problems.* Prev. Med. 5:176–186, 1976.
58. *Preventive Medicine USA,* op. cit.
59. *Disability prevention and rehabilitation.* WHO Chron. 30:324–328, 1976.
60. Smart, R.: *Social Policy and the Prevention of Drug Abuse: Perspectives on the Unimodal Approach,* in Glatt, M. (ed.): *Drug Dependence.* University Park Press, Baltimore, 1977.
61. Lee, P., and Franks, P.: *Primary prevention and the Executive Branch of the Federal Government.* Prev. Med. 6:209–225, 1977.

87

62. Boden, L. I.: *The Economic Impact of Environmental Disease on Health Care Delivery.* J. Occup. Med. 18(7):467–472, 1976.
63. *Preventive Medicine USA,* op. cit.
64. Brenner, M. H.: *Health costs and benefits of economic policy.* Int. J. Health Serv. 7:581–623, 1977.
65. Eyer, J.: *Does unemployment cause the death rate peak in each business cycle? A multifactor model of death rate change.* Int. J. Health Serv. 7:625–663, 1977.
66. Milio, N.: *The Care of Health in Communities: Access for Outcasts.* Macmillan, New York, 1975.
67. Eckholm, E. P.: *The Picture of Health—Environmental Sources of Disease.* W. W. Norton, New York, 1977.
68. Miller, M., and Stokes, C.: *Health Status, Health Resources and Consolidated Structural Parameters: Implications for Public Health Care Policy.* J. Health Social Behav. 19:263–279, 1978.
69. Henderson, J. B., and Enflow, A. J.: *The coronary risk factor problem: a behavioral perspective.* Prev. Med. 5:128–148, 1976.
70. Fein, R.: *Prevention: fiscal and economic issues.* Bull. N.Y. Acad. Med. 51:235–241, 1975.
71. McKinley, J.: *A case for refocusing upstream—the political economy of illness,* in Enelow, A., and Henderson, J. (eds.): *Applying Behavioral Science to Cardiovascular Risk.* American Heart Association, Washington, D.C., 1975, pp. 7–17.
72. Sapira, J.: *Contemporary use of the disease concept.* J.A.M.A. 239:1634–1637, 1978.
73. National Center for Health Statistics: *National Ambulatory Medical Care Survey: Symptom Classification.* Rockville, Md., 1974.
74. McKeown, T.: *The Role of Medicine: Dream, Mirage or Nemesis?* Nuffield Provincial Hospital Trust, London, 1976.
75. Powles, J.: *On the limitations of modern medicine.* Sci. Med. Man. 1:1–30, 1973.
76. McKinlay, K., and McKinlay, S.: *The questionable contribution of medical measures to the decline of mortality in the United States in the twentieth century.* Milbank Med. Fund Q., Summer 1977.
77. Mintz, J., et al.: *Predicting the Outcome of Psychotherapy for Schizophrenics: Relative Contributions of Patient, Therapist, and Treatment Characteristics.* Arch. Gen. Psychiatry 33:1183–1186, 1976.
78. Carlson, R.: *The End of Medicine.* Wiley-Interscience, New York, 1975.
79. Mahler, H.: *Health—A demystification of medical technology.* Lancet, November 1, 1975, pp. 829–833.
80. Knowles, op. cit.
81. Halleck, S.: *Politics of Therapy.* Jason Aronson, New York, 1971.
82. Illich, I.: *Medical Nemesis.* Pantheon Books, New York, 1976.
83. Syme, S., and Berkman, L.: *Social class, susceptibility and sickness.* Am. J. Epidemiol. 104(1):1–8, 1976.
84. Sheldon, A.: *Toward a general theory of disease and medical care,* in Sheldon, A. (ed.): *Systems and Medical Care.* MIT Press, Cambridge, Mass., 1970, pp. 84–125.
85. Powles, J.: *The effects of health services on adult male mortality in relation to the effects of social and economic factors.* Ethics Sci. Med. 5:1–13, 1978.
86. *Preventive Medicine USA,* op. cit.
87. Somers and Somers, op. cit.

88. Blum, H.: *From a concept of health to a national health policy.* Am. J. Health Policy 1:3–20, 1976.
89. Lee and Franks, op. cit.
90. Milio, *The Care of Health in Communities,* op. cit.
91. Odum, E.: *The emergence of ecology as a new integrative discipline.* Science 195:1289–1293, 1977.
92. Rogers and Rostenkowski, op. cit.
93. Breslow, L.: *Research in a strategy for health improvement.* Int. J. Health Serv. 3:7–15, 1973.
94. Schaeffer, M.: *Administration of Environmental Health Programmes: A System View.* World Health Organization, Geneva, 1974.
95. Lerner, M.: *The non-health services' determinants of health levels: conceptualization and public policy recommendations.* Med. Care 15:74–83, 1977.
96. Milio, *Low-Cost Health Care,* op. cit.
97. Rall, D.: *Toward an integrated program of governmental action.* Ann. N.Y. Acad. Sci. 198:271, 1976.
98. Ardell, D.: *From omnibus tinkering to high-level wellness: the movement toward holistic health planning.* Am. J. Health Policy 1:15–34, 1976.
99. Blum, op. cit.
100. Cardus, D., and Thrall, R.: *Overview: Health and the Planning of Health Care Systems.* Prev. Med. 6:134–142, 1977.
101. Somers and Somers, op. cit.
102. *Health services in Europe: administration and preventive services.* WHO Chron. 30:407–412, 1976.
103. Minister of Health and Welfare: *A New Perspective on the Health of Canadians: A Working Document.* Government of Canada, Ottawa, 1974.

5

THE EFFECTS OF POLICY ON CHOICE-MAKING BY HEALTH CARE CONSUMERS AND PRACTITIONERS

Policy sets the options for choices that individuals can make. The plausibility of this view is strengthened by looking at the kinds of choices that both consumers and practitioners make as individuals who meet within the context of health services. This chapter will focus on how these choices are made, not on whether they improve people's health.*

This discussion will show through health services studies, how the consumer traverses the system of health care, especially within ambulatory care settings, and how consumers and practitioners decide the ensuing course of events. Both groups are viewed within the same terms of reference: they make choices in an effort to get the largest gain for what they expend. The parameters of their options are set, among other things, by the particular organizational circumstances in which they meet. The administrative and fiscal policies of health care sites are in turn influenced by a spectrum of public policies.

The reasons that people often behave differently than the way they say they should are discussed within these same terms of reference. The costs to people of developing new patterns of behavior based on new knowledge, beliefs, or attitudes are illustrated, suggesting an explanation for the successes and failures of health education as a means to change behavior and thereby promote health. One conclusion is that although knowledge may be highly important as a social value, it is not of prime importance in explaining why people do what they do. This implies that health policy can

---

*Chapters 9 and 11 consider the health effects of health services.

be more effective by focusing first on opening new and ready opportunities for choice-making, rather than by supplying people with information about how they should behave in the face of current opportunities.

HEALTH SERVICES BEHAVIOR

People seek out health services in ways not so much related to what health professionals advise as best for their health, but more related to the alternatives open to them at any given time.

Many studies, for example, show that higher-income people use more preventive health services than do those of more modest means.[1-5] Some interpret this to mean that wealthier people are more interested in preventing illness, are more concerned with health, and have more positive attitudes about health and health services than do poorer people. However, looking more closely, the "preventive health" activities include getting physical examinations, dental and eye check-ups, and buying health insurance. All of these measures require discretionary income and out-of-pocket payments even when facilities are conveniently located, as they often are not, especially for the poor.[6] In this way the true costs of engaging in "preventive health" activities are higher for those with lower income. Their options are fewer and more difficult. Only when illness, especially severe illness, occurs can their priorities for using limited funds shift so that time, distance, and money become less important than getting to a medical setting.[7-11]

The cost to individuals who seek medical services is less for a sick person than a well one, even when the dollar amount is the same. For the sick, the expected gain is immediate and tangible in the form of relief from pain and discomfort, if not cure. Even so, of course, if a person is poor, his or her cost is certain to be higher when compared with a sick affluent person. As a result, with the relative price low for the affluent and high for the poor in this country, higher-income people use health services more often than medically necessary as judged by physicians; lower-income people use them less often than they need.[12,13]

The cost to consumers of preventive or non-sickness health services, such as immunizations, routine check-ups, and contraceptive services, is higher in relative terms than that of symptom-related care. This is because insurance almost invariably covers only sickness. However, when the costs to individuals of these two kinds of services are equalized, as they are under health maintenance organizations (HMOs) or prepaid group practice insurance plans, the result is that lower-income persons, blue-collar workers and others, blacks and whites alike, increase their use of preventive services.[14-16]

In other words, once the opportunities for economic access and ready availability of a regular source of care are the same for lower-income people as for the affluent, their choices for using preventive services become similar, although still not identical. This is especially so for those with young families who expect to use services frequently. However, young families who are affluent and already have a private physician continue to exercise that option even when an HMO is available.[17]

Because poorer people often do not have a regular physician, they frequently use hospital emergency rooms for non-urgent health services, thus taxing the system. Some health professionals have called for educating them on the appropriate use of emergency services. Yet, when middle-class people in a suburban, semi-rural community found that they had no readily accessible private physicians, they began to use the local hospital emergency room for their non-urgent health services. This occurred regardless of their occupational status or the extent of their insurance coverage.[18,19] In effect, their alternatives for health care were reduced to the range typically available to poorer people. The choices of these middle-income people had to be made within the options available to them, and their health services pattern became like that of poorer people.

When the economic opportunities for paying for health services were increased in the mid-1960s through Federal policy initiatives, the poorer social groups exercised their new options, especially women in their child-bearing years and children. As a result, about a third more poor people now have had at least one visit to a physician within a two-year period than prior to the new policies. Since, however, these new opportunities did not include dental care, the poor have not changed their use of dental services, which remains at a lower rate than that maintained by middle-income groups. Even with more medical care, poor people have no fewer sick days lost from work and school, and their days of restricted activity and days in bed from illness have increased.[20] More health care has not resulted in better overall health for the poor. However, special subgroups, such as pregnant women and infants who received adequate services, have shown some improvement. These health gains were not as large as might have occurred had their opportunities for living under health-promoting circumstances been improved, along with medical services (see Chapters 9 and 11).

When economic options are narrowed for people by imposing on them deductibles and coinsurance under Medicare, Medicaid, Blue Cross, or HMO insurance plans, the poor, especially women, are the first to have to change their health services behavior. They are forced to choose *not* to use services which they otherwise would, if the opportunity were open to them. Affluent people are not likely to use fewer services until the deductible payment is fairly large.[21-24] Contrary to conventional wisdom, paying a fee does not seem to be related to how quickly people recover from illness or respond to treatment.[25]

In these ways the policies of governmental and health care organizations, which are increasingly interrelated, set the range of options for individuals, in this case restricting the opportunities for health care for some more than for others.[26,27]

Consumers in the System

Having once sought out health care, people then face a number of new decisions, their choices again delimited by the options open to them. Often, for example, drugs are prescribed by practitioners, but are not used properly by patients.[28-32] One of the most frequent reasons for this apparent choice not to comply is that patients had no alternative; they did not understand their illness or the drug's action.[33-35] Upon further consideration, however, intellectual comprehension seems not as important for patients as having explicit instructions about what to do. For behavior that is as specific as using medications, specific information is most effective. More importantly, however, when people have limited incomes, they are simply not as likely to buy any or all of the drugs they may need.[36] They cannot comply.

Even among those who can afford financially to follow their prescribed treatment plan, there are other costs in their personal situation. The price in time, pleasure, and family approval may not seem worth the potential benefit of choosing to follow treatment-oriented behavior over their normal patterns.[37]

This personal calculus, which is involved in the decisions of individuals to change their routine activities, suggests the importance of medical practitioners, physicians and others for helping to set the range of options available to their patients. They can make the choices that they ask patients to make less costly. This can be done by giving complete information, by explaining the pros and cons of alternatives, and especially by planning a regimen suited to peoples' circumstances at home and at work.[38]

The quality of such practitioner-patient communication is sometimes damaged by practitioners' views of patients—as "problem-patients," "neurotic," "ignorant," or "low-class"—in reaction to patients who may be less educated, female, or poor.[39-45] Lack of needed information may also be to blame when practitioners do not know, or fail to use, the most efficacious therapy.[46]

The decisions people make which form their patterns of health services behavior—when they will seek health care and how they will respond to the advice given them—are not a matter of free choice. No decision is.

Rather, they are choices made among a limited range of options open to them. They are likely to make the "easiest" choices, the ones promising the greatest gain for the least cost. The limitations on those opportunities come both from their personal social and economic circumstances and from the system of health services available to them.

Choice-Making by Practitioners

The other side of health services behavior also bears attention in a discussion of health care choice-making. This concerns the decisions of practitioners, most often studied with respect to physicians. Although they are far less than 10 percent of all health personnel, physician decisions determine how almost 80 percent of all health care dollars are spent.[47-49] The choices they make, concerning the "how" and "where" of treatment, affect not only the options of individual patients, but also the opportunities available for alternative patterns of service for the entire system of health care. These include the scope of activities and the income of nonphysician care-givers.[50]

Although prospective patients have relative freedom to choose to seek out health services initially, thereafter physicians' choices carry greater weight, especially for symptom-related care. Physician decisions determine the utilization of health services, including the number of diagnostic tests, drugs, follow-up visits, referrals, and inpatient or outpatient sites of care. This is true in several Western countries.[51,52]

In principle, similar options are open to most physicians most of the time concerning the type and length of treatment. Yet their patterns of choice, their health services behavior, differ widely and systematically.

The quality of care rendered by physicians as judged by their peers—for example, the decisions they make concerning patients with specific disorders—is not primarily related to *what they know,* as indicated by the kind of training they have had or their field of specialty.[53-58] Most important is the *setting* in which they work, the hospital and its organization, or the type of ambulatory care setting, whether solo or group practice. The administrative policies of organizational settings are important for affecting the quality of nurses' work in hospitals and ambulatory care settings as well.[59]

The choice physicians make between hospital and ambulatory forms of treatment is further related to the kind of ambulatory practice site in which they work. In health maintenance organizations, in which the HMO and its physicians are financially liable for incurring excess expenditures, physicians tend to rely on less costly ambulatory forms of care, especially when hospital beds are in limited supply.[60,61] In such settings they also tend to require fewer follow-up visits and prescribe fewer drugs as a result. They may choose a narrower spectrum of drugs when the HMO has its own pharmacy. These kinds of decisions result in savings for the HMO and third-party payers, including Medicaid. There has been, at the same time, no apparent loss in quality of care in the not-for-profit HMOs.[62,63]

However, at the same time that their decisions about hospitalization and drugs decrease the total costs of care in HMO settings, physicians' decisions about the use of their time does not necessarily make them more productive, in the conventional economic meaning of that term. The number of visits to each physician does not increase, and may decrease, even though a lesser fraction of his or her time need be spent in hospitals.[64] This has been found where physicians are salaried or where they otherwise have high, steady practice incomes, such as in fee-for-service group practices.[65]

Concerning the choice of diagnostic technology in the primary care practices of internists, it can be shown that if they choose to prescribe more procedures and tests—especially of a complex and energy-intensive nature—as in-office services, their net income or profits will be higher. Charges to patients and insurers will, of course, also be higher.[66] This applies to solo practices, and especially to group practice arrangements, when they are based on fee-for-service.

Thus, as occurs with consumers and individuals generally, the underlying calculus in physicians' choices—concerning site, length, and type of treatment—may also be interpreted as their seeking the greatest gains for least cost among the options available to them. When medically unnecessary use of hospital care is likely to involve their own financial risk, physicians are more likely to rely on less expensive ambulatory care. When seeing more patients is not likely to increase their income, they tend not to do so, as in salaried HMOs or large fee-for-service group practices.[67] When fee-for-service payments provide, in effect, an economic incentive for using more diagnostic services within private practice arrangements, they choose to acquire and use more of such technology, even in primary care settings.

Contexts for Individuals' Choices: Organizational Options for Action

The foregoing findings show that decisions affecting professionally judged patient care are more influenced by the settings in which physicians and nurses work than by their training. This suggests the importance of the working environment, its constraints and possibilities, for establishing the immediate opportunities for practitioners' choice-making. What practitioners have learned in training is not most influential. Group practice physicians, as a further example, are often judged by their peers to provide better quality care than solo physicians, whose practice by nature does not have the built-in option for consulting other opinions or for being monitored. This means that a physician who opts for lesser quality of care, in a group practice setting, does so at a higher personal cost than in a solo practice. The opportunities to be judged by one's peers are greater in group practice. In addition, personal economic risk may be involved in the group practice arrangement when excessive services are involved. In a more positive sense, a better quality of care becomes possible in a primary care or HMO setting as compared, for example, with an emergency room. This is because the former offers more options to both physician and patient to become better acquainted, to share more information over a period of years, and therefore to make choices based on the richness of that information without having to rely as heavily on technologically acquired test data.

The organizational arrangements of health services—which are heavily influenced by policies that affect the modes of financing and managing programs and settings—may be thought of as options for action, or opportunities for decision-making. The range of opportunities and the costs of each, as well as the ease with which practitioners may choose one over others, differ according to the service setting—hospital or ambulatory, solo or group. Related opportunities for economic rewards differ for the practitioner, depending upon whether the method of payment is fee-for-service, capitation, or salary. The fee method provides an "easy" option (one with low cost-for-gain to the practitioner) to prescribe more services than may be needed.

Although the array of available options, each having a certain net gain or cost to the chooser, will shape the *direction* of choices made by practitioners or by consumers, this does not mean that they are wholly *determinative*. Rather this suggests that only a small portion of any group of people may be expected to choose an option that requires a high cost to themselves in return for what they gain. In a fee-for-service practice, a practitioner may indeed scrupulously prescribe only needed services, even though he or she knows that this will keep earnings lower than they might otherwise be.

Most people will most often choose the least costly options available. Thus, as long as Federal health care financing and other insurance policies maintain fee-for-service as the primary method of payment, it will continue to be the easiest, least-costly method of reimbursement for physicians to select. It is therefore the most used, even though it is the most inflationary and the highest in economic costs to public and private payers.[68,69]

Other Federal policies which provide easy, high-gain-for-cost opportunities for physicians concern tax shelters and the tax benefits derived from incorporation. The effect has been, predictably, that an increasing proportion of physicians choose to practice as incorporated organizations and to

97

use tax shelters to expand their non-medical incomes. In corporate practice they gain a larger net income from working fewer hours than those who choose solo or unincorporated practices, and who also work longer hours and see more patients.[70-72]

Personal Choices of Professionals

It is possible to interpret other kinds of professional choices, such as decisions on which form of education to seek, what specialty to select, or where to locate geographically, as individuals' attempts to gain most of what they want at the least cost to themselves from the opportunities available to them. This includes not only physicians, but other health personnel as well.[73-77]

For example, Federal policy permits educational loans to be forgiven for new practitioners who choose to work in medically underserved communities. The policy has not been attractive or effective among physicians. For them, the easier choice, given the high income they can expect, is to pay off their loans in cash rather than service. For others, such as optometrists, the more difficult choice has been to pay off their loans in cash. They are thus more likely to render service.[78]

For many historical reasons, including documented sex discrimination, women have made the "easier" choice of a professional career in nursing instead of medicine.[79] Within those more limited professional opportunities, they too seek the highest-gain-for-cost option when they choose the location and setting for work. The range of economic opportunities available to nurses is often narrow because of hospital-controlled wage ceilings within geographic areas. They also experience constraints on relocation which are imposed by family responsibilities and particularly by the jobs and views of spouses. These are costs that many nurses cannot afford. The easier choice is often not to move into somewhat higher-paying regions or settings, or into areas of greater need, as some nurses say they would prefer to do.[80,81]

Preferences, Attitudes, and Action

Preferences should be distinguished from choices. What people prefer is what they say they would choose if they had the opportunity. In this sense, preferences are like attitudes or beliefs. They express what people think and feel but do not reliably predict what people will do when faced with decisions to act. This is because a decision to act—choice-making—depends on the options available at the time the decision is made.

In one attitude survey, for example, people expressed strong interest in all aspects of health insurance coverage. However, when faced with additions to their monthly premiums for each aspect, their decisions changed. Those with lowest incomes and smallest families were least willing to choose higher premiums for coverage which they had previously said was "very important" in principle.[82] In a similar way, three out of four Americans who do *not* get annual physical examinations nevertheless think it a good idea to do so.[83] Their attitude is a positive one, but the opportunities open to them appear to carry too great a cost in comparison with other priorities which require expenditure of their time, effort, or money.

Attitudes and satisfactions themselves often *develop from* the circumstances people face, from the opportunities for choice which they have experienced. It is not surprising that the people who are most dissatisfied with current forms of health services are those who have the most difficulty in gaining access to them: those who must travel farthest, wait longest, or pay most relative to their income, especially when they have no insurance coverage.[84,85] More of the poor and the uninsured want Federal insurance extended to the entire population, with more services covered, including drugs and dental care.[86] People in all income categories are critical of the cost of health services.[87] They disagree, however, on how best to rearrange current patterns, since the relative cost of different options will vary for different segments of the population.

Another example of how available opportunities can influence attitudes occurred among health administrators. A majority of administrators in one survey favorably viewed the new nurse practitioners as an asset to the delivery of health services. However, when asked how employable they believed these practitioners to be, less than a majority said they were willing to hire them. Those who were willing to employ the nurse practitioners were in health departments with clinic facilities and a relatively large professional staff, and often were themselves nurse administrators.[88,89] In effect, the administrators most willing to hire the practitioners were those who had a budgetary option to do so.

People's attitudes and opinions about issues often derive from experiences they have had as a result of making choices among the options available to them, and from their gains or losses in selecting one alternative over others. Their experiences influence what they think they stand to gain or lose when changes are proposed. It is therefore to be expected that the views and attitudes of the consumers and providers of health services often differ as well. They disagree about what the major problems are and, even more, what to do about them.[90] Consumers seem to prefer general practitioners, community-wide health planning, and universal national health insurance. Providers emphasize the importance of specialists, program-specific planning, and national health insurance for special groups, such as the poor and the aged.[91,92]

Among themselves, of course, providers differ, as various groups have different interests at stake whenever options for changing programs and policies are raised.[93] Changes in financing, reimbursement, licensure laws, and the composition of decision-making bodies can potentially shift the current dominant influence of hospitals and physicians toward ambulatory services and new types of practitioners. Thus the positions taken on these issues by different types of providers are often in conflict.[94]

Consumers, too, differ among themselves, as already noted. Their opinions derive not only from their socioeconomic position, but also from the amount of health care they think they need. The first-choice types of services desired by the ill differ from those desired by the well, as do the costs they are willing to bear, including the psychological ones, such as dissatisfaction with the system. Thus the views of the ill as to acceptable and unacceptable solutions to today's health and health care problems differ somewhat from the views of those who are healthier.[95,96]

Summary

The patterns of health services behavior of practitioners and patients show how each group makes decisions by the same rule of thumb: each seeks, within the limits of their awareness, what will bring the largest gain in return for cost. To each, "costs" and "gains" may have different meanings. In the decisions made between individual physician and patient, the choices they make for action among available options are those which each sees as promising greatest gains in relation to what each must expend of their valued resources: time, effort, money, anxiety, or personal dignity. Prior to making the choice of seeking health services, the prospective consumer's opportunities for care are set by his or her own socioeconomic circumstances, including the urgency of illness, by the nature of health services available in the community, and by the individual's knowledge of the system. Once the patient enters the system, the practitioner's choices, primarily those of the physician, become relatively more important for what will happen to the patient within the system. The physician further delimits, or expands, the range of opportunities available to the patient.

Physicians' choices, however, are also constrained. The options available to them through the organization and financing of their settings of practice render certain kinds of decisions relatively more costly for them to make. Economic costs are important, but not exclusive, in the calculus made by consumers and individual practitioners. The economic cost becomes a lower priority in their choice-making as their income or income security increases. Then other costs, such as convenience, comfort, and personal dignity, enter more largely into the gain-for-cost calculation of individuals' choices.

The policy choices made by organizations, which were not discussed here, also involve a gain-for-cost calculation but do not, in practice, include the intangible costs that influence the choices that individuals make. Thus individuals can choose to do, for love or loyalty, what may ruin them economically, or may literally kill them. Organizations are less likely to act knowingly in this way. Organizational issues are taken up in Chapters 6 and 12.

CHANGING BEHAVIOR THROUGH HEALTH EDUCATION

Attitudes can be changed, almost as feasibly as knowledge can be changed. People can learn to think and feel differently, to view their circumstances differently. However, whether knowledge and attitudes translate into behavior is quite another matter. Changed attitudes are not likely to produce changes in behavior unless opportunities for new choices are available at relatively low cost and are easy to choose when compared with current habitual choices. Habits include the use of health services or other patterns that make up the routine of daily life.

This view of the connection between what people know, feel, or believe, and what they do, is in line with recent findings on the successes and failures of health education to change people's behavior. As interest among policy-makers has increased in this health policy strategy, health education programs have likewise increased. Through community-oriented, mass media campaigns and small group or individual methods, such programs have succeeded in expanding people's knowledge. To some extent, they have also changed popular attitudes about smoking and drug use; food additives, obesity, high-fat diets, and exercise; and about home safety, auto seat belt use, and drunk driving, as well as childhood fluoride treatment, immunizations, and physical checkups.[97-115]

In general, however, the effectiveness of health education in changing people's behavior has been scant. There has been virtually no reduction in smoking or drug use among youths in health education programs. Only about 2 or 3 in 10 adult smokers remain abstainers 1 or 2 years after participating in quit-smoking programs. In special, self-selected health education groups, up to 40 percent of participants maintain a 5-pound weight loss over 18 months.[116] More often, however, no appreciable weight loss occurs, and up to two-thirds of participants drop out after a year of group weight-reduction sessions.[117] Despite health education campaigns, traffic safety habits and drunk driving incidence have remained largely unchanged, and seat belts continue to be used by only about 15 to 30 percent of car occupants.[118-123]

Health education has affected behavior when, along with new information, new or easier opportunities for choice-making are offered to people, giving them greater benefit for cost or providing current benefits at less cost.

Mothers, for example, responded not to media information, but to psycho-logically rewarding invitational appointment cards, to obtain immuniza-tions which were readily accessible.[124,125] Children continued topical fluo-ride treatments at school when offered small rewards.[126] The incidence of childhood falls from apartment windows was reduced by 50 percent after free, easily installed window guards were provided to parents.[127]

Seat belt use increased to 75 percent when made mandatory and en-forceable by law.[128] Fewer cases of childhood poisoning were reported when the use of safety caps was instituted for drug bottles.[129] When closely counseled by their physicians, smoking cessation was maintained by over 60 percent of adults who had experienced heart attacks.[130] This higher rate of success often occurs among people who are already ill and are con-scious of the discomforts caused by their illness.[131,132] As already noted, the gain-for-cost among the ill for choosing alternative ways of living is higher than for the well.

An Experiment as Illustration

Many complexities are suggested by the foregoing studies about what does and does not produce behavioral change as a result of health education. These matters were clarified somewhat in a recent study which was per-haps the largest and most thorough experiment of its kind in this country. The citizens of three semi-rural towns in northern California were involved in a 2-year health education program to reduce their risk of cardiovascular disease. In one town, the control, no special education was offered. The other two towns had a mass media campaign to discourage smoking and dietary fat, and to encourage weight loss and exercise. One of those towns also had special behavior modification groups for adults aged 35 to 50, who, because of hypertension, obesity, and other characteristics, were at high risk for heart disease.[133]

After 2 years, this high-risk group showed a beneficial drop in their risk-factor index of about 30 percent. However, those at high risk who did not attend the special sessions had a similar drop in risk factors, presumably as a result of mass media education. For the rest of the population in the two mass-media towns, the reduction in risk was about 20 percent. These were the vast majority who were not at risk of heart disease and included spe-cifically the spouses of the high-risk group members.[134,135]

Thus the method of small-group behavior modification did not add to the success of the mass education campaign among high-risk persons, al-though it was much more expensive. There was less success in risk reduc-tion among people who were at normal levels of risk. This was mainly be-cause high-risk people were able to reduce their smoking to a greater extent, by about two to six cigarettes a day. Normal-risk persons reduced their habit by less than two cigarettes a day.

Knowledge about risk factors increased for all participants by about 35 percent, with somewhat higher scores for the high-risk people who attended the group sessions.[136]

None of the subgroups in the populations, however, changed their weight or exercise patterns. Nevertheless, the towns with the mass campaigns did know more and did show more changes in diet, smoking, and blood pressure reduction than the control town which had not had the media blitz.[137]

To further qualify the findings, the investigators point out that they were only able to observe fully just over half of the eligible sample populations. Secondly, the extent of food changes is questionable since blood cholesterol did not drop as much as the reductions in dietary fats, which people reported, should have produced. Moreover, some of the change in eating habits, such as the drop in egg consumption and dietary cholesterol, might have resulted from an increase in egg prices which occurred at the time of the study.[138,139]

Two unintended effects were observed. The first was that hypertensive people became more consistent in taking their prescribed medications as a result of the group sessions, thus reducing their blood pressure. A second and undesired effect was that the towns actually *decreased* their use of unsaturated fats as well as saturated fats, bespeaking the problem of making a complex message clear over mass media. People apparently did not distinguish the primarily unsaturated vegetable fats from saturated animal fats.[140]

The greatest successes, beyond gains in knowledge, seemed to occur in patterns of behavior which were fairly specific and could be isolated from current activities, such as taking antihypertensive drugs, egg consumption, and smoking. These were, relatively, more under the control of individuals. In addition, alternatives for behavior in these areas were more likely to be chosen when special circumstances reduced their costliness to individuals: current illness combined with two years of mass media reminders (for taking antihypertensive drugs); the market price of eggs (for egg consumption); and high-risk status together with behavior modification group support (for smoking). In other words, among those groups of people for whom available opportunities became "easier" to choose, their decisions about engaging in some activities changed.

There was little or no success in changing behavior for patterns which were more general, complex, and integrated into everyday living, and thus less under the control of individuals, such as weight loss and exercise. Nor were there successes when the gain-for-cost was small, as with smoking among normal-risk people who had no group support. Weight loss—in contrast to the decrease in consumption by two or three eggs per week which occurred—involves changes for most people in the amounts and types of food they eat. This, in turn, affects family patterns and feelings, budgets, work relationships, and other social and cultural patterns. It thus comes at high cost. Perhaps to a greater degree, exercise in a semi-rural town usually requires a special allocation of time taken from family responsibilities, which itself entails a cost. Presumably, jobs and shopping facilities require transportation by car, including the time in transit, without benefit of convenient public transportation. Here again, exercise comes at increased cost to the individual. This cost was not changed through education about the risk-reduction benefits of exercise.

Such costs remained high even among those who were most intimately aware of the possible consequences of continuing risky habits. These were the spouses of the high-risk people in the group sessions. Their behavior changed no more than that of the general population.[141] They were like the wives in another study who continued to smoke after their husbands had had heart attacks and had quit smoking.[142] Apparently, intimate knowledge alone is not sufficient to reduce the cost to individuals of making new choices for their behavior.

A 20 percent reduction in the risk of heart disease for a population, as in the California experiment, is surely better than no reduction. But before generalizations can be drawn about the efficacy and cost-effectiveness of such mass health education campaigns for other communities, more needs to be known. For example, the economic levels of the three California towns and their citizens were not disclosed. Presumably, the towns were composed largely of middle-income families. If so, lower-income communities may not be able to respond to a similar campaign with even a 20 percent success in risk reduction. This is because they may have fewer economic and social opportunities to replace current patterns of smoking, eating, and medical treatment.[143,144] Questions have also been raised as to whether the degree of risk reduction which the participants achieved, such as smoking two to six fewer cigarettes a day, would actually make a difference clinically in their medical condition, especially in the older age groups.[145,146]

In sum, the greatest gains in this well-organized, community-oriented experiment in health education were in secondary prevention. The people it helped most were those who were already ill or were at high risk of cardiovascular illness.

New Knowledge and New Behavior

Knowledge and attitudes can indeed be changed, but they are not sufficient to change most behavior for most people.[147-149] If knowledge about health-promoting personal activities were sufficient, then surely educators and health professionals, as a group, would have changed their smoking habits. Science and physical education teachers, physicians and dentists have largely done so. Guidance counselors and nurses have not. Their actual behavior notwithstanding, the vast majority of all these professionals, and of the public, believe that they should set a good example by not smoking.[150-152]

Not only are new knowledge and attitudes not *sufficient* to induce new choices in behavior, they are often not *necessary*. With little or no new knowledge or alteration in attitudes, women, for example, have changed birth control practices and food patterns. They have gotten Papanicoulau smears and immunizations when these services were made readily available to them; that is, when new opportunities were provided at low relative cost.[153-159] As already noted, drivers are more likely to use seat belts, whatever their knowledge of safety or attitudes about seat belts, when their use is mandatory.[160] Similarly, people use fluoridated water regardless of their knowledge or attitudes about the health-promoting value of fluoride. They also use contaminated water and breathe polluted air without knowing the impact or source of the contaminants. They buy new, hazardous products and adopt new foods that may not be health-promoting, without being aware of the policies of agribusiness, manufacturing, or government which put those items on the market.

Changes in knowledge or attitudes are often neither necessary nor sufficient to change the patterns of choice which make up everyday behavior. Not only may knowledge or attitudes change quite apart from behavior, but they also may, and often do, change *after* new patterns of behavior have been adopted, bringing them into line with people's actual experience. Racial attitudes improve, for example, *after* blacks and whites work and live in proximity; and people become satisfied with HMO services *after* they have used them, contrary to their attitudes prior to the experience.[161-163]

Knowledge as Social Value and as Explanation for Behavior

As a variety of evidence suggests, a basic principle for inducing changes in patterns of choice is to provide new opportunities and eliminate or alter current options, such that certain ones require a lesser cost than others, regardless of popular understanding or attitudes. Of course, as an often-expressed social value, *informed* choice is highly important. This is so even though, in practice, persons who are informed and who, among others, actually have numerous alternatives from which to choose are not necessarily a majority, nor are they equally represented among various segments of the population. While knowledge, understanding, and "free" choice—which

105

often unrealistically implies the absence of constraints—may be necessary as ideals in a modern democracy, they are not essential to interpret the patterns of choice which compose everyday behavior. Nevertheless, as an ideal, the language of voluntarism and its overtones of "free" choice will continue to be brought into policy-making debates on how best to improve modern health (see Chapter 12).

Summary

Patterns of behavior, in many contexts, eventually have a marked effect on the modern health problem. Among these patterns are those which health professionals study most often: selected personal habits and health services patterns. What people know and believe, and what they actually choose to do—whether as consumers or practitioners in their professional or private lives—often diverge dramatically. People are more likely to make choices that bring them a larger gain for their costs. Therefore policy thrusts that seek to provide new knowledge as a principal means of encouraging health-promoting behavior are not likely to be effective. Policy that creates new, lower-cost health-making opportunities for the individual, or for organizations which in turn program the options for individuals to choose, will be more effective.

REFERENCES

1. Kar, S.: *Communication interventions in health and family planning programs: a conceptual framework.* Int. J. Health Ed. 20:1–15 (Suppl.), 1977.
2. Richards, N.: *Methods and effectiveness of health education.* Soc. Sci. Med. 9:142–156, 1975.
3. Coburn, D., and Pope, C.: *Socioeconomic status and preventive health services.* J. Health Social Behav. 15:76–78, 1974.
4. Steele, J., and McBroom, W.: *Conceptual and empirical dimensions of health behavior.* J. Health Social Behav. 13:382–392, 1972.
5. Salkever, D.: *Economic class and differential access to care: comparison among health care systems.* Int. J. Health Serv. 5:375–395, 1975.
6. Milio, N.: *The Care of Health in Communities: Access for Outcasts.* Macmillan, New York, 1975.
7. Steele and McBroom, op. cit.
8. Berki, S., and Kobashigawa, B.: *Socioeconomic and need determinants of ambulatory care use: path-analysis of the 1970 Health Interview Survey data.* Med. Care 14:5, 1976.
9. Haisinger, E., and Hobbs, D.: *The relation of community context to utilization of health services in a rural area.* Med. Care 11(4):509–522, 1973.
10. Greenlick, M., et al.: *Comparing the use of medical care services by a medically indigent and a general membership population in a comprehensive prepaid group practice.* Med. Care 10:187–200, 1972.

11. Bice, T., et al.: *Socioeconomic status and use of physician services: a reconsideration.* Med. Care, May–June 1972.
12. Taylor, O., et al.: *A social indicator of access to medical care.* J. Health Social Behav. 40–49, 1975.
13. Anderson, R., and Smedby, B.: *Changes in response to symptoms of illness in the U.S. and Sweden.* Inquiry 12:116–127, 1975.
14. Ashcraft, M., et al.: *Expectations and experience of HMO enrollees after one year: an analysis of satisfaction, utilization and costs.* Paper presented at the American Public Health Association Annual Meetings, Washington, D.C., October 30, 1977.
15. Slesinger, D., et al.: *Effects of social characteristics on the utilization of preventive medical services in contrasting health care programs.* Med. Care 14:5, 1976.
16. Wells, S., and Roghman, K.: *GM inpatient utilization before and after offering prepayment plans.* Paper presented at the American Public Health Association Annual Meetings, Washington, D.C., October 30, 1977.
17. Berki, S., et al.: *Multivariate analysis of HMO enrollment decisions.* (abstract) University of Michigan School of Public Health, Ann Arbor, 1977.
18. Kelman, H., and Lane, D.: *Use of hospital emergency rooms in relation to use of private physicians.* Am. J. Public Health 66:1189–1191, 1976.
19. Wan, T. T. H., and Gray, L. C.: *Differential access to preventive services for young children in low-income urban areas.* J. Health Social Behav. 19:312–324, 1978.
20. Wilson, R., and White, E.: *Changes in morbidity, disability and utilization differentials between the poor and the nonpoor: data from the Health Interview Survey: 1964 and 1973.* Med. Care 15(8):636–646, 1977.
21. Scitovsky, A., and McCall, N.: *Coinsurance and the demand for physician services: four years later.* Soc. Sec. Bull. 40:19–27, 1977.
22. Peel, E., and Scharff, J.: *Impact of cost-sharing on the use of ambulatory services under Medicare, 1969.* Soc. Sec. Bull. 36, October 1973.
23. Ginsburg, P., and Manheim, L.: *Insurance, Copayment and Health Services Utilization: A Critical Review.* J. Econ. Bus., Spring, 1975.
24. Friedman, B., et al.: *Influence of Medicaid and previous health insurance on early diagnosis of breast cancer.* Med. Care 11:485–490, 1973.
25. *Fees 'good for' client? study raises doubts.* Innovations 40:32, Fall, 1976.
26. Stevens, R., and Stevens, R.: *Welfare Medicine in America: A Case Study of Medicaid.* Macmillan, New York, 1974.
27. Cooper, B., and Worthington, N.: *Comparison of Cost and Benefit Incidence of Government Medical Care Programs, FY 1966 and 1969.* Staff Paper No. 18. Social Security Administration, Washington, D.C., September 1974.
28. Mitchell, J.: *Compliance with medical regimens: an annotated bibliography.* Health Ed. Monogr. 2:75–87, 1974.
29. *Drug use in health care.* State of the Art (University of North Carolina) 4:7–9, December 1977.
30. Hulka, B., et al.: *Communication, compliance and concordance between physicians and patients with prescribed medications.* Am. J. Public Health 66:847, 1976.
31. Parkin, D.: *Survey of the Success of Communications Between Hospital Staff and Patients.* Public Health 90(5):203–209, 1976.
32. Ward, G.: *Changing Trends in Control of Hypertension.* Pub. Health Rep. 93(1):31–34, 1978.

33. Werner, A.: *Health related concerns of college students.* J. Am. Coll. Health Assoc. 24:276–282, 1976.
34. Ward, op. cit.
35. *Why patients don't follow orders.* Med. World News, April 21, 1972, pp. 45–55.
36. Kirsch, J., and Rosenstock, I.: *Patients adherence to antihypertensive medical regimens.* J. Comm. Health 3(2):115–124, 1977.
37. Weiss, S. (ed.): *Proceedings of NHLI Working Conference on Health Behavior, May 12–15, 1975.* National Institutes of Health, Washington, D.C., 1976.
38. Barro, A.: *Survey and evaluation of approaches to physician performance measurement.* J. Med. Ed. 45(Suppl.):1047–1093, 1973.
39. Fabrega, M., et al.: *Low income medical problem patients.* J. Health Social Behav. 10:334–343, 1969.
40. McKinley, J.: *Who is really ignorant—physician or patient?* J. Health Social Behav. 16:1–11, 1975.
41. Henry, W., et al.: *Public and Private Lives of Psychotherapists.* Jossey-Bass, San Francisco, 1973.
42. Walsh, J., and Elling, R.: *Professionalism and the poor,* in Friedson, E., and Lorber, J. (eds.): *Medical Men and Their Work.* Aldine, Chicago, 1972, pp. 267–287.
43. Goodman, J., et al.: *Factors affecting psychiatric diagnosis.* Can. J. Public Health 67:397–400, 1976.
44. Lennane, K., and Lennane, R.: *Alleged psychogenic disorders in women—a possible manifestation of sexual prejudice.* N. Engl. J. Med. 288:288–292, 1973.
45. Mechanic, D.: *Sex, illness behavior and the use of health services.* J. Hum. Stress 2:29–40, 1976.
46. Ward, op. cit.
47. Luft, H.: *National health care expenditures: Where do the dollars go?* Inquiry 13:344–363, 1976.
48. Congressional Budget Office: *Expenditures for Health Care: Federal Programs and Their Effects.* Washington, D.C., August 1977.
49. Dyckman, Z.: *A Study of Physicians' Fees.* Staff Report, Council on Wage and Price Stability, Washington, D.C., 1978.
50. Milio, op. cit.
51. Dutton, D.: *Organizational and professional characteristics of health care settings and their impact on patient utilization.* Paper presented at the American Public Health Association Annual Meetings, Washington, D.C., November 1, 1977.
52. *Use of health care: an international study.* WHO Chron. 30:403–406, 1976.
53. Rhee, S.: *Relative importance of physicians' personal and situational characteristics for the quality of patient care.* J. Health Social. Behav. 18:10–15, 1977.
54. Riedel, D., et al.: *Determinants of physician performance in ambulatory care.* Paper presented at the American Public Health Association Annual Meetings, Washington, D.C., November 1, 1977.
55. Patrick, D.: *Primary care treatment of emotional problems in an HMO.* Med. Care 16(1):47–60, 1978.
56. Ross, C., and Duff, R.: *Quality of outpatient pediatric care: the influence of physicians' background, socialization and work/information environment on performance.* J. Health Social Behav. 19:348–360, 1978.
57. Flood, A. B., and Scott, W. R.: *Professional power and professional effective-*

ness: the power of the surgical staff and the quality of surgical care in hospitals. J. Health Social Behav. 19:240–254, 1978.
58. Dieter-Haussmann, R., et al.: Monitoring Quality of Nursing Care, Part II. Division of Nursing, Bureau of Health Manpower, Washington, D.C., July 1976.
59. Williams, C.: Family Nurse Practitioner. Worksite Influences on Practice. Unpublished research report, University of North Carolina School of Nursing and School of Public Health, Chapel Hill, 1978.
60. Weil, P.: Comparative costs to the Medicare program of seven prepaid group practices and controls. Milbank Mem. Fund Q. 54:339–365, 1976.
61. Holahan, J.: Foundations for medical care: an empirical investigation of the delivery of health services to a Medicaid population. Inquiry 14:352–379, 1977.
62. Rabin, D.: Drug prescription rates before and after enrollment of a Medicaid population in an HMO. Public Health Rep. 93(1):16–23, 1978.
63. Bush, P., and Osterweis, M.: Pathways to medicine use. J. Health Social Behav. 9:179–189, 1978.
64. Luft, H.: Trends in medical care costs: Do HMOs lower the rate of growth? Paper presented at the American Public Health Association Annual Meetings, Washington, D.C., November 1, 1977.
65. National Center for Health Statistics: National Ambulatory Medical Care Survey, May 1973–April 1974. Rockville, Md., 1975.
66. Schroeder, S., and Showstack, J.: Fiscal incentives to perform medical procedures and laboratory tests. Paper presented at the American Public Health Association Annual Meetings, Washington, D.C., November 1, 1977.
67. Goldberg, L., and Greenberg, W.: The Health Maintenance Organization and Its Effects on Competition. Staff Report, Federal Trade Commission, Washington, D.C., July 1977.
68. Sloan, F.: The Geographic Distribution of Nurses and Public Policy. Division of Nursing, Bureau of Health Manpower, Bethesda, Md., 1975.
69. Expenditures for Health Care, op. cit.
70. Office of Research and Statistics: Study of Physicians' Income in the Pre-Medicaid Period—1965. Social Security Administration, Washington, D.C., 1976.
71. Luft, op. cit.
72. Thorndike, N.: 1975 net incomes and work patterns of physicians in five medical specialties. Social Security Administration, Research and Statistical Notes, 13, July 21, 1977.
73. Women and Minorities in Health Fields: A Trend Analysis of College Freshmen Interested in the Health Professions. Report No. 77–44, vol. 1. Health Resources Administration, Washington, D.C., 1977, pp. 1–47.
74. Women and Minorities in Health Fields: A Trend Analysis of College Freshmen Interested in Nursing and Allied Health Professions. Report No. 77–46, Vol. 2. Health Resources Administration, Washington, D.C., 1977, pp. 1–30.
75. Hesselbart, S.: Women doctors win and male nurses lose: a study of sex roles and occupational stereotypes. Social Work Occup. 4(1):49–63, 1977.
76. Gray, L.: The geographic and functional distribution of black physicians. Am. J. Public Health 67:519–526, 1977.
77. Reitzes, D., and Elkhanialy, H · Black Physicians and Minority Group Health Care—The Impact of NMF. Med. Care 14(12), 1976.
78. CONSAD Research Corporation: An evaluation of the effectiveness of loan forgiveness as an incentive for health practitioners to locate in medically un-

derserved areas, in *Health Manpower Training and Nurse Training, 1974 Hearings.* House Subcommittee on Public Health and the Environment, Washington, D.C., 1974, pp. 1325–1330.
79. Milio, op. cit.
80. Nash, P.: *Evaluation of Employment Opportunities for Newly Licensed Nurses.* Division of Nursing, Bureau of Health Manpower, Bethesda, Md., 1975.
81. Sloan, op. cit.
82. Acito, F.: *Consumer Decision Making and Health Maintenance Organizations: A Review.* Med. Care 16(1):1–13, 1978.
83. National Heart and Lung Institute: *The Public and High Blood Pressure. Survey Report, June 1973.* Washington, D.C., 1975.
84. Pereda, C.: *Under- and over-demand and the use of personal health services: the problem of differential accessibility.* Ethics Sci. Med. 3:107–128, 1976.
85. *A new survey on access to medical care.* The Robert Wood Johnson Foundation Special Report, 1, 1978.
86. Aday, L., et al.: *Social surveys and health policy: implications for national health insurance.* Public Health Rep. 92:508–517, 1977.
87. Fleming, G., and Anderson, R.: *Health Beliefs of the U.S. Population: Implications for Self-Care.* Background Paper, Conference on Self-Care Programs, National Center for Health Services Research, Washington, D.C., 1976.
88. Fottler, M., and Pinchoff, D.: *Acceptance of the nurse practitioner: attitudes of health care administrators.* Inquiry 13:262–273, 1976.
89. Fottler, M. D., et al.: *Physician attitudes toward the nurse practitioner.* J. Health Social Behav. 19:303–311, 1978.
90. Lebow, J.: *Consumer assessments of the quality of medical care.* Med. Care 12:328–337, 1974.
91. Milio, op. cit.
92. Strickland, S.: *U.S. Health Care: What's Wrong and What's Right About It.* Potomac Associates, Washington, D.C., 1973.
93. Milio, N.: *Health Planning and Administration with the Consumer in View and Involved. I. Planning for the "Consumer-as-Citizen" and for the "Consumer-as-Patient,"* University of Cincinnati Program in Community Health Planning/Administration, 1976.
94. Milio, 1975, op. cit.
95. Flexner, W.: *Involving the Consumer in Health Care Through Marketing Research: Applications to Abortion Service Design.* Ph.D. dissertation, University of North Carolina School of Public Health, Chapel Hill, 1976.
96. Milio, 1975, op. cit.
97. Thompson, E.: *Smoking education programs, 1960–1976.* Am. J. Public Health 68(3):250–257, 1978.
98. West, D., et al.: *Five-year followup of a smoking withdrawal clinic population.* Am. J. Public Health 67:536–544, 1977.
99. Mossman, P.: *Changing habits—an experience in industry.* J. Occup. Med. 20(3):213, 1978.
100. Leppink, H., and deGrassi, A.: *Changes in risk behavior: two-year followup study.* Paper presented to the Society of Prospective Medicine, San Diego, October 2, 1977.
101. Smart, R.: *Social policy and the prevention of drug abuse: perspectives on the unimodal approach,* in Glatt, M. (ed.): *Drug Dependence.* University Park Press, Baltimore, 1977.

102. Green, L.: *Determining the Impact and Effectiveness of Health Education as It Relates to Federal Policy*. HEW Office of Planning and Evaluation, Washington, D.C., 1976.
103. Dershewitz, R., and Williamson, J.: *Prevention of childhood household injuries: a controlled clinical trial*. Am. J. Public Health 67(12):1148–1153, 1977.
104. Scherz, R.: *Restraint systems for the prevention of injury to children in automobile accidents*. Am. J. Public Health 66:451–456, 1976.
105. Spiegel, C., and Lindaman, F.: *Children can't fly: a program to prevent childhood morbidity and mortality from window falls*. Am. J. Public Health 67:1143–1147, 1977.
106. Robertson, L., et al.: *A controlled study of the effect of television messages on safety belt use*. Am. J. Public Health 64(11):1071–1080, 1974.
107. Wigglesworth, E.: *Injury control: a state of the art review*. Aust. N.Z. J. Surg. 47(2):248–251, 1977.
108. Robertson, L.: *Estimates of motor vehicle seat belt effectiveness and use: implications for occupant crash protection*. Am. J. Public Health 66(9):859–864, 1976.
109. Holtzman, N.: *The goal of preventing early death*, in *Papers on the National Health Guidelines. Conditions for Change in the Health Care System, September 1977*. Health Resources Administration, Washington, D.C., 1977.
110. Lund, A., et al.: *Motivational techniques for increasing acceptance of preventive health measures*. Med. Care 15:678, 1977.
111. U.S. Senate Select Committee on Nutrition and Human Needs: *Diet Related to Killer Diseases. Obesity Hearings II*. Washington, D.C., 1977.
112. Maccoby, N., et al.: *Reducing the risk of cardiovascular disease: effects of a community-based campaign on knowledge and behavior*. J. Comm. Health 3(2):100–114, 1977.
113. Yarnell, J.: *Evaluation of health education: the use of a model of preventive health behavior*. Soc. Sci. Med. 10:393–398, 1976.
114. National Heart and Lung Institute: *The Public and High Blood Pressure. Survey Report, June 1973*. Washington, D.C., 1975.
115. Williams, A., and Wechsler, H.: *Interrelationship of preventive actions in health and other areas*. Health Serv. 87:969–976, 1972.
116. Leppink and deGrassi, op. cit.
117. Senate Select Committee, op. cit.
118. Wigglesworth, op. cit.
119. Robertson et al., op. cit.
120. Holtzman, op. cit.
121. Fhaner, G., and Hane, M.: *Seat belts: factors influencing their use—a literature survey*. Accident Anal. Prev. 5:27–43, 1973.
122. Plant, M.: *Alcoholism: Evaluation of the 1976 Campaign in Scotland*. Royal Edinburgh Hospital, 1977.
123. Robertson, L., and Zador, P.: *Driver education and fatal crash involvement of teenaged drivers*. Am. J. Public Health 68:959–965, 1978.
124. Yarnell, op. cit.
125. Vernon, T., et al.: *An evaluation of three techniques for improving immunization levels in elementary schools*. Am. J. Public Health 66:457–460, 1976.
126. Lund et al., op. cit.
127. Spiegel and Lindaman, op. cit.
128. Robertson, op. cit.
129. Barry, P.: *Individual versus community orientation in the prevention of inju-*

111

ries. Prev. Med. 4:47–56, 1975.
130. Thompson, op. cit.
131. Conte, A., et al.: *Group work with hypertensive patients.* Am. J. Nurs. 74:910–912, 1974.
132. Rosenberg, S.: *A Case for Patient Education.* Hosp. Form. Mngt. 6:1–4, 1971.
133. Maccoby et al., op. cit.
134. Senate Select Committee, op. cit.
135. Farquhar, J.: *Community education for cardiovascular health.* Lancet 1:1192–1195, 1977.
136. Ibid.
137. Ibid.
138. Stern, M., et al.: *Results of a two-year health education campaign on dietary behavior—the Stanford Three-Community Study.* Circulation 54(5):826–833, 1976.
139. Maccoby, N.: *Achieving Behavior Change via Mass Media and Interpersonal Communication.* Study Report, American Heart Association Symposium, Stanford, Cal., January 30, 1975.
140. Stern et al., op. cit.
141. Maccoby et al., op. cit.
142. Croog, S., and Richards, N.: *Health benefits and smoking patterns in heart patients and their wives: a longitudinal study.* Am. J. Public Health 67:921–928, 1977.
143. Belloc, N.: *The relationship of health practices and mortality.* Prev. Med. 2:67–81, 1973.
144. Rodnick, J. E., and Bubb, K.: *Patient education and multiphasic screening: it can change behavior.* J. Fam. Pract. 6:599–607, 1978.
145. Pomerleau, O., et al.: *Role of behavior modification in preventive medicine.* N. Engl. J. Med. 292:1277–1282, 1975.
146. Holtzman, op. cit.
147. Richards, N.: *Methods and effectiveness of health education.* Soc. Sci. Med. 9:142–156, 1975.
148. Green, L.: *Determining the Impact and Effectiveness of Health Education as It Relates to Federal Policy.* HEW Office of Planning and Evaluation, Washington, D.C., April 30, 1976.
149. Duncan, G., and Morgan, J.: *Five Thousand American Families: Patterns of Economic Progress.* Institute of Social Research, Ann Arbor, 1975.
150. Wakefield, J.: *Public Education About Cancer: Recent Research and Current Programs.* International Union Against Cancer, Geneva, 1977.
151. *Smoking behavior and attitudes of physicians, nurses and pharmacists, 1975.* Morbid. Mortal. Weekly Rep. 26:1, 1977.
152. National Cancer Institute: *Adult Use of Tobacco, 1975.* National Institutes of Health, Washington, D.C., 1976.
153. Stycos, J.: *The Clinic and Information Flow.* Cornell University, Ithaca, N.Y., 1974.
154. Bendick, M., et al.: *Toward Efficiency and Effectiveness in the WIC Delivery System.* Urban Institute, Washington, D.C., 1976.
155. Yarnell, op. cit.
156. Vernon et al., op. cit.
157. Robertson et al., op. cit.
158. *Program evaluation.* Fam. Plann. Digest 3:13, 1974.
159. Wan, T. T. H., and Gray, L. C.: *Differential access to preventive services for*

young children in low income urban areas. J. Health Social Behav. 19:312–324, 1978.
160. Robertson, op. cit.
161. Selltiz, C., et al.: *Research Methods in Social Relations.* Holt, Rinehart & Winston, New York, 1964.
162. Berki, S., et al.: *Multivariate Analysis of HMO Enrollment Decisions.* (abstract) University of Michigan School of Public Health, Ann Arbor, 1977.
163. Ashcroft, M., et al.: *Expectations and experience of HMO enrollees after one year: an analysis of satisfaction, utilization and costs.* Paper presented at the American Public Health Association Annual Meetings, Washington, D.C., October 30, 1977.

PART 3
THE HEALTH EFFECTS
OF PUBLIC POLICY

6

ENVIRONMENTAL, ENERGY, AND
ECONOMIC POLICIES

Modern environments are not "natural." Almost no aspect of them is untouched by industrialized societies. More pervasively than at any time in history, the policy decisions of large organizations—governments and corporations alike—design, by intent or neglect, the environments in which people live, and, in turn, heavily influence their personal behavior. Policy affects the choices that can be made by organized groups and by individuals. In this way, the decisions of industry or agriculture, of consumer, worker, bureaucrat, or entrepreneur, become the patterns of living that result in the contemporary picture of health and illness.

The following discussion will examine three interlinked areas of public policy: environmental and energy policies, and the major components of economic policy. The intent is to show how these governmental courses of action shape the biophysical and socioeconomic dimensions of people's environments, and to suggest as well ways in which they influence the personal choices that people can make.

These policies, through their impact on the animate and constructed parts of environments, have some acknowledged effect on people's health. However, health may be affected more profoundly and subtly through the impact that these policies have on national and personal economic conditions. These *indirect* effects on health will be explored.

Underlying the discussion, and made most explicit in the illustration of environmental policy, are the ways in which public policy affects the policy decisions made by manufacturing and service organizations. Their response, in turn, affects people's health through their impacts on worksite and community environments, wages and jobs, and consumer products.

117

These policies also illustrate a range of design strategies and a variety of instruments that are used to deploy policies, including direct expenditures for public services and the use of indirect, fiscal incentives. The effectiveness of public policies depends not only on *what* they do, but also *how* they do it, how *extensively*, and *where* they are applied. Clues can be found for potential courses of action to improve the health-making effects of public policy by looking at the ways these areas of policy may affect people's prospects for health and illness (see Chapters 8 and 9).

Health policy is almost always assumed to deal primarily with the provision of personal health services. Most policy that affects health is not regarded as "health policy." The policies that may affect health most are least considered to be health-related. They therefore fall outside the official health policy development process in Congress and the health bureaus of government. They are also almost totally excluded from the education of the vast majority of the nation's more than 5 million health personnel. Nevertheless, the development of health-making policy requires attention to "non-health" policies.

PUBLIC AND ORGANIZATIONAL POLICIES: THE CASE OF ENVIRONMENTAL POLICY

Ambient and Worksite Environments

One policy area which has an acknowledged health component is environmental protection and safety. This includes a spectrum of pollution abatement and control measures to reduce or retard air, water, noise, pesticide, and radiation pollutants. The intent of current national drinking water standards and the public surveillance of local water supplies is to improve water quality. These measures were necessary in part because there has been a rise of more than 50 percent in disease outbreaks from contaminated water in the last decade.[1,2] The Toxic Substances Control Act of 1976 additionally provides for banning or placing restrictions on the use of dangerous chemicals.[3] Surveillance of health and safety conditions at workplaces is mandated under occupational safety and health legislation.

These programs have the effect of shifting organizational policies in less health-damaging, if not health-making, directions. They change the options available both to local governments and to corporations as these organizations make policy choices about program emphasis, production processes, and product development. This happens first because national policy forces them (1) to give attention to certain current practices which may have long been neglected, such as disregarding the effects of chemical wastes; (2) to be explicit about what their options are under new stan-

118

dards of health and safety; and (3) to make a clear decision among available options. Organizational decisions that *continue* to neglect or avoid efforts to improve environments, under new national policy, come at a higher cost to the organization than ever before. This cost includes the possibility of civil or criminal penalties, or of court injunction in certain instances.[4]

DIRECT HEALTH EFFECTS

When local governments and businesses make decisions to improve workplace and community environments, the obvious effect on employees and the public is to broaden their opportunities for healthful living compared with their previous circumstances—circumstances over which they could have no individual control. Prior to the emergence of new policies, the options for some residents or workers were to change residence to a less polluted community or to find a safer job. Such choices would clearly come at high cost to the individual. Now free to live in cleaner air, opportunities are opened to individuals to engage in outdoor activity with less fatigue and without eye and throat irritation. Those already ill will have less chance of aggravation of their heart or lung problems, and the elders less likelihood of premature death. Children are less likely to develop acute respiratory illnesses, and adults have less chance of chronic bronchitis, even among those who smoke.[5-7] By maintaining fluoridation of the water supplies, local governments have provided to half of all Americans the opportunity to enjoy a 60 percent reduction in tooth decay over their lifetimes, and up to 75 percent less decay in their school-aged children, without any apparent hazard to health.[8-11]

Health-making opportunities like these are not necessarily assured. Both their design and implementation are crucial to the *real* options placed before organizations and individuals. A policy that is health-protecting in principle may become insignificant in practice. Under occupational safety and health policy, for example, a 1977 rule excluded workplaces with ten or fewer workers. This immediately meant that those worksites, composing 80 percent of business establishments and 87 percent of farms, would not be as likely to make policy choices in favor of more healthful environments: the cost for them to continue any potentially health-damaging practices was no greater than in the past. This, in turn, meant that 12 million people who work in such places, fully 18 percent of the labor force, would not have better opportunities for safe work.[12,13]

The health impact of policy goes beyond the question of which groups are excluded from policy purview. Setting the cost of not complying is crucial. In the mid-1970s, for example, the average fine for minor infractions of occupational health and safety regulations was only $13. Major

119

infractions carried only a $600 penalty. Under such circumstances, it clearly becomes less costly to an enterprise to ignore healthful practices and pay a fine than to adopt new ways at the worksite.[14]

The foregoing cases illustrate some of the important ways in which current environmental policy shapes the options for more healthful patterns of living among large numbers of people, for some more than others. Such policy also has other less direct, though no less significant, effects on prospects for health. These result mainly from the impact of environmental legislation on the economy.

ECONOMIC EFFECTS

Overall, the economic effect of pollution abatement and control policies in the 1970s was stimulative. For every million dollars spent directly by the Federal government, and through its grants and contracts with states and private industries, 70 jobs were created above any that were lost. New jobs totalled 678,000 in the first 5 years, and a 50 percent increase was expected through the decade in some of the most affected industries. Into the early 1980s, the yearly increase in prices resulting from adoption of pollution-control practices was estimated at 0.2 percent, with no net change in employment. A 0.4 percent increase in unemployment was expected, resulting from an anticipated slightly lower rate of real (noninflated) economic growth.[15-19] As control of air pollution makes urban areas more inviting, property values are expected to rise.[19] This benefits landowners but not necessarily lower-income residents or home-buyers.

Figures for 3 years of active enforcement of pollution controls, in the' mid-1970s, show that 117 plants were shut down permanently, some of which were likely to go out of business in any case. Yet job layoffs and jobs lost totalled only 20,000, or about 170 per plant.[20] Furthermore, as the cost of pollution control to industry was passed on in higher prices to consumers, or more directly through the necessity to buy such antipollution items as unleaded gas, the expense amounted to 1.6 percent of family income in 1976. This was expected to drop to less than 1 percent by 1980. However, these out-of-pocket expenditures fell proportionately more heavily on low-income families. Only when portions of clean-air policy were financed through Federal expenditures was there a progressive cost-sharing among all income groups, based more justly on their relative ability to pay.[21]

SUBTLE HEALTH EFFECTS

The experience related above suggests that, in addition to safer environments, there was a favorable overall impact on health which occurred *indirectly* as a result of clean-air policy. For the vast majority of people, the increase in employment and in property values, the relatively low rate of inflation (0.2 percent) and direct cost of personal antipollution expenditures meant a net increase in their disposable income.* This, in turn, meant wider, potentially healthful options for personal behavior as well as greater economic security.

For a minority—those who lost jobs, were laid off, or whose disposable income was otherwise constricted because of rising property values, higher prices, or new expenses—the cost of cleaner air was much higher. For them, a drop in purchasing power would mean fewer opportunities to maintain healthful living conditions and behavior patterns. The uncertainty of employment, without compensating adjustments in income, would bring added distress and the greater likelihood of illness, as discussed in earlier chapters. Again, the burden of a higher risk of health-damage would fall more heavily on those whose options were already limited: persons with lower incomes, families with infants or elders, many ethnic minorities, and the ill.

Viewed in this way, environmental protection policy, of itself, contributes health-making options to most of the people through its impacts on their biophysical and socioeconomic environments. At the same time, it may create health-damaging options by creating or contributing to deficits among some segments of the population when compensating policy measures are not taken.

Environmental policy may indirectly affect health in one further way. Recent legislation has explicitly allowed a degree of monitoring of the laws and has made legal action possible by consumers, including employees.[22-24] These provisions may be thought of as a form of social support or social approval in the form of administrative and legal tools. Such allowances are opportunities for consumers to go beyond mere awareness of their rights and the problematic conditions in their workplaces or communities, to act in organized ways in order to affect those problems. They are opportunities for individuals to cope more effectively with environmental problems by providing them with resources for collective action. Within this context, health education may indeed contribute to improvement of health, for it would serve to inform consumers not only of health hazards and of their rights, but also of the means, not available in the past, to claim those rights. (See Tables 4 and 5 in the Appendix.)

Housing and Urban Environments

Other policies intended to improve living environments have apparently failed in their purpose, and in so doing have also narrowed the opportuni-

---

*Income remaining after taxes and interest payments.

121

ties for a healthy lifestyle among some people, especially those with lower incomes. In the 10 years following the early 1960s, housing, urban development, and highway construction policy was intended to enhance residential living, especially for low-income families. Through direct Federal grants to the states and formulation of national public housing standards, there was to be an expansion of public housing units. Federal policy further provided fiscal incentives to business in the form of low-interest loans for building low-cost rental housing. To families it granted low-interest mortgage loans and tax deductions for mortgage interest, property taxes, and depreciation.[25]

The net effects of these urban policies, however, were that old urban neighborhoods were cut up by expressways, and there was a net drop in housing available to low- and middle-income groups. Fully seven times more middle- and upper-income housing units were supported as low- and moderate-income units. In addition, the tax deductions cost the government five times more than the loan subsidies, thus favoring those who could afford home ownership.[26]

The disruption of social networks in neighborhoods and the increase in substandard housing for low-income people meant a further narrowing of their already-limited options for protective housing and social support. The likelihood of illness and injury became enlarged. At the same time, it is not likely that the health prospects of middle- and upper-income families would have improved. Their circumstances had already allowed them to enjoy higher levels of health (see Fig. 4, p. 45).

One national environmental policy that tends to favor low-income families concerns lead-paint control. Through grants to the states, which widen their budgetary options, inspections of old housing became possible in the 1970s, although not of housing built before the Second World War. As a result, over half of the dwellings inspected were found to have lead-based paint, which is toxic when ingested. By 1977, almost 80 percent of the landlords complied with orders to remove the paint. The effect is that children in these dwellings now have fewer health-damaging risks. However, of the 14 percent of children who were found with high levels of blood lead, those for whom prevention came too late, only 39 percent were actually treated, dooming the others to prospects of retardation.[27]

A final example of environmental protection policy is the Federal requirement which narrows the options of the automobile industry by requiring seat belts in new cars. In doing so, it grants a new opportunity to auto users for protection from injury. Of the one in five who choose to use seat belts, there has been a 50 percent drop in their risk of death from car accidents.[28]

122

Summary

This review of several diverse national environmental protection policies illustrates how policy sets up options from among which choices are made by both public and private organizations. These decisions, in turn, affect the opportunities available for choice-making by citizens, consumers, and employees. The design of policy and the variety of policy instruments which are chosen shape the costs of the options that are made available. Strong incentives, reducing the costs of some options, may come through direct expenditures in grants and contracts to states and private groups, for research and development or for monitoring and enforcement of regulatory standards and other controls. Less apparent, but no less important, are the fiscal incentives granted to individuals or organizations in the form of direct subsidies, or tax exemptions, in the form of deductions and exclusions (see Fig. 8, p. 78).

Thus the impact of policy on the health of large numbers of people depends, first, on which groups are excluded either by intent or by ineffective implementation. Second, the net economic impact on some segments of the population may make the difference as to whether a policy promotes or narrows their chances for health, regardless of the stated intent of the policy.

ENERGY POLICY

If environmental protection is generally seen as a form of health policy only to a limited extent, other policy areas, to which it is increasingly related, are even less so regarded. Energy is one such area.

Assuming that the general direction of national energy policy is to reduce dependence on oil and develop alternate sources of energy, both the design and speed of policy change will have important effects on the health of Americans. During the current development period, as oil prices continue to rise, analysis has shown that a policy of domestic oil price controls would be the most equitable sharing of the cost burden: it would benefit most those in the lower 60 percent of the income scale. By comparison, to reduce oil consumption through conservation alone, using various tax incentives, would be less equitable, benefiting all except the richest 20 percent of the people. The least equitable policy option is to rely on increased tariffs for imported oil: this would benefit only the wealthiest fifth of the population.[29]

Rising energy costs reduce the disposable income of lower-income groups, with all the health-damaging risks that entails, particularly in the short term. The poor are also disproportionately burdened by conservation measures because they are already low users of fuel. Thus when their use of fuel is further curtailed by shortages or allocations, they are more likely to develop increased illness due to exposure to extremes of temperature at home or in travel. Their already limited options become still more limited.

Lower-income people may pay a higher cost for energy policy in yet another way, if compensating measures are not taken. There will inevitably be job losses in the industries most affected by energy changeovers. Those with less education, who are more likely to have low incomes, will be most affected. They will be in greatest need of retraining opportunities and temporary income support.

The forms of energy which Federal policy will foster and allow to predominate, will affect the opportunities for healthful living for the vast majority of people, and for certain occupational groups in particular.[30] The most discussed paths are expanded use of coal and nuclear power. A proposed shift to coal, increasing consumption by a third, would significantly increase the risks of mine injuries. More pervasively health-damaging is the likelihood of exposure to higher levels of air pollution. This would result in more acute and chronic heart and lung disease, if coal is not "washed" with the efficient "scrubbers" now available. Nuclear energy poses cancer risks from low-level radiation for uranium miners and, more widely, for children and plant workers. More publicized are risks of accidents, sabotage, and a mushrooming of the unsolved problem and threat of nuclear waste disposal.[31]

Consistent with the national energy conservation effort was at least one immediately health-making policy. It set motor vehicle speed at a maximum of 55 miles per hour. One year after it was in force, auto fatalities dropped by 17 percent, the largest decline since cars became the principal means of passenger travel in the early 1940s. About 9 percent of the reduction was attributable to slower driving, and the remainder to fewer passenger miles associated with higher gasoline prices.[32] However, in those states that do not enforce the speed limit, auto death rates are highest.[33] There is also evidence that less driving reduced air pollution in some parts of the country, resulting in a drop in death rates from chronic heart and lung disease.[34,35]

Federal policy will make some energy sources more costly, or less costly, for researchers and industry to develop and, in turn, for people to use. In this way policy will affect the costs in health for people who have almost no choice but to live in an increasingly energy-scarce society.

ECONOMIC POLICY AND ITS COMPONENTS

Energy policy is important to health prospects as it affects biophysical and

124

workplace environments, jobs and incomes, personal consumption patterns and prices, residential construction and protection from temperature extremes, and patterns of travel and exercise. It also influences the design and effectiveness of environmental policy. At the same time, energy policy itself is developed with consideration for larger economic policy, those decisions which involve monetary (money supply) and fiscal (budgetary) issues (Fig. 9).

Do decisions about the speed of economic growth, measured as increases in the value of all goods and services produced each year, or gross national product (GNP), affect prospects for health? To the extent that they make health-making choices by large numbers of people easier, or harder, they do. Even so, consideration of the health consequences of economic policy is almost as far removed from the thinking of health professionals as from the average person or policy-maker.

Without attempting to draw conclusions about issues on which economists cannot agree, the effects of some economic policy decisions can at least be summarized. In the first 7 years of the 1970s, the average yearly rate of growth of the GNP in *real* terms, that is, after adjusting for inflation, was 2.4 percent; unemployment increased by 6.2 percent, and consumer prices by 6.5 percent each year. These rates compare with yearly averages of 3.9, 4.7, and 3.2 percent, respectively, in the two previous decades.[36]

It is known that for every 1 percent *increase* in the GNP there is a 0.29 percent *drop* in unemployment, and somewhat more for women and blacks. With a 1 percent *decrease* in the GNP there is a *rise* of 0.61 percent in unemployment, somewhat less for women but two times higher for blacks, or 1.24 percent.[37,38] Economic growth or decline, measured in the GNP, thus affects prospects for employment and unemployment, as well as prices. A major area of controversy is how much the real GNP is affected by Federal economic policy, which includes control of the money supply through the independent Federal Reserve Board, and control of government spending and revenues through the Federal budget. The issue, in other words, is the degree to which economic policy affects noninflationary growth, and thus jobs, income, and prices—the basic ingredients that combine to form opportunities for choice-making by the vast majority of people.

Government Spending: Restrictive Economic Policy

According to some economists, restrictive economic policy, deployed through *high* interest rates by the Federal Reserve Board and through *reductions* in Federal budgetary spending, has shown no evidence of achieving its supposed purpose of reducing inflation. Such policy, in fact,

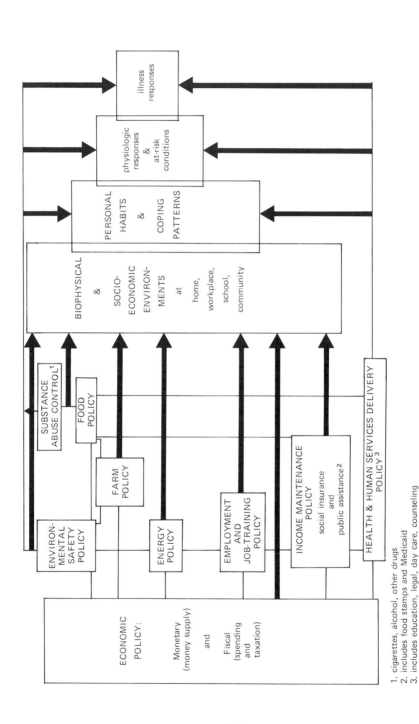

FIGURE 9. Public socioenvironmental policy which shapes American environments, personal behavior, and prospects for health.

1. cigarettes, alcohol, other drugs
2. includes food stamps and Medicaid
3. includes education, legal, day care, counseling

126

has fostered an idling of up to 29 percent of manufacturing capacity, maintained a high rate of unemployment, reduced incentives to invest, and kept the GNP at slow growth.[39] At best, a $10 billion budget cut will reduce inflation by only about 0.1 percent.[40]

The consequences of unemployment are obviously costly, including severe losses to the economy. In the mid-1970s, every 1 percent of unemployment represented $60 billion lost in the output of goods and services per year. It also required $6 to 9 billion in *added* spending from government budgets. Over half of this increase in public spending was for unemployment insurance, a third for public assistance payments, and the remainder for Medicaid (7 percent) and food stamps (3 percent).[41] Sustained over 5 years, each 1 percent in unemployment represents additional consequences in illness and its costs in treatment, disability, and death at the rate of almost a billion dollars per year, based on 1975 figures.[42,43]

The painful irony of restrictive economic policy is that cutting public expenditures contributes to unemployment, which in turn increases the need for public services by the unemployed.[44] Those caught in this policy vice have exceedingly few options for healthful living, and are then understandably more vulnerable to illness and its reverberating effects.

Inflation indeed is more burdensome to the poor than to the affluent. A 1 percent rise in the cost of living for those who are well off is equivalent to a rise of 1.13 percent for the poor.[45] Yet it is not clear that restrictions of public expenditures are helpful to poor persons in any respect. Failing to reduce inflation, except in their extreme application, budgetary restrictions further narrow the opportunities for health-making choices, including job prospects, among people in low-income groups.

Government Spending: Expansionary Policy

An expansionary fiscal policy, by contrast, has stimulative effects on economic production, employment, and public services. For each additional billion dollars spent by the Federal government in 1976, 66,600 jobs were created. This produced almost 82,000 new jobs for each billion dollars spent through government enterprises, including the military, and more than 47,000 jobs per billion dollars contracted through private industry. About 70 percent of the new jobs came as a result of Federal allocations to state and local governments. Sixty percent of the private jobs and more than 80 percent of the government jobs developed in this way.[46]

It is notable that the type of programs developed made a difference in the number of jobs that were created. In 1974, a billion dollars spent on defense, a high energy-intensive, capital equipment field, created 51,000 jobs. The same amount spent on more labor-intensive programs, such as veterans' health care and civilian manpower training, created about 89,000 and 137,000 jobs respectively. These new jobs in non-military programs are brought about through additions to the payroll of agencies which administer programs (55 percent of the jobs) and through purchases made by these agencies to related industries—the "second-round" effects—which then create the remaining 45 percent of the jobs.[47]

ECONOMIC POLICY AND CHOICE-MAKING

The importance of Federal spending to private businesses and local economies, as well as to employees and job-seekers, is readily apparent. Such factors as *where* Federal dollars are placed, in which *types* of programs, and in which *geographic* areas will influence the options for decision-making about programs and products by public and private organizations, as well as by individuals in communities.

The fact that rates of job creation differ for the same amount of Federal expenditure, depending on where and on what it is spent, suggests that the impact on inflation of governmental and private spending may be related not so much to the *amount* spent as to the *ways* and the *ends* for which it is expended, an issue taken up in Chapters 8 and 9.

ECONOMIC POLICIES AND HEALTH

Much of the importance of economic policy for the prospects for health has to do with its effects on livelihoods that are adequate for maintaining health. This connection occurs through employment opportunities, especially for the unskilled, consequent living conditions, and related personal habits and coping patterns: the things that stable employment makes possible and that unemployment disallows.

Changes in opportunities for healthful choices can also occur among those who are steadily employed when their disposable income changes. Interest payments, which are directly related to inflation, can conceivably be avoided. Most taxes for most people cannot. Again, the design of tax policy, a component of economic policy related both to the national money supply and budgetary deficits, is important in assessing the effects of economic policy on health prospects.

Taxation

The purpose of progressive income tax policy is to collect revenue on an equitable, ability-to-pay basis. In practice, the effect of current policy is quite different, as witnessed in the 1976 Federal returns. Income taxes took only 1.7 percent of the 82.1 percent of national income going to the affluent half of the population. It increased by just that amount—1.7 percent—the 17.9

128

percent of all national income going to the poorer half of the population, increasing their share to only 19.6 percent after taxes.[48] It is doubtful that such minimal shifts would either enhance the health-making opportunities of the less affluent or alter the options of the wealthier half of American society.

TAX SUBSIDIES

To improve the fairness of taxation, tax expenditures—the tax subsidies which become expenditures to government—are designed to reimburse taxpayers or exclude from taxation some expenses of income earners, corporate or individual. These provisions also serve as fiscal incentives for certain activities.

The effect of current practices is to benefit the more affluent far more than others. For example, of $124.4 billion in tax subsidies granted in 1978, there were $9.8 billion in tax deductions for health insurance and medical expenses; $11.6 billion for pensions, while for all forms of public assistance, disability, tax credits, and other support for the disabled, poor, or workers with children, the subsidies totalled only $6.2 billion. Charitable donations meant $6.6 billion in deductions, offering most relief to the affluent, while pollution control and community development were granted tax subsidies of only $0.15 billion combined.[49,50]

REGRESSIVE TAXATION

A heavier burden than this uneven distribution of tax subsidies consists in flat rate taxes, such as Social Security and sales, excise, and property taxes, which regressively take their toll: they require the same amount from people, regardless of their size of income. This places a larger burden on those with lower incomes. In 1977, these taxes constituted almost a third of all taxes paid by people who earned as little as $8000 or as much as $50,000 a year, and severely limited the remaining disposable income of lower-income groups. Moreover, since three-quarters of state revenues derive from such taxes, state and local revenue-raising are inherently less equitable than Federal taxation, constricting low incomes more than higher ones. State, local, and excise taxes took 11 percent from households earning less than $5000, and only 4 percent from those making $50,000 or more in 1976.[51]

One of the most regressive and potentially health-limiting forms of taxation is the sales tax on food, relied on in almost half the states for 5 to 10 percent of their revenues. The effect on low-income consumers comes not only through its regressive impact on disposable income, but also because such persons must spend a larger share of their disposable income on food. The working poor spend 37 percent of earnings on food, compared with 18 percent spent by the American population overall. The point has been

129

made that food stamps used in these states become, in effect, a Federal payment of state taxes.[52] If the effects on health of such a policy were taken into account, more equitable and health-promoting ways to assist the states would be found.

GOVERNMENT REVENUES IN SUM

Just as the expenditures side of fiscal policy has a potential health impact, so also does the revenue side, the design of tax policy. It may disproportionately constrict personal disposable income through leveling regressive taxes, or by overly subsidizing more affluent taxpayers. The resulting variations in tax burdens contribute, in turn, to differences in ways of life and the typical profiles of health and illness associated with them.

Just as Federal budgetary *expenditures* affect economic growth and employment, and so may be used to effect stimulative or restrictive economic policy, *taxation* may also be used in a similar way, namely to influence economic growth and employment.

Employment

When the objective of economic policy is, for political reasons, to reduce unemployment and create jobs during economic downturns, as was the case in 1975, tax policy may become an instrument for promoting employment. A 1975 *income tax cut,* for example, with two-thirds of the cut going to individuals and one-third to corporations, was projected to produce an initial 8,000 to 15,000 jobs at a net Federal budget cost of just under 1 billion dollars. This would affect the unemployment rate by a negligible 0.01 to 0.02 points. By contrast, direct Federal *expenditures* or allocations to the states, as noted earlier, would have had larger effects, creating two to four times as many jobs, reducing unemployment at faster rates, and costing 10 to 20 percent less to the Federal budget. However, with maximum employment as the objective, the most effective means would be *public service employment,* creating 10 times as many jobs as a tax cut, and reducing unemployment most rapidly, at about two-thirds the cost.[53]

To the extent that employment provides options for individuals to make healthful choices, public service employment seems an obvious choice for health-making employment policy in periods of increased unemployment. However, in the longer term, the type of job and its stability may be as important for health as the fact of holding a job.

"Secondary jobs," those that require little skill, offer no real upward mobility, and are low-paying and often unpleasant, are considered inherently "unstable." Worker turnover is rapid and absenteeism is high. Both are

130

frequently attributed to worker attitudes, prompting the formation of personnel adjustment programs. Such programs are sometimes successful. Attitudes do change. But new "positive" attitudes have not affected job stability.[54] This is another example of how changes in attitude do not effect changes in behavior unless altered circumstances, in this case improved working conditions, encourage those changes (see Chapter 5).

The instability of secondary jobs, whether in public or private sectors, is found to be the result *not* of worker attitudes, but rather of low wages which discourage the commitment of workers to their jobs. The resulting rapid rate of job turnover reflects the fact that personnel often do not have time to develop skills on the job, while at the same time their employers become unwilling to invest in their training and upgrading.[55] This vicious circle has its counterpart in the personal living patterns of workers. Unstable jobs mean uncertain lifestyles, which contribute to irregular work patterns. These, in turn, help perpetuate the low-income status of many within the labor force and reduce their prospects for health.

Job Training

Policies which focus on job-creation have primarily sought to ease "cyclical unemployment," job loss associated with upturns and downturns in the market economy. They have not made, and have not tried to make, a difference in "structural unemployment," the *sustained* lack of jobs and underemployment of segments of the labor force, particularly teenagers, women, Hispanics, and blacks. In the last decade, some policy attention has been given to these groups. A shift in economic and employment policy in this direction offers health-promoting possibilities.

The national experience with employment policy since 1969 suggests that job training and worker support services yield net gains to the economy, savings in the Federal budget, and economic benefits to individual participants, contrary to sometime conventional wisdom. Earnings were compared among work-eligible people enrolled in Aid to Families with Dependent Children (AFDC), who participated in Federal job training under the Work Incentive Program (WIN) administered by local governments through the Comprehensive Employment and Training Act (CETA) in the mid-1970s. A year after their participation, men's income was 10 to 25 percent higher, and women's was 30 to 50 percent higher (ranging from $330 to $470). These gains resulted both from higher wage rates and more weeks of work, or less underemployment. At the same time, average AFDC payments dropped by over $100 per adult. The amounts of money involved per person were obviously not enough to effect a marked reduction in the AFDC rolls, which was the political objective of the program.

Nevertheless, the gains in earnings exceeded program costs by about 25 to 50 percent through the second year, even after taking inflation into account and assuming a one-third drop in workers' continued ability to maintain their job-acquired incomes.[56]

These averages conceal important differences. Under CETA, the strategies found to be most effective for improved employment were on-the-job training, under subsidies (amounting to $2.5 billion) to private industry, and public service employment. Through these two strategies, participants earned between $1500 and $1900 above their income levels prior to entering the program. By comparison, when simple counseling and job placement services were provided, the income of participants *dropped* $600 to $1200 below previous levels. Even so, this was the most politically appealing strategy since it was cheapest to deploy and tallied the largest number of "people served." Classroom training, the fourth strategy, brought rises ranging from $500 to $800 net increased income.

These differences in the effectiveness of the four policy thrusts were directly related to the amount spent on each type of program. The program costs, per individual, were about $1100 for classroom training, $2550 for on-the-job training, and $6650 for public service employment. The participants who gained most were those with *least* recent work experience, in contrast to the prevailing practice of giving priority to the more recently unemployed.[57,58]

Although overall gains in income between men and women workers were similar, blacks gained only a third to a half as much as whites. By 1978, women and poor workers were receiving fewer benefits. It may or may not be coincidental that when these programs were conducted under Federal, instead of local, administration in the early 1970s, women and blacks were the greatest gainers.[59,60]

A final illustration of the health-promoting potential and limitations of the job training component of employment policy concerns vocational rehabilitation, which is intended to help those with long-term disabilities to return to work. In recent years, workers who obtained such training enjoyed significant increases in their earnings in the year following their participation in the program. However, the impact of this policy thrust was more limited than it might have been because only 27 percent of those who were occupationally disabled actually were trained in 1972.[61,62] Nevertheless, even the restricted services of this program reached greater numbers of people than in comparable efforts. Only 6 percent of eligible unemployed people received job training under CETA, and only 9 percent got public service employment in 1976.[63]

It remains to be seen whether the full-employment goals enacted in the

1978 legislation can be accomplished without major changes in economic policy (see Chapter 8).

Income Support

There are, of course, other important problems that limit one's ability to work besides long-term disability and business downturns. Chief among these additional limitations are age and sickness. These are recognized to some extent in the fringe benefits that are granted to the majority of the working population. Such entitlements to workers are also in the interests of the employer, who gains from having a stable labor force. Employees with a steady and basic income are, of course, protected from both the potential physical stress and the emotional distress of interrupted and uncertain income. In 1975, fringe benefits amounted to one-fourth of all employee compensation in large firms (those employing 100 persons or more) and 30 percent in Federal enterprises.[64] Much of this is paid for by government either through direct contributions in the form of unemployment insurance and workers' compensation, or through tax subsidies to business and employees, in a variety of private wage and disability insurance programs.

There are important limitations, however, to the potential these cash benefits have for maintaining health-promoting options for incapacitated workers. Based on the "low-income standard budget" announced by the Department of Labor each year, an urban family of four needed over $10,000 to meet all its expenditures in 1976.[65] By comparison, the deficiencies of a variety of income maintenance programs become evident. For example, average payments in 1976 to a permanently disabled worker in a family of four were $4630 under Social Security Disability and $4030 for a retired couple. They were $3900 for an unemployed worker under Social Security, covering just half of his or her average earnings. People who were out of work because of *non-work-related* sickness or injury received just 37 percent of their wages under various temporary disability insurances (less than two-thirds of the labor force have any such protection). Those disabled from *work-related* causes had about 22 percent of their wage losses replaced under the workers' compensation plan of the Social Security System; 40 to 60 percent of states do not even require this protection for agricultural or casual workers or servants. These benefits might have been supplemented, for those who dropped into eligible low-income levels, by food stamps, which averaged $900 in value, and Medicaid payments, amounting to about $650 per recipient.[66-74]

Considering these significant declines in income, it is not difficult to understand either the distress or the health-limiting constriction of options remaining to the unemployed, those who otherwise have had steady and predictable earnings.

PUBLIC ASSISTANCE

The foregoing approach to wage replacement, embodied in the Social Security Act, is one in which employer-employee payroll contributions are combined with government funds. It is thus a form of *social insurance*. With an expenditure of $134 billion in 1976, it is by far the largest form of income maintenance. Income maintenance policy is also deployed through *public assistance* programs in which benefits are financed *solely* from government revenues. This amounted to almost $119 billion in 1976, including food stamps and tax credits for the poor.[75]

Those who cannot enter the labor force for reasons of child care or disability, or who otherwise cannot earn more than a poverty-level income (defined as $5800 for an urban family of four in 1976), may become the receivers of public assistance. The intent of this component of income support policy is to maintain the human needs of young families, through the AFDC program, and of low-income aged, blind, and permanently disabled persons, through the Supplemental Security Income program (SSI). About 11 percent of American families had poverty-level incomes in 1976. About half of these families received AFDC payments averaging $3600; another 2 percent received SSI payments. Even with the increments represented by Medicaid and by food stamps, which less than half of these families received, their health protection was tenuous. The opportunities for healthful choice-making available to these persons may be imagined by comparing their income with the $10,000 that is estimated by government as the family income necessary to maintain a low-income living standard.[76-83]

INCOME SUBSTITUTES

Some additional services, which may substitute for income beyond food stamps and health care financing, are directly available under Federal policy. In principle, these services are available to persons whose income or disability keeps them outside the mainstream of the market economy, unable to reach purchasable goods and services. The assumption is that human services can assist people to cope with circumstances that they cannot control. Regardless of the degree of efficacy of these services, their potential is limited by tight budgetary allocations which severely restrict the extent of their deployment. Although one of the best records of policy deployment has been shown in providing education for handicapped children, only 40 percent of eligible children were served in recent years. Of the preschoolers who are eligible for Headstart education, only 22 percent

134

were served. No more than 20 percent of seasonal farmworkers received migrant health services. Just 9 percent of eligible elders were served congregate meals, less than 1 percent received home-delivered meals, and about 15 percent were provided with social casework services.[84]

Regardless of the design and strategy of any potentially health-promoting policy—whether concerning environmental protection, job-creation and training, or income maintenance in cash or in kind—it is fiscal policy that determines the actual size of budgetary allocations, thus setting the limits of the possible (see Fig. 9).

FOOD STAMPS: ECONOMIC IMPACTS

One of the most extensively deployed income supplement policies in recent years has been the food stamp program. Because of its size ($2.7 billion in bonus stamps in 1974) and its extent (reaching about half of the people who are eligible), it has potential impacts on health, both directly and through its effects on the economy. The economic impacts flow from the increased purchasing power of the 12 million households who use stamps. Purchases made with food stamps account for about 4 percent of the dollars spent on food. For every additional dollar in income that participants receive from food stamps or other sources, families in poverty spend about 45 to 55 cents on food. When the poor buy 10 percent more food through the new opportunity afforded them by food stamps (thus increasing total U.S. retail food spending by 10 percent), retail food prices rise between 0.08 and 0.8 percent yearly. The rate at which food prices may rise as a result of the new purchasing power of the poor depends on the relative abundance of such foods as meat, dairy products, and cereals in any given year.[85,86]

Other economic consequences associated with the added food purchases made possible by food stamps include, for 1974, a net $1.2 billion in business receipts, generating 76,500 jobs and adding $427 million to the GNP. These economic benefits accrued in spite of the costs in higher taxes, required to support the program, that were levied on non-food stamp households. Furthermore, a full 96 percent of the income gained from the newly created jobs went to those non-food stamp families.

The net economic effects for 1974 were minor increases in inflation (0.015 percent), because of new consumer demand in the food industry, and in unemployment (0.03 percent), because of a slight drop in demand in nonfood industries, such as the services sector. Overall, the economic benefits outweighed the costs for the food stamp users and for the economy as a whole, while the economic cost was borne by the more affluent segments of the population.[87,88] Additional but uncalculated benefits, as a result of presumably better nutrition and health among food stamp users (see

135

Chapter 7), include the savings from employee productivity that would other-wise be lost in sick days and the savings from medical care that was not needed. Most of these costs would eventually have been borne by taxpayers.

Some Net Effects of Economic Policies

The numerous policies that affect income maintenance through various social insurance and public assistance programs, as well as in-kind sup-port contributed by food stamps and other services, are intended to set a floor below which people need not fall, and at which they may be as-sured of survival. In other words, in spite of the vast gaps in wealth be-tween the richer and poorer segments of the U.S. population—a larger disparity than is found in most modern industrialized nations[89-92]—the Federal government, through its fiscal policy, may redistribute some of the wealth in order to assure a minimum existence for the poorest. As noted, the shift in income after taxes are paid is almost negligible. After transfer payments are distributed in cash or in kind, under social insurance or through public assistance, the shift of monies toward the poorest groups is slightly greater. However, even this comes not at the expense of the rich-est, but rather of the middle-income groups. The wealthiest 20 percent of Americans show *no* decline in their 44 percent share of national income after transfer payments are made, while the poorest fifth increase their share from 5 percent to 8.2 percent as a result of such transfers. The cost then is borne by the middle-income 60 percent of Americans.[93]

The net effect of the variety of policies which result in transfers of in-come may be said to broaden the opportunities for minimal survival of the poorest, although not to guarantee a "low-income standard." At the same time, the effect on the richest is to allow them to retain their very wide array of options for choosing "too much of the good," which is potentially health-damaging.

The effects on the health-making options of the 60 percent middle-in-come majority are more speculative. Their choices will be made out of the remaining 48 percent of national income which is theirs to grasp after transfer payments are completed. Although their health is better than that of the poorest Americans, it is likely to be among these mainstream people—especially the working poor and those on fixed incomes—that *changes* in health will first be measurably affected. Their balance between "health" and "illness" may be so tenuous that when policies produce health-limiting changes, however temporary, in their biophysical or socioeconomic envi-ronments, greater numbers of them will fall into illness. The medical or economic costs of these probable health consequences are rarely if ever part of the "impact statements" that are now required of many Federal policy proposals.

SUMMARY

Federal policy, with the related policy of other public jurisdictions, is far-reaching and pervasive in establishing the health-promoting potential of people's environments. Environmental protection, energy, and economic policies affect the health-making quality of the "natural" biophysical environment—including air, water, and food purity—in communities, workplaces, and homes. These areas of policy are interlinked in several ways. Today they are all likely to affect the pace of national economic growth and so influence inflation, employment, and unemployment. As a result, there are likely to be tradeoffs in design among them as they are moved through policy development negotiations. This may be to the detriment of the health of some community populations, workers, or income groups, if adequate compensating policies are not included. Federal fiscal or budgetary policy itself has long been large enough to affect national economic growth. The directions of its allocations, and the amount and sources of its revenues, affect the economy as well.

These policies and others which are likely to be subordinate to them, including employment and job training, income maintenance, and human services, can affect health in subtle ways. They frame the opportunities faced by public agencies and private commercial or nonprofit organizations when they develop programs and products. Federal policy, in its impact on organizational policies, affects the options that are available to the public for such diverse "goods" as clean air, safe jobs, and energy-efficient transportation.

The public's opportunities are also affected by Federal policy in more direct ways. One is by its effects on the actual supply of available health-sustaining resources, including fuel, housing, and food, irrespective of people's capacity to pay for such essentials. A second way, perhaps the most important, volatile, and well-recognized, is through the effects of Federal policy on real disposable income: income may be enlarged or constricted by inflationary prices, interest rates, and taxation; by employment; or by transfer payments through Social Security or public assistance, food stamps, or Medicaid. A third way is by giving people entitlement to budgeted services which might help those who cannot otherwise get what they need for health-protection, such as health and human services, including legal assistance for helping them lay claim to their legislated rights.

Policy flows along these paths, deployed by a variety of instruments, including direct budgetary expenditures and the provision or financing of goods and services, a variety of regulatory tools, and less obviously, through fiscal incentives in the form of subsidies, taxes, or tax exemptions.

Most of the policy strategies described here have focused on environmental change or environmental regulation: they attempt to produce shifts in the distribution of desired resources, including money, jobs, services, and clean air. Within the context of policy that can change the distribution of resources, supportive policy strategies that provide people with information and education, and with group-support services for getting what they are entitled to, may add to the effectiveness of the environmental strategy.

Whether or not people are aware of them, the opportunities for health-making environments are set in these ways. These large-scale contexts, in turn, set the range of the possible for people's immediate social networks, their interpersonal relations. All are part of their repertoire for coping with the world. These environments, large and small, are prime determinants of their chances to develop and sustain health-making ways of living and acting, in workplaces, homes, and communities.

REFERENCES

1. *Safe Drinking Water Act of 1974.* New York Times, June 21, 1977.
2. *Statistics Needed for Determining the Effects of the Environment on Health.* Report of the Technical Consultant Panel to the U.S. National Committee on Vital and Health Statistics. No. 77–1457. National Center for Health Statistics, Washington, D.C., 1977.
3. *Toxic Substances Control Act of 1976* (PL 94-469).
4. Ibid.
5. Environmental Protection Agency: *Health Consequences of Sulfur Oxides: Summary and Conclusions Based Upon CHESS Studies of 1970–71.* Research Triangle Park, N.C., 1974.
6. Federal Interagency Task Force on Air Quality Indicators: *A Recommended Air Pollution Index.* Environmental Protection Agency, Washington, D.C., 1976.
7. Lave, L., and Seskin, E.: *An analysis of the association between U.S. mortality and air pollution.* J. Am. Statistics Assoc. 68(342):284–290, 1973.
8. Subcommittee on Health and Environment: *Child Health Assessment Act. Hearings, August 8–9, 1977.* House Committee on Interstate and Foreign Commerce, Washington, D.C., 1977.
9. Walsh, D.: *Fluoridation.* N. Engl. J. Med. 296:1118–1120, 1977.
10. Doll, R.: *Fluoridation of water and cancer mortality in the USA.* Lancet 1:1300–1302, 1977.
11. Tokuhata, G., et al.: *Fluoridation and mortality—an epidemiologic study of Pennsylvania communities.* Public Health Rep. 93:60–68, 1978.
12. *Impact on OSHA exemptions.* Occup. Health Safety, 30, June 16, 1977.
13. AFL-CIO, Industrial Union Department, personal communication, January 23, 1979.
14. *Impact of OSHA.* New York Times, December 20, 1976.
15. *Manpower Report of the President.* Washington, D.C., 1975.

138

16. Segel, F., and Dreiling, F.: *Pollution Abatement and Control Expenditures, 1972–76.* Surv. Curr. Bus. 58(2):12–16, 1978.
17. Council on Environmental Quality: *Macroeconomic Impacts of Federal Pollution Control Programs.* Environmental Protection Agency, Washington, D.C., 1975.
18. Hornblower, M.: *Major U.S. industries discover profits fighting pollution.* Washington Post, April 3, 1978.
19. Smith, V.: *The Economic Consequences of Air Pollution.* Ballinger, Cambridge, Mass., 1976.
20. Segel, F., and Dunlap, B.: *Capital expenditures by business for pollution abatement, 1976 and planned 1977.* Surv. Curr. Bus. 57(6):13–15, 1977.
21. Dorfman, R.: *Incidence of the benefits and costs of environmental programs.* Am. Econ. Rev. 67(1):333–341, 1977.
22. *Impact of OSHA exemptions,* op. cit.
23. *Safe Drinking Water Act,* op. cit.
24. *Toxic Substances Control Act,* op. cit.
25. *Studies in Human Need: Rural Housing.* U.S. Senate Select Committee on Nutrition and Human Needs, Washington, D.C., 1972.
26. Ibid.
27. *Surveillance of childhood lead poisoning—United States.* Morbid. Mortal. Weekly Rep., February 11, 1977.
28. Robertson, L.: *Estimates of motor vehicle seat belt effectiveness and use: implications for occupant crash protection.* Am. J. Public Health 66(9):859–864, 1976.
29. Brazzel, J., and Durden, G.: *Estimating the Effects of Energy Policy on the Distribution of Income: A Methodology.* Working Paper, Office of Economic Impact Analysis, Federal Energy Administration, Washington, D.C., 1977.
30. Olsen, M.: *Assessing the Social Impacts of Energy Conservation.* Battelle Human Affairs Research Center, Seattle, 1977.
31. Shy, C.: *Health Consequences of Alternative Energy Systems.* Paper presented at Workshop on Energy and the Social Sciences, University of North Carolina, Chapel Hill, November 19, 1977.
32. Holtzman, N.: *The goal of preventing early death,* in *Papers on the National Health Guidelines. Conditions for Change in the Health Care System, September 1977.* Health Resources Administration, Washington, D.C., 1977.
33. Washington Post, February 1, 1979.
34. Brown, S., et al.: *The Fuel Crisis of 1974: Effects on Mortality.* Paper presented to the American Public Health Association, Los Angeles, October 1978.
35. Brown, S., et al.: *Effects on mortality of the 1974 fuel crisis.* Nature 257(5524):306–307, 1975.
36. Joint Congressional Committee on Taxation: *Estimates of Federal Tax Expenditures.* Washington, D.C., March 1978.
37. *Full Employment and Balanced Growth Act of 1976 Hearings.* Senate Committee on Labor and Public Welfare, Washington, D.C., May 1976.
38. Okun, A.: *Efficient disinflationary policies.* Am. Econ. Rev. 68(2):348, 1978.
39. Thurow, L.: *Inequality, inflation and growth in the American economy.* The Economist, December 24, 1977.
40. Congressional Budget Office, reported in the New York Times, February 26, 1979.
41. *Full Employment and Balanced Growth Act,* op. cit.
42. *Estimating the Social Costs of National Economic Policy: Implications for Mental*

139

and Physical Health and Criminal Aggression. Joint Congressional Economic Committee, Washington, D.C., 1976.
43. Marshall, J. R., and Funch, D. P.: *Mental Illness and the Economy: A Critique and Partial Replication* J. Health Social Behav. 20:282–289 (Sept. 1979.
44. *Inflation and the Consumer, 1974.* Joint Congressional Economic Committee, Washington, D.C., 1975.
45. Ibid.
46. *Employment and Training Report of the President, 1977.* Washington, D.C., 1977.
47. *Manpower Report of the President,* op. cit.
48. Joint Committee on Taxation, reported in the Washington Post, March 27, 1978.
49. U.S. Treasury, reported in the Boston Globe, May 27, 1975.
50. *Estimates of Federal Tax Expenditures,* op. cit.
51. Ibid.
52. *Sales tax on food hits the poor hardest.* Am. Freedom from Hunger Fd. Bull. 3(7), July 1977.
53. Congressional Budget Office: *Temporary Measures to Stimulate Employment: An Evaluation of Some Alternatives.* Washington, D.C., 1975.
54. *Low-Income Labor Markets and Urban Manpower Programs: A Critical Assessment.* Research and Development Findings No. 12. U.S. Department of Labor, Washington, D.C., 1972.
55. Ibid.
56. *The Impact of WIN II: A Longitudinal Evaluation of the Work Incentive Program.* U.S. Department of Labor, Washington, D.C., 1976.
57. Ibid.
58. *Estimates of Federal Tax Expenditures,* op. cit.
59. Kiefer, N.: *The Economic Benefits from Manpower Training Programs.* Technical Analysis Paper No. 43. U.S. Department of Labor, Washington, D.C., 1976.
60. Baumer, D., et al.: *Explaining benefit distribution in CETA programs.* J. Hum. Resources 14(2):172–196, 1979.
61. Greenblum, J.: *Effects of Vocational Rehabilitation on the Earnings of Disabled Persons.* Staff Paper No. 27. Social Security Administration, Washington, D.C., 1977.
62. Treitel, R.: *Rehabilitation of disabled adults, 1972,* in *Disability Survey 72: Disabled and Non-Disabled Adults.* Report No. 3. Social Security Administration, Washington, D.C., 1977.
63. *Calculating human services shortfalls.* Eval (Special Issue), Fall 1978, p. 27.
64. *Employee Compensation in the PATC Survey Industries, 1974.* Report No. 464. U.S. Department of Labor, Washington, D.C., 1977.
65. Bureau of Labor Statistics: *Standard Budgets, Autumn 1976.* News release, April 27, 1977.
66. Hribal, A.: *Workers' compensation laws.* Month. Labor Rev. 25:26; 1977.
67. Social Security Administration: *Monthly Benefit Statistics.* January 19, 1978.
68. *Program data tabulations.* Soc. Sec. Bull. 41(3), March 1978.
69. *Characteristics of Food-Stamp Households, September 1976.* Report FNS-168. U.S. Department of Agriculture, 1977.
70. House Subcommittee on Health and the Environment: *Data on the Medicaid Program, FY 1966–77.* Washington, D.C., 1977.
71. Price, D.: *Cash benefits for short-term sickness, 1948–1976.* Soc. Sec. Bull. 41(10):3–13, 1978.

72. *Data on the Medicaid Program: Eligibility, Services, Expenditures, Fiscal Years 1966–1978.* Health Care Financing Administration, Washington, D.C., 1978.
73. Social Security Administration: *Social Security Programs Throughout the World.* Research Report No. 50. Washington, D.C., 1978.
74. Berman, D.: *How cheap is a life?* Int. J. Health Serv. 8(1):79–99, 1978.
75. *Social Services USA—Statistical Tables, Summaries, and Analyses of Services Under Social Security Act Titles, XX, IV-B, and IV-A/WIN for the Fifty States and the District of Columbia.* HEW Office of Human Development Services, Administration for Public Services, Publication No. (OHDS) 77-03300, Washington, D.C., 1976.
76. *Monthly Benefit Statistics,* op. cit.
77. *Social Security Programs,* op. cit.
78. *Standard Budgets,* op. cit.
79. *Employment and Training Report,* op. cit.
80. Bureau of the Census: *Current Population Reports, P-60* (Nos. 102 and 103). Washington, D.C., 1976.
81. *Characteristics of Food-Stamp Households,* op. cit.
82. *Data on the Medicaid Program,* op. cit.
83. *Data on the Medicaid Program: Eligibility Services, Expenditures, FY 1966:78* Health Care Financing Administration, Washington, D.C., 1978.
84. *Calculating human services shortfalls,* op. cit.
85. *Administration's Welfare Reform Proposal.* Joint Hearings, House of Representatives (Part I, Series 95–47). September 19–21, 1977.
86. Schrimper, R.: *Food Programs and the Retail Price of Food.* Paper presented at the Fourth Food Policy Seminar, U.S. Department of Agriculture, Washington, D.C., February 14, 1978.
87. Nelson, F., and Cochrane, W.: *Economic consequences of Federal farm commodity programs, 1953–1972.* Agri. Econ. Res. 28:52–64, 1976.
88. Belongia, M., and Boehm, W.: *The food stamp program and its impact on the price of food.* Agri. Econ. Res. 30(4), 1978.
89. *Distribution of personal wealth in the United States.* New York Times, July 30, 1976.
90. Pyatt, G.: *Distribution of income and wealth: on international comparisons of inequality.* J. Am. Econ. Assoc. 67:71–75, 1977.
91. Farnsworth, C.: *Taxes for Dutch highest in West: average income in three nations now greater than in U.S.* New York Times, June 6, 1976.
92. Economic Council on Latin America: *Income Distribution in Latin America.* New York, 1971.
93. *Estimates of Federal Tax Expenditures,* op. cit.

7

FOOD AND FARM POLICIES

Although humankind cannot live by bread alone, without it the richness of human experience becomes little more than an academic word game. Major components of Federal policy have direct effects on the supply, health-promoting balance, quality, and availability of food and farm products from which Americans develop their patterns of consumption. An awareness of both the health and economic impacts of major food and farm policies, and of their links to other areas of policy, is basic to any attempt to develop them in more health-making directions (see Chapters 8, 11, and 12).

The review of policies that follows will show that food programs are important to the health of the disadvantaged Americans whom they reach. In this respect they alleviate, to a degree, the deficits resulting from the nation's employment, income support, and related policies. Nevertheless, it is farm policy that has the greater effect on the health of all Americans. These health connections will be made in the discussion that follows. It will show some of the ways in which agricultural policies influence people's consumption habits, within the context of other social and economic changes. A discussion of tobacco, a major health-important, nonfood aspect of farm and other Federal policy, will illustrate the variety of policy-related influences that can promote or restrict its use by Americans.

Farm policy also has widespread economic effects on the small farmer and retailer, the hired hand, and the food system corporation. It is now extensive enough to affect foreign trade and the balance of payments, the national supply of petroleum-based energy, and the overall rate of inflation. It thus impinges on policy development in these areas as well. Such linkages between policy and health-important habits, and between diverse areas of policy, strengthen the case for a broad health policy strategy that supports health-promoting producer and consumer choices.

FOOD POLICY

As part of slowly developing food and nutrition policy, the health-promoting effects of food stamps and similar programs are being studied. This attention, unprecedented in the Department of Agriculture until the 1970s, is a step toward the development of health-making policy.

Contrary to common opinion, low-income families—whose per capita food spending is two-thirds that of other groups—actually get greater nutrient value per food dollar, measured in calories, protein, calcium, and some vitamins. Forced to be economically efficient, their food-buying is nutritionally sound. This nutritional efficiency occurs because they spend only about half of what others spend on foods prepared away from home, and they buy less processed food generally. This pattern also holds for persons over 65, who rely on limited government payment programs for almost half their income, and for American blacks who, though constituting 11 percent of the population, receive only 7 percent of national earnings. *Within* each income group, however, food purchasing patterns are about the same, especially with regard to beef, fresh fruits and vegetables, and the share of food eaten at home.[1,2] This is another way of saying that people make choices, from among the options available to them, options most readily seen in the size of their disposable incomes, regardless of race.

Food Stamps

When the food-buying opportunities of lower-income people are expanded with food stamps, they buy not only more food, but also a more health-promoting variety of foods than the average family. They spend proportionately less on beef, ice cream, cheese, baked goods, snack items, and restaurant foods, and more on poultry, milk, and flour. Soft drink habits remain about the same.[3-5]

School Feeding Programs

Another Federally subsidized food project, the School Breakfast Program, has improved the attentiveness and performance of children in the classroom. However, the School Special Milk Program, offering free or low-cost milk, has not been uniformly successful. Children, like adults, make their choices among available options: when soft drinks are among their op-

144

tions, they choose milk less often.[6,7] Seventy to 80 percent of the children eligible to use the free or reduced-price School Breakfast and Lunch Programs do so, as do four in ten preschoolers eligible for the similarly subsidized Child Care Feeding Program.[8]

These programs and their wide use provide the potential vehicle for an explicit health-making food policy, rather than serving simply as an appendage of farm policy, long used to siphon off surplus commodities. Feeding programs can do more than merely broadening young families' opportunities to add food to their diets. More can also mean better—if the most health-promoting eating patterns are fostered among children. This means that low-fat, low-cholesterol, low-sugar, high-fiber, and fresh foods and drinks could be made at least as available, attractive, and palatable as their less healthful food counterparts, and at a relatively lower cost. In other words, the health-promoting options could be made the easier ones for children to choose.

Supplemental Foods

One supplemental food program which may be variously interpreted as part of income support policy, food and nutrition policy, or health and human services policy, is the Food Supplement Program for Women, Infants, and Children (WIC). Begun in the 1970s, it was made available to only one in five of the pregnant or nursing women and their preschool children who were eligible—those living at a low income and "at nutritional risk." Two-thirds of the participants were below the poverty income level in the mid-1970s.[9]

Compared with similar women and children who did not get the Program's monthly food packages (which were balanced for each age group), WIC women gained more weight, reaching the "ideal" for pregnancy. Fewer became anemic, and their babies were born heavier, with fewer having low birth weights. Their infants and children were less anemic; they grew heavier and taller, but, like their mothers, did not become overweight. Thin women, and children who were underweight for height, were especially likely to gain. Among the children who benefited most in growth rates and reduced anemia were those whose diets had *previously met* recommended nutritional standards, and those whose families' incomes were 50 percent *above* the poverty level.[10-12]

These results call into question the adequacy of both nutritional standards and economic measures of poverty, at least for children.[13] For if children's health can be improved by food when they are living 50 percent *above* the poverty floor, what deficits to their health are they incurring under government policy that is intended to support them at the poverty level?

145

Most women in the WIC program shared their food packages with their entire family and said the supplement also allowed them to buy additional food. This occurred even though about half of these families were using food stamps, and over a third of their school-age children got free school lunches.[14] WIC participants, and particularly the preschoolers, increased their vists to the clinics where the supplements and health services were provided. WIC program expenses in 1974–75 included monthly food costs of $20 for each woman and child, plus about $5 per person for administration. Overhead was half again more costly in programs run by hospitals as compared with health centers.[15]

Food Safety

WIC directly affects only a tiny fraction of Americans. The entire population is affected by food policy deployed through Food and Drug Administration regulations. Here policy affecting food safety can make for "either/ or" options for all people, determining whether health-damaging additives, such as cyclamates, nitrates and nitrites, certain food dyes, saccharin, or unnecessary antibiotics or hormones will be allowed without restriction in the food supply; whether they will be banned; or whether they will be made available, at a higher cost, to certain users.

Each FDA decision forms the calculus and sets the odds—the health risks and costs of avoiding the risks—for the entire population. These risks exist for those people who are aware of the costs, and for the majority who are not. Each policy decision can mean that avoiding cancer risk, as in the case of cyclamates, will no longer be difficult because they are banned. It can also mean that risks will be almost impossible to avoid, as with some additives, because their use is permitted to be pervasive. In other instances, policy decisions can mean that, for those who choose to accept the risk, the choice of individuals will be made at higher cost to themselves than previously, as, for example, if saccharin were to be marketed only by prescription.[16-18]

The economic impact of FDA decisions results from limiting the options of food producers and processors. The costs are often measured in lost profits or income, and in higher food prices. For example, the cost of an immediate ban on cancer-causing nitrites, used in curing bacon, is estimated as a net 2 percent drop in farm income, and a 0.3 percent increase in food prices (resulting from greater demand for other meat products). This excludes the possibility that another bacon-curing substance might be found. The economic costs of illness, including work-disability and medical care, are rarely if ever calculated to compare the cost of *not* restricting health-damaging additives in the food supply. However, an estimate of the increased risk of food poisoning would also have to be calculated as a cost of banning nitrites.[19]

The industrial costs of decisions to remove health risks from the national food supply appear to be relatively self-contained and transitory. For example, a more restrictive policy on the use of antibiotics and other potentially cancer-causing drugs in animal feed, while not without economic consequences, would have little or no impact after 5 years. By that time, livestock consumption might drop by just over 0.5 percent as meat and poultry prices increase commensurately. At the same time, lower livestock weights and cheaper feed would mean higher incomes for farmers by about 5 percent. This in turn would spur animal production and bring down consumer prices.[20] Thus food safety policy, which focuses on improving human health, need not bring the dire economic consequences which some industry officials suggest.[21]

FARM POLICY

Farm policy has far greater consequences for health, intended or not, than current food and nutrition policy. As with other "non-health" policy, it may affect people's health through its effects on the disposable income of farmers, other workers, and consumers, and more impressively through its direct effects on the types of food available and their supply. Farm, rather than food, policy has the most important effect on changes in the costs of production. Production costs, in turn, have a greater impact on farm profits—and thus on what farmers produce and in what amounts—than changes in consumer demand, whether that demand is induced by governmental food assistance programs or by market forces.[22]

The principal aim of farm policy is to protect farm incomes, buffering the effects of production costs and stabilizing food supply at a level to guarantee a fair economic return to farmers in relation to their costs of production. The nutritive balance of farm production or the food supply has not been a consideration in the development of agricultural policy.[23,24]

To a considerable extent, farm policy met its economic objectives in the first 25 years following World War II. Net farm income was almost 6 percent higher than it otherwise would have been, as a result of various price support, loan, purchase, and payment arrangements with the Department of Agriculture. Into the early 1970s, up to 30 percent of farm income accrued through government sources. The overall food supply for Americans expanded, with up to 16 percent of it diverted to government-subsidized storage. This surplus was doled out, at low cost or free, to the poor in this country and to selected nations. An increasing share of farm produce was exported.[25-27]

Unintended Effects

Farm policy had its less favorable economic impacts as well, the importance of which became visible in the 1970s as energy and food shortages fueled widespread inflation. Over the years, most Federal price guarantees to farmers had required that they, in return, take acreage out of production. Having done so, farmers then cultivated their approved allotments more intensely, increasing crop yields per acre and likewise their profits. In order to increase production on fewer acres, they used more energy-intensive methods, methods which were low-cost options for them because Federal policies subsidized water for irrigation, placed price controls over natural gas, and kept fossil fuel prices low.[28,29]

This set of circumstances spurred the development of petroleum-based fertilizers, pesticides, and large-scale machinery, thereby reducing the need for farm workers. The effects of these changes on farm labor, both hired and family workers, was compounded in the decade of the sixties, as 92 percent of Federal support program benefits went to landowners, not workers.[30]

These conditions also favored farm consolidation. Small farms were bought up, expanding the average size by the early seventies to over 50 percent of its acreage at mid-century.[31] The larger the farm, the more of its acreage was rented. About half again as much land from farms of 1000 or more acres is now rented as against farms of 100 acres or less. Ninety percent of the rented land is owned by non-farmer landlords.

Similarly, concentration of farm income also developed. Farms with highest gross earnings (i.e., $40,000 or more) are least likely to be owner-operated; more than two-thirds are not.[32] Almost two-thirds of the farm population live on farms earning less than $20,000 in annual sales. Together these farms account for only a tenth of farm production. Almost a third of the 8.3 million white farm people and almost half of the 400,000 blacks live on the smallest farms, grossing under $2500 per year by 1975.[33]

About three-fourths of some 2.7 million hired farm workers do not live on farms, and up to a fifth of them are migratory. The income of these laborers was less than $2900 per person in 1976, and averages $5000 for each household.[34,35]

These figures foreshadow the state of today's agriculture and its dilemmas. While the food supply mushroomed during the fifties and sixties, the seeds were being sown in the agricultural sector for farm production inflation in the seventies. Then, in 1974–75, once-cheap energy became costly at the same time that world food demand increased sharply because of crop failures elsewhere, and farm-food prices became important public issues.

148

Policy Interlinks

Today the economic importance of agriculture, and thus the political importance of the Federal policies which shape it, lies far beyond what is denoted in farm receipts. These were $94.3 billion in 1976 and represent less than 3 percent of all business receipts. But in the international arena, U.S. agriculture produces over a third of the world's wheat and tobacco, almost a fifth of its feed grains, and almost half of its high-protein meals, such as soybeans, used by affluent nations for livestock and by poor nations for direct human consumption.[36-39] The farm sector also has ramifying effects on the rest of the domestic food system. This includes the processing industries, trucking, wholesale and retail trade, as well as consumer consumption, whether done at home or away from home. Moreover, since the nation's food system uses about 16 percent of U.S. energy expenditure, it, like other sectors, is a focal point of energy policy.[40]

FARM AND ENERGY POLICIES

Farm policy has more central links to energy policy issues. Not only have farm exports increased in value, but because the U.S. exports more than twice what it imports in farm products, the agricultural trade balance is positive. This has come to mean, in the 1970s, that the balance of payments deficit, created by growing U.S. imports of oil, has been partially offset, by more than half, because of farm exports. Without them, for example, the trade deficit in 1976 would have been over $21 billion instead of under $10 billion.[41,42] Because a balance of payments deficit affects the desirability and value of the dollar in international money markets, the spiraling effects of overseas farm trade are political as well as economic, and flow back into considerations of U.S. monetary as well as agricultural policy.

ECONOMIC AND FARM POLICIES

Further links to economic policy result from current modes of agricultural and food production. Because of its increasing dependence on energy-intensive technologies, and their capital-intensive nature, farm production continues to be vulnerable to the inflation in the national economy, inflation which derives from the costs of energy and of money, a probable fact of national life for the foreseeable future.[43] Beyond this, a larger share of the food supply is processed for eating both at home and away from home. This requires greater use of energy.[44,45] Add the fact that both food production and marketing are done increasingly through very large, market-controlling corporations, and the result is accelerated rises in food prices.[46-48]

149

The price of food now represents almost 18 percent of the Consumer Price Index, which means that 18 percent of the consumer dollar is spent on food. Thus a 10 percent rise in the cost of food in any one year adds 1.8 percentage points to the overall cost of living.[49] This directly affects the amount of food available to poorer segments of the population. Worse yet, since inflationary prices take larger shares of poorer people's budgets than are taken from the more affluent, the poor are left with still fewer opportunities for obtaining health-sustaining necessities, much less for having health-promoting recreational options.

At every step in the contemporary food chain, Federal policy shapes the likelihood of what food producers will or will not do, and what people will or will not eat.

Making the Health Connections

With the growing economic and political importance of agriculture, it is no surprise that the development of farm policy has excluded any major consideration of its consequences, directly or otherwise, for the nutrition and health of people.[50] Such consideration, however, would yield significant findings, as the following discussion suggests.

Based upon the numerous population and clinical studies discussed in the first section of this book, and as analyzed within the nation's principal policy-making body, the Congress, the profile of health and illness for the American people would be measurably improved if their dietary and smoking patterns changed. Specifically this would mean consuming less fat, especially animal fats, which are saturated; less cholesterol, which is derived from animal sources; less refined and processed carbohydrates, particularly pastry products, salted products, sugar, and corn sweeteners; and fewer calories overall, including those in alcoholic and soft drinks. It would also mean concomitant increases from vegetable sources of protein and fats, yielding more grain and other dietary fiber, and more fresh foods, including those with "naturally occurring sugar."[51] Ideally, cigarette smoking would cease.

What impact does agricultural policy have on the eating and smoking habits of Americans? The recommended health-promoting changes in habits, if translated into basic agricultural commodites, have to do with beef cattle, dairy herds, eggs, the principal feed grains of corn and sorghum grain, tobacco, sugar cane and sugar beets, wheat, soybeans, peanuts, and potatoes. All are among the 25 leading U.S. farm commodities. Together they amounted to two-thirds of farm receipts in 1976. Other related commodities in the top 25 are fresh fruits and vegetables, accounting for another 6 percent of farm receipts. Cattle and corn alone contribute almost a third of

150

total farm value, dairy products about 12 percent, wheat and soybeans together about 15 percent, and the others from 1 to 3 percent each.[52]

FARM SUPPORT: ANIMAL EMPHASIS

These economically vital and health-important commodities, and their production costs, supply, and price to consumers, are specifically tied to agricultural support programs. Livestock sales, for example, are protected from foreign competition by an adjustable import quota hovering around 4 percent of the meat consumed in the U.S. annually. Livestock producers get highest profits from grain-fed and corn-fed beef that receive higher government grades for their meat; it is well marbled with saturated fat, in contrast to leaner, grass-fed cattle.

Responding to these potential high profits, beef producers now use commercial animal feedlots for about two-thirds of all slaughter cattle, instead of slower, and lighter-weight-producing, range-feeding methods. These feedlots then are dependent on the ability of producers to purchase grain and corn feed. Thus low feed-grain prices become an incentive for heavier, high-grade, high-profit beef production.[53-57]

Feed-grain prices, particularly of sorghum and corn, are tied directly to the Federal price support system. Through the Department of Agriculture's Commodity Credit Corporation, the government grants loans to individual farmers, with crops as collateral, or makes purchases of the commodity when market prices drop below a predetermined "target" price, based on a profit-after-production cost. As is true for wheat, feed-grain production is then controlled by government-required crop acreage "set-asides," for which farmers are paid up to $40,000 a year. The land that is set aside may also be required to be planted with another specific commodity—a vegetable protein crop, such as sunflower seeds, for example. Such authority, however, has not been used by the Secretary of Agriculture since it was legislated in 1974.[58-60]

In these ways, Federal farm policy not only encourages beef production, but also, through meat grading and feed-grain price supports, gives incentives for less health-promoting forms of meat (favoring livestock over poultry) and beef (favoring marbled over lean). In addition, this policy has consequences for energy consumption, since feedlot cattle require over six times the energy of range-fed cattle, pound for pound of retail beef sold. Although only 1 percent of the nation's meat and meat products is exported, it represents about 10 percent of the value of agricultural exports, and so becomes a political as well as an agricultural policy consideration.[61,62]

Like livestock, milk and milk products are protected from competition by an import quota, set at less than 2 percent of national consumption. The

151

Department of Agriculture determines the amounts to be produced each year and maintains milk prices at 80 percent of the Congressionally defined target price. The price on the open market is established through the government's purchase, from milk producer associations, of amounts of fluid milk and butter that are large enough to influence the supply in relation to consumer demand. Government standards also maintain milk fat content. This was recently raised in order to qualify some grades of milk for higher prices.

The production of milk is affected by feed-grain prices. Lower feed costs are an incentive to farmers to enlarge their dairy herds. More grain also brings more milk per cow. When other sources of income for farmers compete with what they can earn from dairy production, such as job opportunities off the farm, total milk production drops. This suggests that the increasing amounts of unused, high-fat milk produced in recent years, requiring high price supports to assure farmers' income, would be reduced if dairy farmers had other opportunities for earning a livelihood within the rural areas of the nation.

Another important factor that influences the prices of dairy products is the amount of milk bought by cheese producers. Cheese consumption by Americans has increased as their disposable income has risen. Cheese also serves as a substitute when retail meat prices increase. The milk supply remaining after the demand for cheese is met, in a marketing year, then affects the supplies of butter and nonfat milk products and their prices.[63,64]

POLICY, PRODUCERS, AND CONSUMERS

These relationships of livestock, feed-grain, and milk production, along with the deployment of Federal policy, serve to affect supplies, nutrient content, and the prices of these commodities. They interact, in turn, with other economic factors in the marketplace, including changes in consumer income. Together they clearly affect patterns of consumption, including changes in "consumer tastes," meaning that, when necessary, consumers substitute lower-priced for higher-priced foods. The working assumption behind all this, which is used reliably to predict producer and consumer response to current policy, is that producers will seek the highest return on their investment, if not through farming, then from nonfarm work. Moreover, consumers will buy costlier foods only within the limits of their real disposable income. Both groups choose the greatest gain-for-cost options, based on their experiences and resources.

Among consumer food patterns, beef buying is the most responsive to changes in price. A 10 percent price rise will usually mean a drop in the dollar value of beef-buying of about 6 percent. Similar rises in cheese, milk, or potatoes would bring down consumption by about 4.5 percent for

152

cheese and 3.5 percent each for milk and potatoes. For bread the drop would be 2.5 percent.[65]

Part of the reason for the persistent policy support of choice beef and whole-milk prices may be that, of the major food commodities, the farmers' share of the final retail price is largest at between 53 and 64 percent. This compares with their shares of the final prices for bread (19 percent) and potatoes (30 percent), where wholesale/retailers get the largest share, and for vegetable oil (30 percent), where processors take the largest share. [66] For all domestically produced foods, the farmers' share of the retail price is about 38 to 40 percent. When imported foods are included, the farmers' share is 26 percent.[67-69]

FARM SUPPORT: PLANT COMMODITIES

The two principal commodities which are sources of vegetable protein and unsaturated vegetable fat, in addition to wheat, are soybeans and peanuts. They also receive Federal price supports in return for acceptance by farmers of restrictions on the amount they place on the market in any given year. The price guarantee, however, covers a smaller share of production costs than for animal products. When market prices for corn-fed beef rise faster than people's disposable income, consumer "tastes" shift to leaner and ground beef, which is made cheaper still (and more nutritious) by the use of soy-protein extenders.[70,71] Soybean oil, the predominant ingredient in vegetable fats and cooking oils, is itself readily substituted by consumers for peanut and other oils, depending on their prices.[72]

The peanuts and soybeans that are not placed on the market are stored in government-subsidized warehouses, owned by producer organizations, until consumer demand will command a higher price. This system is similar for tobacco growers and sugar producers. In addition, there is a protective import quota and a price-raising tariff placed on foreign-grown sugar.[73,74]

Consumers respond quickly to higher prices for these plant commodities when their disposable income does not rise at comparable speed. A 10 percent increase in prices for peanut butter, for example, reduces purchases by over 6.5 percent. A similar price rise for candy or soft drinks brings declines of 4.5 to 5 percent. Cigarette consumption may be one of the most volatile of these price elasticities, with a 5 to 7 percent drop in buying for every 10 percent increase in price. This drop is more likely to occur among prospective smokers.[75-78]

COMMODITY SUPPORTS, ENERGY COSTS, AND FOOD INFLATION

The costs in energy of these government-subsidized commodities vary widely. Feed grains and wheat require about the same energy consumption per pound grown, but tobacco requires 16 times more. Of the pro-

153

cessed foods, beet sugar requires most energy, consuming almost six times the share used by flour and grain mill products (8.5 vs. 1.5 percent) among all energy used in food processing.

One effect of government price support policy applied to such energy-intensive products is to add even further to the inherent inflationary impact that most energy-intensive products now have on prices. At the same time, policy protects producers from wide-range changes in retail prices that might otherwise occur; for consumers would normally respond to erratic rises in wholesale or retail prices by reducing their consumption, thus forcing prices down. In this way policy protects producer profits and sustains consumption of relatively health-limiting commodities, such as refined and processed sugars and cigarettes.[79]

STORAGE AND OTHER COSTS

The annual production of all these basic agricultural commodities is consumed mainly in this country. However, for some, a large share is exported. This was about 20 to 25 percent of peanut and soy product production and about 30 to 45 percent of feed-grain, wheat, and soybean production in 1976.[80-84]

After export demand is met, varying shares of the annual production of these commodities may enter government-subsidized storage. Wheat and feed-grain stocks change according to worldwide demand. The more consistent stockpiling in recent years has been amassed by butter and nonfat milk, 13 and 25 percent, respectively, of the amounts produced in 1976, and by sugar and tobacco, with 8 and 12 percent, respectively, of their production placed in storage. The total value of Federally supported farm stocks was over a billion dollars that year, almost a third of it in tobacco holdings.[85,86] Another $700 million was paid directly to farmers for setting aside cropland and other purposes.[87] In addition, agricultural tax subsidies cost the Federal treasury $1.2 billion by 1978.[88]

The Net Health Balance

If five of the leading farm commodities—beef, corn, grain, sugar, and tobacco—are viewed as potential health-limiting commodities, and if wheat, soybeans, peanuts, dairy products, and potatoes are viewed as more health-promoting, then the net balance of the health-making potential of the nation's food supply can be estimated. The first group of commodities, largely as a result of farm policy, accounted for 36 percent of farm receipts, and the second group for 29 percent, in 1976. This gives a negative net health balance of about 7 percent.[89] Thus the overall impact of government policy provides greater incentive for the production of potentially health-limiting commodities than for the relatively more health-promoting ones.

154

Policy, Prices, and Eating Patterns

Farm policy, through a variety of subsidies, fiscal incentives, and regulations, importantly shapes the options available to farm producers as to the nature, quantity, and nutritional quality of their produce. The resulting supply of food and plant products is further shaped by retail pricing. Prices, in turn, are influenced by Federal policies that regulate supplies and that support production practices and purchasing patterns, especially for the most potentially health-limiting and health-promoting commodities. The impact of prices is of course especially important for the amount and quality of food available to people who have limited or fixed incomes.

The ways in which Federal policies affect food prices have been analyzed by the Federal Trade Commission. The price support component of farm policy alone influences about 16 percent of the overall price of food. If, for example, food prices rose by 10 percent in a year, price support policies could control 1.6 percent of the increase. Federal control of farm production further influences prices.[90] An additional price impact occurs through other, non-farm, policy, such as regulation of trucking and rail transportation, which compose another 13 percent of food prices. Much of the remaining price spread, related to processing and marketing, is also influenced by Federal tax expenditures and government regulation of energy use, conglomerate expansion, toxic substances, and food safety.[91]

Taken together, Federal policy covers the farm-food system at every phase, to an extent sufficient to shape the food supply and nutritional balance, its quality and availability in the marketplace and, in turn, Americans' consumption of health-important commodities.

RECENT HISTORY AS ILLUSTRATION

The role of Federal policy becomes still clearer in historical perspective, through a closer look at food consumption patterns over a 20-year span. The relationship between Federal policy and people's eating patterns is apparent within the context of the growing affluence of Americans and the changes in their family patterns during the two decades.

Between 1948 and 1968, people's overall consumption of fat increased by about 12 percent. However, fat from animal sources declined by 25 percent, and increased from vegetable sources by more than 40 percent.[92] The most likely reason for this health-promoting shift to less saturated fats, which to some observers might account for recent declines in cardiovascular deaths, is not simply the greater nutritional concern of the public or of policy-makers. If health were the concern, the shift among protein

155

sources would not have been toward more beef buying, which increased by 58 percent, while pork and eggs dropped by 25 percent each, and cheese nearly tripled. These animal food shifts keep people's daily dietary intake of cholesterol at a high 500 mg. per person, the same as it was 75 years ago.

Most of the saturated fat reduction came, in fact, through an almost two-thirds drop in the purchase of fluid whole milk and cream, and an almost fivefold rise in consumption of fluid low-fat milk, in response to price fluctuations and to changes in family size. Most significant was the more than 50 percent drop in the use of butter, lard, and edible beef fat. This shift occurred because of the lower price of vegetable oils and margarine, and especially because food processors and fast-food outlets increasingly used liquid vegetable oil for salad dressings and cooking.[93] This change in the use of fats was a successful response by commercial food enterprises to the increased affluence and mobility of Americans, who now spend over 40 percent of their food budget on away-from-home eating, much of it in "fast-food" establishments.[94,95]

"Fast-food" restaurants provided widely available opportunities for Americans to eat larger amounts of processed foods. This development combined with other social factors, such as larger disposable incomes, smaller families, and greater numbers of singles, working women and youths, influenced people to change their food choices. The increasing use of pro-cessed and convenience foods, including a myriad of new snack items, produced shifts in the amounts and types of fats and sugars in the national diet. For example, well over half of all potatoes are now consumed as chips or fries, and well over a third of all refined sugar is used in the manufac-ture of candy bars and similar products, 27 percent of it in the form of soft drinks.[96,97] In fact, while refined sugar consumption increased by less than 8 percent among all foods (excluding soft drinks) since 1960, its consump-tion in soft drinks alone rose by over 100 percent. Sugar intake is espe-cially high in preadolescent and teenage boys and in young males to age 35. They eat between 25 and 50 percent more sugar than the average adult.[98] These food habits portend a continuation of patterns of overweight and other cardiovascular risks which men, in particular, exhibit in their mid-life decades.

The options that made possible, and provided the incentives for, these significant changes in food production and personal behavior were set through Federal farm policy—which affected every food whose consump-tion has altered—as well as government policy concerning energy costs and the regulation of industry. The result has been, however unintended, not only an increase in the share of the food dollar for large food manufactur-ers at the expense of farmers and small retailers, but a decided change in eating habits and nutritional intake by the U.S. population.[99]

Substance Abuse Control

While Federal policy is most often used to promote the supply and availability of farm products, other fiscal or regulatory methods are used to restrict the consumption of selected products, such as alcohol and cigarettes. The purposes of such substance abuse control policies are not necessarily consistent with farm policy, nor are they necessarily successful.

The regulation of people's access to commonly abused substances does not seem to reduce their use on an overall, per person basis. Restrictions on age or on the time and place of sales of cigarettes, alcohol, or drugs, and the strict enforcement of penalties for driving while intoxicated, have not lessened the per capita use of these substances.[100-102] Together they cost the economy—in direct damage from illness, accident, crime, correction or treatment, and through lost productivity from disability, imprisonment, or death—about $50 billion in 1975. The leading costs are from alcohol ($32 billion), followed by drugs ($10.3 billion).[103] In addition, Social Security payments amounted to $11.3 billion in 1975. These were made to people who were disabled because of alcohol and smoking-related illnesses, with more than 75 percent of the funds going for smoking-related disability.[104]

Only real price increases—higher prices in relation to disposable income—appear to reduce consumption of alcohol or cigarettes per person.[105,106] The reasons for the success of this strategy become clearer by looking at the factors affecting cigarette consumption between 1950 and 1970.

During the two decades after 1950, Americans increased their cigarette purchases each year by about 20 cigarettes per person aged 14 and older. The principal factors affecting consumption were rising income, cigarette advertising, cigarette prices, and public education concerning the health effects of smoking. Each of these, however, had different degrees of influence on buying patterns.

The relative price of cigarettes (i.e., the variation in price in relation to changes in income) was clearly most important, accounting for about 50 percent of the total change in consumption. Rises in income increased cigarette consumption by almost 3 percent per year, while the very small cigarette price rises that occurred depressed consumption by 0.2 percent each year. By comparison, cigarette advertising raised consumption by only 0.5 percent annually, probably affecting most the new smokers who had increases in their disposable incomes. The U.S. Surgeon General's report of 1964 reduced buying by more than 3 percent, and the "counter-commercials" on television resulted in a drop of more than 7 percent between 1968 and 1970.[107]

While the income/price ratio was most important, particularly in comparison with the influence of advertising, the impact of information, especially when dramatically presented as it was in the counter-commercials, had a decided effect on consumption, at least for the short term.

During the later 1960s, however, other changes were also occurring. In 1965, twice as many state and local jurisdictions had levied cigarette taxes as in any previous year. By the mid-1970s, these taxes had increased the price of cigarettes by 55 to 130 percent over the market price, a hike sufficiently large to outpace rises in income. As a result, cigarette consumption between 1965 and 1975 was 22 percent lower than it would otherwise have been.[108] Whether the primary intent of these excise taxes was to control cigarette use or to raise revenue, the effects were to lower consumption among adults, especially middle- and upper middle-income men, and to increase public revenues by about $6 billion in 1976.[109]

The degree of impact on cigarette buying depends on the design of pricing policy. For example, a 1 cent excise tax per package would produce a drop in cigarette purchases more than five times greater than that resulting from an increase in the Federal price support for tobacco. The use of price supports would add to government-subsidized stocks and would eventually raise retail prices and reduce sales. By contrast, the excise levy is cheaper to administer and brings in revenue as well.[110]

SMOKING, TAXES, AND PUBLIC EDUCATION

These figures on the recent history of cigarette consumption invite interpretation. The slowing down on the growth of cigarette-buying, especially in the last decade, was mainly the result of a real rise in prices, making cigarettes a more difficult choice to buy compared with other items of consumption. This slower growth was not due mainly to the health concerns of smokers or would-be smokers. However, the price rise was the result of a shift in public policy, of decisions to apply taxation to cigarettes rather than to some other item, as well as to place other restrictions on smoking. That kind of policy choice derived from public support for such a shift, if not by a majority, then by a large minority of the public. These were people who had been convinced by the health education conveyed through the Surgeon General's report and through the counter-smoking campaign on television, made possible by a Federal communications policy ruling.[111]

This suggests that anti-smoking health education measures worked most effectively in an *indirect* way, and not primarily by persuading smokers to quit. They helped to mobilize groups of people who, in turn, influenced tax and related policy in ways that made cigarettes a relatively less easy item to buy and use. The price increases made health admonitions easier for consumers to follow, especially for the majority of smokers who say they have tried to quit. Of the 29 million persons who have quit since 1964, 95 percent did so without special support. They were, however, provided an incentive through the real rise in cigarette prices. They were thus enabled to make a health-promoting switch in behavior.[112]

Tax policy as an instrument to control substance abuse clearly has its limitations. Levied on cigarettes at highly uneven rates among the states, taxes have fostered organized smuggling.[113] In the context of Federal tobacco support policy, taxation has slowed the growth of, but not reduced, cigarette consumption, measured in sales dollars. This impact has been especially limited among lower-income people. Even though they bear a heavier burden of such a flat rate tax, they continue to show high rates of cigarette use. This is perhaps because their budgetary and other alternatives for dealing with distress or having pleasure are fewer than for more affluent people, who now smoke less. Moreover, current policy is not deterring adolescents or women from adopting cigarette smoking in growing numbers,[114] although there is some indication that when the real income of teenagers declines, the tax deters their taking up the habit or pursuing it heavily.[115]

SUMMARY

Farm policy has a more profound effect on the health of Americans than food policy, essential as food programs are to some people. By supporting some options and controlling others that are open to farmers and food system industries, farm and related policies affect the nutrient composition and safety of foods, as well as their prices, making some more costly than others. One result is a predictable set of food, tobacco, and alcohol purchase patterns by Americans. Taken together, current policies favor agricultural commodities and products that have health-limiting, and sometimes health-damaging, effects on the national profile of health and illness. Policies do not now induce farmers to produce, or manufacturers to develop, a more health-promoting food supply, one that could protect Americans from currently high risks of illness.

At the same time these food system policies have important consequences for the national economy as well as for individuals' incomes. Thus they have the potential to affect people's prospects for health through the less direct route of changing their real purchasing power, the final denominator that shapes the patterns of choice for most Americans.

This review of some major health-important areas of public policy, encompassing large-scale economics and agriculture, shows that the effects of policy on health cannot be estimated by assessing policies individually. The sum of the components is different than the whole. The options that policy shapes for healthful environments and health-promoting patterns of behavior are never the result of any single policy. They are rather the net effect of a wide variety, only some of which are health-making in intent or effect. The search for policy that can make for better health will have to include ways to combine otherwise segregated types of policy, as well as ways to develop them along lines that make health-promoting decisions by organizations and individuals easier and less costly to them than health-damaging ones.

REFERENCES

1. Gallo, A., and Boehm, W.: *Food purchasing patterns of senior citizens.* Natl. Food Rev. 4:42–45, 1978.
2. Gallo, A., et al.: *Does race influence food purchasing?* Natl. Food Rev. 4:34–37, 1978.
3. *Administration's Welfare Reform Proposal.* Joint Hearings, House of Representatives, Part I, Serial 95–47, September 1977.
4. Walker, C.: *Poverty by Administration: a review of supplementary benefits, nutrition, and scale rates.* J. Hum. Nutrition 32:5–18, 1978.
5. West, D.: *Effects of the Food Stamp Program on Food Expenditures.* U.S. Department of Agriculture, Washington, D.C., 1978.
6. *Special Milk Program Evaluation.* U.S. Department of Agriculture, Washington, D.C., November 1978.
7. National Research Council: *Nutrient Requirements of Dairy Cattle.* (ed. 5 rev.) National Academy of Sciences, Washington, D.C., 1978.
8. House Committee on Science and Technology: *Nutrition-Related Oversight Review* (Hearings, July 26–28, August 2–4, 1977). Washington, D.C., 1977.
9. Edozien, J., et al.: *Medical Evaluation of the Special Supplemental Food Program for Women and Children (WIC).* University of North Carolina School of Public Health, Chapel Hill, 1976.
10. Ibid.
11. Center for Disease Control: *CDC Analysis of Nutritional Indices for Selected WIC Participants.* Washington, D.C., 1978.
12. Bendick, M., et al.: *Toward Efficiency and Effectiveness in the WIC Delivery System.* Washington, D.C., Urban Institute, 1976.
13. Scrimshaw, N.: *An analysis of past and present recommended dietary allowances for protein in health and disease.* N. Engl. J. Med. 294:136–142, 1976.
14. Edozien et al., op. cit.
15. Bendick et al., op. cit.
16. Robinson, K.: *Food programs and farm policy—what are the issues?* Paper presented at the Fourth Food Policy Seminar, Washington, D.C., February 14, 1978.
17. U.S. Senate Subcommittee on Agricultural Research and General Legislation: *Food Safety and Quality: Use of Antibiotics in Animal Food* (Hearings, September 21, 22, 1977, Part II). Washington, D.C., 1977.
18. Pollitt, E.: *Educational benefits of the U.S. School feeding program: a critical review of the literature.* Am. J. Public Health 68:477–481, 1978.
19. *Nitrite in Bacon: A Summary Analysis of a Ban on the Use of Nitrite in Cur-

ing Bacon. Report No. ESCS-44. U.S. Department of Agriculture, Washington, D.C., 1978.

20. Burbee, C.: *Economic Impacts of a Ban on Selected Animal Drugs.* Natl. Food Rev. 5:42–44, 1978.
21. *Food Safety and Quality,* op. cit.
22. Pollitt, op. cit.
23. Agriculture Stabilization and Conservation Service: *Price support and other loan, purchase and payment programs.* BI No. 4, May 1976.
24. Hardin, C.: *Agricultural price policy.* J. Pol. Studies, Summer 1978, pp. 467–472.
25. Nelson, P., and Perrin, J.: *Economic Effects of the U.S. Food Stamp Program, 1972 and FY 1974.* Agricultural Economic Report No. 331. U.S. Department of Agriculture, Washington, D.C., 1976.
26. Heady, E.: *The agriculture of the U.S.* Sci. Am. 235:3, 1976.
27. Rosine, J., and Helmberger, P.: *A neoclassical analysis of the U.S. farm sector, 1948–1970.* Am. J. Agr. Econ. 56:717–729, 1974.
28. *Energy Policy and Strategy for Rural Development.* (Senate Committee on Agriculture Hearings, July 13, 14, 1977, Part I) Washington, D.C., 1977.
29. Van Arsdall, R., and Devlin, P.: *Energy Policies: Price Impacts on the U.S. Food System.* Economic Report No. 407. U.S. Department of Agriculture, Washington, D.C., 1978.
30. Heady, op. cit.
31. Rosine and Helmberger, op. cit.
32. *Farmland Tenure Patterns in the U.S.* Economic Research Service Report No. 249. U.S. Department of Agriculture, Washington, D.C., 1974.
33. Bank, V.: *Farm Population Trends and Farm Characteristics.* Report No. 3. U.S. Department of Agriculture, Washington, D.C., 1978.
34. Rowe, G.: *The Hired Farm Working Force of 1974.* U.S. Department of Agriculture, Washington, D.C., 1975.
35. Smith, L., and Rowe, G.: *The Hired Farm Working Force of 1976.* Agricultural Economic Report No. 405. U.S. Department of Agriculture, Washington, D.C., 1977.
36. *FATUS* (Foreign Agricultural Trade, United States). U.S. Department of Agriculture, Washington, D.C., October 1978.
37. *World Agricultural Situation* (No. 17). U.S. Department of Agriculture, Washington, D.C., 1978.
38. *Foreign Agricultural Situation.* U.S. Department of Agriculture, Washington, D.C., November 1978.
39. *Tobacco Situation.* Report TS-166. U.S. Department of Agriculture, Washington, D.C., 1978.
40. *Energy Policy and Strategy,* op. cit.
41. *FATUS,* op. cit.
42. Manfredi, E.: *Agriculture's contribution to the balance of payments,* in World *Economic Conditions in Relation to Agricultural Trade.* Report No. WEC-14. U.S. Department of Agriculture, Washington, D.C., 1978.
43. *Changing Character and Structure of American Agriculture: An Overview.* General Accounting Office, Washington, D.C., 1978.
44. Belongia, M., and Manchester, A.: *Total food expenditures.* Natl. Food Rev. 5:20–22, 1978.
45. Marston, R.: *Nutrient content of the national food supply.* Natl. Food Rev. 5:28–33, 1978.

46. Marion, B.: *Market structure and performance in food retailing.* Econ. Issues, No. 24, August 1978.
47. Robbins, W.: *The American Food Scandal.* Morrow, New York, 1974.
48. *What Causes Food Prices to Rise? What Can Be Done About It?* General Accounting Office, Washington, D.C., 1978.
49. Boehm, W.: *The role of food prices in inflation.* Natl. Food Rev. 5:49–52, 1978.
50. Office of Technology Assessment: *Nutrition Research Alternatives.* Washington, D.C., 1978.
51. Senate Select Committee on Nutrition and Human Needs: *Dietary Goals for the United States (ed. 2).* Washington, D.C., 1977.
52. *State Farm Income Statistics.* Statistical Bulletin No. 576 (Suppl.). U.S. Department of Agriculture, Washington, D.C., 1977.
53. Agricultural Stabilization and Conservation Service: *Sugar Statistics and Related Data.* Statistical Bulletin No. 293. U.S. Department of Agriculture, Washington, D.C., 1975.
54. House Committee on Agriculture: *Export of U.S. Agricultural Commodities* (Hearings, October 12, 1977). Washington, D.C., 1977.
55. *Livestock and Meat Situation.* Report No. LMS-223. U.S. Department of Agriculture, Washington, D.C., 1978.
56. *General Farm Bill* (House Committee on Agriculture Hearings, March 1–4, 1977). Washington, D.C., 1977.
57. *Food and Agriculture Policy Options.* Congressional Budget Office, Washington, D.C., February 1977.
58. Agricultural Marketing Service: *Sugar and Sweetener Report,* Vol. 3, No. 8, August 1978, p. 130.
59. *State Farm Income Statistics,* op. cit.
60. Personal communication, Office of the Secretary, U.S. Department of Agriculture, October 15, 1978.
61. *World Agricultural Situation,* op. cit.
62. *FATUS* (Foreign Agricultural Trade, United States). U.S. Department of Agriculture, Washington, D.C., March 1978.
63. *Dairy Situation.* Report No. DS-372. U.S. Department of Agriculture, Washington, D.C., October 1978.
64. *Program data. Natl. Food Rev.,* September 1978.
65. George, T., and King, G.: *Consumer demand for food commodities in the U.S.* California Agricultural Experiment Station, Giannini Foundation Monograph No. 26, March 1971.
66. *Cost Components of Farm-Retail Price Spreads.* Report No. 391. U.S. Department of Agriculture, Washington, D.C., 1977.
67. King, S.: *Farm income.* New York Times, January 25, 1979.
68. Penn, J.: *The food price outlook for 1979.* Natl. Food Rev. 5:2–6, 1978.
69. *What Causes Food Prices to Rise?* op. cit.
70. Nix, J.: *Retail Meat Prices in Perspective.* Report No. ESCS-23. U.S. Department of Agriculture, Washington, D.C., 1978.
71. *Indexes of Total Beef, Total Ground Beef and Soy-Beef Blends Sold, 1973.* Economic Research Service Report No. 485-74(2). U.S. Department of Agriculture, Washington, D.C., 1974.
72. Hacklander, D.: *Price relationships among vegetable and related oils prices,* in *Fats and Oils Situation.* Report No. FOS-293. U.S. Department of Agriculture, Washington, D.C., 1978.

73. *Sugar Statistics,* op. cit.
74. Ibid.
75. George and King, op. cit.
76. *Dynamics of the U.S. Tobacco Economy.* Technical Bulletin No. 1499. U.S. Department of Agriculture, Washington, D.C., 1974.
77. Hamilton, J.: *The demand for cigarettes: advertising, the health scare, and the cigarette advertising ban.* Rev. Econ. Stat. 54(4):401–411, 1972.
78. Warner, K.: *The effects of the anti-smoking campaign on cigarette consumption.* Am. J. Public Health 67:645–650, 1977.
79. *Energy Policy and Strategy,* op. cit.
80. Report No. FOS-291. U.S. Department of Agriculture, Washington, D.C., 1978.
81. Report No. ASDE-3273-11. U.S. Department of Agriculture, Washington, D.C., 1977.
82. Report No. WS-244. U.S. Department of Agriculture, Washington, D.C., 1978.
83. Report No. ESCS-23. U.S. Department of Agriculture, Washington, D.C., 1978.
84. *FATUS.* (March 1978), op. cit.
85. Commodity Credit Corporation: *Charts Providing a Graphic and Tabular Summary of Financial and Program Data through September 30, 1977.* U.S. Department of Agriculture, Washington, D.C., 1978.
86. *Tobacco Situation.* Report TS-162. U.S. Department of Agriculture, Washington, D.C., 1977.
87. *State Farm Income Statistics,* op. cit.
88. Joint Committee on Taxation: *Estimates of Federal Tax Expenditures.* Washington, D.C., March 1978.
89. *State Farm Income Statistics,* op. cit.
90. King, op. cit.
91. Connor, J.: *Public policies toward conglomerate firms in food processing.* Natl. Food Rev., December 1978.
92. Marston, op. cit.
93. Ibid.
94. Boehm, op. cit.
95. Belongia and Manchester, op. cit.
96. National Potato Council: *Statistical Information Booklet.* Denver, 1978.
97. Agricultural Marketing Service: *Sugar and Sweetener Report,* Vol. 1, No. 8, September 1976.
98. *Program data.* Natl. Food Rev., September 1978.
99. Connor, op. cit.
100. Holtzman, N.: *The goal of preventing early death,* in *Papers on the National Health Guidelines. Conditions for Change in the Health Care System,* September 1977. Health Resources Administration, Washington, D.C., 1977.
101. Zylman, R.: *A critical evaluation of the literature on 'alcohol involvement' in highway deaths.* Accident Anal. Prev. 6:163–204, 1974.
102. Smart, R.: *The relationship of availability of alcoholic beverages to per capita consumption and alcoholism rates.* J. Studies Alcohol 38(5):891–896, 1977.
103. Rufener, B., et al.: *Management Effectiveness Measures for NIDA Drug Abuse and Treatment Programs. Vol. II. Costs to Society of Drug Abuse.* Alcohol, Drug Abuse, and Mental Health Administration, Washington, D.C., 1977.
104. House Subcommittee on Social Security: *Disability Insurance Legislation Hearings* (February 21, 22, 28; March 1, 5, 9, 16, 1979). Washington, D.C., 1979.
105. Smart, R.: *Social policy and the prevention of drug abuse: perspectives on the*

unimodal approach, in Glatt, M. (ed.): *Drug Dependence.* University Park Press, Baltimore, 1977.
106. Warner, op. cit.
107. Hamilton, op. cit.
108. Warner, op. cit.
109. *Cigarette Taxes as a Percentage of Basic Cost.* Tobacco Tax Council, Richmond, 1977.
110. *Dynamics of the U.S. Tobacco Economy,* op. cit.
111. Warner, op. cit.
112. *Highlights of the Surgeon General's Report on Smoking and Health.* Morbid. Mortal. Weekly Rep. 28(1), January 2, 1979.
113. *Miscellaneous Measures to Discourage Cigarette Smuggling* (House Subcommittee on Miscellaneous Tax Revenues, Hearings, March 21, 1978). Washington, D.C., 1978.
114. *Adult and teenage cigarette smoking patterns—U.S.* Morbid. Mortal. Weekly Rep., May 13, 1977.
115. *Promoting Health, Preventing Disease: Objectives for the Nation. Working Papers: Smoking.* Office of Smoking and Health, Washington, D.C., 1979.

8
HEALTH-MAKING ALTERNATIVES
TO CURRENT POLICY

Human progress in the last century, if measured by modernization through industrial growth, was sped by cheap fossil-fuel energy supplies. Progress in the future will more likely depend on using other sources of energy and on finding new ways to use them. Led by the United States, the energy-intensive economies of the advanced industrial nations, because they are dependent on nonrenewable, shortage-prone types of fuel, will continue to be inherently inflationary for foreseeable decades.

A major focus of economic policy will therefore continue to be the containment of inflation. This objective, if it is to be met, will require substantial changes in both *what* nations produce and *how* they produce their goods and services. Depending on their direction, these new policy decisions could improve the health-making potential of public policy over the current situation.

Ideas for economic and social development are abundant, but they usually remain near their origins, within circles of academics, philosophers, and visionaries. They are not likely to become translated into usable planning material. Rarely do they enter policy-making arenas.

Nevertheless, because of the magnitude, complexity, and crucial nature of contemporary public policy questions, these ideas have, in recent years, found entry into policy development to some extent. Hitherto "impractical" ideas are being recommended, and adopted, as alternatives to customary policy in many affluent Western countries, and in a variety of jurisdictions in the United States. Some of these proposals, developed in the 1970s and by no means millenarian, will be reviewed here and assessed for their health-making potential. They support the plausibility, importance, and timeliness of attempting to move public policy in more health-promoting directions.

NATIONAL CHANGE, POLICY CHANGES, AND RESPONSIBILITY FOR AMERICAN HEALTH

New directions in policy will be taken in the 1980s that would not have been predicted two decades before. They may be ad hoc and untimely, but ideally they will be comprehensive and farsighted. In any case, their effects on people's health will depend on which paths are followed, as well as on how long decisions are deferred by policy-makers.

The discussion that follows takes up several economically oriented proposals concerning energy, growth, environmental, and farm-food policies. It suggests how the pursuit of new paths to the generally agreed-upon goals of less inflationary growth and less dependence on fossil fuels could improve the prospects for American health.* By rewarding new technologies that are more labor-intensive and based on renewable and safe forms of energy, including that most pervasive form—people's learning and organizing skills—policy can reshape patterns of choice by producers and consumers. Among the probable results are new products, including more health-promoting crops and foods; new forms of housing and transportation; new job opportunities and worksites; and less pollution, as well as less inflation. Environmental changes such as these, in turn, support more healthful ambient conditions, help maintain stable socioeconomic prospects for people, and offer them more healthful options for the food-buying and other lifestyle choices they make. The discussion will also suggest how large-scale policy can reshape people's immediate interpersonal situations and so influence their feelings of satisfaction and distress, and the very patterns of work and leisure that are scheduled during everyday living.

The changes implied by the proposals that are reviewed in this and later chapters are of great magnitude. Large-scale and widespread changes in the next decade will occur, in any case, whether or not public policy makes plans for them and helps make the course of events smoother. The virtual inevitability not only of rapid changes, but also of historically new and less predictable directions of change, is related of course to worldwide problems in the distribution of funds, fuel, and food resources.

There is a clear implication here for those who have responsibility and concern for the health of Americans. Some basic changes in ways of living are in the offing and, indeed, have been underway in recent years. If it

---

*One specific policy proposal is discussed in greater detail in Chapter 11.

is reasonable to expect these changes to elicit far-reaching public policy responses, then it is also both necessary and timely for health authorities and others to give attention to "non-health" areas of policy and to the policy options that are most health-promoting.*

A further policy implication is that these important changes will place health-limiting economic strains on some segments of Americans more than on others. Adequate transitional policies can lessen these strains and prevent much of their health-damaging effect. These kinds of policies, which exist in several affluent countries, will be contrasted with recent proposals made in the United States. Their costs to the public in these other nations do not appear to be very much larger, proportionate to GNP, than comparable total public expenditures in the U.S., especially in view of the better health status of their populations.

The obvious interlinking of the policy areas to be discussed, and their consequences for people's health, calls for an effort to design them jointly and comprehensively, rather than ad hoc and isolated from each other. This sets aside for now the question of whether such an approach is politically feasible in the U.S. However, in the real worlds of several modern industrial nations, more comprehensive policy development has occurred and will be illustrated.

ECONOMIC GROWTH, ENERGY, AND ENVIRONMENTAL POLICY

To move toward the economic goals of low inflationary growth and full employment, while reducing unemployment and environmental deterioration, a series of studies was commissioned by Congress in the mid-1970s. A basic policy recommended to Congress was that the nation support the development of abundant and renewable resources, and that it conserve nonrenewable resources. In the most generic sense, the most *abundant and renewable* resource is knowledge, embodied in people and what they can learn, and, more formally, institutionalized as information and organization. *Nonrenewable* energy supplies, generically, consist of fossil fuels or earth-based energy sources, whether in raw, processed, or manufactured forms, such as durable goods.[1-3]

To deploy such a policy would mean investing increasingly in the renewable capacity of people, through a continuous development of their knowledge and skills derived from *all* the ways in which they learn, including formal education, avocational or voluntary activities, and socially necessary paid work. It also means combining the growing numbers who

*It also suggests a strategy for securing support for health-making policy (see Chapter 12).

seek work—especially first-time workers, young and old; re-entry workers; job losers and job leavers—with the array of currently unmet, community-specific requirements for services that are notably lacking in rural and central city areas. These services might include health care, recreation, nontraditional education, housing, transportation, and other municipal responsibilities.

The money for investing in this shift to a more labor-intensive form of economic growth would come by rewarding both consumers and businesses when they do not overconsume nonrenewable resources. Their reward, or economic advantage, would derive from their choices to purchase non-energy-intensive products (such as fresh, instead of processed, foods), or to develop biological farm management processes, simplified packaging, and energy-efficient manufacturing processes. This reward system could be accomplished by shifting the present basis of taxation from *income* to a progressive tax on *consumption,* taxing the more energy-intensive products more highly, including the products and raw materials purchased by businesses.

Energy Use and Labor-Intensive Production

Any such economic policy is, of course, inextricable from energy policy. Policy purposes with respect to energy would be not only to use energy more efficiently, but, more importantly, to develop less energy-intensive products and more renewable energy sources.

According to changes proposed by national and international studies, current trends in the ways goods and services are produced would be reversed. The labor-intensive sector of a less-inflationary, growing economy would be enlarged. A high-capital-investment, research-intensive production sector would be maintained, but as a smaller share of total productive resources than at present. This would allow and promote the continued development of new technologies—more effective ways of solving problems—that are appropriate to do the job with the least expenditure of nonrenewable energy. The innovations would include organizing technologies as well as "hard" instrument-based types.

NEW PATTERNS AND NEW PRODUCTS

The new economic goals would quite likely mean an expansion of publicly supported, nonprofit or nonprofitable goods and services in local communities. A number of researchable problems may be cited. How might this best be done? What is the most workable balance between national authority and local control? Furthermore, incentives would have to be designed to alter other patterns of activity. What are the most effective? If energy-efficient patterns of living are to be developed, what are the best technical and organizational means to design and implement new programs in communities, such as minibus systems, bicycle paths and walkways; more multifamily housing units and fewer disposable items; more vegetable and less meat protein; and more home and neighborhood-based activity, including paid or voluntary work and learning? One technological solution proposed here is the use of a variety of communications links to schools and employers that could promote modern "cottage industries," based in a network of people's homes and small community sites. These would provide new opportunities for families, working women and men, students, elders, and disabled people.

In addition to such new patterns of work and learning, new industries would emerge. These might include more consumer-run businesses to provide collectively used services, such as food-gardening, clothes-making, equipment repair, child care, libraries, and supper shops.

As a result of these changes, employees and consumers may find more satisfaction in their transactions. Workplaces would be more personalized and services could be more tailored to individuals, including health, educational, leisure-time, and other personal services. The associated savings of nonrenewable energy would result from people's not having to travel long distances to work or to buy and sell. And there would be less need to construct and maintain large facilities, which are a major source of inflation because of their large capital requirements and energy use.[4,5]

The extent of savings in energy that these shifts in community development would bring has been estimated in part. Today two-thirds of the stock of housing from which Americans choose their types of residence consist of single-family dwellings. These units require at least twice the heating fuel of apartments. Policy incentives that would spread investment in housing equally among the four main types of dwellings—including low-rise and high-rise apartments and townhouses—would allow people wider options for housing and, at the same time, reduce gas and electricity requirements by 25 percent. By localizing businesses, out-of-community travel could be reduced by 15 percent, and bicycling or walking would save 2 percent of the energy used at 1977 levels.[6,7]

Policies will achieve savings in fossil fuel resources when they reward the development and use of new kinds of products—foods, housing, and equipment—and new ways to deliver commercial and nonprofitable services in local communities. At the same time, these changes will slow down inflation and provide new job opportunities, especially for people who are most vulnerable to unemployment and low income; this includes women and small farmers who cannot, or do not want to, leave their families and communities. These shifts in policy will also prevent increases in environmental pollution, which, at bottom, is the result of energy-intensive agricultural, mining and manufacturing practices.

NEW EFFICIENCIES AND ENERGY SOURCES

A third path to energy savings is to reward greater *efficiency* in current production processes in industry, agriculture, construction, and sales. If, for example, the efficiencies achieved in Sweden in the early 1970s were implemented in the United States, overall U.S. energy consumption would drop by almost half.[8]

Along with greater efficiencies in the use of energy and new ways to use it in goods and services, economic growth that contains inflation and creates jobs requires the development of *new sources* of energy. The most efficient forms of energy are perpetual, safe, and nonpolluting. They are also the most health-supporting. For example, solar energy-producing technologies would create more than twice as many jobs for each unit of energy as nuclear energy technologies, and they are without question safer in both the short and long terms.[9]

Another, more immediately available energy option is the use of biomass residues for fuel. Gasohol, composed of 90 percent gasoline and 10 percent grain or ethyl alcohol, is a source for vehicular fuel and has been adopted for mass production in other countries. About a tenth of U.S. gasoline consumption yearly could be produced from farm field residues or surplus corn and distressed crops, thus reducing the petroleum fraction in gasoline by 10 percent. Gasohol would also reduce air-polluting emissions and increase mileage per gallon. The retail price of gasohol, if Federal excise taxes were waived, would be about the same as that of regular gasoline.[10-12]

Removing the excise tax, in effect, makes possible a new opportunity for consumers, one that is at least no more costly to them than their current options are. This illustrates in a simple way how the changes in the economy outlined in these proposals would be likely to bring about new patterns of behavior. Changes in ways of living would derive from planned, and phased, shifts away from the directions pursued in current policies—embodied in the Federal expenditures, regulations, and fiscal incentives now in force. The foci of present policies make today's patterns of choice, by public and private producers and consumers, relatively less costly to themselves than choosing new ways. New policies can make new choices less costly, or more rewarding, to organizations and individuals as they make their decisions about what to sell and what to buy.

HEALTH POTENTIAL OF ENERGY POLICY

Public policy can avoid energy overkill in the United States. It can limit the use of fossil fuels to the minimum amounts needed to solve the ongoing problems of public and private production and use of goods and services. It can encourage less reliance on energy-intensive products and processes, and develop new energy sources. By doing so, public policy will also help to prevent human overkill: the unnecessary incapacity and death experienced by Americans from chronic and acute illness. Less reliance on nonrenewable energy means, in effect, more reliance on people, on their ingenuity and organizing ability, on their capacity to continue to learn, as well as on a healthful increase in the use of their physical potential in work, transportation, and recreation. Balanced exercise becomes more feasible when activities are localized and daily schedules can be more flexible.

Control of nonrenewable energy would also improve environmental safety. The production of goods and services through low energy-intensive methods, ranging from biomass conversions to modern cottage industry linkages, means less pollution from industrial concentration and toxic wastes. Bikeways, car pooling, and mini-mass transit mean not only energy savings and more exercise, but also cleaner air and fewer serious accidents. These may, in turn, improve prospects for instituting safer highway traffic policies, such as requiring passive restraint systems in vehicles; use of air bags or automatic safety belts can reduce auto deaths by a third and auto insurance premiums by almost $2 billion.[13-18] Integrated housing work-service units would not only save heating and transportation costs, but also would be likely to reduce the incidence of childhood and adult illness.[19]

Policy that avoids energy overkill also implies that people increase their reliance on each other, both in their daily face-to-face contacts—their immediate interpersonal contexts—and between community organizations, public and private. All have a larger vested interest in cooperation, since they must be mutually reliant when more of the goods and services necessary to business and community life are provided directly by individuals and by enterprises close to home. The services of elders and children become more necessary as well, especially within family contexts.

All this does not mean that public economic policy that avoids energy overkill will bring either utopia or a return to the primitive. It does, however, offer the opportunity, at a crucial period in human history, to use high technology—and not just technically oriented and equipment-based high technology—to achieve very sophisticated, healthful, and humane patterns of living. In a more practical way, this discussion also illustrates how public policy that affects the forms and uses of energy underlies people's environments, influencing their air, water and food; their housing and income; and their patterns of activity and interpersonal relationships. Therefore, the coming changes in public policy, by reshaping the community, workplace, home, and school environments, can improve the health prospects for Americans.

171

Transitional Policies

Changes in patterns of production and consumption often place the sharing of costs and benefits inequitably among segments of the population. They burden more heavily those who are already disadvantaged, whether the changes are planned and comprehensive, or, more typically, like current ad hoc measures. For example, as an ad hoc, energy-saving measure, a policy that encourages more use of wood or coal for home heating would, without compensating changes, burden poor and black households more than others. This is because, with added use, wood and coal prices would rise. And since more than twice as many poor and black households already use these fuels compared with other households, more of them, proportionately, would bear the brunt of higher prices.[20]

In a more extensive way, changes in production, whether of food or heavy equipment, would adversely affect the jobs of large numbers of workers during a transitional period. Thus employment, job training, and income maintenance policies become essential components in any economic development strategy that is to be energy-saving, less-inflationary, and, at least, non-health-damaging.

EUROPEAN STRATEGIES

Employment policy in the most affluent western European nations has succeeded in holding unemployment to half or less of what it is in this country. One successful strategy is work-sharing, in which work time is reduced for all employees in a firm or an industry instead of laying off only some of them. Workers' pay is then a portion—up to 100 percent—of their wages that they lose because of their reduced work time. Various financing arrangements pay for this program, including work-sharing insurance, an employee tax, and partial benefits allowed under unemployment insurance programs. As a result of this policy in West Germany, the short-term work force grew faster than the ranks of those who became unemployed during the 1975 recession, avoiding 175,000 layoffs, and with no more than 3.8 percent unemployment for the year. This meant, in effect, that the impact of recession was more equitably shared. There were smaller cutbacks in consumer spending; workers maintained their job loyalty and skills, and they retained all their fringe benefits.[21]

To deal with job issues in Sweden, the central government provides wage subsidies to local governments to allow them to release employed personnel for advanced education leaves. This represents an investment in continuous learning. In return, local governments hire replacement personnel, for periods of months or even years, from among young and, sometimes, first-time or disabled workers. In 1975, this form of income protection supported 94,000 employees and held the actual number of unemployed people to less than 40,000, or 1.6 percent of the labor force. This compares with 8.5 percent unemployment in the United States for that year.[22]

Great Britain provides travel allowances to unemployed workers, in addition to business subsidies for the recruitment of school dropouts and for employee retraining. Travel pay provides an opportunity for people to move to higher-employment regions without bearing all of the costs themselves. The 1975 rate of unemployment was 4.7 in Britain.[23]

When employment is not possible because of mismatch in needed skills or for other reasons, such as family duties, work injury, sickness or long-term disability, and old age or retirement, most affluent nations have recourse to income maintenance policies which provide up to 90 percent of workers' usual wages. Policy is based not on the severity of the personal *problem*, such as the seriousness of a disease, but rather on the severity of *impact on the capacity* of the person to earn, measured against what comparable persons otherwise earn.[24] In addition, regardless of income or job status, public income support provides up to $500 per child each year as a family allowance. Public long-term payments, such as disability, old age, and retirement, are protected from inflation through adjustments annually, or as often as monthly.[25-27]

THE PUBLIC COSTS OF TRANSITIONAL POLICIES

These programs are based on a policy of people's entitlement or right to basic resources, rather than politically arbitrary means or income tests that determine whether people are eligible to receive them. The effect is that "welfare" or "public relief" spending is less than half the proportion of public funds that are spent on public assistance in this country.[28] In spite of the less restrictive policies in these countries, their range of government spending is comparable to that of the United States. As a share of the 1975 gross domestic product, it is 51 percent in the Netherlands and 42 percent in West Germany, both nations having a highly capitalistic economy. For Sweden and Great Britain it is 49 and 44 percent, respectively. The comparable U.S. figure for all levels of government is 34 percent.[29] Europeans spend proportionately more on transfer programs and less on military defense. Still, social or nonmilitary spending, as a percentage of GNP, is within the same range for all five nations, including the U.S.—roughly 20 to 32 percent.[30]

The amount of social spending is not necessarily related to national wealth in these countries. Income per person varies widely. Compared with the United States, per capita income ranges from only half as much, in the United Kingdom, to about 11 percent higher, in Sweden. The energy use in each country is about half what it is per person in the U.S.[31]

Regardless of the extent of private enterprise within these European nations, ranging from 78 percent of the economy in Sweden to 85 percent in the Netherlands, all have a large degree of public ownership of certain sectors of the economy. This includes full ownership of mail, telecommunications, and rail services, and from half to full ownership of electricity, coal, gas supplies, and airlines. Ownership of motor and shipbuilding industries ranges from fully private to fully public. All of these nations provide public financing, although not necessarily ownership, of 30 to 40 percent of the housing supply, and they finance or own almost all health services.[32]

PUBLIC POLICY AND THE PUBLIC'S HEALTH

In contrast with current U.S. policy, people's disposable income in the most prosperous western European nations is clearly secure, made possible through their entitlement to essential health-sustaining environmental resources or in-kind benefits, such as housing, fuel, health care, transportation, and communication services. Based on considerations discussed earlier, these policies should contribute to the health prospects of the populations overall, and to their otherwise more illness-vulnerable subgroups. National figures for general health status in all these countries, some of which have older populations than the U.S., tend to support this expectation.[33] Life span is longer and age-specific death rates are lower in the middle decades of life. Occupational disease rates are lower, and so are infant deaths and prematurity.[34-40]

This is not to suggest that health-making policies are either optimal or fully shared among the people in these countries. It is only to say that policies which make health-promoting options relatively less costly to individuals than health-damaging ones can improve the health profile of modern populations.

U.S. Reforms for Income Transitions

Congress has heard recommendations to adopt European strategies. However, the proposals for improved employment and income security that it has given most attention are those that call for more modest reforms of customary practice. These include, for example, providing more subsidized on-the-job training and public service employment and less classroom training and job placement; improving the quality of less-preferred, secondary jobs and opening the preferred, primary jobs to the subgroups of Americans with the highest rates of unemployment.[41,42]

One long-recommended reform, intended to upgrade agricultural jobs, is to extend unemployment insurance to farmworkers. This program, under

Federal-state regulation, is financed in part by an employer tax of 0.5 to 5 percent on taxable wages, based on a state-imposed ceiling, and on an industry's experience with unemployment. It applies only to employees who work at least 20 weeks a year. Extending this to farmworkers may benefit employers, because it would very likely increase the labor supply and reduce job turnover, at a minimal cost. It would also be an incentive for them to avoid seasonal hiring whenever possible, thus benefiting some workers.[43] However, the "average" farm wageworker would not be eligible for coverage under the 20-week work rule. Both migratory and nonmigrant farmworkers did less than 90 days of farmwork a year in the middle 1970s.[44-46] Here, these modifications of usual practice can have only a minimal health-enhancing effect because they still exclude those who have least income and are most vulnerable to illness.

Other reforms proposed for U.S. income maintenance policy, specifically the public assistance component, are more likely to have the effect of improving administrative efficiency than of expanding health-making options for people whose income is restricted. No recent proposals seek to bring income up to the Federal low-budget standard.

The Carter Administration welfare reforms of 1977 proposed that all welfare payment and food stamp programs be replaced with a system of basic income support. This would guarantee $4200 to a family of four when members were unable to work, and $2300 when one member could work. Additional earnings would be allowed until $8400 was reached, after which support payments would stop. Public service employment would be available to some extent, and earned income tax credits for low earners, as well as veterans' pensions, housing assistance, and Medicaid would continue. The entire program was estimated to add $6 billion to Federal expenditures.[47,48]

Underlying this approach to income maintenance is a long-held, and undocumented, assumption that people do not work because they do not want to, and that if required to do so, they will be able in any case to find jobs. These beliefs have been amply critiqued, as well as contradicted, by a wealth of evidence. One example is the adverse effects, noted earlier, of low-wage jobs on working and living patterns *in spite of* workers' "positive attitudes."[49]

IMPACTS ON SOCIOECONOMIC CONTEXTS AND HEALTH PROSPECTS

It is difficult to see how this administrative reform of public assistance would have healthful effects for most of the poor any more so than current measures. The work requirement would formalize in law what is already a burdensome fact of life among low-income people. It is that the poor must pay more to earn a living, at lower wages, than others. They face higher relative costs, when seeking and holding jobs, than more affluent people. For them, finding and keeping a job may require moving residence or breaking up family and friendship ties. Employment almost always means unpleasant, low-wage work, often in unsafe and uncomfortable environments, with few fringe benefits, little assured tenure, and little possibility of advancement. Such circumstances may dissolve workers' sources of support for coping with difficult conditions, and make harder still the building of new networks. Finally, within the reform framework, all this brings the low-income family to only about three-fourths of the official low-budget standard of living.

Such reforms are likely to continue to expose most people who receive public income support to health-limiting environments at work, home, and community; to the breakup of their social networks; and to constricted everyday personal choices from their minimal disposable incomes. These prospects will make them vulnerable to illness and aggravate the more than average burden of illness that is already part of their lives.

FARM-FOOD-NUTRITION POLICY

Issues of economic growth, energy use, and environmental safety are joined most clearly with the prospects for health in the area of farm and food policy. Recent recommendations to control inflation and save energy in the food system, made by the Department of Energy and other agencies, also have potentially far-reaching effects on the health of Americans.

A number of these proposals concern farm production methods that can reduce energy consumption. These include (1) use of biological fertilizers, such as nitrogen-fixing legumes, and of agricultural byproducts, such as stalks and manure, for fuel production; (2) solar-powered systems for pumping, heating, and drying processes that are used for peanuts and for curing tobacco; and (3) more labor-intensive farming methods and more use of small, less-costly, energy-efficient machinery, as is used in other affluent countries whose farming efficiency exceeds that of the U.S.[50-53]

Adoption of these technologies would save half to two-thirds of the energy currently used for crop drying and on-farm fertilizer production. Additional savings could come from the production of pen-fed cattle by substituting currently used, energy-intensive feed grains (corn and sorghum) with residues such as citrus pulp, whey from butter, and the "tankage" remaining from animal slaughter. Large energy gains could occur if more cattle were range-fed, instead of pen-fed, on the nation's abundant, non-farmable grazing land. This would also increase the supply of beef and, at the same time, lower its fat and cholesterol content.[54,55]

These measures to conserve energy in agriculture will also help to hold down food prices, increase farm employment, and with it, rural develop-

176

ment. They would help reduce toxic residues which result from production processes and seep into the soil, run off into water supplies, and enter the national food supply. Moreover, they would make greater amounts of lean beef available. All of these changes represent new opportunities for people to make important, health-promoting choices.

Changing the Health Balance

Greater gains in health may occur by changing the variety of products that farms produce and the shares of the consumer dollar that these products now have. The lesser used, but potentially more healthful, commodities and products could be expanded. At the same time, this reordering would help to save energy and food costs.

CROP SUBSTITUTES AND NEW PRODUCTS

Soybean and peanut planting, for example, could substitute in ecological terms for high-energy-intensive tobacco (85 percent of which is used for cigarettes), according to information on the growing conditions for cash crops gathered by government agricultural scientists.[56] For corn and sorghum (the major cattle feed grains), the more health-promoting and less energy-expending alternatives are wheat, potatoes, and soybeans. Where the sources of refined sugar—sugar cane and sugar beets—are grown, alternate saleable crops include citrus and rice, or wheat and soybeans, among others.[57-59]

In addition to promoting new crops, expanded food uses of the more health-promoting crops would also be a health-making policy direction. This might include greater use of soybeans as flour, in curd foods, or processed as non-cholesterol, high-protein blends with beef, egg substitutes, or in milk, desserts, cheeses, yogurt, mayonnaise, and dressings. Peanuts, as a vegetable fat, can substitute for cream and for milk fat in ice cream-type desserts and beverages. High-protein corn can be cultivated for use as flour, and corn oil for vegetable fat. To add fiber and protein to refined white wheat bread, the green pea legume, used as a flour, could substitute for 15 percent of the wheat.[60-62] These changes would reduce animal fat, cholesterol, and calories in the overall food supply, and would increase high-quality protein in both animal and vegetable food products.

The supply of the relatively health-limiting products, such as beef and related feed grains, sugar, and tobacco, would be reduced. This drop may be offset not only by substituting alternate crops and food uses, but also by turning some of them toward nonhuman consumption. Both sugar cane and corn, highly energy-intensive when processed for food use, can be shifted toward the production of gasohol, as noted earlier. Tobacco leaf, without

177

very extensive changes in cultivation, can be used for processing as edible protein of a quality comparable to that of soybeans. It may also be developed for several medical uses, such as protein feedings for patients with gastrointestinal diseases, for reducing the frequency of renal dialysis for kidney patients, and as a milk replacer for children who are allergic to cow's milk.[63-68]

These are a few of the technologically feasible ways in which today's more energy-intensive, inflationary, and health-limiting agricultural products might be reserved for special use, when lesser amounts are produced for eating and smoking. These would then be replaced—if health-making policy were deployed—by health-promoting alternatives.

NEW FOOD-BUYING OPPORTUNITIES

Changes in public policy could produce gradual changes in the nutrient balance of the farm and food supply. In the process, the array of food options currently available to American consumers would be changed. The food supply from which they made dietary choices in 1978 derived almost 70 percent of its protein, and over half its fat, from animal sources. Forty percent of its carbohydrates came from refined and processed sugars alone.[69] This current weighting of food commodities encourages a national dietary pattern which is typically about 25 percent higher in calories than what people need for modern activity. Food-buying opportunities for consumers are a result of the profits that can be obtained through current production patterns. Producers could not sustain these profits without the support of the Federal farm, regulatory, and fiscal policies discussed in previous chapters (see also Chapters 11 and 12).

The implications of all this for developing health-making policy are quite clear. Beef, corn, grain, sugar, and tobacco are more profitable for growers to produce, by over $6.5 billion a year, than wheat, soybeans, peanuts, potatoes, and dairy products. Policies which now make production of these potentially health-limiting commodities more profitable than the more health-promoting ones could be reversed. This would change what now amounts to a negative net health balance.[70]

POTENTIAL HEALTH EFFECTS

Changing a negative balance to a positive one would mean establishing a food supply that would move toward dietary goals within the nutrient ranges set by the Senate Committee on Nutrition and Human Needs in 1977. Shifts in farm products and processes of the sort reviewed here would then make more likely a daily diet which met these health-promoting goals. Translated from commodity changes into food products, this means that eating patterns would consist of less beef, but more textured-soy beef; more chicken, but fewer eggs; more or similar amounts of dairy products, but with a greater share of the low-fat and textured-soy varieties. It would mean fewer fats overall, and larger shares from peanut, soy, or corn oil sources; more breads and cereals to which whole wheat, soy, or corn meal were added; more unprocessed potatoes, fruits, and vegetables; more peanut products and beans; and less sugar, syrups, soft drinks, and candy.

This dietary pattern, computed for calories and nutrients, meets the nutrient recommendations made by health scientists in virtually all industrially advanced countries (see Chapter 2),[71-72] including a reduction of cholesterol in the diet to less than 300 milligrams a day.[73] The diet derives about 40 percent of its protein and fat from animal sources. If the national food supply were balanced in this way, it would also have the less obvious, healthful effect of freeing more of the world's grain stocks for its 500 million to 1 billion hungry people.

This food supply has another health-important prospect for the average American man and woman, who are currently 16 to 21 pounds overweight.[74] It is the potential for, or even likelihood of, weight loss that might occur because of this dietary shift. When the diet is computed on the basis of the same number of calories per person, averaging 3300 a day, that are currently consumed, the weight of food in the more healthful prototype diet just described would be almost 1¼ pounds heavier. It would weigh about 5½ instead of an average 4⅓ pounds. Assuming that many people would not eat an additional 1¼ pounds of food a day, and would reduce the excess bulk and protein from vegetable fiber foods, retaining their customary 4⅓ pounds, they would then be eating about 600 calories fewer each day.[75] As a generalized pattern, this means that Americans might lose excess weight. The amount, on average, could bring them very close to their statistically "ideal" weight, the one which, in relation to size and height, holds the best chances for long life.[76,77]

Comprehensive Policy Thrusts

The complex interconnections between issues of health, nutrition, the food supply, agricultural production, economic growth, and world food requirements are being faced in some Scandinavian countries through joint development of these policy areas. The European Economic Community has also recognized the need for a more comprehensive approach in order to deal effectively with the issues. Comparable approaches have not been proposed in U.S. policy arenas. There is as yet no consensus, or even significant support, for the goals or means for a food and nutrition policy. At most, policy advice urges expansion of food supplement programs and more nutritional education for all Americans.[78-85]

FARM AND FOOD POLICY

The new policy framework in Norway, for example, has three prongs. The first develops subsidy programs which are interrelated and will help meet national goals. Subsidies are made to food producers for commodities which will develop rural areas. Consumer subsidies help keep domestically produced food at a lower price than imports, *if* they contribute to nutritional goals. This means that in seeking to increase the nation's consumption of complex and nonrefined carbohydrates, Norway's policy subsidizes potatoes. In order to decrease fat consumption, especially of animal fat and cholesterol, it sets margarine and butter, whole and low-fat milk, and meat and fish subsidies concurrently to favor the more health-promoting options. To further decrease animal fat, it decreases support for concentrated animal feeds, which also lowers milk production and encourages roughage in cattle feed.[86,87]

The second facet in Norway's policy framework is to plan economic programs to deal with the problems of transition in farm production. Thirdly, that nation is using public and professional education and information which goes far beyond delineating the health effects of nutrition. Its intent is to improve people's understanding of food production, of the private and public policy determinants of the food that is available, of the price of food, and of popular purchasing patterns.[88]

The early results of some of these policies show beginning shifts toward more healthful patterns of food choices in some of the Scandinavian countries.[89,90]

SMOKING AND ALCOHOL ABUSE

If health-making redirections of farm and food policy were begun in the United States, they would go beyond altering the nutritional balance of the food supply. They would also reduce the production of tobacco and divert it to nonsmoking uses. Many affluent countries of Northern Europe, the Common Market, and some non-market countries have adopted substance abuse control policies to eliminate cigarette smoking entirely. These include an increase in excise taxes to up to $2 per pack, using the revenues for research and education on smoking cessation. Other programs tax cigarettes according to the level of hazardous ingredients they contain, or limit the levels of ingredients. There are bans on sales in vending machines and bans on smoking in public places and transportation facilities. Some countries also support anti-smoking advertisements. In this country a newer strategy is to provide nonsmoker discounts on life insurance policies.[91-94] Such discounts were offered by about 40 companies in 1979. Discounts ranged from 0.4 to over 20 percent of the premium.[95]

The most extensive cigarette-control plan, recommended for implementation over a 10-year period, has been developed in Australia. It seeks to eliminate all specific and general subsidies to the tobacco industry within a decade, while at the same time ensuring an adequate economic transition for that industry. The first step was a 25 percent increase in the excise tax on cigarettes. This reduced consumption by almost 3 percent after 9 months.[96]

In the United States, a policy that could reduce the health risks of smokers would require a significant drop in the consumption of cigarettes. Smokers would use, on the average, a half pack less a day. In effect, heavy smokers (those who smoke more than a pack a day) would become moderate smokers; moderate smokers would become light smokers; and light smokers (who smoke less than a half pack a day) would quit. For the entire U.S. adult population this degree of change in cigarette buying would amount to an average drop of 32 percent in the number bought (4110 in 1976) per person per year.[97] A national excise tax that would raise the real price of a pack of cigarettes—above any percentage gains in average income—by about 17 percent each year could achieve this reduction in 3 years. Alternatively, a lower annual price increase would be as effective if smoking bans and counter-commercials were applied uniformly.

These ad hoc measures would not, however, have a long-term effect on continuous reductions in cigarette consumption, beyond a 32 percent drop, unless price rises were made increasingly higher, as consumer purchasing power increased. Further reductions would require annual price increases, beyond any gains in people's disposable income.[98,99] Such an ad hoc approach also fails to address the wider and complex economic issues related to a marked drop in cigarette use (see Chapters 11 and 12).

Comprehensive policies to reduce alcohol consumption and abuse have been adopted in several industrially advanced countries, as well as recommended and selectively used by some localities in the U.S. In addition to the most effective single measure, an increase in the real price of absolute alcohol regardless of the variety of beverage, France has undertaken other broad measures. These include reducing the total supply of alcohol by giving subsidies to growers who shift to other crops; upgrading minimum standards of quality; controlling sales and advertising; promoting nonalcoholic drinks; educating health professionals and public officials; aligning alcohol treatment programs, not with mental health, but with nutrition programs; and penalizing drunk driving more severely, as a misdemeanor.[100-104]

These policies, taken together, clearly change the cost of alcohol for producers and consumers. They make the continuation of past patterns either less gainful or more costly. The resulting changes in drinking patterns, reducing average consumption per person, can be expected to have an effect on the population's overall health and illness profile. This improvement would result from declines in chronic liver disease and accidental injuries and deaths. In the United States, lower alcohol consumption would mean a drop in some of the 200 calories which the average person adds to his or her daily diet through alcoholic drinks. In reality, the caloric savings and potential weight loss may be larger because about a third of adults do not drink at all, and another third are only light drinkers.[105]

SUMMARY

Federal policy that seeks low-inflationary, resource-conserving economic growth and, at the same time, lower unemployment and safer environments, would also improve Americans' prospects for health. This is because saving nonrenewable energy means more jobs and more integrated communities, more personal networks, and more stable incomes. It means cleaner and safer community and work environments, more healthful exercise, and food that is safer from contamination by toxic wastes. Applied to the farm-food sector, it means producing and processing the more health-promoting commodities, which also help to contain food prices.

The same kinds of policy instruments which now array the options available to people can also be used to redefine those options. The sets of penalties and rewards that shape the likelihood of producer and consumer decisions can be used to alter those decisions, changing current patterns. Federal expenditures, regulations, taxes, and subsidies are unlikely to be health-making policy tools if they are developed in customary, ad hoc ways. Health-making policy requires a more comprehensive approach, a framework that recognizes the interrelationships and the unintended, as well as intended, consequences of such health-important policies as economic growth, energy, and environmental safety, and of farm, food, and substance abuse control. It requires monitoring the ways in which the costs and benefits are shared. Policies to smooth the periods of economic and social transition are also essential. The burden of the costs of change must be shared among people commensurate with the distribution of current resources. Otherwise, those who are already more vulnerable to illness will be exposed to still higher risks.

At a time of national and global scarcity of essential resources, the needed changes in public policy provide an opportunity to redirect governmental programs in ways that promote health. By influencing the array of what it is possible to produce and consume, and by affecting the spectrum of costs associated with various options, policy can redirect the inevitable changes in environments and social behavior along a more healthful course. As organizations and individuals weigh the gains and costs of their new sets of options, public policy will set the odds for what most will choose, most of the time, in health-important areas of choice.

REFERENCES

1. U.S. Senate Committee on Labor and Public Welfare: *Full Employment and Balanced Growth Act of 1976.* Hearings, May 14, 17–19, 1976, Washington, D.C., 1976.
2. Madden, C.: *Toward a new concept of growth: capital needs of a post-industrial society,* in *U.S. Economic Growth from 1976 to 1986: Prospects, Problems and Patterns. Vol. 8. Capital Formation: An Alternative View.* Studies prepared for the Joint Congressional Economic Committee. Washington, D.C., December 27, 1976.
3. Strumpel, B.: *Induced Investment or Induced Employment—Alternative Visions of the American Economy,* in *U.S. Economic Growth from 1976 to 1986: Prospects, Problems and Patterns Vol. 8. Capital Formation: An Alternative View.* Studies prepared for the Joint Congressional Economic Committee, Washington, D.C., December 27, 1976.
4. Galtung, J.: *Alternative life styles in rich countries.* Devel. Dialogue (Stockholm) 1:83–96, 1976.
5. Olsen, M.: *Assessing the social impacts of energy conservation.* Battelle Human Affairs Research Center, Seattle, 1977.
6. Burby, R.: *Saving energy in urban areas: community planning perspectives.* Energy Research, Institute for Research in Social Sciences (University of North Carolina) Newsletter 63(4):1–6, October 1978.
7. Energy Policy Project: *Exploring Energy Choices.* Ford Foundation, New York, 1974.
8. Schipper, L., and Lichenberg, A.: *Efficient energy use and wellbeing: the Swedish example.* Science 194:1001–1013, 1976.
9. Laitner, S.: *Impact of solar and conservation technologies upon labor demand.* Unpublished paper, Conference on Energy Efficiency, Washington, D.C., May 20–21, 1976.
10. Curtis, C.: *Gasohol.* Washington Post, June 28, 1978.
11. *Gasohol.* Illinois Energy Commission, Springfield, Fall 1978.
12. Sugar and Sweetener Report 3(12):6, 1978.
13. Parker, S.: *Decreasing mobile source air pollution.* Unpublished paper, Department of Health Administration, University of North Carolina School of Public Health, April 1978.
14. Stern, A.: *Air Pollution.* Vol. 2. Academic Press, New York, 1976.
15. *Evaluating Transportation Controls to Reduce Motor Vehicle Emissions in Major Metropolitan Areas.* Prepared for the Environmental Protection Agency by the Institute of Public Administration and Teknetron, Washington, D.C., 1972.
16. Carter, L.: *Auto safety.* Science 193:1219, 1976.
17. Robertson, L.: *Estimates of motor vehicle seat belt effectiveness and use.* Am. J. Public Health 66(9):859–864, 1976.
18. Gellman, D., et al.: *The Canadian approach to health policies and programs.* Prev. Med. 6:265–275, 1977.
19. Holma, B., and Winding, O.: *Housing, hygiene and health: a study in old residential areas in Copenhagen.* Arch Environ. Health 32:86–93, 1977.
20. Burby, op. cit.
21. Levitan, S., and Belous, R.: *Work-sharing initiatives at home and abroad.* Monthly Labor Rev., September 1977.

183

22. Moy, J., and Sorrentino, C.: *An analysis of unemployment in nine industrial countries.* Monthly Labor Rev., April 1977.
23. Ibid.
24. Copeland, L.: *Defining Disability: A Cross-Country Study.* Social Security Administration Staff Paper No. 28. Washington, D.C., 1977.
25. *Social Security Programs Throughout the World.* Social Security Administration, Washington, D.C., 1978.
26. Johnson, W.: *Reorganization of workers' compensation.* Paper presented at the American Public Health Association Annual Meetings, Los Angeles, October 14–18, 1978.
27. Goldsmith, F.: *State workers' compensation systems and occupational disease: problems and suggested reforms.* Paper presented at the American Public Health Association Annual Meetings, Los Angeles, October 14–18, 1978.
28. Reinhold, R.: *In Europe more than the poor get welfare.* New York Times, August 7, 1977.
29. *Governments' share of the economy.* New York Times, February 11, 1979.
30. Reinhold, op. cit.
31. *World Development Report, 1978.* World Bank, Washington, D.C., 1978.
32. *Europe's mixed economies.* The Economist, March 4, 1978, p. 92.
33. Wirz, H.: *Economics of welfare: implications of demographic change for Europe.* Future, February 1977, pp. 45–52.
34. Sirard, R.: *World Military and Social Expenditures, 1976.* WMSE Publications, Leesburg, Va., 1976.
35. Powles, J.: *Effects of health services on adult male mortality in relation to the effects of social and economic factors.* Ethics Sci. Med. 5:1–13, 1978.
36. *Occupational Health Programme Report.* 29th World Health Assembly, World Health Organization, Geneva, April 9, 1976.
37. *1974 Yearbook of Labour Statistics.* International Labor Organization, Geneva, 1973.
38. *Chartbook on Occupational Injuries and Illnesses, 1974.* Report No. 460. U.S. Department of Labor, Washington, D.C., 1975.
39. Wegman, M.: *Annual summary of vital statistics—1977.* Pediatrics 62(6):947–954, 1978.
40. Anderson, O.: *Health Care: Can There Be Equity?* John Wiley & Sons, New York, 1972.
41. *Impact of WIN II. A Longitudinal Evaluation.* U.S. Department of Labor, Washington, D.C., 1976.
42. *Low-Income Labor Markets and Urban Manpower Programs: A Critical Assessment.* Research and Development Findings No. 12. U.S. Department of Labor, Washington, D.C., 1972.
43. Holt, J.: *Extending jobless pay to farmworkers.* Manpower, December 1971, pp. 27–31.
44. Rowe, G.: *Hired farmworking force of 1974.* Agricultural Economic Report No. 297. U.S. Department of Agriculture, Washington, D.C., 1975.
45. Smith, L., and Rowe, G.: *The Hired Farm Working Force of 1976.* Agricultural Economic Report No. 405. U.S. Department of Agriculture, Washington, D.C., 1977.
46. *Migrant Farmworker Survey Report.* U.S. Department of Agriculture, Washington, D.C., March 1976.
47. *Administration's Welfare Reform Proposal.* Joint Hearings, House of Representatives, Part I, Series 96–47, Washington, D.C., September 19–21, 1977.

48. *Highlights of the President's plan to revise the Nation's welfare system.* New York Times, August 8, 1977.
49. Piven, F., and Cloward, R.: *Regulating the Poor: Functions of Public Relief.* Random House, New York, 1972.
50. *Department of Energy Programs and Objectives: Energy Conservation in Agricultural Production.* U.S. Department of Energy, Washington, D.C., 1977.
51. Pimenthal D.: *Energy and agriculture.* Science, November 1973.
52. Youngberg, G.: *The alternative agricultural movement.* J. Policy Studies, Summer 1978, pp. 524–530.
53. Nair, K.: *Blossoms in the Dust.* Frederick A. Praeger, New York, 1962.
54. King, S.: *The good news is cows eat grass: The bad news is they prefer grain.* New York Times, June 18, 1978, p. E-7.
55. *German use of soybean meal hits record while EC debates use of nongrain foods.* Foreign Agriculture, February 5, 1979.
56. *Tobacco Situation.* Report No. TS-161. U.S. Department of Agriculture, Washington, D.C., 1977.
57. Duke, J., et al.: *Economic Plants and Their Ecological Distribution.* USDA Plant Genetics and Germplasm Institute, Beltsville, Md., June 1976.
58. Siceloff, B.: *Protein called key to tobacco's future.* News and Observer (Raleigh, N.C., October 7, 1978, p. 23.
59. Jones, G., Crop Science Specialist, School of Agriculture and Life Sciences, North Carolina State University: Personal communication, November 16, 30, 1978.
60. Hoover, M.: *Frozen dessert and beverage from roasted peanuts.* Proc. Am. Peanut Res. Ed. Assoc. 9(1):104–106, 1977.
61. Shurtleff, W.: *New food from old ways.* AID Agenda 1:8, 1978.
62. *Pea flour fortifies wheat flour in breads.* USDA News, January 12, 1978.
63. Wildman, S., et al.: *Production and biological evaluation of crystalline fraction I protein from tobacco leaves.* Paper presented at the National Science Foundation Meeting, Washington, D.C., November 1977.
64. Tso, T.: *Tobacco as potential food source and smoke material.* Beitr. Tabakforschung 9(2):63–66, 1977.
65. DeJong, D.: *Recent advances in the chemical composition of tobacco and tobacco smoke,* in Proceedings of American Chemical Society Symposium, New Orleans, 1977, pp. 78–103.
66. DeJong, D.: *The future of tobacco as I see it.* Paper presented at the Tobacco Growers' Information Committee Annual Meeting, Raleigh, N.C., October 6, 1978.
67. *Gasohol,* op. cit.
68. Sugar and Sweetener Report, op. cit.
69. Marston, op. cit.
70. *State Farm Income Statistics.* Statistical Bulletin No. 576 (Suppl.) U.S. Department of Agriculture, Washington, D.C., 1977.
71. U.S. Senate Select Committee on Nutrition and Human Needs: *Dietary Goals for the United States.* ed. 2. Washington, D.C., 1977.
72. Norum, K.: *Experts link heart disease and diet.* J.A.M.A. 237(24):2593, 1977.
73. Milio, N.: *Daily diet in the United States: current and proposed nutrient and food intake.* Unpublished paper, University of North Carolina Health Services Research Center, Chapel Hill, January 1979.
74. *HANES (Health and Nutrition Survey) 1971–74,* National Center for Health

Statistics, Height and Weight of Adults 18–74 Years, U.S. Advancedata 3, November 19, 1976.
75. Milio, op. cit.
76. Metropolitan Life Insurance Statistical Bulletin, 39–49, 1958–1961.
77. Milio, op. cit.
78. Winikoff, B.: *Nutrition and food policy: The approaches of Norway and the United States.* Am. J. Public Health 67:552–557, 1977.
79. Ringen, K.: *The Norwegian food and nutritional policy.* 67:550–551, 1977.
80. Pushka, P.: *All-out effort cuts Finn's heart illness.* New York Times, April 3, 1977.
81. McGovern, G.: *National Preventive Medicine, Health Maintenance and Health Promotion Act of 1977 (S.1191),* March 31, 1977.
82. Karpoff, E.: *EC commission reviews milk dilemma.* Foreign Agriculture, December 12, 1978, pp. 13–16.
83. Blix, G., et al.: *Activities in Sweden to improve dietary habits.* Bibl. Nutr. Diet. 19:154–165, 1973.
84. National Advisory Council on Child Nutrition: *1976 Annual Report.* U.S. Department of Agriculture, Washington, D.C., 1976.
85. National Advisory Council on Maternal, Infant and Fetal Nutrition: *1977 Annual Report.* U.S. Department of Agriculture, Washington, D.C., 1977.
86. Winikoff, op. cit.
87. Ringer, op. cit.
88. Ibid.
89. Guest, I.: *Preventing heart disease through community action: The North Korelia Project.* Devel. Dialogue (1):51–58, 1978.
90. Powles, op. cit.
91. Guest, op. cit.
92. National Cancer Institute: *The Smoking Digest.* National Institutes of Health, Washington, D.C., 1977.
93. Kennedy, T.: *Smoking Deterrence Act of 1978 (S.3118),* May 19, 1978.
94. *Smoking, health and related problems in Australia: official recommendations,* in *Report from the Senate Standing Committee on Social Welfare. Drug Problems in Australia,* Canberra, 1978.
95. *Antismoking Initiatives of the Department of Health, Education and Welfare.* Hearings, February 15, 1978. House Subcommittee on Health and the Environment, Washington, D.C., 1978.
96. *Drug Problems in Australia,* op. cit.
97. *Tobacco Situation,* op. cit.
98. Hamilton, op. cit.
99. Warner, op. cit.
100. National Institute on Alcohol Abuse and Alcoholism: *French prevention effort takes varied approaches.* Information and Feature Service 35, April 27, 1977.
101. National Institute on Alcohol Abuse and Alcoholism: *Alcohol abuse prevention strategies.* Information and Feature Service 30, November 23, 1976.
102. National Institute on Alcohol Abuse and Alcoholism: *Projects seeks to end serving of drunk patrons.* Information and Feature Service 47, April 26, 1978.
103. Yamamuro, B.: *Combating alcohol abuse in Japan,* in *Selected Translations of International Alcoholism Research.* National Clearinghouse for Alcohol Information, Washington, D.C., 1978.
104. Corcoran, S.: *Reducing alcohol-related problems in a prototype community.*

Unpublished paper, University of North Carolina School of Public Health, Department of Health Administration, Chapel Hill, April 1978.
105. *Summary of third report on alcohol and health.* National Institute of Alcohol Abuse Special Report, November 30, 1978.

9

HEALTH CARE POLICY
AND ITS IMPACTS

Is the purpose of what is currently regarded as health policy to improve people's health? Except in recent years, the answer to that question was given in local communities, in the charters and programs of myriad state and local health organizations, more of them private than public. The answers were not necessarily in agreement, nor were the effects of agency programs, if known, necessarily consistent with their goals. Today Federal health care policy heavily influences the delivery of health services. It shapes the options for state and local health service and related organizations. It sets the parameters for what health care will be: its components, the supply and distribution of its services, and its impact on people.

Federal policy, however, has not yet provided a clear answer to whether its primary purpose is to deliver health services or to improve Americans' health. While these purposes are not mutually exclusive, the determination of which is to have priority is crucial. The answer has profound importance for evaluating current policy and for changing that policy, in scope, emphasis, and component strategies, to most effectively solve that which is determined to be the principal policy problem.

The definition of a clear and consistently followed national policy goal, and the determination of an organizational focus of responsibility for its deployment, is doubly important as the influence of Federal policy grows. That growth is virtually inevitable as the rising costs of health care become increasingly financed by public funds, especially from Federal sources.

This chapter will summarize the major consequences of current policy,

189

suggesting the implied purpose of present strategies. The analysis reveals, among other things, the after-the-fact emphasis of health care policy, ameliorating people's illness after it develops. It shows the inflationary effects of present policy for financing health services. Basically, policy sustains a delivery system that is dependent on energy-intensive and capital-intensive technologies to deal with health problems. The cost effects spill over into the national economy with burdensome reverberations. They also reinforce the inequities that exist among Americans and, through their economic impact, serve to damage the prospects for health of lower-income people.

Major alternatives to current health care policy will be reviewed here as well. Some of the proposed changes could perpetuate present problems. Other proposals, giving more attention to the prevention of illness and having a broader scope, appeared to have the least political support at the close of the 1970s.

Discussion shows how the development and application of health care policy is likely to be increasingly tied to considerations involving "non-health" policies, economic and budgetary as well as energy-related and environmental.

The fundamental evaluation of health care policy is not based solely on what it costs, but rather on whether its effects are justified by those costs. However, without a clear goal showing what effects are sought—whether primarily improved services or primarily improved health—evaluation remains equivocal. As a result, policy also remains unaccountable to the public interest. This issue centers on the question that is least asked of current and proposed health care policies: what is their effect on the health of Americans?

HEALTH CARE ECONOMICS AND HEALTH CARE POLICY

Size and Scope of Spending

If there is no clearly articulated agreement on the goal of health policy, it may nevertheless be surmised from the way the nation's health resources, both private and public, are allocated collectively under this rubric. Of the total $163 billion spent in fiscal 1976, 40 percent was for hospital care and 20 percent for physicians' services; 8 percent went for drugs and 6 percent for construction and research. Another 2 percent was spent on public health measures.[1-4]

The basis for many of these expenditures can be seen by looking more closely at the largest—hospital care. The percentage of small hospitals (those with fewer than 100 beds) that have energy-intensive and capital-

190

intensive technology (e.g., electroencephalography, intensive care units, and respiratory therapy departments) doubled between 1970 and 1975. At the same time, hospital care also became more labor-intensive, increasing from an average 2.9 employees to 3.4 per patient. Part of this increase was not to provide direct care to patients, but rather to make use of the new technology. As a result, the number of tests performed for each hospital patient increased by 8 percent a year from 1972 to 1977. These services, in turn, increased the daily cost of care. For example, the average cost per patient day in 1975 was 10 percent higher than it would have been without intensive care or the other specialized units.[5]

This picture of expenditures is of an industry whose size in dollar terms is about 9 percent of the GNP. It is increasingly energy-intensive through its high investment in, and use of, large facilities and specialized, hard technologies. At the same time, it somewhat paradoxically provides personal services to over 20 million people in hospitals and to perhaps 150 million people through a billion ambulatory care visits each year. Such labor intensity, employing over 5 percent of all working people, makes it the third largest labor force in the nation. Nevertheless, as some of the foregoing evidence suggests, that labor force may be dealing increasingly with equipment rather than people. Physicians themselves engage proportionately less in the direct care of patients than was the case even a decade ago.[6,7]

FEDERAL ALLOCATIONS AND EMPHASIS

The Federal share of national health expenditures now is about 40 percent of the total. The principal use of Federal dollars, 70 percent of them, is for the financing of personal health services; another 14 percent goes to the direct provision of services, such as through the Veterans Administration; about 4 percent is expended to train health personnel, and 3 percent to prevent and control illness, such as through immunization and screening programs. The remainder is for research.[8]

Almost all biomedical research is now Federally financed. Close to two-thirds of those funds deal with biological and health services problems, about half of this amount with cancer and heart-lung disease, mainly concerning diagnostic and treatment questions.[9,10] The remaining research dollars are spent on environmental problems (30 percent) and lifestyle issues (4 percent).[11-13]

If Federal health spending is categorized somewhat differently, according to strategies to affect health, over 90 percent goes to the delivery of health services, with less than 1 percent of this for prevention and disease control services. Five percent is allocated for environmental control, with half of this for prevention. The remainder is for human biology and life-

191

style impact, virtually all in basic laboratory research, or in health education research and professional training programs.[14] In a rather similar budgeting pattern, the 50 state health departments, which derive over a fifth of their funds from Federal sources, allocate almost three-quarters of their spending for personal health services, and less than 7 percent for environmental health measures.[15]

Health Strategies

As these allocations of public funds show, the overwhelming emphasis in health policy is on the delivery of personal health services, denoting this as the principal means for dealing with health problems. Moreover, the predominant form of services that are financed consists of those that deal with serious acute or complex chronic illnesses, requiring specialized equipment, treatments, and personnel, as well as in-hospital care. Such secondary-level care is in greater supply compared with simpler, ambulatory, primary-level services that are suited to the self-limiting, uncomplicated health problems that people most frequently experience (see Chapter 2).

One major effect of policy is to deal with health by treating diseases, particularly the more advanced and serious types. This leaves only a small share of resources for either personal services or environmental changes which could prevent illness, or for research which might find new ways to prevent, rather than merely treat, illness. Allocating the Federal health budget in these ways both reflects and reinforces national patterns and priorities for services that are over a half-century old.

Sources of Inflation

Beyond the amount and directions of Federal health expenditures, a more immediately important and far-reaching effect of policy on health care results from the legislated guidelines under which Federal funds may be allocated. The legislation that established financing and reimbursement policy was initially embodied in the Medicare-Medicaid legislation of the 1960s. This aspect of health policy received increasing attention in the 1970s. The reason, of course, is widespread and growing concern over the containment of health care costs. These costs are both a reflection of, and a contributor to, inflation in the national economy, as the following discussion shows.

FINANCING METHODS

A major reason that today's hospital care takes the largest share of all health dollars spent nationally is that hospital costs have risen faster than other medical care costs, and faster than national inflation, at 16 percent annually in the mid-1970s. This acceleration, running at twice the rate of the Consumer Price Index over a decade, had its impetus from the Medicare-Medicaid legislation of the 1960s.[16]

The spurt in the demand for medical care that resulted from this law was not, however, a principal source of the cost problem. Rather the problem lay in the form of financing and reimbursement devised by Congress in its well-intentioned purpose to subsidize the most economically burdensome types of health care for elders and low-income people. In order to do so, it obtained hospital and physician cooperation by setting up various reimbursement arrangements. The most important of these was to pay hospitals on the basis of their declared costs for providing care, thus setting no upper limits on what hospitals would spend. Physicians, too, were to be paid at "usual" or "customary" fees for each service rendered, without a ceiling.[17-20].

These policies reinforced earlier Federal guarantees on loans and reduced interest rates for hospital construction. The effects of such subsidies had been to reduce incentives, by hospitals and private lenders, to analyze the financial feasibility of enlarging hospitals or of making other capital investments. Private medical facilities and banks had little to lose in building large and costly institutions. The subsidies also were incentives for hospitals to spend more on equipment instead of on personnel. The operating cost for each piece of hard technology now equals the original cost with 2½ years, compounding costs. Investment patterns like these resulted in unused hospital beds. Over 25 percent of the nation's hospital beds were empty by 1975. Just to maintain these empty beds, the yearly cost was up to three-fourths of their original $75,000 to $100,000 price.[21-23]

FOCUS OF TRAINING

Other aspects of Federal health care policy, intended to support the health services which public monies were financing, increased the supply of health professionals, beginning in the mid-1960s. After a decade, with over 60 percent of medical school costs funded by public money—40 percent by Federal funds—there was a 50 percent increase in physicians and an 80 percent increase in registered nurses. However, without incentives or requirements to do otherwise during most of that period, all health professionals became increasingly specialized, led by physicians. Almost 85 percent of physicians are now specialists. Even such "primary care" physicians as those in pediatrics and internal medicine or obstetrics-gynecology continue to subspecialize.[24,25]

Specialized personnel not only cost more to train, and more to retain, but they also use more expensive technology and more hospital services. In

193

these ways the average physician was generating over $250,000 a year in health expenditures in 1972, or over $315,000 in 1977 dollars.[26,27] Thus the type of training, technology, and place of practice, combined with Federal reimbursement for physician services according to "usual or customary" fees, resulted in inflation of doctor fees at a rate 40 percent above the cost of living in the 1965–76 decade. Moreover, when ceilings were set on some fees, many physicians then subdivided their services and so increased the number of fees they charged.[28] The effects of such financial incentives on patterns of patient care were discussed earlier (see Chapter 5).

TAX INCENTIVES

Beyond these subsidies for hospitals and physicians, a final component of Federal health policy that has made cost containment a focal policy issue today is the income tax deduction for health insurance premiums paid by individuals and employers. Where Medicaid-Medicare most often assists non-taxpayers or low-income people, these tax expenditures favor high-earners and, in effect, the private health insurance companies. This subsidy is equivalent to about 18 percent of the dollar value of all private health insurance premiums paid. It is *more than* the difference between the total premiums paid into companies and the total benefits paid out on behalf of consumers. The effect is that government bears all of the fees (profits) of private insurance companies and also offsets part of their cost of providing their insurance service to the insured.[29]

SUMMARY

Federal health policy, particularly since the 1960s, reinforced the nation's system of health services, one which had been expanding its secondary care-hospital-specialist capacity since the origins of private hospital insurance in the 1930s[30] With the assurance of Federal financing, and without adequate controls on spending, this service complex mushroomed in size and in the intensity of the methods of care it developed. Technologically advanced and oversized in relation to what is medically needed by Americans, it became vulnerable to inflation. It is now an important contributor to inflation. In 1976, for example, because of high energy and capital costs, high-technology equipment was the most inflationary component of hospital costs. Once acquired, of course, advanced equipment and specialized personnel must be used in order to be financially justifiable. These circumstances then set up the likelihood of overusing, or using in medically unneeded ways, the more expensive services.

All this meant that in an industry in which consumers have little to say about what they need to buy, 100,000 people were unnecessarily hospitalized in 1977. Others were kept longer than needed; 2.4 million surgeries were performed that were not medically necessary. Such excess services brought $2 billion in profits to proprietary hospitals and in a surplus of income over costs to nonprofit hospitals. The surplus provides them with a reserve—an incentive, in effect—for further expansion. The total excess costs were over $16 billion for the year.[31,32]

National Economic Impacts of Health Care Costs

With health care now a significant part of the economy, and its hospital component so predominant, it is no surprise that hospital inflation alone in the 1975–77 period added 0.3 percent to the overall cost of living each year.

Rising hospital costs reverberate through the economy in several major ways. First, since government funds now pay for over half of all hospital costs (private insurance pays for almost all the remainder), government health spending increased by 20 percent, and Medicare-Medicaid alone by 25 percent, between 1967 and 1978. Second, families are affected through the insurance and direct out-of-pocket medical expenses they pay, which amount to 5 or 6 percent of their total expenditures.

Hospital inflation moves through the economy in more subtle ways as well. It results in higher auto and liability insurance and in larger Medicare payroll taxes affecting both employers and workers. Along with higher health insurance premiums, this represents an increase in production costs to employers which are passed on in higher prices to consumers. To employees, rising hospital costs mean that a larger share of their compensation is in fringe benefits, which may then diminish their chances for wage increases. To individual taxpayers, hospital inflation means a smaller disposable income because of the income tax increases needed to pay for it. Finally, rises in the consumer price index add still further to national inflation through increasingly used wage and income adjustment clauses that call for a half percent increase for each 1 percent rise in the CPI. These cost-of-living adjustments now affect half of all income payments, including many private and public pensions, union contracts, and public assistance programs.[33] Inflation is thus reinforced.[34,35]

In the later 1970s, Federal estimates showed that hospital inflation, sustained over the 1978–83 period, would mean added total health spending of about $120 billion each year. Half of this would come from family income, through higher insurance premiums, payroll and income taxes, and direct medical payments. A third would come from employers, through payroll taxes and higher premiums. The remainder would be the added state and local government shares for Medicaid and increases in their public hospital budgets.[36,37]

INEQUITIES

The burden of inflationary hospital costs is clearly not shared equitably. Most of the excess cost is borne by family incomes. This not only reduces disposable income and limits the options for remaining purchasing power, it does so regressively. The flat-rate nature of premiums, payroll taxes, and direct payments is inherently regressive. Flat rates require the same rate of payment regardless of people's income. Hence those with lower incomes bear a larger burden.

An often-used means to control rising Medicaid and public hospital spending is simply to reduce the number of services covered, make eligibility more stringent, or require partial payment from those with low incomes. In any case, the people most affected are the ones most vulnerable to illness and least able to afford treatment. To require a larger share of the income of lower-income groups, and at the same time reduce their access to health services, compounds their share of the burden of inflation. This, in effect, further restricts the already limited options for a healthful life inherent in the circumstances of poor people. It removes one form of material support—health care—which might help them cope with their health-limiting environments, if only by repairing the health damage they incur.

For the more affluent majority of the people, inflationary medical costs not only restrict their personal purchasing power, they preclude other public uses for those excess expenditures. Used nationally, these funds could be invested in the health care system in ways that would reduce costs, enhance access, and deploy more health-effective strategies.

POLICY SOLUTIONS TO RISING HEALTH COSTS

Ad Hoc Regulation

Efforts to change health policy in order to contain rising costs, however piecemeal, have been made since the early 1970s. Among them was certification-of-need legislation. It required hospitals to show the community need for new beds before new construction would be approved by Federally funded planning agencies—the areawide comprehensive health planning bodies—and more recently, by health systems agencies (HSAs). The result was indeed some reduction in the construction of hospital beds, along with an associated drop in the use of inpatient services. At the same time, however, hospitals increased their investments in new and complex equipment, increasing the price and intensity of service. The net effect was an actual increase in the cost of each day of care.[38]

A related effort, the establishment of physician-run professional standards review organizations (PSROs) was intended to control the excessive use of hospital care, at least the care that physicians ordered for patients covered by Medicare-Medicaid. By 1976, the PSROs showed no overall impact on rates of hospital use. However, in the relatively few PSRO areas in which the attending physician's decision to hospitalize a patient was reviewed prior to, instead of after, admission, there were some declines.[39,40] A 1977 evaluation showed a net savings of $5 million from fewer hospital days among Medicare patients.[41] However, since this approach concerns decisions about elders, poor, and permanently disabled people, it burdens them with an uncertainty as to whether or not they will enter hospitals, that does not exist for other patients who are not under PSRO purview.

Another measure, mandatory medical care wage and price controls, was used to control inflation between 1971 and 1974. These controls slowed rises in costs by almost 40 percent. They were, however, more effective in containing wages than hospital prices; and only 8 months after controls were lifted, the rate of medical price increases more than doubled.[42,43]

Another attempt to reduce hospital costs, as well as deploy energy policy, was a proposed adoption of Energy Management Programs by hospitals and nursing homes which together account for 55 percent of the $120 billion spent on personal health care in 1976.[44] Their energy costs were estimated as $1.65 billion. Energy conservation could reduce this expenditure by up to 20 percent in the fifth year of implementation without incurring new capital costs.[45] Incentives or requirements for using these measures were not, however, part of the proposal. In any case, the potential annual savings of $330 million is but a tiny fraction of the $16 billion in excess costs that result from the unnecessary use of hospitals.

Because of their minimal or transitory potential, such ad hoc cost-containment measures to control hospital construction, utilization, wages, and energy consumption drew less attention toward the end of the 1970s. Policy focused on more direct strategies to contain hospital inflation.

One of these strategies was to have the Federal government set the level of hospital price increases, or approve hospital proposals for price changes, similar to the ways public utilities are regulated. Of several states which independently deployed this approach and made it *mandatory,* the rate of hospital inflation was 14 percent below the national average. In states which instituted this policy on a *voluntary* basis for hospitals, the rate was 9 percent above the national average. In states with *no* cost-containment programs at all, hospital inflation was 11 percent above the nation's average.[46]

Comprehensive Alternatives

Side by side these anti-inflationary efforts were proposals spanning the decade for a more comprehensive revamping of health care. These proposals encompassed *financing* schemes calling for minimal government involvement, as well as attempts to secure Federal control of universal national health insurance. More ambitious proposals sought to use Federal financing as a tool to *reorganize* the delivery of health services, emphasizing primary care through health maintenance organizations, and redistributing services to underserved areas and populations. Toward the end of the decade, still others called for *public ownership,* with either local community or central control, and *integration* with broad preventive programs.

FINANCING PLANS

At one end of the spectrum of national health financing proposals was the minimal governmental approach, supported by the American Medical Association. It would cover all persons who requested insurance coverage. A set of limited benefits included some primary care services. Deductibles and coinsurance would be part of the financing plan, which proposed private insurance for most people, and government payments for services to low-income groups. There would be no changes in the patterns of delivery of services or in methods of reimbursement.[47]

At the other end of the spectrum was a financing approach which would increase Federal involvement. It was supported by the large labor unions and many consumer and health professions groups. It proposed universal coverage for the entire population as a matter of entitlement, providing comprehensive services, financed half by employer-employee payroll taxes and half by Federal revenues. There would be no deductibles or coinsurance. Funds would provide incentives for the redistribution of services to underserved communities, emphasizing primary-level care in HMO settings, and other than fee-for-service forms of reimbursement for physicians. Hospitals would be required to have their budgets approved, doing away with cost-based reimbursement. Consumers would be able to participate, individually and collectively, in the development of the system.[48-50]

By comparison, the overall costs of these two approaches are quite similar, although the distribution of the burden and benefits is different. The minimal public approach would bring costs, projected for 1980, to about 9 percent above the $180 billion that personal health services were otherwise expected to cost without changes from 1976 legislation. The increased governmental approach would be 11 percent higher in total spending.[51]

Under the first proposal, people would pay for the new costs through larger private insurance premiums (by 23 percent), but with lower (by 15 percent) out-of-pocket payments, lower state and local taxes (by 27 percent), and higher Federal taxes (up to 40 percent). Under the second plan, all private spending would drop, by half for out-of-pocket costs, and by 90 percent for insurance premiums. Costs to taxpayers, through state and local

198

taxes, would drop by half, but would increase by three times through Federal income taxes.

Of the two approaches, the second, which emphasizes less regressive sources of payment, is the more equitable. It spreads the costs more in relation to the consumer's ability to pay.[52] Because it does not require people to pay at the time they seek health care, the second plan provides lower-income people, in particular, with improved access to services.

The *added costs* in each plan derive from the added services that would be financed, and from new administrative expenses. The minimal approach, with half as many new services, would have twice as large an administrative expense, mainly because many public and private insurance programs and eligibility systems would be involved. Sources of *savings* from both plans would come from controls on utilization and hospital spending, and limits on fees. About nine times more would be saved from the second, increased public approach, because it more effectively encourages less expensive forms of financing, reimbursement, and delivery of services.[53]

Without compensating measures, the economic impact of national health insurance could have additional less obvious, inequitable effects, beyond the degree of cost-sharing among Americans which will affect the distribution of income. These inequities result mainly from the multiple-source insurance arrangements embodied in the first, minimal government approach. Under it, several types of public and private insurance programs would continue, covering different categories of people, according to their employment status, income, and age. Employers would be required to provide limited private insurance for *currently uninsured,* and usually lower-paid, workers. This would increase their production costs and could, in turn, reduce the employment opportunities they offer to low-wage workers. At the same time, the Federal budget would have to expand to pay for related employer tax credits and tax subsidies for individuals; for premiums to private insurers for low-income, elderly, and disabled persons; and for reinsurance for private insurance companies in order to cover their risks, overhead, and, for the commercial insurers, a portion of their profit margin. There would be an increase in demand for health services that would have to be met, in part, by more expensive secondary levels of care, because primary care would not be as readily available as needed. These effects would contribute to overall inflation which, in turn, erodes purchasing power and is most burdensome for people with lower incomes.[54]

In contrast, the prospect for containing health care inflation is more likely under the alternate expanded public plan. It has many similarities with Canada's universal national health insurance program. After 7 years' experience from 1968 to 1975, Canadian rates of health cost increases had dropped, as did rates of surgery, lengths of stay in hospitals, and numbers of hospital beds.

199

At the same, lower-income people increased their office visits to physicians, and more affluent and healthier people made fewer visits. The overall average visit rate, however, did not change.[55] In the late 1970s, a growing source of inflation in the Canadian system appeared to be the increase in the supply of physicians coupled with the use of fee-for-service reimbursement.[56]

Whether planned and intended or not, the financing of health care clearly affects not only the supply, but also the types and patterns of services—the inflation potential of the system. It influences where services will exist, by whom they will be rendered, and to whom they are available. The effects of financing may mean an in-kind addition to the resources of lower-income groups. But if financing policy supports an inherently inflationary system of care, it can also diminish people's disposable income.

REORGANIZATION PLANS

Other national health care proposals, appearing later in the decade of the seventies, sought to affect the type and patterns of services more directly than through financing methods. These plans called for varying forms of public ownership and control. One proposal emphasized regionalization of planning and budgeting of nationally collected funds. This would be comparable to consolidating several adjacent health systems agencies and funneling national health insurance and other developmental funds through them, along with Federal guidelines for their use. The central purpose of this kind of arrangement would be to redress a variety of imbalances in the way in which health expenditures are currently used. Monies would be reallocated, for example, to give gradual priority to ambulatory and non-hospital forms of care. Funds would be directed more toward segments of the population in greatest need, rather than to those who could pay for care. Prevention would be emphasized over cure, and comfort-bringing care over heroic measures.

This approach has similarities with totally owned governmental health services, such as those in Britain and Sweden, and with extensive national health insurance programs, as found in France and West Germany. In all four nations, the share of the GNP taken by health spending in the early 1970s was between 5.8 and 7 percent compared with the U.S. share of 7.7 percent.[57]

A second approach to the reorganization of health care emphasized local control. It proposed that all health services be provided through public health services districts. Modelled after the nation's local school districts, each health district would have a duly elected board invested with taxing and bonding authority. Its task would be to establish and maintain comprehensive health services, adopting an annual budget, and using salaried professional and other staff, as well as performance standards, as some local

200

health departments now use. Funds from Federal sources would also become part of the local budget. Comparable arrangements are used in Swedish counties, some Canadian provinces, and in Japanese district governments. Two states, Arizona and Minnesota, have passed enabling legislation for this approach as well.[58] It implies full entitlement to services by people in the district, and allows flexibility for adapting services to local conditions, as well as more public participation in the development and operation of the system.

A third alternative for revamping this country's health care focuses on the integration of types of services in a national health system. It would combine, at Federal, state, and local levels, all of the planning and services programs which are responsible for health promotion, protection, maintenance, and treatment. These include both environmental and personal health services. Moreover, it would use national health insurance as a fiscal incentive for communities to develop programs to prevent illness, ranging from effective air pollution control to extensive immunization programs.[59] A system roughly similar to this exists in Finland.

This approach appeared to be embodied in Congressional policy in the national health planning legislation which established the health systems agencies in the mid-1970s. It also seemed to be the explicit intent of the Congressional sponsors of HSAs during that period.[60-62] That intent, however, has not yet materialized within the health systems planning network (see Chapter 12).

THE HEALTH EFFECTS OF HEALTH CARE POLICY

What Is the Goal?

The wide variation in the possible future direction of health policy that is suggested by these proposals clearly reveals a lack of consensus about the goal of health policy. The basic issue is whether its principal purpose is to improve people's health or to provide them with personal health services, on the long-held assumption that these services will significantly improve their health.

Whichever the answer, the implications are far-reaching. If the primary goal of health policy is to improve health, in view of today's profile of health and illness, the strategies will have to go beyond the delivery of personal health care. They will have to include, and emphasize increasingly, environmental changes (see Chapter 4).

As previous discussion showed, other "non-health" policies have vast potential for affecting health, in both health-promoting and health-damaging ways. Thus one effect of using broader health strategies would be that when national health expenditures were added up, they would no longer consist solely of personal health services, traditional public health activities, health care facilities construction, and research. Nor would the account of national health expenditure, whatever its composition, show fully 86 percent of its spending devoted to personal health services, as has long been the pattern.[63] Rather, public health activities would expand as a proportion of all expenditures. They would include programs to change Americans' environments, including the ambient air and physical character of living and working sites and of modes of transport and other goods, as well as those that can make people's social and economic conditions health-promoting. Facilities construction expenditures would include small, community-based units, integrated with local patterns of activity and suited to day and nighttime uses, such as information-sharing, personal services, and community planning and organizing. Congregate housing would also be among the spectrum of health-promoting facilities. Research spending would show a growing emphasis on finding environmental strategies, taken in the broadest sense, to improve people's health (see Chapter 11).

The necessity of a broader policy framework for effective health-making is acknowledged, and to some extend advocated, by a minority of Congressional policy-makers.[64-66] Yet the lack of consensus on health policy goals (that makes it little different from many major policy areas) is one of the things that impede its development. Much of the basis for continued disagreement may lie not only in the tenacity of the groups whom current policies favor, but also in their imposing organizational capacity to influence policy development and to help elect sympathetic policy-makers (see Chapter 12).

Whether or not a national health policy goal is agreed upon in the foreseeable future, health policy will get increasing policy-making attention. This is, of course, because of the growing economic and political consequences of health care costs, a problem grounded in current and past policy. Like other policy areas, the cost problem in health care policy joins it to other types of policy. Whatever the resolution of the cost issue, effective or not, it is not likely to be determined apart from large-scale policy issues.

Policy Interlinks

The rising costs of health care, particularly hospital care, occurring at a rate that added to the growing pace of the overall inflation of the 1970s, made it an issue in national economic policy (see Chapters 6, 7, and 8). Part of the goal to dampen inflation was to contain hospital costs. At the same time there was a change in the spectrum of national health plans proposed at the

202

beginning and at the end of the decade. The proposals became significantly more conservative, reflecting political fears of inflation. Some of the proposals became more radical, based on the assumption that the severity of the health cost problem warranted fundamental solutions, ones that were grounded in more effective ways to prevent illness and in more open and participatory means of determining health policy.

Thus the direction of national economic policy, as it shifts between stimulative and restrictive strategies, is very likely to influence the direction that health policy will take.

Health care costs clearly affect, and are affected by, Federal fiscal policy, both on the expenditure and revenue sides of the budget, as the initial discussion showed. Energy and employment issues are intertwined as well. This will be particularly apparent as changes toward more labor-intensive primary care services begin to occur, while energy-intensive hospital services experience a relative decline. Should a major refocus toward primary-level care actually take place, hundreds of thousands of personnel would not be needed in hospitals. At a minimum, they would require some degree of retraining, and perhaps income maintenance. This would enable such persons, after a transition period, to work where they would be needed: to render health services outside hospitals, in clinics, homes, and other community sites. But without a planned and adequately funded transition period, the burden of lost income will very likely fall heaviest on lower-income personnel, consisting predominantly of blacks and women.[67]

Hospitals are also important sites for the application of environmental safety policy, affecting millions of personnel and patients. Because of the sheer size of their labor force, they have the largest share of all occupational injuries and illnesses among the service industries, 40 to 50 percent of the total. They also, however, have a 25 percent higher rate of illness and injury per hundred full-time workers. These rates for hospital personnel are more than three times higher than for personnel who work in ambulatory care facilities.[68]

Among the environmental conditions that make hospitals more hazardous than ambulatory care centers are the concentrated presence of radiation, viruses, and other pathogens, and the use of shift-work scheduling. These are a still larger risk for pregnant workers, as noted earlier (see Chapter 2).[69-73]

Hospital environments also pose health risks to patients. The hazards may, of course, be the same as those for personnel. Up to 5 percent of hospitalized patients, for example, incur hospital-induced infections.[74] Additional health risks stem from unnecessary amounts or types of treatment, including surgery, particularly for women and children; drug-induced labor; artificial rupture of membranes at delivery; elective cesarean sections; diagnostic x-rays; cancer chemotherapy; antibiotics; sedatives; and tranquilizers.[75-85] Other risks are imposed by unreliable diagnostic tests or missed diagnoses.[86-89] Risks to health come also from the iatrogenic or untoward effects of appropriately used medical therapy, such as oral contraceptives and other drugs.[90-94]

These risks that are imposed on patients, only some of which may be balanced by benefits, may occur in any health care setting. Nevertheless, they are likely to be compounded within the complexity of a hospital. As a large facility, a hospital is by nature error-prone. It deploys numerous personnel per patient, utilizes large numbers of tests, drugs, and treatments around the clock, and becomes continuously more intensive technologically. The ways in which various kinds of health care settings can affect the kinds of options available to both personnel and patients, thus limiting or promoting certain patterns of behavior, were discussed in some detail in Chapter 5.

Health Care and Health

Questions on the cost or amount of health care, or concerning the settings in which it is provided, do not speak to the impact of health policy on the health of Americans. The foregoing discussion has shown that health policy, like other policy, has its more subtle effects on health through its impact on the economy, on the purchasing power of individuals, and on the immediate service-rendering environments of health personnel and patients. But what is the effect of health policy on today's profile of health and illness as experienced by the American people?

The answer to this is really the answer to another question: What is the effect of *personal health services* on contemporary problems of health and illness? For health policy in the United States is really a health care policy. Its principal strategy, consuming over 86 percent of all health expenditures and over 90 percent of Federal health spending, is the delivery of personal health care.

SECONDARY PREVENTION

There will be little disagreement that, at a minimum, personal health services are a material support for helping people to cope with illnesses and related changes at either earlier or later stages of their development. To this extent, health services are, in general, health-promoting. The sad irony is that for those segments of the population that are likely to be most ill or most vulnerable to illness, this support is least accessible. Despite almost 15 years of ad hoc policy measures to relocate and finance health services suited to the requirements of low-income, minority, rural, ghetto, or elderly people, their access to this form of support is still not nearly comparable to that of their social and economic counterparts, who are also healthier.[95]

The most prominent form of help that consumers of health services receive is treatment for the illnesses which result from their living conditions. This is the purpose of almost 80 percent of the one billion visits made to ambulatory care settings each year.[96,97] The effect is often relief from symptoms and some reduction of disability, rather than cure. Family physicians estimate that about 6 in 10 of their patients improve, and about 7 percent become worse. More specialized physicians, such as obstetricians, internists, and pediatricians, say that from 4 to 18 percent improve and 5 to 15 percent become worse.[98] Others estimate that about a fourth to a third of visits make a beneficial difference in the course of the disease.[99] These estimates are plausible, considering that prescription drugs, the most commonly used form of treatment, are used either unnecessarily or have no proven efficacy at least 25 percent of the time.[100]

With impetus from the recognition by policy-makers of the higher costs of delayed and longer-term care, some national attention has been given to identifying those who have "at-risk" disorders, such as high blood pressure, in hopes of providing early treatment and preventing more serious disease. In this way, secondary prevention, through its efficacy for containing selected illnesses, can avoid some of the higher costs of secondary care (see Fig. 9, p.126).

Such general statements about the impact of personal health services on controlling illness cannot be made much more specific, because the answers are not known.[101] However, the cost issue has again provided the impetus necessary to seek more specific answers. In very recent years, the new Congressional Office of Technology Assessment, among others, has undertaken planning for research into the efficacy and safety not only of drugs and medical devices, but of other diagnostic and treatment techniques and procedures as well.[102]

PRIMARY PREVENTION

When and if answers are found concerning the efficacy of personal health care in terms of how much it can do in the essential tasks of secondary prevention—detecting, treating, and containing illness, as well as providing comfort and care for the ill—another question remains. This concerns primary prevention—the prevention of illness before it begins, especially the illness experienced most frequently and severely by Americans.

The basic tools of primary prevention that are used within the personal health services are immunizations, principally for childhood diseases and influenza; drugs, for selected conditions, for birth control and for some

205

maternity disorders; and fluoride, for preventing tooth decay. A third tool is health counseling or education concerning smoking, drug use, diet, and exercise. The health service technologies affecting children and childbearing are highly efficacious; 90 percent or more of those served are successfully protected.[103] The low efficacy of health education for changing personal behavior, particularly among healthy people, has already been discussed at length in Chapter 5.

This suggests that personal health services can prevent certain important health problems. Nevertheless these problems compose a diminishing part of today's illness profile. To prevent the enlarging portion—the chronic illnesses that are most disabling for most people—the health care delivery system has only the technique of health education, a not very effective tool for primary prevention.

Furthermore, even when highly efficacious techniques exist, for prevention or for treatment, the limitations for health improvement inherent in personal health services become apparent. In order to affect people's health in a community, the techniques must get to the individuals. People must make choices to seek out services. Even when policies remove the financial and geographic costs involved in people's choice-making (and when they increase the supply of community-based, primary level care which will make such choices easier), and even when the current fragmenting of services between screening, treatment, and other processes hopefully is changed in favor of "one-stop" care, making health-service seeking easier still, individuals must nevertheless make an active choice. What this means, inevitably, is that health care cannot reach everyone. Those less likely to be reached are those who, at any given time, have other problems and priorities that make them vulnerable to illness, and who make other choices for their time and resources.

The Limits of Health Services and the Limits of Health Policy

Recognition of the inherent limitations of personal health services implies, first, that health care policy must do far more to make health-service seeking—especially for the more efficacious services—less costly to individuals, financially and otherwise. They must be easier to choose than they have been. Making the more efficacious services more accessible will also make them more effective, for they will reach larger segments of the population (see Chapter 11). Most of these services are deployable at the primary level of care and in community settings, clinics, schools, worksites, and homes. Their effectiveness can be increased by links with health care organizations on the HMO or health district model. In this way, the most health-improving services also become the safest, and the least inflationary, in comparison with more complex hospital care.

The delivery of personal health services, including its most health-promoting and cost-containing component, primary care, has its inherent limitations for dealing with the profile of modern health problems. That too must be recognized. But those limitations must not become the limits of health policy. Such a development surely would not be in the public interest, nor would it be likely to be acceptable to Americans if the issue were intelligibly put to them.

Nevertheless, the potentially most health-promoting policy strategies—those that have greatest promise for the primary prevention of today's illness profile—are developed and deployed in isolation from each other and from health care policy-makers (see Chapters 10 and 12). This haphazard state of affairs is not only wasteful of resources, it also deters forward movement in the development of health-making policy: policy that can measurably affect today's health problems in the American population.

SUMMARY

Health care policy, like other areas of public policy, has indirect and subtle effects on people's health. This impact results from its effects on their spendable earnings and on the health care environments that it helps shape. The more direct effects on policy on the health of Americans result from the deployment of its principal strategy, personal health services. These health benefits are limited. They mainly involve the amelioration and containment of illnesses for which people seek out professional care. In the face of the long-term and disabling forms of illness that increasingly restrict people's lives, and that compose a growing share of known illness, the tools and tactics of the personal health care strategy are relatively impotent. This is especially true of its capacity to prevent the onset of illness. It is also a less than optimal approach when compared with strategies that could reshape people's environments in health-making ways; given such a strategy, personal services would be used supportively, and more effectively than at present.

By the end of the last decade, proposals for changes in health policy became increasingly conservative, focusing on regulation and narrow fiscal measures, and disregarding their potential impact on American health. Only a few, scarcely publicized proposals offered a broader, prevention-oriented approach.

The absence of a clear health policy goal; reliance on a personal care strategy; lack of an organizational focus of responsibility for health; failure to assess the health impact of directly health-related and "non-health" policies; and failure to design health-promoting policy options—all poorly serve the health interests of the public. This implies that the prospects for people's health will brighten significantly when national policy sets a consistent goal of health-making and fixes responsibility in a publicly accountable unit of government, a unit required to evaluate the impact of public policy on Americans' health and to design health-making policy options. Once adopted, policies would be implemented through several executive departments, including transportation, housing, labor, and a reorganized Department of Health and Human Services.

As formidable as these implications are, they may be the more manageable parts of the task of health-making in the United States. The other facet of the job is to gain political support for the adoption of policies that are health-making. These aspects of policy development—the problems of design and adoption—are the focus of the last section of this book.

REFERENCES

1. Council of Economic Advisors: *Hospital Cost Containment Data*. Unpublished report, Washington, D.C., September 1978.
2. Somers, A., et al.: *A proposed framework for health and health care policies.* Inquiry 14:115–170, 1977.
3. Congressional Budget Office: *Expenditures for Health Care: Federal Programs and Their Effects*. Washington, D.C., 1977.
4. Gibson, R., and Mueller, M.: *National health expenditures, fiscal year 1976.* Soc. Sec. Bull. 40:3–22, 1977.
5. Congressional Budget Office, op. cit.
6. *Controlling the Cost of Health Care*. National Center for Health Services Research, Washington, D.C., 1977.
7. Somers et al., op. cit.
8. Robert Wood Johnson Foundation: *Special Report: Federal Health Expenditures*. Washington, D.C., 1977.
9. *Appropriations FY 1977*. U.S. Department of Health, Education and Welfare, Washington, D.C., 1977.
10. *NCI Fact Book 1976*. National Cancer Institute, Washington, D.C., 1977.
11. Council of Economic Advisors, op. cit.
12. Somers et al., op. cit.
13. Congressional Budget Office, op. cit.
14. Robert Wood Johnson Foundation, op. cit.
15. *Expenditures of 55 state health agencies for public health programs, FY 1974.* Nation's Health, October 1976.
16. Mushkin, S., et al.: *The cost of disease and illness in the U.S. in the year 2000.* Public Health Rep. (Suppl.) 93(5), 1978.
17. Council of Economic Advisors, op. cit.
18. Congressional Budget Office, op. cit.
19. *Controlling the Cost of Health Care,* op. cit.
20. Somers et al., op. cit.

21. *Controlling the Cost of Health Care,* op. cit.
22. Somers et al., op. cit.
23. Congressional Budget Office, op. cit.
24. *Controlling the Cost of Health Care.*
25. Somers et al., op. cit.
26. Ibid.
27. Milio, N.: *The team delivery of primary care: better health compared to what?* in *Policy Issues in the Team Approach to Primary Health Care Delivery,* University of Iowa Health Services Research Center, Iowa City, 1978, pp. 180–274.
28. *Controlling the Cost of Health Care,* op. cit.
29. Ibid.
30. Mushkin et al., op. cit.
31. Council of Economic Advisors, op. cit.
32. Congressional Budget Office, op. cit.
33. Shiskin, J.: *A new role for economic indicators.* Monthly Labor Rev., November 1977, pp. 3–100.
34. Council of Economic Advisors, op. cit.
35. Congressional Budget Office, op. cit.
36. Council of Economic Advisors, op. cit.
37. Joint Subcommittee on Health: *President's Hospital Cost Containment Proposal.* Joint Hearings, House Ways and Means Committee, Parts I and II, May 11–13, Washington, D.C., 1977.
38. *Controlling the Cost of Health Care,* op. cit.
39. *Evaluation of PSROs.* Special Report. PSRO Letter, December 1977.
40. Congressional Budget Office, op. cit.
41. *New evaluation shows PSROs produce savings.* Health Law Proj. Lib. Bull. 4:57, 1979.
42. Joint Subcommittee on Health, op. cit.
43. *Controlling the Cost of Health Care,* op. cit.
44. Gibson and Mueller, op. cit.
45. Joint Subcommittee on Health, op. cit.
46. Council of Economic Advisors, op. cit.
47. *NHI Cost Estimates from HEW, 1976.* NHI Reports, November 8, 1976.
48. Ibid.
49. *HEW proposal for a 'National Health Plan.'* Medicine and Health Legislative Newsletter, February 12, 1979.
50. American Public Health Association: *Resolution on a National Health Program.* Washington, D.C., 1978.
51. NHI Reports, op. cit.
52. Bowler, M., et al.: *The Political Economy of National Health Insurance.* J. Health Politics Policy Law 2:100–133, 1977.
53. NHI Reports, op. cit.
54. Califano, J.: *Lead Agency Memorandum on a National Health Program.* U.S. Department of Health, Education and Welfare, Washington, D.C., April 1978.
55. Hatcher, G.: *Canadian approaches to health policy decisions: national health insurance.* Paper presented at the American Public Health Association Annual Meetings, Washington, D.C., October 31, 1977.
56. Badgley, R., and Wolfe, S.: *The inflation of Canadian health insurance and unresolved issues of inequality.* Paper presented at Meeting of the Association

of University Programs in Health Administration, University of Toronto, May 7, 1979.

57. Abel-Smith, B.: *Value for money in health services.* Soc. Sec. Bull. 37:17–28, 1974.
58. *The Health Service District.* Project Narrative Committee for a National Health Program, American Public Health Association, Washington, D.C., October 1978.
59. National Environmental Health Association: *A proposed recommendation for a national health services system.* J. Environ. Health 39:214–223, 1976.
60. *National Health Planning and Resources Development Act of 1974* (PL 93-641), December 1974.
61. Committee of Interstate and Foreign Commerce: *National Health Policy, Planning and Resources Development Act of 1974.* Committee Report 93-1382, U.S. House of Representatives, September 26, 1974.
62. *Health Services Extension Act of 1977 (PL 95-83),* August 1977.
63. Mushkin et al., op. cit.
64. Rogers, P., and Rostenkowski, D.: *The National Leadership Conference on America's Health Policy: Proceedings.* National J., 1976, pp. 5–6.
65. Kennedy, E. M.: *Disease Prevention and Health Promotion Act of 1978.* U.S. Senate, May 17, 1978.
66. McGovern, G. S.: *National Preventive Medicine, Health Maintenance and Health Promotion Act of 1977.* U.S. Senate, March 31, 1977.
67. Milio, op. cit.
68. Bureau of Labor Statistics: *Chartbook on Occupational Injuries and Illnesses in 1976.* Report No. 535. U.S. Department of Labor, Washington, D.C., 1978.
69. Hunt, V.: *Occupational Health Problems of Pregnant Women: Report and Recommendations for the Office of the Secretary.* U.S. Department of Health, Education and Welfare, Washington, D.C., 1975.
70. Stellman, J., and Dawn, S.: *Work is Dangerous to Your Health: A Handbook of Health Hazards in the Workplace and What You Can Do About It.* Random House/Vintage, New York, 1973.
71. Chapple, C.: *Developmental defects.* Birth Defects (Original Article Series) 8:1–79, 1972.
72. Wilson, J.: *Environmental effects on development—teratology,* in Assali, N. (ed.): *Pathophysiology of Gestation.* Vol. 2. Academic Press, New York, 1972, pp. 269–320.
73. Winget, C. M., Hughes, L., and LaDou, J.: *Physiological effects of rotational work shifting: a review.* J. Occup. Med. 20(3):204–210, 1978.
74. National Heart, Lung and Blood Institute: *Respiratory Diseases, Task Force Report on Prevention, Control and Education.* U.S. Department of Health, Education and Welfare, Washington, D.C., 1977.
75. House Subcommittee on Oversight and Investigations: *Cost and Quality of Health Care: Unnecessary Surgery.* Washington, D.C., 1976.
76. Patterson, J., et al.: *Ambulatory surgery in a university setting.* J.A.M.A. 235:266–268, 1976.
77. McCarthy, E., and Widmer, G.: *Effects of screening by consultants on recommended elective surgical procedures.* N. Engl. J. Med. 291:1331–1335, 1974.
78. Arms, S.: *Immaculate Deception.* Houghton-Mifflin, Boston, 1975.
79. *Exposure of patients to ionizing radiations.* WHO Chron. 29:90, 1975.
80. Costanza, M.: *Problem of breast cancer prophyllaxis.* N. Engl. J. Med. 293:1095–1098, 1975.

81. Grimm, R., et al.: *Evaluation of patient-care protocol use by various providers.* N. Engl. J. Med. 292:507–511, 1975.
82. Ase, J.: *Environmental causes of birth defects.* Cont. Ed. Fam. Physicians 3:39–46, 1975.
83. National Institutes of Health, reported in New York Times, April 10, 1975, p. 48.
84. Sterling-Smith, R. S.: *Alcohol, marihuana and other drug patterns among operators involved in fatal motor vehicle accidents,* in Israelstam, S., and Lambert, S. (eds.): *Alcohol, Drugs and Traffic Safety. Proceedings of the Sixth International Conference on Alcohol, Drugs and Traffic Safety. Toronto, September 8–13, 1974.* Addiction Research Foundation of Ontario, Toronto, 1975, pp. 93–105.
85. Gove, W. R., and Tudor, J. F.: *Sex roles and mental illness.* Am. J. Sociol. 78:812–35, 1973.
86. Lennane, K., and Lennane, R.: *Alleged psychogenic disorders in women—a possible manifestation of sexual prejudice.* N. Engl. J. Med. 288:288–91, 1973.
87. Sartwell, P.: *Oral contraceptives—another look.* Am. J. Public Health 68(4):323–326, 1978.
88. Sanazaro, P., and Williamson, J.: *Physician performance and its effects on patients.* Med. Care 8:299–309, 1970.
89. Sanazaro, P., and Williamson, J.: *End results of patient care.* Med. Care 6:123–130, 1970.
90. Doll, R.: *Epidiology of cancer.* Am. J. Epidemiol. 104:396–404, 1976.
91. Jick, H., et al.: *Noncontraceptive estrogens and nonfatal myocardial infarction.* J.A.M.A. 239(14):1407–1408, 1978.
92. Jick, H., et al.: *Oral contraceptives and nonfatal myocardial infarction.* J.A.M.A. 239(14):1403–1406, 1978.
93. Austin, G. A., et al. (eds.): *Drug Users and Driving Behaviors.* National Institute on Drug Abuse, Rockville, Md., 1977.
94. Mather, H., et al.: *Acute Myocardial Infarction: Home and Hospital Treatment.* Br. Med. J. 3:334–38, 1971.
95. Milio, op. cit.
96. *The National Ambulatory Medical Care Survey: 1973. Summary, U.S., May 1973–April 1974.* Series 13, No. 21, DHEW(HRA) 76-1772, Washington, D.C., October 1975.
97. *The Nation's Use of Health Resources.* Health Resources Administration, Washington, D.C., 1976.
98. Sanazaro and Williamson, op. cit.
99. Cochrane, A.: *World health problems.* Can. J. Public Health 66:282–288, 1975.
100. Silverman, M., and Lydecker, M.: *Drug Coverage Under National Health Insurance: The Policy Options.* U.S. Department of Health, Education and Welfare, Washington, D.C., 1977.
101. *Health Technology Management of the Department of Health, Education and Welfare. Final Phase I, Report to the Secretary.* Washington, D.C., December 1977.
102. Office of Technology Assessment: *Development of Medical Technology—Opportunities for Assessment.* Washington, D.C., 1976.
103. Milio, op. cit.

PART 4

DEVELOPING
HEALTH-MAKING POLICY:
FACT-FINDING PROBLEMS AND
POLITICAL ISSUES

10

MEASURING PREVENTION
AND ITS WORTH:
THE BENEFITS OF
HEALTH-MAKING POLICY

What would happen to the current profile of health and illness if the health impacts of public policy were known? What are they, and how can we know them? Said another way, what data are available, and what would a framework for analyzing them look like? How might the data be used to produce useable estimates?

Answers to these questions would allow comparisons to be made between traditional health care policy and socioenvironmental policies: to find those which could bring greatest gains in health, relative to the costs entailed; to discover which among the components of personal health services, and among social and economic policies, do the best job; to learn which ones, when combined, could afford incremental or even multiplier improvements in the health of Americans.

These are central questions evoked by previous discussions of the nature of modern illness in its American context. Today's health problem is a measurable set of people's responses to contemporary environments that result in long-term but preventable restrictions on their lives. Those environments, with their inseparable biophysical and socioeconomic facets, are shaped increasingly by public and corporate policies, themselves very much interrelated. The result is an array of options from which the public makes its choices for livelihood and leisure, a result that becomes, in effect, the shape of health and illness in the population, the amount and type of disability and vigor, of death and life.

Needless to say, making health from the standpoint of public policy is an exceedingly complex problem. Traditional disease-by-disease solutions, or the more recent efforts to convince people to alter individual risk factors, do not offer much hope for overall gains in health extensive enough to be reflected in the national profile of health and illness.[1,2] By implication they are not very potent strategies for a national health policy. This and the next chapter will illustrate a more comprehensive, "ecological" approach to guide the design of more health-effective policy (see also Chapter 4). The assumption, for now, is that if the impact of current and proposed policies on people's health could be estimated, this might make some difference in the kinds of policies that would actually be adopted (see Chapter 12).

The initial discussion concerns some practical uses of a broad framework for comparing the consequences of health policy strategies. An ecological scope also implies that far more than traditional health professionals and health care provider organizations would be involved in the development of health policy.

Next to be considered are the problems of measuring the effects of public policies on the general health of Americans. This is followed by the even more difficult issues involved in estimating the value, especially in dollar terms, of improvements in health. Dollar assessments are one important measure of health benefits because, at some point in policy development, these benefits will be related to the public and private costs of bringing them about. The criterion of economic efficiency is given high priority by some policy-makers and their most influential constituencies.

Some basic understanding of the problems of measuring policy-related changes in health status, concerning both the kinds of data that are used and the conceptual lacunae that exist, can help avoid misinterpretations of the findings and, hopefully, avoid choices of less than health-effective policies. At a minimum, a comparative, systematic approach to analyzing the health effects of policy can provide some explicit common denominators for their evaluation by policy-makers and, potentially, by the public.

COMPARATIVE EVALUATIONS OF HEALTH STRATEGIES

The principal goal is to find ways to bring the greatest gains in health relative to cost: it is the primary prevention of illness. Second is to find ways to detect and contain disability once illness has occurred, especially among those most at risk because of prior illness or social circumstances.

Context for Policy Choices

Decisions about whether a health policy should be adopted or expanded require information that answers questions about its effectiveness "compared to what?" This is a vacuum in policy development, in part because of the lack of a comprehensive policy framework. It is increasingly recognized in Congress and the Executive Branch.[3-9] The dearth shows up also as an absence of organizational responsibility for recommending Federal health priorities and policies. Food, housing, and environmental safety policy is far removed from the Department of Health, Education and Welfare and its successor, the Department of Health and Human Services.[10-14] Attempts to consolidate some health promotion tasks have failed. A recent effort, in 1979, was to house much of the technical analytic expertise in an HEW Office of Health Research, Statistics and Technology.[15] But further linkages to sources of health-related policy development were not planned.

Making a Case for Prevention

In addition to providing a context for evaluating health-important policy, a broad, comparative approach to analyzing policy could also address some of the arguments that are voiced against the feasibility of primary prevention. A more substantive response, at least, would be available to answer those who say, for example, that the public, and therefore politicians, are unwilling to pay now for distant and uncertain gains in health. There is no guarantee that specific individuals will be less disabled in their later lives because they pay now, in taxes or price increases, for health-making policies. Those who pay and those who gain may be quite different persons and social groups.[16,17] This argument maintains, in effect, that dollars on hand and useable today are the most preferable. It neglects to note that while this is mainly true when individuals, in their personal lives, and profit-oriented groups, make gains-for-costs decisions, this generalization is by no means accurate in all contexts. For individuals, as citizens addressing public issues, have clearly been willing to support policies that defer benefits for the years ahead. This is especially so among people who are reasonably assured of an adequate current standard of living.[18]

Others say that preventing contemporary illness will only mean that other illnesses will occur which are now unknown. "People will die of something."[19] While the latter is probably true, the first is not necessarily so, for at least two reasons. The longer the onset of modern illness—particularly the chronic forms—is deferred in the population, the less complicated future illnesses are likely to be, because of the reverberating nature of illness. This also means a less debilitating old age, a shorter "end stage" of life. It means more vigorous life in the middle decades, which has both personal and economic value, and thus potential political value. This line of argument, while skeptical of primary prevention, is ironically antithetical to the previous one, held by those who prefer current to distant gains. They would argue that if "people will die of something," better to acquire

217

it later than sooner. One group prefers to take its chances now and pay later. The other says that even if you pay now, you'll have to pay for something else later. Again the critique is posed as though it were an individualistic issue, and is contrary to the public's record of decisions on issues that are posed within a social context (see Chapter 12). Still others claim that preventing illness will actually increase the cost of health care.[20,21] The reasoning behind this is that, if more people live longer, there will be more elders. Their health care, in turn, would raise the total health bill, since older people use more services and hospital care. This assumes that elders would have the same severity of illness as now. This, as just noted, would not necessarily be so. Nor would the normal biological aging process, without serious illness, require hospital care. Less expensive, congregate arrangements would be appropriate and socially preferable.

Other reasons for presumed increases in medical costs are that people of all ages would use more services, especially the "preventive" ones. This assumes that these services are the best preventive tactics for modern illness, and is an unwarranted assumption (see Chapters 9 and 11). Moreover, presumed *new kinds* of health problems are said to add to the costs of health care. However, if public policy, particularly in socioenvironmental areas, were adequately undertaken to actually and measurably prevent some of modern illness, it seems unlikely that new and unique health problems would emerge: they, as always, result from health-damaging excesses or deficits in biophysical and socioeconomic environments.

Another view is that the costs of preventing illness are quite separate from the costs of medical care: that prevention monies would be found from other than the current categories of the national health budget, and that, as just noted, the societal savings from prevention would not produce significant savings in health services expenditures.[22] This view assumes, of course, that health policy, in its development and execution, will remain essentially a policy of health care in principle and organizational practice. However, if health policy were in fact to become effectively directed toward primary prevention, it could not remain predominantly a health care policy in principle or practice.

To these and other claims there have been responses, often as conjectural and well-intended as those of their critics. Other responses are more substantive, but based on narrowly defined studies.[23-26] All, however, have lacked either sufficiently sound data or adequate scope to be able to compare one health-important strategy, or a group of strategies, with others. A comprehensive approach could make this possible. It could also help unloose the understanding of primary prevention from the limited definition of "preventive medicine," which concerns "slowing the progress of disease and conserving maximal function," and thus represents secondary prevention.[27] Policy aimed at health improvement, if it is confined to *secondary prevention*, may well produce what the skeptics of prevention claim will happen.

Timeliness

Even as controversy over the goal and strategies of health policy continues, the rising cost and limited success of the current principal strategy—the provision of personal health care—continue to be felt. So does the reality of other industrial nations, and of groups of Americans, who are doing a better job of improving health than the U.S. as a whole. It is timely, if not belated, to make a serious effort to compare policy strategies for their health-effectiveness and for their obvious, and subtle, costs for achieving measurable gains in the prevention of today's illness.

To illustrate what such an analytic framework would include, this discussion now takes up the problems of comparing the health impact of two major health improvement policy strategies. One is the traditional delivery of personal health services. Its focus is on the impact of primary level care under the kinds of financial and geographic access currently available, and also under the more extensive access that might be possible for Americans with a national health insurance program (see Chapter 11). The second policy thrust is a socioenvironmental strategy that would alter the national farm-food supply (see Chapter 11).

Any number and variety of policies might be included in a comparative analysis. These could range from a guaranteed income floor and full employment to full use of air pollution control authority, completion of water fluoridation, and enforcement of national highway safety laws. Most usefully, a mix of policies would be analyzed, with goals ranging from modest ones to more optimistic reaches, and requiring different levels of national and local administration. Some might affect organizations most, while others would emphasize options for individuals. Each might use a range of means for deployment, including public information, fiscal incentives, and administrative action. Each would represent also a range of political feasibility.[28-30]

ESTIMATING CHANGES IN HEALTH

The measure of health status against which the effectiveness of all policy strategies would be compared is the annual profile of health and illness in America. This includes the total occurrence and distribution of illness, the associated days of disability and deaths, and the "at-risk" conditions that place people at increased risk of illness, such as obesity, smoking, anemia, low income, or exposure to toxic substances.

219

Illness and Restricted Activity

Measuring the changes that occur in total annual illness of the population, the incidence and prevalence alone, does not, of course, tell anything about its severity. However, changes in the number of days during which people's activity is restricted by illness do speak to this issue. These can be further categorized as days of bed disability and days lost from work or school. Days of disability are the most immediately felt impact of illness for most people, a readily understood indicator of how illness disrupts their lives.[31] Use of this measure is also a good way to communicate to the public the comparative impact of various policy strategies on their own lives.

Days of disability can be correlated with various degrees of limitation on activity in daily living and at work. They can also be related to the *amounts*, or numbers, of health problems people have and their *perceptions* of their own health, whether they view it as good, fair, or poor.[32] These relationships can show not only how restricting different forms and amounts of health problems are in terms of what people can do at home or at work, they also indicate what various kinds of restriction mean to people for the way they view their relative state of health. This in turn implies a dimension of their "quality of life." In this way, both the personal and the economic costs of illness, or the value of prevention, can be estimated in terms that have meaning to several audiences, including the general public, employers, and policy-makers.

Deaths

Although a change in death rates is an additional measure to be used, it is not a very good measure of the health of a population. It bears little relationship to amounts of acute illness or of disability from existing chronic or acute conditions.[33,34] Because death is a rare event in the context of most lives, and may be far removed in time from the initiation of any policy intervention, it is not a very timely measure of evaluation. Nor can it capture the *breadth* of impact on people's lives that a change in health status can make.[35]

Nevertheless, death rates are probably the most used indicator for comparing the health of one population with another. In industrialized nations they are highly reliable figures and are readily available. Refinements in their use could add to understanding the longer-term health impact of various health strategies.

It is possible, for example, to estimate the proportion of a large population that will ultimately die from specific causes by using the known life expectancy at birth of a particular group. White females born in 1974, for instance, had a life expectancy of over 76 years; for other females it was about 72 years. Using extrapolations from historical and international data, this means that about 0.8 percent of these whites would die from certain diseases of infancy, and over 18 percent eventually from cancer. By comparison, 1.3 percent of other females would be expected to die from infant causes, and less than 16 percent from cancer.[36-38] Changes from these expected patterns might then be one indicator of the effect of specific health-related policies.

A more immediate use for death rates is for estimating the potential for prevention, comparing them with other national populations or with various groups of Americans. This becomes, in effect, a way to formulate realistic objectives for health improvement. By comparing differences in deaths between age-sex groups that live in different communities or at different levels of income, an estimate of premature death—the unnecessary burden of terminal illness and injury—can be made. Policy strategies can then be directed to reducing these differences, and evaluated over time.[39-42] Overall differences in deaths among men, for instance, may be over 40 percent higher in lower-income groups. They can range from 1 to 30 percent higher, depending upon the specific causes, between low- and high-income white men, regardless of their residence in central cities or suburbs.[43,44]

PREVENTION AND LONGEVITY

Reaching for a closing of the gap, even measured by so gross an indicator as death rates—or by more sensitive indicators of illness frequency and disability—brings efforts at primary prevention out of the realm of utopian visions and into the region of achievable public policy objectives. At the same time it helps to nullify the skeptics' critique of seeking to live "forever."

In fact, the significant lengthening of *average* life expectancy in any of the advanced industrialized countries is probably neither technically nor biologically achievable in the foreseeable future. It seems that even in the impossible case of immediately saving people from all cardiovascular deaths, the average life span in the United States, based on the population profile of 1970, would not be more than 84 years. With the total elimination of cancer deaths, it would be about 74 years, and if all motor vehicle deaths were prevented, not more than 72 years. This is a limited impact, considering that these deaths are from causes that now account for three-fourths of all deaths. Clearly, eliminating them will not make centenarians of all Americans. This is mainly because the two chronic diseases mainly affect older people and are the predominant causes of death. At the same time, although vehicle fatalities affect younger people, they are not a pervasive cause of death.[45]

221

Thus the total years of life saved do not add very much to the average span of life.

As greater proportions of the population reach older ages, by avoiding death in infancy and youth, the average life span lengthens more slowly, until its *rate* of improvement becomes almost insignificant.[46,47] Thus the more practical health policy objective is to close the persistent and unwarranted gap in death and disability between segments of the American population. A second important objective is to enhance the vitality of the mid-life decades. This means to prevent, in the primary sense, those forms of illness that disable and disrupt lives, such as heart-lung disease, but that are now sufficiently controllable or containable through medical care to defer death—but not disability—until the later years of life. In one sophisticated, although admittedly imperfect, study an estimate was made of the meaning of survival for people who faced disabling illness and its treatment, in this case people who had had a stroke. The impact was found to be equivalent to a loss of 1½ years from their lives. Their "quality of life" was diminished by that much.[48]

Moreover, hopes for survival from cancer, even under good medical care, may be somewhat misplaced because of the way relative survival rates are computed. Although comparisons are made between age-sex groups that continue to live under medical treatment and those that live without treatment, their economic status is not taken into account. Thus the continued life of those who have medical care, their seemingly improved prognosis for survival, may be the result of the advantages of higher income, rather than the efficacy of cancer treatment itself. This does not discount the fact that for some forms of cancer early treatment seems to lengthen survival for some people.[49]

Monitoring Risks

It is important to measure changes in the amount and severity of overall illness in order to judge the comparative health effects of policy strategies. It is also necessary to monitor the "risk factors," the environmental conditions, activities, and biochemical changes that increase the likelihood of illness within a population. The most important of these, which have been discussed in some detail in earlier chapters, are summarized in Table 7 in the Appendix. They are estimates for all Americans, and for special age, sex, or other subgroups that are exposed to health hazards in their environments (including the fetal environment), through their personal practices, or within their physiology. Collectively, these risks become manifest as today's profile of health and illness, represented as percentages of the more than 3000 health problems occurring per 1000 persons annually (see Chapter 2).

In principle, any health strategy which could reduce the prevalence of risk factors would have the effect of preventing the illnesses associated with them. In order to estimate this impact it would be necessary to know how many of those persons with specific risk factors actually develop illnesses. Epidemiologic studies can provide information relating the prevalence of risks, such as smoking, and the frequency of associated health problems, such as acute or chronic respiratory illness, within a population. Such relationships could be translated into rates per thousand and, adjusting for population differences in age, sex, and economic level, applied to the demographic makeup of the United States. This would then permit an estimation of what a certain percentage of decline in smoking, for example, would mean for an overall reduction in acute or chronic lung disease.

To put forward this fairly typical methodological approach is to immediately invite a number of problems which exist whenever apparent statistical relationships are found within a population. Among these are issues deriving from that which cannot be known through this method, such as which subgroups are the most, or solely, affected; whether the relationship between risk and resulting illness is a direct one, is dependent on other factors, or is simply spurious; how many people may be under treatment to reduce their risk; and how long certain risks have existed, such as whether lifelong patterns of diet or smoking may have been only recently changed.[50-52] Other problems occur because of differences in defining "low" or "high" risk and identifying the point at which a set of symptoms or physiologic indicators becomes diagnosed as illness.[53,54]

One of the most important problems with currently available epidemiologic data is its limited scope. The "disease by disease" tradition of medical care has become a "risk factor by risk factor" approach to health improvement. Most often studies measure very few risk factors and do so, almost invariably, for just one disease or a very few specific conditions. The result is the misleading implication—or the mistaken interpretation—that changing one or two risk factors in the individuals who have those risks, such as through counseling overweight people to eat less fat, or smokers to quit smoking, will be an effective strategy for lowering the risks of illness for the population.[55,56]

The potential consequences of such a misreading have been illustrated for coronary heart disease, which constitutes less than 2 percent of annual illness. Almost 40 percent of men aged 35 to 65 have two or more of the risk factors known to be associated with coronary heart disease, namely, high blood pressure, cigarette smoking, raised blood cholesterol, and overweight. These factors increase their susceptibility to heart trouble by at least 4½ times over other men of the same age. Just under 60 percent of all cases of coronary heart disease occur in this age group of men. Thus, if all men aged 35 to 65 were screened, and all with two or more risk factors were appropriately counseled and treated, such that half of them effectively reduced their risks to normal, the incidence of coronary heart disease would drop by 25 percent.[57] Others estimate the decline to be only 10 to 20 percent.[58] A policy that targeted screening, patient education, and drug therapy for this age group of men would be a highly expensive, and necessarily continuous, effort. It still would have no effect on younger adults, or on women, who would continue to incur the same risks and so require the same kind of counseling and treatment once they too became "high-risk."

POLICY IMPLICATIONS

Epidemiologic, single-disease studies have so far not been modelled after what epidemiologic data have shown: "risk factors" are not independent of each other or of people's environments; illnesses are interrelated, often cumulative or synergistic responses to environmentally induced hazards and habits. This implies that targeting a health strategy toward a narrow risk factor and the individuals in whom it exists, without concomitant environmental changes, is at best a tenuous, "finger in the dyke" effort. It provides questionably sustainable improvement for the individuals involved, and little, if any, measurable health improvement for the overall population.

What is needed is information not only on the proportion of people who are exposed to specific health-damaging risks, but on the combinations of risks involved. How many exposed persons, for example, have low incomes or high incomes *and* breathe polluted air, *and* live in unsafe housing, *and* have hazardous jobs? Which of them are sedentary *and* underweight, or obese *and* have high cholesterol diets, *and* smoke, *and* take alcoholic drinks, *and* have elevated serum cholesterol, *and* high blood pressure? Which persons, having various combinations of risks, also manifest which acute and chronic forms of illness, especially the most disabling? Such information, based on a national random sample, could provide reliable evidence on the cumulative and synergistic relationships among environmental and personal risks, and among illnesses. All of this would then indicate the prevalence of those who are truly at high risk of illness, the segments of the population to which they belong, and the regions in which they live. It would also suggest more effective approaches to health improvement by showing what environmental conditions and patterns of activity, if altered, might bring the greatest gains in health, including those changes which, if combined, might produce synergistic health improvement. In this way, health-promoting changes in environments not only would help the people who are already at high risk of illness, but also would prevent their counterparts from becoming "high-risk."

224

Current Capabilities

The means for allowing this kind of data collection exist in the National Center for Health Statistics. Its ongoing surveys are based on large random samples of the U.S. population and are analyzed along demographic, geographic, and socioeconomic lines. Continuous gathering of illness and disability information is undertaken, as well as special surveys on physiologic measures, and on dietary, smoking, drinking, and exercise patterns, and plans include the addition of ambient environmental data.

This vast source of health-related population data is not, however, cross-tabulated in ways that could answer questions about the prevalence of *combined* risks and their consequences for *clusters* of illness. Such a reordering of the data could provide a statistically reliable and epidemiologically sound basis for estimating the impact of current and proposed national health policies. Where such estimating procedures have been used in special studies to predict the effects on health status for certain combinations of risk factors in a small community, the predicted results have been in accord with what actually occurred in the population.[59,60] Thus an organized, technical capability exists to develop a sound basis both for developing health-making policy thrusts and for measuring the health impact of policy.

Until this potential is realized, however, currently available national data can be used. In addition to the random sample surveys just noted, a corroborating source is the relatively new National Ambulatory Medical Care Survey that has information on patients' visits to private physicians. The data indicate the prevalence of persons who have more than one illness. The Survey's limitation is that it excludes people who do *not* visit private doctors. However, until better data are available, these could be arranged for age/sex/income groups, and would be especially useful if correlated with occupation, region, diet, and personal habits. Such information is generally available in the properly protected patients' records from which this survey is drawn.

PLAUSIBLE ESTIMATES

A few studies have recently tried to estimate the degree of impact that selected risk factors have on several forms of illness and deaths from certain diseases. These are summarized in Appendix Table 8, which also shows the profile of all annual deaths, illness, and related days of disability. Alongside are the estimates of how much smoking, dietary excesses or deficits, air pollution, hazardous jobs, and other implicating factors contribute to each type of illness. Smoking and dietary excesses stand out as the major contributors to deaths and illness from cardiovascular and lung disease, cancer,

225

and diabetes, being implicated as causes in 30 to 60 percent of these ill-nesses and deaths. Food deficits contribute to most deaths and illness but to an unknown extent, except for resulting in low-birth-weight babies in over half the cases. Hypertension accounts for about 13 percent of deaths from diabetes and from cardiovascular disease, including half of the deaths from stroke.[61]

Adding these selected risks to estimate their combined impact on all deaths, illness, and disability cannot, of course, be done without knowing what proportion of Americans are exposed to multiple risks. However, using what little is known about the prevalence of individuals who have more than one major risk, some plausible and conservative estimates are made in Table 8. The combined impact of the selected environmental and personal factors account, for example, for about half of all deaths from cardiovascular dis-ease, cancer, and accidents, and for 15 to 65 percent of major acute and chronic illnesses, and the days of disability associated with them. Appropri-ately weighted, the overall combined impact of these risks results in about 40 percent of all annual deaths, 30 percent of illness, and 30 percent of all days of disability.

These kinds of estimates, and more precise ones which could be made from available current data, can be used to help evaluate the potential ef-fects on the total profile of American health of various policies, those in-volving either the delivery of personal health care or changes in socioenvi-ronmental conditions and ways of living. A policy that is known to result in a drop in the prevalence of selected risk factors or diseases, such as drug treatment for persons with a diastolic blood pressure of 105 or higher, could be evaluated for its potential impact on the overall occurrence of illness, disability, and death among Americans, in addition to the improvement that it would bring to hypertensive people.

THE DOLLAR VALUE OF BETTER HEALTH

Once the effects of a specific health improvement policy on people's health are estimated, the impact in dollar terms may be calculated, in this case the savings to be had from prevention. This immediately invites a host of fre-quently discussed problems. The most common are concerned with how to validly attach a dollar sign to changes in health.

The customary technical approach is to estimte the *direct* savings in the costs of medical care that are made possible because illness was avoided. In addition, *"indirect"* savings are derived from the fact that people who are not ill or disabled can continue to go about their daily lives at work, home, and school, thus continuing their contribution (valued in dollar terms) to the production of goods and services. Taken together, these direct and indirect sources of savings would, without the prevention of illness, become what is

226

regarded as the "total economic cost of illness." These total costs have been estimated for all annual illness, as well as for some specific types of disease.[62-75]

Direct Savings: Medical Care

Once the reduction in the amount of illness by an effective health policy is estimated, the cost of treating that illness in people through direct medical care—that is, the *direct* source of savings—can be estimated from the personal health care expenditures data compiled annually by the Social Security Administration.[76] For example, at the national level, if a policy had prevented 20 percent of American illness in 1976, it would have saved almost $25 billion in medical costs, assuming that people who were ill that year would have sought medical care. However, adjustments in the estimated savings could be made for the fact that different proportions of people seek care for different types of illness, and that certain types of illness involve varying amounts of more costly hospital and nursing home care.[77,78] Further refinements can be made to estimate additional savings from preventing complications in persons who are already ill.[79]

Indirect Savings: Less Disability

A far more complex issue concerns the estimation of *indirect* costs that are avoided whenever illness is prevented, for this presumes to measure the value of lives in dollars. According to the conventional method, the reduction in days of disability resulting from prevention is subdivided into its components, days saved from what would otherwise be work loss or school loss, and from confinement to bed at home or in hospital.[80-83] The dollar value of these days saved from restricted activity is then estimated separately.

DAYS SAVED FROM LOSS OF PAID AND UNPAID WORK

To estimate the value of fewer days lost from work, the composition of the labor force is taken into account, adjusting for unemployment, as well as differences in work force participation by men and women, and the average value of daily wages and fringe benefits (about 15 percent). (Instead of wages, worker productivity, which is the dollar value of goods and services produced per worker, may be used.)[84,85] A working year of disability is equivalent to 255 to 300 days, varying between employed and self-employed workers.[86]

Until very recently, it was customary to stop at this point in estimating the indirect savings from prevention, assuming that the major impact was accounted for. The value of services rendered in the home is now being recognized, for these services would have to be bought, if not provided by the employed person's spouse, or the employed person.

On the basis of survey data and market prices, the value of full-time housekeeping, including a portion for child care, was about $6600 for a 365-day year in 1976 dollars.[87] The value of these services, which is saved when illness is prevented, is estimated by the drop in the number of days of disability that the housekeeper would otherwise have spent in bed. This is further adjusted according to the composition of the housekeeping population. For purposes of calculation, housekeepers include women who are not in the labor force but who keep house (42 percent of all American women); women who are in the labor force; and married men with children under 18 years. The last category is used because it is the only available information on men who do not live alone and are therefore assumed to do household work.[88] The value of housekeeping services done by persons living alone is excluded because there is as yet no reliable basis from survey data for estimating the value of their household work.[89]

Further sources of savings when illness is prevented are found among those who would be in the labor force if they were not ill.[90,91] Another source involves those who, because of illness, are in long-term care facilities, assuming that if they were not, they would be doing the same share of employed and household work as their healthier age-sex counterparts.[92]

DAYS SAVED FROM LOSS OF SCHOOL TIME

One final source of savings which illness prevention may tap is a reduction of days lost from school, and a related one, the loss of work by the parent who must stay home to care for a young child who is too ill to attend school. These are rarely taken into account as a cost of illness, or its reciprocal, savings from prevention. Declines in days lost from school because of illness in children under 6 years of age have been valued at the average daily wage of mothers in the work force who have children under 6. This assumes that they would attend their children at home.[93] These mothers make up about 13 percent of women workers.[94] School days for older children and youth might be valued at the daily costs of public schools and colleges. These amounted annually to about $1460 and $1750 per student, respectively, in 1976.[95] In strict economic terms, these public costs, or savings, are to government. They are transfer payments rather than losses or gains in the total production of goods and services.

DATA SOURCES

The sources of information for these kinds of estimates, of the dollars that are saved by preventing disability in adults and children, are readily and systematically available from the Bureau of the Census, the Social Security Administration, and the Bureau of Labor Statistics.

Some recent attempts have been made to measure people's perception of their health, whether "good," "fair," or "poor"; their capacity to act, physically and emotionally; and their ability to relate these to the degree of paid work or personal care they can do.[96-100] In order to estimate, in dollars, the value of improvements in how people feel and what they can do when their illness is prevented, these indicators would have to be related to *days* of work disability and bed disability. Again, this potential exists, as shown in two national health and social security disability surveys, but has not yet been put to use.[101]

Undervaluing Prevented Disability

Measuring changes in disability by these means nevertheless understates the impact of disability in several ways, and so underestimates the value of prevention. The indicators do not include the effect of disability on the *quality* of work or other valued activity, although such changes must be a concomitant to some extent. Nor is disability measured beyond the first year, since the only indicator that is used conventionally is the occurrence of illnesses annually.[102] What account can be made of longer-term disability as its effects accumulate?

A partial answer, at least, lies in using new Social Security surveys which allow estimates to be made of how many, among those who are newly disabled, become worse, improve, or recover completely after a year of disability. This includes those who return to normal work or to household activity.[103] Comparable information exists for people who have longer-term disability.[104,105] Moreover, a measure of the savings from preventing the cumulative consequences of illness and disability can be had from national data showing changes in income, marriage and divorce, and the occurrence of new illness among persons who are disabled.[106,107]

More extensive analysis of this sort on the longer-term effects of illness and disability, which are actually part of the cost of *not* preventing illness, would reveal more profoundly some unstated but measurable losses. These include the costs to the economy through people's lost productivity, as well as costs to government, such as wasted school resources, workers' compensation, Social Security disability payments, early retirement benefits and other income maintenance programs, and subsidies for private disability insurance, sick leave, and pensions.[108-110]

Assessment of the long-term consequences of disability also suggests more accurately the costs, both economic and less tangible ones, to the individuals who are ill. These personal "intangibles" costs are always noted as important but not amenable to a dollar value, and then dismissed, rarely if ever to be studied.[111] At a minimum, they might be specified alongside the dollar values of more tangible savings, for the "intangibles" may indeed differ as a result of deploying different national policies.

Prevention of illness, for individuals, could mean not only less pain, grief, discomfort, or loss of family, but also more "free' time—time unencumbered by the requirements of illness—for noneconomic, widened options for personal growth, pleasures, achievements, family and social relationships, and concomitant personal dignity.[112] Strategies, undertaken to prevent illness, that emphasize "targeted" groups and risk the stigma of labeling them, as compared with strategies applied to the total population, may indeed have quite different "intangible" consequences. These also ought to be made explicit when other impacts on illness, disability, and dollar savings are compared (Fig. 10).

Indirect Savings: Fewer Premature Deaths

The remaining measure that is used for estimating the dollar value of prevention is a change in death rates, the other source of indirect savings besides changes in disability. It is the only measure conventionally used to estimate savings beyond the first year of prevented illness.

The dollar value is first estimated in the same way as for savings from reduced disability. In addition, the expected number of years of life remaining are tallied, as are the expected lifetime earnings, for the age-sex categories of persons whose deaths are prevented. This total dollar amount is then adjusted, first, for inflationary changes which would *annually reduce* the value of dollars saved (10 percent is now commonly used). Second, *yearly* increases in productivity, which *enhance* the value of dollars, are accounted for, usually by using the recent average of about 1.7 percent. The net difference, about 8 percent, is then the *effective discount rate*. This figure, applied to the lifelong productivity or expected earnings of people whose deaths were prevented, provides the dollars saved at current value, known as net present value.[113]

Not surprisingly, this method of setting the value of human lives generates a good deal of controversy.[114] One major criticism is that it has the effect of making short-term gains in health the most important ones. Priority, in effect, is given to short-term solutions to problems. This approach tends also to place greater value on those who are currently best situated, that is, men over women, high-paid over low-paid workers, the better educated over the less educated, and whites over blacks. This results from basing the value of lives saved on lifetime earnings. Thus the "value" of an infant boy whose life was saved in 1972, discounted at 6 percent, was $51,000 if white, and $31,000 if black; a white infant girl was valued at $31,500, and a black infant girl at $27,000.[115] If alternative policies were

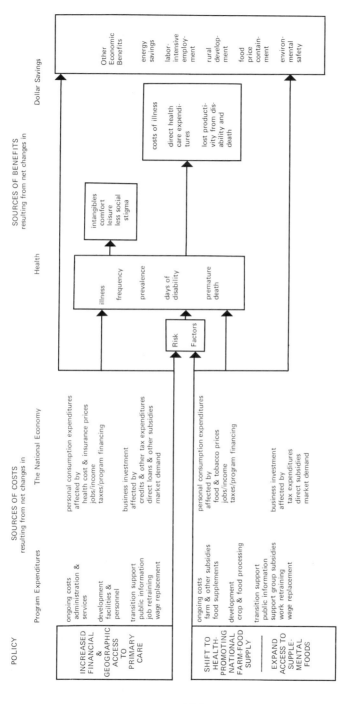

FIGURE 10. Measuring the comparative effects of two health policy thrusts: the sources of their costs and the benefits resulting from net health and economic changes.

231

judged solely in relation to dollar benefits, those selected would be the ones that are most advantageous to white, upper middle-class males.

Another approach suggested for valuing lives is to base the monetary amount on people's willingness to pay for programs which would increase their chances for longer life. In the one attempt that was made to test this method, the individuals surveyed said they were, in effect, willing to pay up to 50 percent more to prevent their dying from heart disease and stroke than the dollar value that was theoretically derived from their expected lifetime earnings. In other words, valuing their lives in terms of the economy understated their own estimates of value. Moreover, they showed no distinction in the value of men's over women's lives. Older people—who were, of course, at higher risk of death—were willing to pay more to extend their lives; so were people with higher incomes.[116] It should be noted that the question of their willingness to pay was put to them in individualistic terms: their own money for their own lives.

THE DOLLAR VALUE OF HUMAN LIVES

This study illustrates many of the problems involved in using individual preferences for evaluating savings from prevention. First are the more obvious. People's attitudes and intentions that are elicited through surveys do not directly relate to what they do in actual experience. Because attitudes vary in such polls, depending on media events among other things, the "value" as stated is not necessarily enduring. Furthermore, the people interviewed in surveys are almost invariably different as a composite population than those who vote policy-makers into office. More subtly, the social composition of the survey may bias the responses, bringing into question the equity of this approach. For not only are the more affluent and the ill willing to pay more than others: *adults* were willing to pay relatively *less* for the heart conditions that affect children, who, of course, were excluded from the survey.

Carrying the implications further, the effect, if policy followed these preferences, would be to use short-term, curative, high-technology solutions to health problems, rather than longer-term, primary prevention strategies, and to do so with little regard for those who were not able to pay. The totaling of individuals' preferences, necessarily based on their perceived personal interests, is not equivalent to a measurement of the interests of society overall, nor in particular of the health interests of future generations.

Both the "willingness to pay" and conventional lifetime earnings methods for putting lives in dollar terms are thus discriminatory for segments of the population. One further major bias, in both methods, is the choice of a discount rate for determining the present value of net future dollar savings.

A low rate, say 2 percent, has the effect of making future net savings "more valuable" today; a high rate makes such savings appear less so. The usual method for deciding which rate to use (in addition to taking inflation and productivity into account) is essentially to determine what policy funds (derived from taxes) would earn if invested elsewhere (i.e., not taxed and retained in the private sector), earning, say, 10 percent in dividends or interest. This compares with the 2 percent effective interest these dollars might earn if put out in short-term government borrowings.[117,118] The important point is that the criteria used to select a discount rate are those of the private, profit-making economy. The use of money is judged competitively against what it would bring in the profit-oriented market over its use in the public interest. These uses, however, are not comparable. In the market orientation, profit is the principal goal for the production of goods and services. By contrast, the public interest is not simply to accumulate money, but to enhance people's lives, whether or not the largest possible return is obtained in dollar benefits (affected by the choice of a discount rate) in relation to the funds that are expended. From the point of view of the public interest, a more equitable distribution of resources through the public purse is in the long-term interests of all.

To illustrate the different effects that the selection of a high or low discount rate may have, consider use of a hypothetical $10 billion proposal to prevent maternal-child health problems. The total costs in treatment, illness, and death for these problems in 1975 was about $15 billion, discounted at 2.5 percent, and about $4.5 billion when discounted at 10 percent.[119] Assuming that the $10 billion policy could prevent all these problems, it would appear to be a persuasively efficient investment, using the savings figure derived at 2.5 percent. In other words, benefits over costs would be 1.5 to 1. However, based on the higher discount rate, program costs of $10 billion would save only $4.5 billion, or would reap only 45 cents in benefits for every dollar spent. In economic terms—which now weigh increasingly in the use of public funds—the policy would not be cost-beneficial using the high-discount figure, and so the $10 billion would either be used for other public purposes or not taxed at all.

The Value of Prevention

In sum, the value of prevention of illness to society in dollar terms depends on how the costs of death and disability are estimated. The value is very much understated when the cumulative costs of illness are excluded. The value of prevention also depends on how the value of money is determined, which is an implicit indication of what the dollar's most appropriate use ought to be: profit-making or human welfare. Every society maintains that some monies ought not to go for profit-making endeavors. In the United States, this amount is about a third of the gross national product, in the form of monies that are allocated for public uses. This fact alone would presumably justify a discount rate that is at least one-third lower than the current, market-oriented 10 percent, if not far lower, when evaluating the efficiency of new public expenditures. A lower discount rate, in turn, would "increase" the value of benefits for illness-prevention policies.

In practice, some of the issues concerning estimation of savings from prevention have been partially dealt with by using a range of rates, rather than a single discount rate, a method called sensitivity analysis.[120]

For addressing the further problem of simplistically emphasizing death-avoidance while underestimating the costs of prolonged, disabled living, a "quality of life" method has been used. It subtracts, from the dollar value of lives saved, the added costs of the side-effects from medical treatment and the costs of treatment for other illness incurred during prolonged survival.[121,122] The effect is to convey, in dollar terms, that a longer life accompanied by disability is worth less than a longer life that is free from disability. Here the dollar value approximates what most people would be presumed to agree with intuitively.

If longer life without disability is "worth more," this means, when translated into a policy goal, that the prevention of illness is more valuable than detecting and treating illness, and should therefore have increasing priority. By implication, the public may be willing to pay for its achievement, even if total costs to initiate it may be higher than traditional approaches in the short term (see Chapter 11). Another modified approach is simply not to attempt to value lives in dollars after about age 65. Rather, benefits can be enumerated simply as the number of years of life saved, since most people are not likely to be willing, or able, to value their later lives in terms of their economic productivity.

Whatever improvements can be made in attaching a dollar figure to people's lives, the simplest, most straightforward approach, and the one most useful to both policy-makers and the public, is to forego the attempt to value lives in dollar terms. Instead, efforts could focus on making clear the initial, intermediate, long-term consequences, and the ramifying effects, of disability. The effects should also be described according to how they may affect major age, sex, socioeconomic, ethnic, and geographic groups.

An important distinction should be made when prevention policies are being compared and evaluated. This is whether the health improvement, as indicated in changes in days of disability, is a gain in illness-free days (and therefore disability-free days) or in disability-free days *after illness has occurred*. This distinction is, of course, the difference between successful primary prevention and secondary prevention strategies. Primary prevention aims at achieving more illness-free days, especially in the young and prime decades of life when this freedom can most likely be increased.

Since the success of secondary prevention is the early detection and treatment of illness, it is more likely to achieve more disability-free days because the illness that is discovered may be cured, tempered, or controlled.

Presumably, all people would prefer prospects of more illness-free days over more disability-free days following illness. Yet this distinction is not made when disability days are used as an indicator of the potential health improvement to be had from alternate health strategies. "Disability days" encompass both illness-free and post-illness categories.

If more intuitively understandable kinds of health indicators were developed and used, helping to clarify the spectrum of impact on people's health of proposed policies, then the costs of those policies could be related to their projected effects. This would avoid disagreements over methods of computing dollar benefits, which tend to deflect attention from the major issues concerning the merits of the policies that are being debated.

SUMMARY

This discussion has set forth some of the major problems involved whenever changes in health status, and the dollar benefits of primary or secondary prevention (or conversely, the costs of illness), are measured. An awareness of the assumptions that underlie the figures is crucial for policy-makers. This is also important for the public, if it is to speak in its own interest, and for the media as well, as it so often sets the parameters of public information. These assumptions concern the indicators of health that are included, and those that are omitted, from typical policy studies; the biases concerning sex, age, job types, and income groups; and the valuing of money itself over time. Without this basic understanding, the "benefits" and their relationship to costs appear misleadingly objective and certain when, in fact, they are only a partial measure of but one set of the criteria used to evaluate policy—those of economic efficiency.[123,124] Other criteria are taken up in Chapter 12.

In spite of these necessary qualifiers, the systematic analysis of alternate public policies to estimate their potential or actual effects on health, with some modification of conventional methods, has the advantage of making their possible consequences explicit. The effects that should be made explicit include changes in various indicators of illness, death, and disability, including distinctions between increased freedom from illness and increased freedom from disability due to illness. The dollar value of these changes may also be estimated as another common denominator for comparing alternate policies, and their intangible, currently unmeasured concomitants, that cannot satisfactorily be given a dollar value. These impacts can then be viewed from three fundamental perspectives: that of the total economy and population; that of the public purse; and that of the population subgroups that are likely to be most affected. Most importantly, this approach to policy analysis places alternate or complementary policy proposals within the same frame of reference and allows a common basis for comparing gains (or declines) in health in relation to costs.[125] The findings, however, have different meanings depending upon which policies are being compared and what is included in their costs, as the next chapter will show.

REFERENCES

1. Dick, T., and Stone, M.: *Prevalance of three major risk factors in a random sample of men and women and in-patients with ischemic heart disease.* Br. Heart J. 40:617–626, 1978.
2. Glueck, C. J., et al.: *Diet and coronary heart disease: another view.* N. Engl. J. Med. 298(26):1471–1474, 1978.
3. *Report: Health Services Extension Act of 1977.* Committee on Conference, U.S. Congress, Washington, D.C., August 1977.
4. Office of the Assistant Secretary for Planning and Evaluation: *Health Technology Management at the Department of Health, Education and Welfare. Final Phase I Report for the Secretary.* Washington, D.C., December 1977.
5. Office of Technology Assessment: *The Development of Medical Technology.* Washington, D.C., August 1976.
6. Waters, W. J., and Kelley, B. C.: *Health systems priority setting: key concepts and factors.* Am. J. Health Policy 2:34–38, 1977.
7. Gori, G., and Richter, B.: *Macroeconomics of disease prevention in the United States.* Science 200:1124–1130, 1978.
8. Highland, J. H.: *Public interest groups.* Bull. N.Y. Acad. Med. 54(4):444–445, 1978.
9. Winikoff, B.: *Nutrition, population and health: some implications for policy.* Science 200:895–902, 1978.
10. Lee, P., and Franks, P.: *Primary prevention and the Executive Branch of the Federal Government.* Prev. Med. 6:209–225, 1977.
11. *Health services in Europe—1. Administration and preventive services.* WHO Chron. 30:407–412, 1976.
12. Williams, C. A., et al : *Family Nurse Practitioner Program: Feedback Report No. 3: Salary Data on UNC–Chapel Hill Family Nurse Practitioner Program Graduates Practicing in North Carolina.* University of North Carolina, Chapel Hill, 1977.
13. Steiner, G.: *The Children's Cause.* Brookings Institution, Washington, D.C., 1976.
14. *Symposium on environmental effects of sulfur oxides and related particulates.* Sponsored by the Subcommittee on Public Health Aspects of Energy and the Committee on Public Health of the New York Academy of Medicine, March 23–24, 1978. Bull. N.Y. Acad. Med. 54(11), 1978.
15. *Briefing Memorandum No. 27, Cooperative Health Statistics System.* U.S. Department of Health, Education and Welfare, Washington, D.C., February 1979.
16. Warner, K.: *The economic implications of preventive health care.* Paper presented at the 106th Annual Meeting of the American Public Health Association, Community Health Planning Section, Los Angeles, October 16, 1978.
17. Holtzman, N.: *The goal of preventing early death,* in *Papers on the National*

Health Guidelines. Conditions for Change in the Health Care System, September 1977. Health Resources Administration, Washington, D.C., 1977.
18. Akerman, N.: *Can Sweden be shrunk?* Dialogue, Fall 1979, pp. 71–114.
19. Gori and Richter, op. cit.
20. Holtzman, op. cit.
21. Gori and Richter, op. cit.
22. Holtzman, op. cit.
23. Mushkin, S., and Wagner, D.: *Expected mortality as a criterion in health policy evaluation, Report No. B12.* Paper presented at the 106th Annual Meeting of the American Public Health Association, Los Angeles, October 17, 1978.
24. Gori and Richter, op. cit.
25. Keyfitz, N.: *Improving life expectancy: an uphill road ahead.* Am. J. Public Health 68:954–956, 1978.
26. Boden, L. I.: *The economic impact of environmental disease on health care delivery.* J. Occup. Med. 18(7):467–472, 1976.
27. *Definition of Preventive Medicine.* American College of Preventive Medicine, Washington, D.C.
28. Henderson, J. B., and Enflow, A. J.: *The coronary risk factor problem: a behavioral perspective.* Prev. Med. 5:128–148, 1976.
29. Bonnie, R. J.: *Law and the discouragement of unhealthy personal choice,* in *Summary Proceedings of the Tripartite Conference on Prevention,* Alcohol, Drug Abuse and Mental Health Administration, Washington, D.C., 1977.
30. Schmidt, R. W.: *Quit-smoking programs—What really works?* In *Attitudes Toward Smoking in the U.S.* American Lung Association, 1977.
31. McDowell, I. and Martini, J.: *Problems and New Directions in the Evaluation of Primary Care.* Int. J. Epidemiol. 5:247–250, 1976.
32. Nagi, S.: *An epidemiology of disability among adults in the United States.* Milbank Mem. Fund Q., Fall 1976, pp. 439–465.
33. Chen, M.: *A norm-referenced population health status index based on life expectancy and disability.* Social Indicators Res. 5:245–53, 1978.
34. Forster, D. P.: *Mortality, morbidity and resource allocation.* Lancet 1:997–998, 1977.
35. *Quality of Medical Care Assessment Using Outcome Measures.* National Center for Health Services Research Publication No. (HRA) 77-3176, Washington, D.C., 1977.
36. Preston, S. H., et al.: *Causes of Death: Life Tables for National Populations.* Seminar Press, New York, 1972, pp. 1–41.
37. *Expectation of life among nonwhites. Statistical Bulletin* (Metropolitan Life Insurance Company) 58:5–7, 1977.
38. Brotman, H.B.: *Life Expectancy: comparison of national levels in 1900 and 1974 and variations in state levels 1969–1971.* Gerontologist 17:12–22, 1977.
39. Chen, M. K.: *The K index: a proxy measure of health care quality.* Health Services Res. 11;452–463, 1976.
40. Guralnick, L., and Jackson, A.: *An index for unnecessary deaths.* Public Health Rep. 82(2):180–182, 1967.
41. Romeder, J. M., and McWhinnie, J. R.: *Potential years of life lost between ages 1 and 70: an indicator of premature mortality for health planning.* Int. J. Epidemiol. 6:143–151, 1977.
42. Gonella, A., et al.: *The staging concept—an approach to the assessment of outcome of ambulatory care.* Med. Care 14:1, 1976.

43. Saracci, R.: *Epidemiological strategies and environmental factors.* Int. J. Epidemiol. 7(2):101–105, 1978.
44. Yeracaris, C. A., and Kim, J. H.: *Socioeconomic differentials in selected causes of death.* Am. J. Public Health 68:342–351, 1978.
45. Tsai, S. P., et al.: The effect of a reduction in leading causes of death: potential gains in life expectancy. Am. J. Public Health 68:966–971, 1978.
46. Brotman, op. cit.
47. Keyfitz, op. cit.
48. Weinstein, M., and Stason, W.: *Hypertension: A Policy Perspective.* Harvard University Press, Cambridge, Mass., 1976.
49. Hakulinen, T.: *On long-term relative survival rates.* J. Chron. Dis. 30:431–443, 1977.
50. Cornfield, J., and Mitchell, S.: *Selected risk factors in coronary disease: possible intervention effects.* Arch. Environ. Health 19:382–394, 1969.
51. Hemminki, E., and Starfield, B.: *Prevention of low birthweight and pre-term birth: literature review and suggestions for research policy.* Milbank Mem. Fund Q. 56(3):339–361, 1978.
52. Paffenberger, R., and Hale, W.: *Work activity and coronary heart mortality.* N. Engl. J. Med. 292:545–550, 1975.
53. Anderson, T.: *Reexamination of some of the Framingham blood pressure data.* Lancet, November 25, 1978, pp. 1139–1140.
54. Graham, S., and Mettlin, C.: *Diet and colon cancer.* Am. J. Epidemiol. 109(1):1–20, 1979.
55. Glueck et al., op. cit.
56. Dick and Stone, op. cit.
57. Winkelstein, W.: *Contemporary perspectives on prevention.* Bull. N.Y. Acad. Med. 51(1):27–38, 1975.
58. Marmot, G.: *Epidemiological basis for the prevention of coronary heart disease.* Bull. WHO 57(3):331–347, 1979.
59. Truett, J.: *A multivariate analysis of the risk of coronary heart disease in Framingham.* J. Chron. Dis. 20:511–524, 1967.
60. Walter, S.: *Calculation of attributable risks from epidemiological data.* Int. J. Epidemiol. 7(2):175–182, 1978.
61. Louria, D.: *The epidemiology of drug abuse and drug abuse rehabilitation,* in Glatt, M. (ed.): *Drug Dependence.* MTI Press, Baltimore, 1977.
62. Cooper, B., and Rice, D.: *Economic cost of illness revisited.* Soc. Sec. Bull. February 1976, pp. 21–36.
63. Berk, A., and Paringer, M.: *Economic cost of illness, fiscal 1975.* Med. Care 16(9):785–90, 1978.
64. Senate Select Committee on Nutrition and Human Needs: *Dietary Goals for the United States.* ed. 2. Washington, D.C., 1977.
65. Luce, B. R., and Schweitzer, S. O.: *Smoking and alcohol abuse: a comparison of their economic consequences.* N. Engl. J. Med. 298:569–571, 1978.
66. Stamler, J.: *HBP in the U.S.: An Overview,* in *National Conference on High Blood Pressure: Edited Report of Proceedings,* January 1973, pp. 11–66.
67. Luce and Schweitzer, op. cit.
68. Rufener, B. L., et al.: *Costs to Society of Drug Abuse,* vol. 2 in *Management Effectiveness Measures for NIDA Drug Abuse Treatment Programs.* National Institute on Drug Abuse, Rockville, Md., 1977.
69. Mills, E., and Thompson, M.: *The economic costs of stroke in Massachusetts.* N. Engl. J. Med. 299(8):415–418, 1978.

70. *Report of the National Commission on Diabetes to the Congress.* Vol. 3, No. 76–1024. National Institutes of Health, Washington, D.C., 1975.
71. Cerra, F.: *Cost of spinal injuries.* New York Times, December 25, 1976.
72. Rendtorff, R. C., et al.: *Economic consequences of gonorrhea in women: experience from an urban hospital.* J. Am. Venereal Disease Assoc. 1(1):40–47, 1974.
73. Cohen, M. L., et al.: *An assessment of patient-related economic costs in an outbreak of salmonellosis.* N. Engl. J. Med. 299(9):459–460, 1978.
74. *Development of Medical Technology—Opportunities for Assessment.* Office of Technology Assessment, Washington, D.C., August 1976.
75. Lansky, S., et al.: *Childhood cancer: nonmedical costs of illness.* Cancer 43:403–408, 1979.
76. Gibson, R., and Mueller, B.: *National health expenditures, fiscal year 1976.* Soc. Sec. Bull. 40:3–22, 1977.
77. Scitovsky, N.: *Changes in the Costs of Treatment of Selected Illnesses.* National Center for Health Services Research, Washington, D.C., 1976.
78. Ma, P., and Piazza, F.: *Cost of treating birth defects in state crippled children's services, 1975.* Paper presented at the 106th Annual Meeting of the American Public Health Association, Los Angeles, October 15–19, 1978.
79. Report of the National Commission on Diabetes, op. cit.
80. *Current Estimates from the Health Interview Survey, U.S., 1976.* National Center for Health Services, Washington, D.C., 1977.
81. *Health—United States, 1976–1977.* Health Resources Administration, Washington, D.C., 1978.
82. Bureau of Labor Statistics: *Occupational Injury and Illness Chartbook, 1974,* No. 460. U.S. Dept. of Labor, Washington, D.C., 1976.
83. Hedges, J.: *Absence from work—measuring the hours lost.* Monthly Labor Rev. October 1977, pp. 16–23.
84. Bureau of Labor Statistics: *Employee Compensation in the Private Nonfarm Economy, 1976.* Summary 77-7. U.S. Dept. of Labor, Washington, D.C., 1977.
85. Bureau of Labor Statistics: *Employee Compensation in the Private Nonfarm Economy, 1977.* Summary 78-7. U.S. Dept. of Labor, Washington, D.C., 1978.
86. Price, D. N.: *Cash benefits for short-term sickness, 1948–76.* Soc. Sec. Bull. 41(10):3–13, 1978.
87. Brody, W.: *Economic value of a housewife.* Res. Stat. Note 9, August 28, 1975.
88. Bureau of Labor Statistics: *Women in the labor force by presence and age of children under 18 years.* U.S. Dept. of Labor, Washington, D.C., 1978.
89. Mushkin and Wagner, op. cit.
90. *Employment and Training Report of the President, 1977.* Washington, D.C., 1977.
91. Cooper and Rice, op. cit.
92. Mushkin and Wagner, op. cit.
93. Lansky et al., op. cit.
94. *Women in the Labor Force,* op. cit.
95. Bureau of the Census: *Recent Social and Economic Trends,* in *Statistical Abstracts of the United States, 1977.* Washington, D.C., September 1977.
96. Nagi, op. cit.
97. Kane, R. L., et al.: *Medex and their physician preceptors: quality of care.* J.A.M.A. 236:2509–2512, 1976.
98. Chambers, L. W., and West, A. E.: *The St. John's randomized trial of the family practice nurse: health outcomes of patients.* Int. J. Epidemiol. 7(2):153–161, 1978.

99. Kane, R. L., et al.: *A method for assessing the outcome of acute primary care.* J. Fam. Practice 4:1119–1124, 1977.
100. Ibid.
101. Krute, A., and Burdette, M.: *Disability survey.* Soc. Sec. Bull. 41(4):3–17, 1978.
102. Mushkin and Wagner, op. cit.
103. Schechter, E. S., and Bye, B.: *Demographic and economic correlates of changes in disability status among the newly disabled,* in *Disability Survey 72,* Disabled and Nondisabled Adults, Report No. 12. Publication No. (SSA) 78-11717. Social Security Administration, Washington, D.C., 1978.
104. *Termination Experience of Workers' Disability Insurance Benefits Awarded 1957–67.* Social Security Administration, Washington, D.C., 1977.
105. *Termination of OASDI Benefits, 1975.* Res. Stat. Note 11, August 22, 1978.
106. McManus, L. A.: *The Effects of Disability on Lifetime Earnings.* Staff Paper No. 30, Publication No. (SSA) 78-11860. U.S. Department of Health, Education and Welfare, Washington, D.C., 1978.
107. Burdette, M., and Frohlich, P.: *Effect of disability in unit income,* in *Disability Survey 72,* Report No. 9. Social Security Administration, Washington, D.C., 1977.
108. Berman, D.: *How cheap is a life?* Int. J. Health Services 8(1):79–99, 1978.
109. Social Security Administration Staff Report No. 450, Washington, D.C., 1978.
110. Joint Committee on Taxation: *Estimates of Federal Tax Expenditures.* Washington, D.C., March 1978.
111. Hoos, I. R.: *Analysis of cost and benefits of health care,* in *Systems Analysis in Public Policy.* University of California Press, Berkeley, 1972, pp. 178–192.
112. Forster, D.: *Mortality, morbidity and resource allocation.* Lancet 1:997–998, 1977.
113. Johns, L., et al.: *Guide to Financial Analysis and Introduction to Economic Impact Analysis for Health Planning.* Health Resources Administration, Washington, D.C., 1976.
114. International Bank for Research and Development: *Social Cost-Benefit Analysis: A Guide for Country and Project Economists to the Derivation and Application of Economic and Social Accounting Price.* Working Paper No. 239. World Bank, Washington, D.C., 1976.
115. Office of Research and Statistics: *1972 lifetime earnings by age, sex, race and educational level.* Res. Stat. Note 12, May 20, 1976.
116. Acton, J.: *Measuring the Social Impact of Heart and Circulatory Disease Programs: Preliminary Framework and Estimates for the National Heart and Lung Institute.* Rand Corporation, Santa Monica, Cal., 1975.
117. Mushkin and Wagner, op. cit.
118. Dunlop, D. W.: *Benefit-Cost Analysis: A Review of Its Applicability in Policy Analysis for Delivering Health Services.* Soc. Sci. Med. 9:133–139, 1975.
119. Berk and Paringer, op. cit.
120. Peskin, H., and Seskin, E. (eds.): *Cost-Benefit Analysis and Water Pollution Policy.* Urban Institute, Washington, D.C., 1975.
121. Weinstein, M., and Stason, W.: *Foundations of cost-effectiveness analysis for health and medical practices.* N. Engl. J. Med. 296:716–21, 1977.
122. Schoebaum, S. C., et al.: *The swine-influenza decision.* N. Engl. J. Med. 295:759–65, 1976.
123. Fein, R.: *Fiscal and economic issues.* Bull. N.Y. Acad. Med. 51:235–241, 1975.
124. Fein, R.: *But on the other hand: high blood pressure, economics, and equity.* N. Engl. J. Med. 296:751–753, 1977.
125. Rufener et al., vol. 1, op. cit.

11

THE TOTAL COSTS OF MAKING HEALTH: AN ILLUSTRATION COMPARING TRADITIONAL AND NEW HEALTH STRATEGIES

Policy decisions that affect people's health can be made in the best health interests of the public if policy-makers have information that can help to evaluate one proposal in comparison with alternatives. Which components of current policy and which new approaches will affect health to what extent and for what price? The answers clearly differ, depending, first, upon what is being compared. If policy options are confined to biomedical strategies, policy choices will be quite different than if biomedical options were compared with environmental strategies. Choices will also depend upon the benefits that are included, as well as the costs of initiating a policy.

The evaluation of costs may be made in terms of some overall, predetermined limit. Alternatively, costs may be weighed in the context of anticipated gains, expressed here as the indicators of illness prevention (see Chapter 10). A large, overall cost may be acceptable if the expected benefits are considered to be highly worthwhile, such as the example of living a long life without disability in comparison with an extended but disabled existence.

The indicators of changes in health status have been shown to be describable in several ways, including their dollar benefits, or the savings of what would otherwise be the costs of illness and death. The discussion now turns to an approach for estimating how two different health policy strategies may affect changes in Americans' health, and the costs of these strategies. The two policies are universal access to primary care and a health-promoting shift in the national farm-food supply. Placing them within the same frame of reference, the problems and possibilities of estimating their

241

health improvement potential are taken up. This is followed by a discussion of the total costs of implementing such policies. These include the direct program deployment costs, such as providing services or granting subsidies, and the indirect costs that result when resources, such as time, personnel, or funds, are not used in a more productive, alternative activity. The designation "more productive" depends, of course, on who is making the judgment. As the discussion in Chapter 10 indicated, this judgment is conventionally made in terms of economic productivity.

Some of these program costs, or the indirect associated costs of foregone opportunities for earnings, may be "hidden," in the sense that they are not made explicit. They also have a redistributive dimension that transfers wealth, in the form of goods, services, jobs, or funds, from one segment of the society to another. This transfer can occur through government budgets, as, for example, the tax revenues from middle-income people that help to pay for Federal tax exemptions for large corporations.

By determining the total costs of strategies for health improvement, support for primary prevention may be strengthened. For, by recognizing the costs to vulnerable groups who may suffer lost income, protective transition policies can be formulated that will hopefully lessen objections to changes in current policy.

As in the previous discussion, the purpose here is to illustrate, in nontechnical terms, how more effective health policies can be designed. The focus is on using an ecological and comparative policy perspective that makes explicit the health-related and social consequences of public policies. The potential synergistic effects for improving health when policies are deployed in combination, and the combinations that are discoverable by using this perspective, are also illustrated.

The two policy thrusts that are used here themselves illustrate the major conceptual and empirical linkages that were developed in Chapters 2 through 6: how national policy, whether health care or farm policy, sets the options for organizations; how they, in turn, provide organizational options for action by their personnel and the consumers of their products; how decisions among organizations, public and private, depend upon the sets of rewards and penalties that are available to them; how a similar gains-for-cost calculation implicitly occurs within interpersonal contexts, as between practitioner and consumer, within organizations; and finally how, given this pyramid of greater to lesser potential for shaping the options for decisions, the less potent, individualistic strategies, such as health education and interpersonal support, are more effectively used in connection with more salient socioenvironmental strategies.

With a wider range of options for health policy, and a fuller view of their costs and benefits, the public and policy-makers may weigh "costs" and "benefits" differently than in the past, and as a result, lean toward new choices for health policies.

THE COSTS OF IMPROVING PRIMARY CARE

Estimating Potential Gains for New Costs

In order to determine the costs of a policy to provide Americans with full access to primary care services, the scope of primary care must be delineated, based presumably on its health-effective services. In order to compare this strategy with others, its health-effectiveness in relation to its cost must also be estimated. The basic question is: what *improvement* in the profile of modern health problems can be expected by *expanding* current policy? That is, by improving access to personal health services, and emphasizing primary-level care, what health gains might occur, along with the attendant savings in treatment and human productivity? What would be the direct, and more subtle, costs to achieve these benefits?

A prior question, posed in Chapter 9, arises again in this context: what is the potential of personal health care, as *currently* available, for improving today's health? The answer is two-pronged. The first concerns the *efficacy* of health services, the "probability of benefit to individuals in a defined population from a medical technology for a given problem under ideal conditions of use."[1] The second is the *effectiveness* of health care, the extent to which its potential is actually applied and achieved in the real world.

EFFICACY FOR PREVENTION

Although the systematic study of medical efficacy is only beginning, a large amount of information is nevertheless available. It could be synthesized to allow a tentative judgment of the health impact of health care now, rather than when "all the answers are in," a point in time that scientists can never reach and that policy-makers almost always outpace.

The questions of efficacy can begin to be answered by asking: what potential do health services have for both the primary and secondary prevention of illness? Specifically this requires taking each acute and chronic condition in the illness profile, and the risk factors associated with each, and asking what the current tools of health services can do to prevent each. The answers would be the best estimates now available from studies in several health and health-related fields, many of which have been summarized.[2-12] This prompts the question: what can the three principal modes of primary prevention in personal health care (health counseling, immunization, and drug prophylaxis) do to prevent the occurrence of each condition or of its related risk factors?[13-19] (See Chapters 5 and 9.)

243

A similar approach can estimate the potential for secondary prevention. Thus, for each risk factor, such as obesity, and each illness, such as colon cancer: what is the efficacy of screening techniques, such as physical examinations, prenatal examinations, and multiphasic testing? Specifically, what proportion of people who are screened are found to have problems; how many problems were not previously known; how many findings are confirmed as true health problems? As many as two-thirds of those screened by a battery of tests show some abnormality, mainly dental, vision, or hearing problems. However, less than 5 percent of their health problems were previously unknown to themselves or to medical practitioners; and large proportions of the presumed problems, as many as 50 to 95 percent, are not confirmed on re-examination.[20-23]

Once a health problem is recognized by those affected, with or without the assistance of practitioners, what is the efficacy of treatment that they seek from the health care system? Whether through counseling, drugs, surgery or other means, what is the potential therapeutic effect for each at-risk condition or disease? Moreover, what kinds of beneficial effects are attainable: cure, control, comfort, or death-avoidance? Studies show, for example, that antibiotics can cure 95 percent of ear infections; antihypertensive drugs can prevent complications in persons with moderately high blood pressure; treatment for asthma can contain its progression for 98 percent of asthmatics; certain symptoms, such as pain, can be mitigated; and coronary care units can reduce the chance of dying by 12 percent for heart patients for up to 3 years after their heart attack.[24-26] Overall, however, only 10 to 20 percent of medical procedures, when tested under rigorously controlled clinical studies, are efficacious,[27] and a large share of care has a neutral effect on health.[28,29]

The efficacy of health services for each acute or chronic health problem can be reduced by the iatrogenic, or health-damaging, effect of treatment. New illness can be caused by such techniques as fetal monitoring, induced labor, unneeded surgery, adverse drug reactions, x-rays, chemotherapy, and physician malpractice.[30-36] In addition, account should be made of the proportion of each type of problem that may be self-limiting, and so would resolve itself without formal medical treatment. This share may range from 10 to 85 percent, depending on the type of illness, based on the conditions that people say they usually self-treat.[37]

DIMENSIONS OF EFFECTIVENESS

The next set of questions involves estimating to what extent this net health-promoting, or efficacious, *potential* of health care is *effectively* brought to bear on the health problems of the population, and not merely on those who seek health care. Only the users of care have been the usual focus for

244

evaluating the effects of health services.[38] To answer the question of health effectiveness for the population means that for each type of problem the actual impact of care will depend on how much of the problem, such as bronchitis, as it occurs in the general population, is dealt with by the system. How much is either detected by or brought to the system of care? And if detected early, what proportion is followed up with treatment? Only 20 percent of eligible children receive Medicaid screening, for example, and of those who are found to have health problems, less than 40 percent are actually treated.[40,41] Furthermore, the incorrect timing of screening or treatment may preclude an efficacious result,[42-44] or practitioners may not follow correct medical practice.[45,46] The organization and financing of health care also may present a barrier between *efficacious* services and *effective* use among the population. The result can be delayed or inappropriate treatment, and therefore a less health-effective impact (see Chapters 5 and 9).[47-49]

In brief, the measure of effectiveness is the proportion of an illness (or at-risk condition) occurring in a population that is actually treated (for primary or secondary preventive purposes) and, of the portion treated, the efficacy obtained from the treatment technologies that are used (each of which has an estimated efficacy).

Effectiveness is still further influenced by the way patients carry out medical instructions. If a treatment is very efficacious, it cannot meet its potential in practice unless both patient and practitioner apply it correctly. Compliance among patients varies, depending upon how ill they are, and how complex and extended the treatment is. Estimates of people's compliance with instructions for preventive purposes are lower (54 percent) than for curative purposes among patients who have symptoms (80 percent). Compliance is least by ill people who have no symptoms (47 percent).[50]

A SIMPLIFIED METHOD FOR ASSESSMENT

This approach to estimating the effectiveness of personal health care can be illustrated, in a simplified form, for one health problem, chronic bronchitis, using data from the National Center for Health Statistics. The occurrence of chronic bronchitis in the U.S. population has a prevalence of 33 cases per 1000 persons. Because cigarette smoking is a major risk factor associated with it, the proportion of smokers with this illness (17 of the 33) is taken into account. Then, taking smokers and nonsmokers separately, the following information is applied to each category of people with chronic bronchitis: the proportion of all cases that are brought to the health care system for treatment (12 of the 33, or about 36 prcent), and of these, the proportion that is treated primarily with drugs (72 percent), and primarily with counseling (8 percent), presumably to advise them to stop smoking.

The efficacy of these treatments, for drugs, is 98 percent, for reducing symptoms or increasing comfort, but not for cure. This efficacy is diminished because only about 54 percent of patients are expected to use the drugs appropriately. About a third of the patients who smoke will benefit from counseling. Of these, almost two-thirds will reduce their habit enough to have fewer lung symptoms. A very few will stop smoking entirely.

Each step in the process has a probability of being completed by the patients involved. Only a percentage will complete each action. Therefore the overall effectiveness of the entire series of events is a product of the probabilities of accomplishing each step. The net effect of the estimates here is that almost a third of smokers who have chronic bronchitis, and somewhat more than a third of nonsmokers with this disease, are helped to some extent by primary care services. Overall, about one-third of Americans who have chronic bronchitis (11 of the 33 per 1000) benefit by having their symptoms relieved through primary care services. This includes about 3 percent of those with this condition who are enabled to live a longer life because they quit smoking as a result of receiving medical counseling through primary care services. The effectiveness of primary care for the secondary prevention of chronic bronchitis can thus be represented.

This approach can be followed for each problem in the profile of modern illness. However, the overall impact of personal health services on the national health problem profile is further complicated by the fact that some combinations of risks have synergistic effects on some forms of illness, and that many illnesses are interrelated. These overlaps may be estimated, as is illustrated in Appendix Table 8. As noted in Chapter 10, there are many problems in making these estimates because of the limited ways that currently available national data are analyzed.

Nevertheless, a plausible, if tentative, estimate of these overlaps can be made, indicating, for example, how a reduction of major risks in the population will contribute to a drop in several major forms of illness. These can then be incorporated into estimates of the effectiveness of health services in reducing each major risk factor and illness. Combined in this way, the result provides a measure of the impact of personal health services on the profile of American health problems.

Additional estimates can next be made of related declines in death and in people's disability. These are derived from current rates, taking into account what would be statistically expected to have occurred in the absence of health services. After determining the total number of days of disability, for example, that were avoided by Americans because they received health services, the economic value of these benefits can be estimated. Thus about 13 percent of all days of disability are absences from paid work, and 39 percent are days spent in bed. Chronic conditions account for 25 percent of this work loss and for 65 percent of days in bed. Acute conditions account for the remaining 75 and 35 percent, respectively.[51,52] Reductions in chronic and acute illness can be expected to lower a proportion of work loss by employees and reduce days of bed disability by employed and nonemployed men and women.

With this information, and using the method discussed in Chapter 10, an overall estimate may be made of the health improvements deriving from health care, or of their dollar benefits with all of the necessary qualifications attached to that method. The gains in health-effectiveness or dollar benefits may then, in turn, be compared with the total costs of providing personal health services. These kinds of findings then become a baseline for estimating the health impact of proposed *changes* in health care policy in relation to their costs.

Based on plausible estimates of the *net* health effectiveness (i.e., improvements minus untoward effects) of technologies used for primary care and more complex services, a clearer delineation of what constitutes effective primary care can be made. A reasonable statement can also be made of what primary care can be expected to achieve in the *improvement* of Americans' health.

The preliminary findings of a feasibility study that follows this approach suggest that personal health care has a limited impact on the profile of American health problems.[53] For example, about 50 to 60 percent of the 3000 acute and chronic conditions that exist among each 1000 persons are treated within the health care system. Of these, about half are improved in some way. A third are prevented before onset: these are almost exclusively communicable and other infectious childhood and some maternity conditions. Almost 10 percent are relieved symptomatically, including less than 1 percent in which the associated risk factors are reduced. An additional 5 percent are cured. The remaining 50 percent of problems that are dealt with by the health care system, through primary-level care or referral to more complex treatment, appear to be unaffected by health care. This does not discount the likelihood that, regardless of effect, people may be comforted merely by receiving attention. All of these findings are based on a series of data that are available for slightly more than half of the profile of American health problems.

These findings can also be stated in terms of the impact of health care on the *total* modern illness profile, and not simply in terms of the illnesses *brought to* the system of care. They suggest that about 18 to 20 percent of all illness is prevented. Another 3 to 4 percent is known to be relieved or controlled, and an additional 2 to 3 percent cured. If national policy granted universal access to primary care, the health impact of health care might be increased by about 30 percent. About 25 percent of illness might be prevented, and, in terms of secondary preventions, 4 to 5 percent relieved or controlled, with perhaps 4 percent cured. This estimate is based on the assumption that lower-income people would increase their visits to primary care practitioners relatively more than other income groups.[54]

The policy implications of these early findings support the increasing calls for a greater emphasis on primary care services. They show that the greatest share of demonstrated health improvement derives from the tools of primary care, or of more complex treatment that could be rendered in nonhospital settings. These kinds of estimates can thus help evaluate, for example, whether the costs of supporting new secondary care technologies are justifiable on the basis of health effectiveness in comparison with expanding access to primary care.

This kind of analysis also reveals the limits of personal health care and of its most effective component—primary care—for being effective in *preventing* the growing share of *chronic* illness that makes up the modern profile of health problems.

The inherent *efficacy* of personal health care—the potential of its tools for preventing much of modern illness—is not likely to increase appreciably in the foreseeable future. However, as implied by the findings above, its *effectiveness* can be increased somewhat. To the extent that its impact on Americans' health is limited because it is *not reaching* those who have health problems that *are* amenable to primary or secondary prevention by personal care methods, then enhancing access for those people will bring gains in overall health. This is presumably one purpose of national health insurance proposals. Any such policy that does not improve access for these groups of Americans, who come mostly from the lower-income and rural sectors, should not be expected to improve health.

Sources of New Program Costs

Although there are numerous descriptions of what a health-effective health care system should include,[55-63] the most debated national health insurance plans recognize that, at a minimum, improved effectiveness requires financial and geographic access to services, and greater availability of primary care. The proposals cover primary care services in varying degrees. These services are generally defined as basic primary and secondary preventive care that is appropriate for up to 90 percent of health problems, that is rendered predominantly in ambulatory facilities, and that represents a continuous source of care, except for referrals to other more complex services for about 5 to 10 percent of visits. These services are delivered by primary care practitioners, including physicians in general and family practice, pediatricians, internists, obstetricians, dentists, nurse practitioners, and physician assistants.[64-68]

CURRENT COSTS OF PRIMARY CARE

Current spending for primary care constitutes about one-third of all personal health expenditures, taking into account hospital outpatient services, dental care, drugs, and other services, as well as the share of office time spent on primary-level problems by primary care physicians. This amounted to about $200 per American in 1976, compared with an additional $375 expended for more complex secondary and tertiary levels of care.[69-77] A thorough review of studies of health care efficacy will show, as noted above, that the vast majority of efficacious procedures for most health problems are, or can be, delivered in primary care settings, including home, day care, or other community facilities, as well as ambulatory care centers.[78]

All this suggests that a health-effective insurance program would increase the share of personal health expenditures for primary care to well above the current 34 percent, by insuring more of those services, doing so for lower-income persons and women, who currently have less such protection, and providing incentives for developing primary care settings, such as health maintenance organizations and home care programs. These ingredients of a national health services policy will help to determine whether people who could most benefit from health services will actually be enabled to use them as they need. This, in turn, will determine whether health care effectiveness will increase.[79-82] As was discussed in Chapter 5, the evidence is that those who need services most are more likely to use them when financial and other barriers are removed.[83-86] And, they do not use them beyond medical necessity.[87,88]

It is mainly this "new" proportion of all health problems—the illness and risks of illness of people who cannot now readily use health care—that will compose whatever improvement in national health will occur, as a result of a national policy of expanded personal health care. The amounts and types of health problems of those who would have newly acquired access to services can be estimated and, in turn, the health impact of health care on such persons can be estimated.

SOURCES OF COST CONTAINMENT

The cost of a policy to expand the availability of primary care and the rate of cost increases are greatly affected by the policy design (see Chapters 5 and 9). The important elements include methods of financing, such as whether private profit-making must be supported; the administrative costs of maintaining multiple public and private insurance programs; and the share of primary care services actually covered.[89-92] Forms of reimbursement, in addition, affect the supply and types of practitioners, their practice arrangements, and their relative productivity.[93-103] Other incentives or disincentives affect the development of comprehensive ambulatory centers, the emphasis on the most cost-effective levels of care and of settings for care,[104-107] as well as whether alternatives to hospital care can be developed, such as in-home care or day centers.[108-125]

These fiscal incentives shape the options for the ways that expanded services can develop and whether they are likely to be inflationary. Policy incentives that show promise for overall savings in personal health care expenditures include those that direct development toward "one-stop" ambulatory care and other nonhospital alternatives, rendered by generalist practitioners in non-profit, simplified organizational arrangements, and that are available to people regardless of their ability to pay.

Program costs may be further contained if there is some decline in iatrogenic illness. This can be expected if primary care replaces some unnecessary amounts of more complex secondary and tertiary levels of care (see Chapter 9). A modest increase in effectiveness, as well as efficiency, might occur if policy strongly encouraged more "one-step" types of primary care. Evidence suggests that a single source of health care, in which patient and practitioner can become familiar with each other, provides the interpersonal and organizational context that improves people's adherence to health care instructions.[126]

Taken together, these sources of costs and effectiveness would properly be part of estimating changes in total expenditures, in health improvement, and in its dollar benefits. Initial cost figures for national health insurance plans are provided by their sponsors and, independently, by the Congressional Budget Office.[127] It is the health impact which is literally never estimated. The few cost-benefit estimates that have been made are limited to the treatment of a few specific diseases and involve such diversity in baseline information and approach that they are not comparable.[128-137]

Hidden Costs

The direct program costs of a policy of expanded national health insurance are estimated as an overall 10 to 20 percent increase over what national health expenditures would otherwise be. As with all policy, there are also related and indirect costs that may not be made explicit when costs are reported. Those that are estimated but not included in personal health care expenses are the costs of prepayment and administration, and the developmental costs of new facilities and personnel.[138]

Important additional expenditures that are not fully, if ever, estimated include the redistributive and other reverberating costs. These are conventionally consigned to "externalities" in policy analysis, and are regarded as uncontrollable, "outside factors."[139-141] The redistributive effects here involve both health personnel and consumers.

REDISTRIBUTIVE COSTS

The design of a national health care policy will affect the relative earnings between the occupational groups of the nation's 5½ million health personnel. Their average annual earnings currently vary at least tenfold among occupational categories.[142-147] In addition, a national policy that significantly shifted the major site of services to community settings—if it is to be health-promoting in the less obvious ways that involve people's income stability—would take into account the job displacement and attendant threat to income of inpatient personnel (see Chapter 9). Job retraining and wage replacement would be part of its initial program costs. Without these, most of the employee groups who are vulnerable to income loss would also become more at risk of illness. Moreover, the public purse would suffer if lost income were extensive, because of lost income tax revenues, in addition to covering the health care expenses and other deficits of unemployed health care personnel.

For the public, even if equal access is built into their provision, the burden of financing health services may be regressive. It may place a relatively larger share of the bill on those who are less able to pay for it. For example, a $10 billion increase for an expanded health care policy, if financed through *personal income taxes,* would take less than 0.1 percent from family incomes under $10,000, and 0.8 percent from those earning $25,000 or more. This represents progressive financing. However, if financed through *insurance premiums,* such programs would *increase* the burden on those lower-income families fourfold and *reduce* it for higher-income families by over a fourth.[148,149] This would be regressive and inequitable financing (see Chapter 6).

To the degree that health care financing widens this income gap, it places lower-income people at further risk of illness. This increased risk is roughly measurable, and with it the added, predictable increased costs of illness, its treatment, and its losses in productivity. Such "externalities" contribute to the total costs of regressive financing. If made explicit, they might bear on policy decisions and on the public's views of desirable policy options.

Summary

The analytic approach put forward here makes an estimate of the impact of health care on health problems, based on the efficacy of its tools and its effectiveness under current conditions of access. Then, for any proposed increase in financial and geographic access to services, it estimates the expected increase in the use of health care by those segments of the population that now have insufficient access. It takes into account any built-in controls on providers or consumers that would affect the use of care and provider productivity. Estimates can then be made of health improvements, measured both in health status and in dollar terms, for this "new" portion of illness that is prevented, detected, or brought for care by those with newly acquired access to services. These effects can be compared with the added costs generated by such expanded access.

Total costs would include the *direct* costs of providing additional services, as well as the transition costs, those potential *indirect* losses, some of which affect both health personnel and consumers if regressive, redistributive effects are not compensated. If these transitional costs in lost income and consequent health problems are to be avoided among the vulnerable groups, they must become added, direct, explicit program costs, costs undertaken to prevent indirect health-damage resulting from policy change.

By comparing the increments in program costs with the estimated new gains in the national health profile, an estimate can be made of the cost-effectiveness of the new health care policy. Valuing these health gains in dollars would provide a benefit-cost estimate (see Fig. 10, p. 231).

THE COSTS OF NEW OPTIONS FOR HEALTHFUL LIFESTYLES

It is almost a truism, though one borne out by epidemiologic studies, that clean air, pure water, adequate housing, and food are health-making, and that excesses or deficits are health-damaging. Just how efficacious they are for health improvement is, however, a matter of disagreement. This is, in part, because the cumulative or synergistic impact of these factors is rarely studied.[150-156]

Estimates have, of course, been made of the health effects of individual air and water pollutants, of the byproducts of nuclear and other energy sources, of modes of transportation, and of variations in housing standards and employment.[157-177] Even their individual efficacies, however, are not fully realized among Americans because current knowledge is applied in only limited ways.

Just as with health services, the effectiveness of what is known to be efficacious for health is delimited by the mediating influence of policy, which sets the parameters of access to health-making circumstances. Furthermore, policy and policy deployment strategies are most often determined by simply comparing expected health benefits with the costs of individual socioenvironmental programs. This approach is less useful for achieving maximum gains in health than making comparisons among alternative policy thrusts.[178-180]

252

The discussion now takes up a new, hypothetical, socioenvironmental policy whose aim is to make a health-promoting shift in the nation's agricultural supply (see Chapter 8). This proposal suggests how the impact of such a policy on Americans' health, and its true costs, might be estimated, and provides a way to compare its effects with those of other environmental or personal health care policies. Information of this kind would contribute to an informed debate on health-making policy. The measurement of impact again centers on changes in the national profile of health and illness and on the reverberating economic and personal consequences of policy changes.

The Policy Proposal

A new farm-food policy, based on the growing affluent-nation consensus on health-promoting dietary changes, would use the Congressional Dietary Goals of 1977 as a guide for national farm-food policy, rather than for merely admonishing individuals to change their eating habits. The policy would change the composition of the farm-food supply and so create a different set of options for consumers. Today's farm supply provides Americans with 42 percent of their daily calories in fat, half of which come from animal sources. These are relatively low in polyunsaturated fats as compared with saturated fats, and supply over 500 mg of cholesterol daily. In addition, 46 percent of calories are available as carbohydrates, including 18 percent from refined and processed sugars.[181-183]

Under new policy, the food supply would be composed of fats that provide about one-third, instead of 42 percent, of daily calories, 30 to 40 percent derived from animal sources. This would afford less than 300 mg of cholesterol daily and provide equal shares of polyunsaturated and saturated fats. Over half of a day's calories would come from carbohydrates, but only 10 percent or less would derive from processed or refined sugars. About 40 percent of protein would come from animal sources, instead of the current 70 percent.[184,185] A nonfood commodity in the farm supply, tobacco, would become less available as well. A final component of the new policy would extend the current supplemental food program to all pregnant or nursing women, and to children up to 16 years, whose families are below 150 percent of the annual official poverty threshold, earning less than $8300 in 1976 dollars (see Chapter 7).

THE DESIGN STRATEGY

The policy strategy to bring about these changes would be to make selected health-limiting commodities less profitable options for producers and less easy to choose by consumers. At the same time, opportunities to use other commodities and foods would be made more rewarding. Policy would narrow producers' options for such potentially health-limiting commodities as beef, corn, grain, sugar, and tobacco. It would widen and ease the options for wheat, soybeans, dairy products, peanuts, and potatoes, the more health-promoting group.

In order to estimate the effects of this shift in farm supply, the complex linkages among these commodities within the farm-food system would have to be taken into account (see Chapters 7 and 8). To address the impact of this policy on Americans' health, the chain of relationships linking the components of the farm-food supply, consumer consumption expenditures, dietary and smoking patterns, and health problems would be measured. These relationships are considered in the following discussion.

Estimating Potential Health Gains

The basis for estimating the changes in health resulting from a shift in the farm-food supply is, again, the best available epidemiologic and clinical evidence. A few studies show specific relationships that can reasonably be adjusted and generalized to the U.S. population.[186,187] For example, a one-third drop in dietary saturated fats, along with an increase in polyunsaturates, is associated with a 10 percent or larger reduction in serum cholesterol.[188,189] This reduction is doubled when accompanied by weight loss in people who are above their ideal weight.[190,191] Americans are about 18 percent above their ideal weight. If the proposed food supply were translated into the actual national eating pattern, it is likely that people would eat about 20 percent fewer calories a day because of the greater bulk and lower caloric density of the foods (see Chapter 8). Even if calories were lowered by only 7 to 10 percent, serum cholesterol levels would be likely to drop to levels of moderate or normal risk for the majority of people who are at high risk. Blood pressures might also be reduced by 8 percent or more, as well as the associated risks of cardiovascular, digestive, and other diseases.[192]

Health improvements from food supplements would be estimated on the basis of experience with the WIC food supplement program for women, infants, and children. These declines in the proportions of Americans who are at-risk of illness from undereating would be likely to produce cumulative and synergistic improvements in the national health profile. These changes might again be captured as in the approach illustrated in Appendix Table 8, which estimates the combined contribution of health risks to illness and death.

There is a more statistically reliable and systematic approach to estimating the health improvement potential of the proposed dietary and smoking patterns. It is, again, to make better use of currently available national data. The national health and nutrition survey data could be reassembled and combined with the special and ongoing national health and illness surveys. Comparisons could then be made, according to socioeconomic/age/sex groups, between those people who consume predominantly more products of a potentially health-limiting character and those who consume more health-promoting products. Their eating patterns, and smoking habits, can then be matched against their at-risk conditions (such as overweight or underweight, serum cholesterol, and high blood pressure) and their acute and chronic illnesses. These subgroups can then be statistically weighted in order to estimate the health impact for all Americans of one set of eating and smoking habits compared with the other.

PROGRAM STRATEGIES

Needless to say, these estimates of the total health impact of changes in national dietary and tobacco patterns are averages and will affect some segments of the population more than others. However, the fact that about two-thirds of those who are overweight try to lose, and a similar share of smokers try to quit, is a good indication that people at higher risk may benefit most from health-promoting policy changes.[193]

To help reinforce the all-encompassing supply policy, supportive components could be provided in the form of public information and readily accessible diet modification and quit-smoking groups. This would not necessarily be done through traditional health care programs. Rather, community, worksite, school, church, and other self-help groups, supported by small subsidies, might be as effective, at lesser public expense. In this way, the tools of health education and of group support, when combined with national policy that provides new health-promoting options for consumption, can reach maximum effectiveness.

This set of policy deployment strategies could be expected both to reduce the health risks of people who are currently at high risk and, more importantly, to deter or prevent the development of risks in younger people. In effect, this socioenvironmental strategy would, as with the personal health care strategy, be measured according to its effectiveness for both primary and secondary prevention.

Although current levels of health risks and of illness are correlated with the national mix of agricultural supplies, altering those supplies does not necessarily mean that health problems will change in direct response. Reducing the supply of sugar by 40 percent, for example, does not necessarily mean that caries will decline by that amount. First, of course, people will have to eat less, and buy less, sugar. In order to translate shifts in national supply into what people can be expected to eat, or smoke, their buying patterns must be taken into account. These, in turn, depend on the type of food involved and its price relative both to their disposable income and in comparison with other foods. These relationships are captured in price elasticities, based on supply and demand trends (see Chapter 7). Thus, if the national supply of animal protein and fat is reduced, while the vegetable protein-fat supply is increased, people's purchase patterns for beef and peanut butter, for example, would change. The extent of the change could be planned and estimated according to their price elasticities. A 10 percent increase in beef prices would *reduce* beef consumption by over 6 percent. A similar drop in the price of peanut butter would *increase* its use by over 6 percent.[194]

This kind of information can then guide the application of Federal policies that affect food and tobacco prices, including those that pertain to growers, processors, and marketers. By identifying the specific Federal farm, regulatory, and tax subsidy programs that affect the major products that are derived from the ten farm commodities, the direct program costs of a change in farm-food policy can begin to be estimated.[195]

Sources of Program Costs

The national farm-food *supply* would be shifted toward more vegetable-source protein and fat, and naturally occurring sugars, by using current policy instruments. This would mean a gradual increase in support (through acreage control, target prices, marketing orders, commodity purchases, and disposal programs) for wheat, peanuts, potatoes, dairy products, and soybeans, and the offering of incentives for their *expanded use.* A new value-added tax for highly processed foods might be added to deter uses that perpetuate the current destruction of food fiber.

At the same time, current, indirect beef production supports would decline. Subsidies might instead support leaner beef and more corn-grain uses for such products as gasohol, polyunsaturated oils, and corn-meal foods. Similar reductions in commodity support for sugar cane and tobacco would occur, except for the amounts that might be diverted to gasohol production or protein uses. Concomitant increases would occur in production supports for wheat, dairy products, peanuts, potatoes, and soybeans.

Fiscal incentives or disincentives could be designed to encourage processors to develop low-fat products and expand soy use in meats, baked goods, and oil products. Initially, either consumer subsidies, which are common in Europe, or disincentives in the form of taxes may be used to keep health-promoting products at sufficiently low prices relative to their health-limiting counterparts. This would help to maintain increased consumption of the new foods until agricultural and marketing incentives achieve a stabilized system of relative prices.

In sum, the principal sources of the new public expenditures required for a new farm-food supply policy are the added costs of farm and other subsidies, over and above present subsidy programs. This net increase may not be appreciable. A second source is the added cost of expanding the current WIC food supplement program. Third are the short-term, developmental costs for encouraging expansion of selected crops and new uses of commodities. These expenditures, in order to minimize redistributive costs, would be directed to the states and regions most affected.

Effects on Regional Development

A close look at the 26 states that are the leading producers of the ten health-important commodities shows that 12 of them already have a net economic balance in favor of the health-promoting commodities. Of the 14 states that produce, in dollar terms, more of the potentially health-limiting supplies, eight are nevertheless also leading producers of at least one of the health-promoting commodities. Of the remaining six states, five of them grow, as secondary farm products, two to five of the health-promoting commodities.[196-199] This suggests that there is a viable agricultural basis from which to develop an alternate mix of farm supplies, if start-up funds and subsidies are appropriately targeted to the most vulnerable states.

Other sources of costs to the public purse may occur through temporarily reduced income tax revenues, if net losses in personal income are allowed. Depending upon the mix of fiscal incentives used, however, these tax losses could be offset by raising present tobacco, sugar, and other excise taxes.[200]

Indirect Costs

EMPLOYEES AND TAXPAYERS

As significant to human welfare as are the added program costs, there are indirect, social costs of a policy to alter the agricultural supply. These are the costs "to the economy," reflected in part in losses to those people whose livelihood is affected, in the farming, food, and tobacco industries. Together these sectors contributed about $160 billion to the domestic economy and employed about 4 million people in 1976.[201-209]

As a result of a new farm-food policy, some parts of these industries would experience a decline, while others would expand. In order to estimate the net impact, as well as develop transition plans to protect the livelihood—and therefore the health—of those adversely involved, each farm commodity and its related processed goods would first be examined.

257

Assume, for example, that after 1 year of the new policy, consumer meat consumption dropped by 25 percent. This would mean, in 1976 dollars, a loss of about $25 billion for animal livestock producers and another $4 billion loss for meat processors, taking into account the price share going to each. These losses, in turn, would translate into job layoffs for about 65,000 workers in each sector, based on economic output per employee.[210-212]

Other losses would occur among tobacco manufacturers and their 80,000 production personnel, as well as tobacco farmers. These farm families compose less than 8 percent of the farm population; this is less than 7 percent of whites and about 23 percent of blacks. Almost half of the black farm population live on the smallest farms, producing less than $2500 annually in 1975. The comparable figure for whites is 31 percent.[213] In addition, the impact on the jobs of hired farmworkers, who are already both economically depressed and health-vulnerable, would be estimated. Many of these farm people work on the diminishing number of small farms in the American agricultural system. They are among those farmworkers who, in any case, have long needed better assistance to sustain a steady and adequate income.

Policy Implications

THE COSTS OF TRANSITION

All of this has a number of implications concerning both the costs and benefits of health-making policy. Analysis may show that, in the intermediate and long term, if not sooner, the total economy may benefit in dollar savings through the development of less energy-intensive crops and food manufacturing, more labor-intensive employment and rural development, and less environmental pollution (see Chapter 8).[214-218] These measures might then increase productivity and help contain food-price inflation. Some of the major costs of disability and premature deaths, owing to national changes in eating and smoking habits, would also be avoided.

However, in the short term, during a transition period, costs will be entailed in order to avoid allowing relatively few people to bear an undue burden of the changes that occur. A more equitable distribution of the burden can be achieved through transfers in government budgets. These, again, become the source of additional program costs which are, nevertheless, essential to health-making policy. In effect, policy that develops a health-promoting farm-food supply must also prevent *indirect* health damage to those whose incomes are adversely affected to an extent that puts them at health risk.

In order to prevent health-damaging consequences, the costs of transition would be borne through the public budget by all taxpayers, rather than only by the affected segments of the population. Explicit transition program costs would include not only expenditures for agricultural and food product development, public information, and consumer group support subsidies: there would also be the costs of farm and production worker retraining and income maintenance at health-sustaining levels, and the costs of improved unemployment insurance benefits or, for some, early retirement programs.

The redistributive effects of policy deployment for the public at large would depend on the mode of financing: the proportion derived through general revenues, and through excise taxes levied nationally, and the share paid by each income group. Similarly, food and tobacco price patterns and their effects on the disposable income of low-income people should be measured to determine whether, in fact, the health-promoting food and nutritional impact on buying patterns is also equitably shared, and is in accord with ability to pay. In general, both price and food equality could be expected to be much improved over present patterns.

FOREIGN TRADE CONNECTIONS

A final set of major economic impacts flowing from an alteration in national farm supply concerns farm-food exports and imports. Currently, the scale of U.S. food-feed grains and tobacco industries could not exist in a free market without domestic Federal support programs and export sales. These sales are also promoted by government. They now account for 50 to 80 percent of cash receipts for these commodities.[219,220] Grains also provide the largest and most stable contribution to the favorable balance of agricultural trade, helping offset the overall U.S. balance of payments deficit.[221-223]

The "costs" and "benefits" entailed in a health-making policy goal may differ, depending on the national or international perspective that is used. Conceivably, for example, surplus U.S. health-limiting commodities might be exported in order to dampen adverse economic impacts in this country. Viewed globally, however, these enlarged food-feed grain and tobacco exports could increase foreign beef production in rich countries, promote cigarette smoking, and deter food-crop development in rural poor nations. As many of these nations now advocate, rather than importing U.S. grains, they might instead pursue a more health-promoting course, such as exporting some of their domestically grown and processed vegetable protein foods, derived from their rich Asian, African, and Latin American food cultures. This would add much-needed value to the balance of trade for poor nations, and would contribute to health-promoting food supplies in affluent countries.

From a health-promoting point of view, the foreign trade aspects of policy would best be decided in a multinational context of consultation, with "costs" and "benefits" allocated accordingly. As was taking shape in the last decade, the 1980s will see a difficult dialogue continuing throughout the world. In the European Economic Community, the concern is over whether their joint agricultural policy should continue to subsidize "mountains of butter" and fat beef herds, while their health ministries advocate lean diets.[224-226] In the United Nations, the Food and Agricultural Organization attempts to negotiate, between rich and poor nations, sufficient food surplus for short-term and emergency needs, while fostering longer-term self-sufficiency in food production.[227] It might be hoped that U.S. domestic farm-food policy would be formulated to contribute to both these short- and long-term world health goals.

Summary

To design a health-promoting farm-food supply policy in the United States requires that its full costs, as well as its benefits, be taken into account, most of which can be reasonably estimated (see Fig. 10). Beyond the costs to the economy that may occur if *net* employment and investment temporarily drop are the more likely, and less acknowledged, distributive costs. These essentially answer "who gains?" and "who pays?" economically, and otherwise, in relation to their need or capacity, and especially in the short term. The health-damaging consequences—and related health services spending—that the inequitable distribution of costs and benefits would bring, can be avoided. The redistributive costs can be absorbed in the Federal program budget as the acknowledged program costs of deploying new policy, as part of the transitional costs of health-making policy (see Fig. 10).

The sources of benefits adding to the nation's economy include the dollar savings from improved national health and individual welfare; the savings in medical treatment and fewer losses in productivity; and the savings that contribute to such national goals and requirements as less-intensive uses of energy, expanded employment, environmental protection, inflation control, and international trade and monetary balances.

HEALTH-MAKING SYNERGIES INVOLVING OLD AND NEW STRATEGIES

Having estimated the costs and benefits of major health policy thrusts within a common framework, as here with universal access to primary health services, and a shift in the national farm-food supply, it becomes possible to make reasonable comparisons that can help guide policy decisions.

Overall comparisons of the effects on health status, their cost-effectiveness, and their short- and longer-term benefits can be made. For example, for purposes of secondary prevention—the detection, control, or amelioration of people's illnesses—it is obvious that some personal care services are irreplaceable, especially for those with a long history of illness. At the same time, a socioenvironmental policy, such as the farm-food supply policy, also has potential for the secondary prevention of illness. Under the policy changes described above, it can reduce the large number of Americans who are at risk of chronic illness, including perhaps 75 percent of those who have high blood levels of cholesterol. It can ameliorate symptoms, as, for example, among smokers who reduce their habit as a result of fewer options to smoke. It can help detect illness by the public information component of the policy; and, by subsidizing self-help groups, it can provide some of the nonmedical personal services sought by individuals who are either ill or at high risk of illness.

The *forte* of personal health services in primary prevention is predominantly infectious illness, and some maternity and infant conditions. However, socioenvironmental strategies, even for these problems, would reduce their incidence, since well-nourished and healthy people are less likely to develop infections or succumb under physiologic stress, such as pregnancy.

A potentially larger impact on health, and the single most significant one from the standpoint of a new farm-food supply policy, is the primary prevention of chronic forms of illness. This alone would include an estimated drop in the incidence of all cancers of 50 percent, and of heart disease and stroke of 15 to 20 percent, based on minimal expected changes among Americans in their average weight, serum cholesterol, and the number of cigarettes they smoke.[228-231] (The scope and extent of other potential improvements in health are suggested in Appendix Table 8.)

These illustrations suggest important implications for health policy. First, if personal health services and socioenvironmental strategies are selected according to their *health-effectiveness,* they can be complementary in their impact on Americans' health. Second, the larger potential for future improvements in health lies in the use of socioenvironmental strategies. This would become increasingly apparent over time as a drop in the *incidence* of chronic illness resulted in a relatively lessening burden of the cumulative effects of illness: less disability, less related acute illness, and less complicated and severe illness. It would also mean that youth would enter adulthood relatively more risk-free than their parents' generation.

In addition to finding complementary health strategies, comparisons of health-important policies can show the *relative* effectiveness of *components* of each thrust. For example, how much prevention is possible within personal health services in relation to the site of care, whether hospital, health center, home, or other community facility? Or, what mix in the food supply brings the greatest health gains at least cost?

It is also possible and realistic to seek out policy components that are *synergistic,* those that, if planned and deployed jointly, bring greater health improvement at lower costs than if either is used separately. Children's dental care, for example, is 50 percent more cost-effective in communities where water is fluoridated. Children in these communities have fewer caries, compared with those in other communities who either have fluoridated water but no access to dental care, or dental care but no fluoridation.[232]

To illustrate more broadly, a primary care system might fully use its primary prevention tools, namely, health counseling concerning diet, smoking, weight control, and pregnancy; and delivery of immunizations and birth control prophylaxis. In communities where health-promoting products were available at lower cost than health-limiting products, and where women and children were well-nourished, its impact on the health profile of the population might well be multiplied. Its secondary prevention technologies for containing illness would also be more effective in such communities, especially for dealing with acute infections and with such chronic conditions as heart and lung disease and diabetes. Furthermore, over a period of time, illnesses brought for treatment might be less frequent and severe, and require less complex and potentially dangerous treatment. In such communities, too, all efforts at health education, whether through news media, schools, workplaces, community groups, or health care settings, could be expected to be more effective as people found that doing the more healthful things was relatively easier, and less costly in numerous ways, than doing the less healthful.

With a comparative, ecological framework for the analysis of health-important policies and their components, such expectations and prospects as these would have a firmer basis for both development and correction.

Weighing Costs and Gains

The complexity of the problem of estimating the health effects of public policy, in order to guide national health-making efforts, obviously requires sophisticated computer modeling. More importantly, it presupposes a national organizational entity charged with the responsibility of providing such information and guidance for public policy to policy-makers and the public. Both the technical capacity and political feasibility of developing such a capability seem to be increasing in some respects (see Chapters 4, 10, and 12).

Some may caution that data of the sort that would be developed in this undertaking would misleadingly appear to be hard and incontrovertible "facts." It is more likely, however, that findings would be thoroughly questioned, hopefully by all parties affected. Yet controversy could be expected to be no more than what occurs over the results of the macroeconomic models that are now used to guide national economic policy; nor would findings be more tenuous than the information systems on which national security policy is based. At a minimum, discussions over health and health-affecting policy would be generated more widely than at present, founded on a firmer information base, and set within a broader, more health-oriented framework of options.

Both policy-makers and the public would become aware of the true costs of major policy changes, whether in the delivery of personal health care or in the national farm-food supply. Full view would be possible, especially of the costs that are well beyond the direct amounts needed to administer specific program services or to develop resources to carry out policy. Public debate could weigh these less obvious costs to the nation, measured as potential losses in national output. the possible short-term drop in personal expenditures when people lose their jobs, and the related drop in business investment. People could judge whether these costs should be borne by the public through explicit transitional programs, thus spreading the burden more equitably, or whether the costs should weigh on the segments of the population that are most adversely affected. The public would be aware that very often these vulnerable people are already at economic or other disadvantages, and would, as a result, be more likely to incur for themselves, and the nation, the additional costs of increased illness. By having a means to make comparative judgments, people would be better informed about their prospects, and those of their children, for living more of their lives free from disability. Policy-makers and the public then would also understand the costs of *not* choosing the most health-promoting policy options.

REFERENCES

1. *Assessing the Efficacy and Safety of Medical Technologies.* Office of Technology Assessment, Washington, D.C., 1978.
2. Fogarty International Center, National Institutes of Health: *Preventive Medicine USA.* Prodist, New York, 1976.
3. Milio, N.: *The ethics and economics of community health services: the case of screening.* Linacre Q., November 1977.
4. Milio, N.: *Self-care in urban settings.* Health Ed. Monogr., Summer 1977.
5. *Development of Medical Technology—Opportunities for Assessment.* Office of Technology Assessment, Washington, D.C., 1976.
6. *Quality of Medical Care Assessment Using Outcome Measures.* National Center for Health Service Research Publication No. (HRA)77-3176, Washington, D.C., 1977.
7. *Assessing the Efficiency,*op. cit.

8. Dickinson, J. C., and Gehlbach, S. H.: *Process and outcome: lack of correlation in a primary care model.* J. Fam. Pract. 7(3):557–562, 1978.
9. Brook, R. H., et al.: *Chapter II—uses of outcome information.* Med. Care 15:(9):16–23, 1977.
10. Milio, N.: *The team delivery of primary care: a comparative analysis of policy approaches to health improvement using available (National Center for Health Statistics) data,* in Proceedings: Policy Issues in Primary Health Care. DHEW Health Planners' Region VII, University of Iowa Health Services Research Center, Iowa City, 1978.
11. Milio, N.: *Health Planning and Administration with the Consumer in View and Involved.* Unit I–VI, University of Cincinnati, 1976–1977.
12. Milio, N. (principal investigator): *The Development of Complementary Policy Options in Primary Care and Ecological Health Improvement Interventions* (Working Papers). Research funded by Health Services Research Center, University of North Carolina, Chapel Hill, under a core grant from the National Center for Health Services Research (1978–1979).
13. Suinn, R. M., and Bloom, L. J.: *Anxiety management training for pattern a behavior.* J. Behav. Med. 1(1), 1978.
14. Werlin, S. H., and Schauffler, H. H.: *Structuring policy development for consumer health education.* Am. J. Public Health 68:596–597, 1978.
15. Schmidt, R. W.: *Quit-smoking programs—what really works?* in *Attitudes Toward Smoking in the U.S.* American Lung Association, 1977, pp. 10–12.
16. Mossman, P. B.: *Changing habits—an experience in industry.* J. Occup. Med. 20(3):213, 1978.
17. Center for Disease Control: *Silver nitrate prophylaxis for gonococcal ophthalmia neonatorum.* Morbid. Mortal. Weekly Rep. 27(13):107, 1978.
18. *Measles—United States: current trends.* Morbid. Mortal. Weekly Rep. 26(14):109–111, 1977.
19. McKinley, K. B., and McKinley, S. M.: *The questionable contribution of medical measures to the decline of mortality in the United States in the twentieth century.* Milbank Mem. Fund Q., Summer 1977.
20. Phelps, C.: *Illness prevention and medical insurance.* J. Hum. Res. 13(Suppl.):183–207, 1978.
21. Collen, M. (ed.): *Multiphasic Health Testing Services.* John Wiley & Sons, New York, 1978.
22. Wynder, E., and Arnold C.: *Mini-screening and maxi-intervention.* Int. J. Epidemiol. 7(3):199–200, 1978.
23. *Health services in Europe—1. Administration and preventive services.* WHO Chron. 30;407–412, 1976.
24. Holtzman, N.: *The goal of preventing early death,* in *Papers on the National Health Guidelines. Conditions for Change in the Health Care System. September 1977* Health Resources Administration, Washington, D.C., 1977.
25. *Assessing the Efficiency,* op. cit.
26. *Quality of Medical Care Assessment,* op. cit.
27. *Assessing the Efficiency,* op. cit.
28. Alpert, J., et al.: *Delivery of health care for children: report of experiment.* Pediatrics 57(6):917–30, 1976.
29. Sanazaro, P., and Williamson, J.: *Physician performance and its effects on patients: a classification based on reports by internists, surgeons, pediatricians, and obstetricians.* Med. Care 8:299–309, 1970.
30. Brinsden, P. R. S., and Clark, A. D.: *Postpartum haemorrhage after induced*

and spontaneous labor. Br. Med. J. 2:855–856, 1978.

31. Banta, D., and Thacker, S.: Policies toward medical technology: the case of electronic fetal monitoring. Paper presented to the American Public Health Association, Los Angeles, October 17, 1978.

32. Stanford Center for Health Care Reseach: Comparison of hospitals with regard to outcomes of surgery. Health Services Res., Summer 1976, pp. 112–127.

33. Rubsamen, D.: Medical malpractice. Sci. Am. 235:18–23, 1976.

34. Campbell, W. H., et al.: Treated adverse effects of drugs in an ambulatory population. Med. Care 15:599–608, 1977.

35. Flaksman, R., et al.: Iatrogenic prematurity due to elective termination of the uncomplicated pregnancy. Am. J. Obstet. Gynecol. 132:885–888, 1978.

36. Corea, G.: The Hidden Malpractice. Morrow, New York, 1977.

37. National Center for Health Statistics: Acute Conditions, July 1974–June 1975. Health Resources Administration, Washington, D.C., 1977.

38. Christoffel, T., and Loewenthal, M.: Evaluating the quality of ambulatory health care: a review of emerging methods. Med. Care 15:(11):877–888, 1977.

39. Data on the Medicaid Program: Eligibility, Services, Expenditures: Fiscal Years 1966–1978. Health Care Financing Administration, Washington, D.C., 1978.

40. Frankenburg, W., and North, A. E.: A Guide to Screening for EPSTD. U.S. Department of Health, Education and Welfare, Washington, D.C., 1974.

41. Luft, H. S.: How do HMOs seem to provide more health maintenance services? Milbank Mem. Fund Q. 56(2):140–165, 1978.

42. Holtzman, op. cit.

43. Measles—United States, op. cit.

44. Pearman, W. A.: Participation in flu immunization projects: what can we expect in the future? Am. J. Public Health 68(7):674–675, 1978.

45. Mushlin, A. I., et al.: Quality assurance in primary care: a strategy based on outcome assessment J. Comm. Health 3:292–305, 1978.

46. Hinds, M. W., and Gale, J. L.: Male urethritis in King County, Washington, 1974–75. II. Diagnosis and treatment. Am. J. Public Health 68:26–30, 1978.

47. Stonehill, E. H.: Impact of cancer therapy on survival. Cancer 42:1008–1014, 1978.

48. Cancer Patient Survival Report Number 5: A Report from the Cancer Surveillance, Epidemiology and End Results (SEER) Program. DHEW Publication No. (NIH) 77-992, National Cancer Institute, Bethesda, Md., 1976.

49. Mather, H. G., et al.: Myocardial infarction: a comparison between home and hospital care for patients. Br. Med. J. 1:925–929, 1976.

50. Sackett, D., and Haynes, R. (ed.): Compliance with Therapeutic Regimens. Johns Hopkins University Press, Baltimore, 1976.

51. National Center for Health Statistics: Current Estimates from the Health Interview Survey, U.S., 1976 U.S. Department of Health, Education and Welfare, Washington, D.C., 1977.

52. Health—United States, 1976–1977. Health Resources Administration, Washington, D.C., 1978.

53. Milio (1978–1979), op. cit.

54. Milio (1978), op. cit.

55. A Taxonomy of the Health System Appropriate for Plan Development. Contract No. HRA 230-76-0105, Health Resources Administration, Philadelphia, 1977.

56. Blum, H.: From a concept of health to a national health policy. Am. J. Pub-

lic Health 1:3–20, 1976.
57. *The Definition of Parameters of Efficiency in Primary Care: Report on Working Group, Reykjavik, July 14–18, 1975.* World Health Organization, Copenhagen, 1976.
58. Mahler, H.: *Promotion of primary health care in member countries of WHO.* Public Health Rep. 93(1):107, 1978.
59. Breslow, L., and Somers, A. R.: *The Lifetime Health-Monitoring Program: A Practical Approach to Preventive Medicine.* N. Engl. J. Med. 296:601–608, 1977.
60. Wallace, H. M., and Goldstein, H.: *The status of infant mortality in Sweden and the U.S.* Med. Care 87:995–1000, 1975.
61. Parker, A., et al.: *A Normative Approach to the Definition of Primary Health Care.* Milbank Mem. Fund Q., Fall 1976, pp. 415–438.
62. *Draft Model Standards for Community Preventive Health Services.* Center for Disease Control, Atlanta, 1978.
63. Eidsvold, G.: *Regionalization of organized ambulatory health services in major urban communities.* Resolution, American Public Health Association, Washington, D.C., November 1977.
64. White, K.: *American medicine.* Science, September 1975.
65. National Center for Health Statistics: *National Ambulatory Medical Care Survey: 1973–74.* U.S. Public Health Service, Washington, D.C., 1975.
66. Milio, N.: *The Care of Health in Communities: Access for Outcasts.* Macmillan, New York, 1975.
67. Scheffler, R. M., et al.: *A manpower policy for primary health care.* N. Engl. J. Med. 298;1058–1062, 1978.
68. *1977 Summary: National Ambulatory Medical Care Survey.* Advancedata 48, April 13, 1979.
69. *Physicians: A Study of Physicians' Fees.* Council on Wage and Price Stability, Washington, D.C., 1978.
70. *Skyrocketing Health Care Costs: The Role of Blue Shield.* Hearings before the Subcommittee on Oversight and Investigations of the House Committee on Interstate and Foreign Commerce, 95th Congress, Second Session, Serial No. 95-106. Washington, D.C., March 21–22; April 5–7, 1978.
71. *Supply and Distribution of Physicians and Physician Extenders.* Graduate Medical Education National Advisory Committee (GEMENAC) Staff Paper. DHEW Publication No. (HRA) 78-11. Health Resources Administration, Washington, D.C., 1978.
72. *Physician Manpower Requirements.* GEMENAC Staff Paper. Health Resources Administration, Washington, D.C., 1978.
73. Thorndike, N.: *1975 net incomes and work patterns of physicians in five medical specialties.* Research and Statistics Note No. 13. Social Security Administration, Washington, D.C., 1977.
74. Gibson, R., and Fisher, C.: *National Health Expenditures Fiscal Year 1977.* Soc. Sec. Bull. 41(7):3–20, 1978.
75. *1977 Summary,* op. cit.
76. Kriesberg, H., et al.: *Methodological Approaches for Determining Health Manpower Supply and Requirements.* Vol. 2. National Health Planning and Information Clearinghouse, Washington, D.C., 1976.
77. Comptroller General's Report to the Congress: *Are Neighborhood Health Centers Providing Services Efficiently and to the Most Needy?* General Accounting Office, Washington, D.C., 1978.

78. Milio (1975), op. cit.
79. Doyle, T., et al.: *The Impact of Health System Changes on the Nation's Requirements for Registered Nurses in 1985.* Health Resources Administration, Washington, D.C., 1978.
80. *Analysis of Physician Price and Output Decisions.* DHEW Publication No. (HRA) 77-3162. Health Resources Administration, Washington, D.C., 1977.
81. Vehorn, C. L., and Landefeld, J. S.: *Projecting health expenditures: year 2000.* Paper presented at the 106th Annual Meeting of the American Public Health Association, Los Angeles, October 15–19, 1978.
82. Mushkin, S., and Wagner, D.: *Expected mortality as a criterion in health policy evaluation. (Report No. B12).* Paper presented at the 106th Annual Meeting of the American Public Health Association, Los Angeles, October 17, 1978.
83. Newhouse, J., et al.: *Policy options and impact of NHI.* N. Engl. J. Med. 290:1345–59, 1974.
84. Luft, op. cit.
85. Kronenfeld, J.: *The great unmet need: a regular source of dental care.* Paper presented at the Annual Meetings of the American Public Health Association, Washington, D.C., October 30–November 3, 1977.
86. Hatcher, G. H.: *Canadian approaches to health policy decisions: national health insurance.* Paper presented at the 105th Annual Meeting of the American Public Health Association, Washington, D.C., October 31, 1977.
87. Kilpatrick, S. J.: *Consultation frequencies in general practice.* Health Serv. Res. 12(3):284–298, 1977.
88. Duchnok, S.: *Disability survey 72, Disabled and nondisabled adults,* in *Health Care Coverage and Medical Care Utilization, 1972.* DHEW Publication No. (SSA) 78-11717, Report No. 11. Social Security Administration, Washington, D.C., 1978.
89. Showstack, J. A., and Schroeder, S. A.: *Potential effects on a university medical center of national "catastrophic" health insurance.* Paper presented at the Annual Meetings of the American Public Health Association, Washington, D.C., November 2, 1977.
90. Broida, J. M.: *Japan's high-cost illness insurance program. A study of its first three years, 1974–76.* Public Health Rep. 93:153–160, 1978.
91. Mitchell, B. M., et al.: *Strategies for financing national health insurance: Who wins and who loses?* N. Engl. J. Med. 295:866–71, 1976.
92. Califano, J.: *Lead Agency Memorandum on a National Health Program.* Office of the Secretary, U.S. Department of Health, Education and Welfare, Washington, D.C., April 3, 1978.
93. Record, J. C., and McCabe, M.A.: *Access, quality and cost trade-offs in substituting PAs for MDs: some empirical evidence from an HMO.* Paper presented at the Annual Meetings of the American Public Health Association, Washington, D.C., October 30–November 3, 1977.
94. Berki, S.: *The economics of new types of health personnel.* Macy Conference on Intermediate-Level Health Personnel, Williamsburg, Va., November 12–14, 1972.
95. Schneider, D. P., and Foley, W. J.: *A systems analysis of the impact of physician extenders on medical cost and manpower requirements.* Med. Care 15:277–297, 1977.
96. Scheffler et al., op. cit.
97. Schweitzer, S. O., Record, J. C.: *Third-party payments for new health profes-*

sionals: an alternative to fractional reimbursement in outpatient care. Public Health Rep. 92:518–525, 1977.

98. Enterline, P. E., et al.: Physician's working hours and patients seen before and after national health insurance: "free" medical care and medical practice. Med. Care 13:95–103, 1975.

99. Willemain, T. R., and Farber, M. F.: Nursing homes and the Roemer-Feldstein hypothesis. Med. Care 14(10):880–83, 1976.

100. Goodman, L. J., et al.: Current status of group medical practice in the U.S. Public Health Rep. 92:430–443, 1977.

101. Physician Manpower Requirements, op. cit.

102. Schonfeld, H., et al.: Numbers of Physicians Required for Primary Medical Care. N. Engl. J. Med. 286:571–576, 1971.

103. Giacalone, J. J., and Hudson, J. I.: Primary care education trends in U.S. medical schools and teaching hospitals. J. Med. Ed. 52(12):971–981, 1977.

104. Pomerance, J. J., et al.: Costs of living for infant weighing 1,000 grams or less at birth. Pediatrics 61(6):908–919, 1978.

105. Dawson, P., et al.: Cost-effectiveness of screening children in housing projects. Am. J. Public Health 66:1192–95, 1976.

106. Lasdon, G. S., and Sigmann, P.: Evaluating cost-effectiveness using episodes of care. Med. Care 15:260–263, 1977.

107. National Institute on Drug Abuse: Alcohol and illicit drug use: National followup study of admissions to drug abuse treatments in the DARP during 1969–71. U.S. Public Health Service, Washington, D.C., 1977.

108. Primary Care Development Project: Prescription for Primary Health Care: A Community Guidebook. Cornell University Medical School, New York, 1976.

109. Miller, C. A., et al.: A survey of local public health departments and their directors. Am. J. Public Health 67:931–938, 1977.

110. Health Planning and Resources Development Amendments of 1978, Part 2. Hearings before the Subcommittee on Health and the Environment of the House Committee on Interstate and Foreign Commerce, 95th Congress, Second Session, H.R. 10460, Serial No. 95-94, Washington, D.C., 1978.

111. Doherty, N., and Hicks, B.: Cost effectiveness analysis and alternative health care programs for the elderly. Health Serv. Res. 12:190–203, 1977.

112. Office of Research and Statistics: Medicare: utilization of home health services, 1974. Health Insurance Statistics HI 79; No. 2, 1977.

113. Moore, F. M.: New issues for in-home services. Public Welfare, Spring 1977, pp. 26–37.

114. Development of Medical Technology, op. cit.

115. Weissert, W. G., et al.: Effects and Costs of Day Care and Homemaker Services for the Chronically Ill: A Randomized Experiment. National Center for Health Statistics Research, Washington, D.C., 1979.

116. Weissert, W. G.: Costs of adult day care: a comparison to nursing homes. Inquiry 15:10–19, March 1978.

117. McNeer, J. F..: Hospital discharge one week after acute myocardial infarction. N. Engl. J. Med. 298(5):229–232, 1978.

118. Congressional Budget Office: Working Papers on Major Budget and Program Issues in Selected Health Programs. Washington, D.C., 1976.

119. Cretin, S.: Cost/benefit analysis of treatment and prevention of myocardial infarction. Health Serv. Res. 12:174–189, 1977.

120. National Heart, Lung and Blood Institute: Respiratory Diseases—Task Force Report on Prevention, Control, Education. Division of Lung Diseases Publica-

tion No. (NIH) 77–1248, Washington, D.C., 1977.
121. Chamberlain, G.: *The maternity services.* Lancet 2:1188–1189, 1976.
122. Stason, W. B., and Weinstein, M.C.: *Allocation of Resources to Manage Hypertension.* N. Engl. J. Med. 296:732–739, 1977.
123. MacNeil, B. J., and Adelstein, S. J.: *Measures of clinical efficacy: the value of case finding in hypertensive renovascular disease.* N. Engl. J. Med. 293:221–226, 1975.
124. Editorial, *Coronary-artery surgery at the crosswinds.* N. Engl. J. Med. 297:661–663, 1977.
125. Feigenson, J., et al.: *Outcome and cost for stroke patients in academic and community hospitals.* J.A.M.A. 240(17):1878–81, 1978.
126. Sackett and Haynes, op. cit.
127. Califano, op. cit.
128. Van Pelt, A., and Levy, H.: *Cost-benefit analysis of newborn screening for metabolic disorders.* N. Engl. J. Med. 291(26):1414–18, 1974.
129. Centerwall, B. S., and Criqui, M. H.: *Prevention of the Wernicke-Korsakoff syndrome—A cost-benefit analysis.* N. Engl. J. Med. 299:285–289, 1978.
130. Kristein, M.: *Economic issues in prevention.* Prev. Med. 6:252–64, 1977.
131. Cohen, M. L., et al.: *An assessment of patient-related economic costs in an outbreak of salmonellosis.* N. Engl. J. Med. 299(9):459–460, 1978.
132. Hoos, I. R.: *Analysis of cost and benefits of health care,* in *Systems Analysis in Public Policy: A Critique.* University of California Press, Berkeley, 1972, pp. 178–192.
133. Kushner, J.: *A benefit-cost analysis of N.P. training.* Can. J. Public Health 67:405–409, 1976.
134. National Institute on Drug Abuse, op. cit.
135. Schoebaum, S. C., et al.: *The swine-influenza decision.* N. Engl. J. Med. 295:759–65, 1976.
136. Sencer, D. J., and Axnick, N. E.: *Established vaccines for regular programmes: cost benefit analysis.* (International Symposium on Vaccination Against Communicable Disease, Monaco.) Immunobiol. Standard. 22:37–46, 1973.
137. Lave, J. R., and Lave, L. B.: *Measuring the effectiveness of prevention: I.* Milbank Mem. Fund Q. 55(2):273–289, 1977.
138. Gibson, R., and Fisher, C.: *National health expenditures, fiscal year 1977.* Soc. Sec. Bull. 41(7):3–20, 1978.
139. Draper, P., et al.: *Micro-Processors, Macro-Economic Policy, and Public Health.* Lancet, February 17, 1979, pp. 373–375.
140. Doherty and Hicks, op. cit.
141. Conly, S.: *Critical Review of Research on Long-Term Care Alternatives—Executive Summary.* Project SHARE, National Clearinghouse for Improving the Management of Human Services, Rockville, Md., 1977.
142. *Profiles of Medical Practice.* American Medical Association, Chicago, 1974.
143. *1971 Survey of Dental Practice. II. Income of Dentists by Location and Other Factors.* J.A.D.A. 84:397–402, 1972.
144. Ibid.
145. Williams, C. A., et al.: *Family Nurse Practitioner Program: Feedback Report No. 3: Salary Data on UNC–Chapel Hill Family Nurse Practitioner Program Graduates Practicing in North Carolina.* University of North Carolina, Chapel Hill, 1977.
146. *Hospital Cost Containment.* Prepared by the Staff for the use of the Subcommittee on Health and the Environment of the House Committee on Interstate and For-

eign Commerce, 95th Congress, First Session, Washington, D.C., 1977.
147. Luft, H.: *National health care expenditures: Where do the dollars go?* Inquiry 13:344–63, 1976.
148. Califano, op. cit.
149. Mitchell et al., op. cit.
150. Kneese, A. V., and Schulze, W. D.: *Environmental problems: environment, health and economics—the case of cancer.* Am. Econ. Rev. 67(1):326–32, 1977.
151. Boden, L. I.: *The economic impact of environmental disease on health care delivery.* J. Occup. Med. 18(7):467–472, 1976.
152. Martini, C. J. M., et al.: *Health indexes sensitive to medical care variation.* Int. J. Health Serv. 7(2):293–309, 1977.
153. Milio (1975), op. cit.
154. National Caries Program: *Preventing Tooth Decay: A Guide for Implementing Self-Applied Fluoride in Schools. Part I: Cost Benefit Analysis Technical Paper.* Alcohol, Drug Abuse, and Mental Health Administration, Washington, D.C., 1977.
155. Cuzacq, G., and Glass, R.: *The projected financial savings in dental restorative treatment: the result of consuming fluoridated water.* J. Public Health Dentistry 32(1):52–57, 1972.
156. Ast, D. B., et al.: *Time and cost factors to provide regular, periodic dental care for children in a fluoridated and nonfluoridated area: Final report.* J.A.D.A. 80:770–776, 1970.
157. *Symposium on Environmental Effects of Sulfur Oxides and Related Particulates.* (Sponsored by the Subcommittee on Public Health Aspects of Energy and the Committee on Public Health of the New York Academy of Medicine, March 23–24, 1978.) Bull. N.Y. Acad. Med. 54(11), 1978.
158. Lave, L. B., and Seskin, E. P.: *An analysis of the association between U.S. mortality and air pollution.* J. Am. Stat. Assoc. 68(342):284–290, 1973.
159. Smith, V. K.: *The Economic Consequences of Air Pollution: Resources for the Future.* Ballinger, Cambridge, Mass., 1976.
160. Environmental Protection Agency: *Health Consequences of Sulfur Oxides: Summary and Conclusions Based upon Chess Studies of 1970–71.* EPA Publication No. 650/1-74-004. Research Triangle Park, N.C., 1974.
161. *Health evaluation of energy-generating sources.* J.A.M.A. 240(20):2193–2195, 1978.
162. Brown, S., et al.: *Effect on mortality of the 1974 fuel crisis.* Nature 257(5524):306–307, 1975.
163. *Safe Drinking Water Act of 1974.* New York Times, June 21, 1977.
164. Kraybill, H.: *Carcinogenesis induced by trace contaminants in potable water.* Bull. N.Y. Acad. Med. 54(4):413–427, 1978.
165. *Hazard Analysis Related to Bicycles.* U.S. Consumer Product Safety Commission, Bureau of Epidemiology, Washington, D.C., 1973.
166. Craun, G. F., and McCabe, L. J.: *Review of the causes of waterborne disease outbreaks.* J. Am. Water Works Assoc. 65(1):74–84, 1973.
167. Holtzman, op. cit.
168. Zylman, R.: *A critical evaluation of the literature on 'alcohol involvement' in highway deaths.* Accident Anal. Prev. 6:163–204, 1974.
169. National Institute on Alcohol Abuse and Alcoholism: *Information Features Service.* Washington, D.C., 1977.
170. National Institute on Alcohol Abuse and Alcoholism: *Information Features Service.* Washington, D.C., 1976.

171. National Institute on Alcohol Abuse and Alcoholism: *Information Features Service.* Washington, D.C., 1978.
172. Robertson, L.: *Estimates of motor vehicle seat belt effectiveness and use: implications for occupant crash protection.* Am. J. Public Health 66(9):859–864, 1976.
173. Duvall, D., and Booth A.: *The housing environment and women's health.* J. Health Social. Behav. 19:410–417, 1978.
174. Holma, B., and Winding, O.: *Housing, hygiene and health: a study in old residential areas in Copenhagen.* Arch Environ. Health 32:86–93, 1977.
175. National Center for Health Statistics: *Current Estimates from the Health Interview Survey, 1973–1974.* U.S. Department of Health, Education and Welfare, Washington, D.C., 1975.
176. Barry, P.: *Individual versus community orientation in the prevention of injuries.* Prev. Med. 4:47–56, 1975.
177. Brenner, M. H.: *Health Costs and Benefits of Economic Policy.* Int. J. Health Serv. 7:581–623, 1977.
178. Dorfman, R.: *Incidence of the Benefits and Costs of Environmental Programs.* Am. Econ. Rev. 67(1):331–341, 1977.
179. *Symposium on Environmental Effects of Sulfur Oxides,* op. cit.
180. Grabowski, H., and Vernon, J.: *Consumer product safety regulation.* Am. Econ. Rev. 68(2):284–89, 1978.
181. Senate Select Committee on Nutrition and Human Needs: *Dietary Goals for the United States.* ed. 2. Washington, D.C., 1977.
182. Winikoff, B.: *Impact of change in American diet on health.* Paper presented at the Lifestyle and Health Conference, San Francisco, January 1979.
183. Marston, R.: *Nutrient content of the national food supply.* Natl. Food Rev. 5:28–33, 1978.
184. Milio (1978–1979), op. cit.
185. Passmore, R., et al.: *Prescription for a better British diet.* Br. Med. J. 1:527–531, 1979.
186. Wilson, R.: *National Center for Health Statistics, Testimony before Regional Forum sponsored by the National Commission for Smoking and Public Policy,* Philadelphia, June 16, 1977.
187. Kleinman, J., et al.: *The effects of changes in smoking habits on Coronary Heart Disease Mortality.* Paper presented at the National Heart, Blood and Lung Institute Conference, October 25, 1978. National Center for Health Statistics, Washington, D.C., 1979.
188. *Fatty acids and ischemic heart-disease.* Lancet, May 27, 1978, pp. 1146–1147.
189. Glueck, C. J., et al.: *Diet and coronary heart disease: another view.* N. Engl. J. Med. 298(26):1471–1474, 1978.
190. Stamler, J., in Carlson, R. (ed.): *Future Directions in Health Care. A New Public Policy.* Ballinger, Cambridge, Mass., 1978, pp. 95–135.
191. Kannel, W. B., and Gordon, T.: *The effects of overweight on cardiovascular diseases.* Geriatrics 28:80–88, 1973.
192. Bennion, L., and Grundy, S.: *Risk factors for the development of cholelithiasis in man.* N. Engl. J. Med. 299(22):1221–23, 1978.
193. *Health—United States, 1976–1977,* op. cit.
194. George, T., and King, G.: *Consumer Demand for Food Commodities in the U.S.* California Agricultural Experiment Station, Giannini Fund Monograph No. 26, March 1971; *Food Prices in Perspective: A Summary Analysis.* Publication No. ESCS-53, U.S. Department of Agriculture, 1979; Salathe, L.: *Household expen-*

diture patterns in the United States. Technical Bulletin No. 1603, U.S. Department of Agriculture, 1979.

195. Meyers, W., and Hacklander, D.: *Vulnerability of soybean and product markets to key supply and demand variables.* Fats and Oils Situation, No. 295, May 1979; Miller, R.: *Estimated economic returns attributable to U.S. tobacco and tobacco products.* U.S. Department of Agriculture, 1978.

196. Milio (1978–1979), op. cit.

197. U.S. Department of Commerce: *Survey of Current Business* 57(7), 1977.

198. Bureau of the Census: *Recent social and economic trends,* in *Statistical Abstracts of the United States, 1977.*

199. *State Farm Income Statistics* (Suppl.), Statistical Bulletin No. 576. U.S. Department of Agriculture, Washington, D.C., 1977.

200. Milio (1978–1979), op. cit.

201. Ibid.

202. Bureau of the Census: *Statistics for States and Metropolitan Areas.* U.S. Department of Commerce, Washington, D.C., 1977.

203. Ibid.

204. U.S. Department of Labor: Data printouts on employment by SIC code, January 1979.

205. Office of Management and Budget: *Standard Industrial Classification Manual.* Washington, D.C., 1972.

206. Bureau of the Census: *Farm Payroll and Employment, 1974.* U.S. Department of Commerce, Washington, D.C., 1979.

207. Bureau of the Census: *Annual Survey of Manufacturers.* U.S. Department of Commerce, Washington, D.C., 1978.

208. Bureau of Labor Statistics: *Employment and Earnings.* Vol. 22, No. 9, March 1976.

209. Bureau of Labor Statistics: *Employment and Earnings.* Vol. 24, December 1977.

210. Milio (1978–1979), op. cit.

211. *Cost Components of Farm-Retail Price Spreads.* Agricultural Economic Report No. 391 Economic Research Service, U.S. Department of Agriculture, Washington, D.C., 1977.

212. Marston, op. cit.

213. Banks, V.: *Farm Population Trends ad Farm Characteristics.* Report No. 3. U.S. Department of Agriculture, Washington, D.C., 1978.

214. *Energy Policy and Strategy for Rural Development.* Senate Committee on Agriculture Hearings, July 13–14, 1977, Part I. Washington, D.C., 1977.

215. Van Arsdall, R., and Devlin, P.: *Energy Policies: Price Impacts on the U.S. Food System.* Economic Report No. 407. U.S. Department of Agriculture, Washington, D.C., 1978.

216. Chapman, D.: *Taxation, Energy Use and Employment.* Department of Agricultural Economics, Cornell University, Ithaca, New York, 1978.

217. *Small-scale farmers: a unique set of problems?* Farm Index, March 1979, pp. 12–14.

218. Leach, G., et al.: *A Low Energy Strategy for the United Kingdom.* International Institute for Environment and Development, London, 1979.

219. General Accounting Office: *The Rising Cost of Food.* Washington, D.C., 1978.

220. Foreign Agricultural Service: *FATUS.* U.S. Department of Agriculture, Washington, D.C., 1978.

221. Manfredi, E.: *Agriculture's contribution to the balance of payments,* in *World Economic Conditions in Relation to Agricultural Trade.* U.S. Department of Agriculture, Washington, D.C., 1978.

222. World Bank: *Annual Report*. International Bank for Research and Development, Washington, D.C., 1978.
223. Triffin, R.: *The international role of the dollar*. Foreign Affairs, Winter 1978/79.
224. *Ashes to ashes, fat to fat*. The Economist (London), December 17, 1977, p. 58.
225. Karpoff, E.: *EC commission reviews milk dilemma*. Foreign Agriculture, December 11, 1978, pp. 13–16.
226. *Europe's agriculture*. The Economist (London), March 18, 1978, pp. 82–83.
227. World Bank, op. cit.
228. Weisburger, J., Gori, G., Schottenfeld, D., and Hegsted, M.: Review articles on cancer and nutrition. Cancer (Suppl.) 43, May 1979.
229. *Preventing Disease, Promoting Health. Objectives for the Nation*. Working Papers, U.S. Public Health Service, Washington, D.C., 1979.
230. Stamler, J., in Carlson, R. (ed.): *Future Directions in Health Care*. Ballinger, Cambridge, Mass., 1978.
231. Milio (1978–1979), op. cit.
232. Ast et al., op. cit.

273

12

DETERMINING THE PROSPECTS
FOR HEALTH

If the health of Americans is their response to the interlinked dimensions of their environments, then policy that helps create those environments has a health-important dimension. If health is inextricable from its environmental origins, then health policy cannot be separated from other major areas of policy. Prospects for significant improvements in the health of Americans depend on the attention that people give to "non-health" policies.

The healthy responses of individuals—their capacity to respond to circumstances in ways that enable them to pursue their chosen round of life without personal restrictions—depend upon the choices of policy-makers in government and corporations. These decisions now create the probabilities for the achievement of clean air, sound housing, stable and safe jobs, and adequate income and food supplies. These policies affect the distribution of health-promoting resources and the concentrations of health-damaging conditions. They therefore affect the odds that families will encounter uncertainties about their livelihood, creating, in turn, interpersonal strains. These large-scale policies shape the likelihood that people who face problems that are beyond their resources can get help—whether the problems result from illness, unemployment, lack of food, or inadequate information. They also determine the relative effectiveness of that help as they shape such options as those that will influence health services and profitable farm production.

In this view, the most salient health strategies are those that affect the larger dimensions of environment—the biophysical and socioeconomic conditions of workplaces, homes, and communities. These measures set forth and define the boundaries of the possible. Supportive strategies, such as educational information and personal services, are effective only when they help people do what is possible within their environments. These supportive efforts are thus effective within the context of policies that create enabling environments. By themselves they are dubious and often "band-aid" efforts.

If health policy is to make health, it must rely on environmental strategies, and must plan and deploy supportive strategies in tandem, such as worker education in the context of the legal and regulatory structure of the Occupational Health and Safety Act; or the detection of risk factors and health education in the context of a more nutritional national farm supply; or admonitions for energy conservation alongside the development of safe, renewable energy supplies. To do otherwise is to invite failure, cynicism, and resentment by the public.

Even though there are great difficulties in evaluating the health effects of public policy, and in estimating the costs of changing to more health-promoting policies, the nation's capacity to develop this kind of information is far greater than that which is currently used or apparently contemplated. At the same time, far-reaching policies with health-important consequences are continuously made, based on information far less sound, as the following sections will show.

The costs and benefits resulting from changes in policy are, of course, inevitable. The only matters in question are how large they will be and who are to be the "gainers" and "losers." The answer to whether "benefits" outweigh "costs" depends on whether all the costs and gains are made explicit; whether they are compared with policy alternatives, and, if so, with which ones; and how all of this is perceived—by the public, by those who have vested interests in things as they are, and by policy-makers. The determination of policies that are "feasible" depends on people's awareness of the full costs and gains, and the specific gainers. More importantly, it centers on identifying which groups among potential gainers and losers can effectively enter the process of weighing costs and gains, and of making the final judgment.

MAKING HEALTH AND MAKING POLICY

This section will attempt to interpret some of the political issues involved in the development of health-making policy. These are the issues that will finally determine the health prospects for Americans. In a real sense, as earlier discussions have shown, one of the most health-important aspects of modern environments is public policy. Therefore, attention to how it is formulated is an inseparable part of health-making efforts. In what follows,

276

the consequences of a deferral of health-making are first pointed out in a scenario based on a recent and extensive forecast of health care costs. The study assumes only modest changes in current policy. Then an assessment is made of the ingredients of the policy-shaping process, and of the relative influence of those who favor present courses of action.

The analysis of some of the ways by which policy is influenced suggests strategies which might also be employed in the health interests of the public. This involves organized action and the necessary related resources to involve the public effectively and directly in health policy decisions. These issues are examined within the context of health systems agencies (HSAs). Also considered is a complementary strategy for assuring that the health interests of the public are adequately represented at the national level, where direct participation is not possible. The strategic political problem for health-making here centers on how to make health-promoting policy choices easier—meaning less "costly"—for policy-makers than they are at present.

Options and Choices, Gainers and Losers

There is no "free" choice. This has been shown throughout these chapters in relation to individuals and social groups, consumers and producers, employees and administrators, as well as organizations and governments. There is only choice within a limited number of options, and there is only a greater or lesser awareness of this reality. At issue is not whether options will be restricted, but rather what the array of options will be, how many there will be, and how broadly available they will be to various societal groups.

Corporations and other organizations are far more conscious than individuals of the nature of their options and of how these affect their survival and viability. They have far more resources, including money, staff, and information sources, both to discover the limits of their options and to make the gains-for-cost calculations to guide their choices—choices which become, in effect, corporate policy. Individuals, in their personal lives, do most of this implicitly, often valuing intangible, noneconomic, nonpolitical gains more highly than concrete, objective advances, sometimes at the cost of survival.

The counterpart of individual "free choice" or "voluntarism," in the societal arena, is the espousal of a "free market" economy, unrestricted by government "interference," unfettered by limited options for selling and buying. In reality, of course, both agriculture and industry have long sought and fought to maintain market controls through government policy, in order to limit the options of competitors and reduce the risks to profit-making, if not the risks to people's health. In other words, the U.S. economy has long since opted for a "non-free" market, just as the public has long supported policy to restrict certain kinds of personal behavior. Just who has been affected, and in what ways, by these public policies has depended on which groups were able to influence the formulation of policy, as the following discussion will show.

The broadening and restricting of options for organizations and individuals—the very essence of public policy—are increasingly pervasive realities in modern life. In the policy-making process the basic issues that will shape prospects for American health are contained in two questions: How health-promoting or health-damaging will the options be? And, which groups will gain, and which lose, in health and wealth? The issue is not one of either/or, but rather one that is measured by the degree to which policy puts the nation's resources where its rhetoric is.

The Public Forum

The foregoing issues are relevant and timely inclusions in the public forum for two basic reasons. The first is that for at least the next two decades public policy will continue to expand in scope, and major policy shifts will occur in order to address urgent, fundamental, and worldwide problems which are the result of traditional policy, namely, energy and food supplies, and environmental protection. Second, these issues enter the broader public arena at a time when health and the provision of health services have become controversial public issues as a result of failures by the private sector that were remedied only piecemeal through Federal funds. Now that escalating health care costs can no longer be ignored, the debate over how best to deal with health problems is somewhat more open to the public.

All of these issues that are basic to survival and welfare, and that require significant policy changes, are now in the public forum. There is, in consequence, at least the possibility that the policy shifts that will almost inevitably emerge can be designed to be more health-making than in the past. At a minimum, whatever the changes in policy, they can be called to account to the public interest. The array of options that these policy changes set for all groups of people will shape the prospects for health in the decades ahead.

A NONPREVENTION SCENARIO

If policy for dealing with modern health continues along its present, traditional course, the consequences for the turn of the century can be predicted. A highly sophisticated and careful forecasting study has shown what could occur in the year 2000.[1] Very briefly, it predicted that the total economic costs of illness, adjusted for inflation and discounted at both high and low rates, would be over twice those of 1975. This estimate encompasses both the cost of health care and the economic loss in production from disability and death. Health care costs alone would be about 11 to 12 percent of the gross national product, or almost 50 percent higher than in the mid-1970s.

These costs would result from changes in patterns of illness and death. According to the panel of experts involved in the study, expected improvements in health care would be countered by increases in environmental pollution, including toxic chemicals, and by increases in smoking and alcohol consumption, especially among women, who would also be more exposed to the stresses of the work-for-pay world. Thus there would be higher rates of heart and respiratory disease, and of liver cirrhosis, most of the increases occurring among women. A larger share of all deaths would result from heart disease and cancer, even though the total death rate is expected to remain about the same as in the mid-1970s.

Because more of the population will be in the work force, the nonmedical costs of illness, resulting from lost productivity, will be sharply higher. However, medical costs will rise at an even faster rate so that they will become 50 percent of the total cost to society of the impact of illness and death. By comparison, medical costs were a third of the total economic costs of illness in 1975, and only 11 percent of total societal costs in 1900.

Another way to say this is that the cost of treating illness is increasing far faster than the productive capacity of the nation. The total costs of illness, both for health care and in productivity losses, are becoming an increasing economic burden, and are doing so at an accelerating rate. These enlarging costs result mainly from growing amounts of chronic illness and lengthening spans of associated disability. Americans increasingly enter their later years of life with disabling illness compounded by an extended life span.

This economic picture of the future is the cost of *not* preventing the kinds of illness which derive from contemporary life. Its dismal nature does not even include the costs to individual and social relations which would also be incurred. This prospect could well be obviated if the nation were to undertake to achieve in two decades the health improvements that other affluent countries have made in the last decade, through policies which could reduce heart and cancer deaths by at least 25 to 35 percent, and possibly by as much as 75 to 80 percent.[2]

Deferred Health-Making and Its Consequences

This scenario of entry into the new century has grave implications beyond the economic and human costs involved. It presents an irony that foretells even more discouraging prospects for health, well into the twenty-first century. For as medical costs assume an increasing share of the total costs of illness, there may be relatively less economic justification for attempting to achieve the primary prevention of illness. This is because, as noted above, the *relative* costs in productivity, stemming from work loss, will become less, and because the ever-looming costs of medical care will impel immediate short-term efforts to contain costs within the delivery system. At the same time, the health care industry enlarges—in facilities, personnel, suppliers, and insurers—expanding the vested interest in continuing policies which emphasize the secondary prevention, or control, of health problems. Furthermore, viewed from the perspective of the national economy, and its profit-making sector in particular, an enlarging personal health care system is actually adding to the gross national product. In the absence of effective public funding, it is increasing the output of goods and services through its "sales" of services, insurance, and drugs, and its investments in facilities and equipment. Thus the longer this policy direction, emphasizing a personal care health strategy, is allowed to continue, the more those who gain economically will increase their material interest in it. Changing course may therefore become more difficult politically.

A major moderating influence in this scenario is that even if public funds were to assume increasing responsibility for health care financing, pressures would still arise from the private business sector to contain health care costs, conceivably through primary prevention strategies. For in order to pay the public bill, money would be sought in taxes or through deficit financing in competition with private borrowing. Such pressures, however, may be modest because private profit-making as well as nonprofit health care providers, suppliers, and insurers increasingly benefit from public health care financing.[3,4]

Thus the prospects for the public's health are unfavorable so long as health policy focuses almost totally on the provision of personal health services with their limited efficacy for the primary prevention of modern illness (see Chapters 9 and 11).[5,6] Time will further strengthen the economic justification and influence of vested interests for perpetuating current policy thrusts, albeit with certain modifications.[7-15]

Continuing the current approach to health policy is also likely to see another set of circumstances that may further deter the use of health-making, primary prevention strategies. For as the American population grows older, as more people enter the later years of life with chronic disabilities, and as more in the mid-life decades succumb to chronic disease, their numbers become a political force opposed to shifting resources into primary preventive, socioenvironmental policies. Rather, their interests collectively must lie in secondary prevention efforts, emphasizing programs which will attempt to contain and control the illness that exists. In essence, if the well do not support true health-making strategies, they will become ill sooner and will be more likely to support the perpetuation of illness-control strategies.

Postponement, then, of the development of a balanced health policy that encompasses socioenvironmental, as well as personal care, strategies may make it less likely to happen over the next few decades. For delay may diminish the economic impetus and political support that are essential to shifting toward a health-making, rather than just a health care, policy.

THE SHAPING OF POLICY DIRECTIONS

Status Quo Forces

The array of groups that are likely to continue to support the current approach to health policy, either by intent or default, is indeed impressive. The basis for influencing policy decisions is to reach the Federal and Congressional sources of public policy with the right information at the right time. The message may be systematically or scientifically based and relatively unbiased. It may be simply a message which, subtly or otherwise, threatens the political survival of policy-makers.

INFORMATION IN THE POLITICAL PROCESS

The systematic data which policy-makers use for their health-important decisions, as already suggested, tend to be flawed by a lack of comprehensive scope, limited analyses, and the fragmented mechanisms for gathering information among the various bureaucracies.[16-18] This is compounded by the absence of any single center of responsibility, much less of authority, to integrate health-relevant information and analyze its implications either in the Executive Branch or in Congress.[19,20] There is little consistency or monitoring of priorities for publicly funded, health-related research, of criteria to evaluate data, or of funding to complete useable studies.[21-26]

The use of available information is also limited because of the way it is presented. Often the language, format, qualifying statements, and vague conclusions are more appropriate to academic readers than to policy-makers or the general public.[27] Policy officials have appealed to university analysts to speak out clearly, early, and in understandable, policy-relevant ways, translating their never-perfect findings for use in the public forum.[28,29] Many scientists and analysts, in their praiseworthy zeal for precision, may dismiss the fact that policy is made, of necessity, on the basis of that which

281

is brought to the policy-makers' attention. This is the reality, in spite of the limitations of the data or their sources, whether they come from intelligence agencies, manufacturers, or universities.

The ad hoc nature of health-information analysis and its use in policy-making, scattered among Congressional committees and government agencies, provides maximum advantage for special interest groups. It increases the likelihood that they can influence policy formulation, implementation, and interpretation.[30-41] There is little question that most of the information used in policy decisions comes from special interests, either within or outside government agencies. Some of it may be systematically collected data, interpreted from a vested interest perspective. Other data have been intentionally misleading. Much information is of a persuasive, politically related type.[42,43]

At issue is not the right of different groups to present different interpretations of problems, data, or policies, or to air these differences. Rather the problem centers on the consequences for the health interests of the public that occur when public issues are defined by special interests and pursued by them in the policy-making process. It is a matter of record that under these circumstances, issues are defined in narrow terms, and policy is effectively set through behind-the-scenes Committee lobbying. This serves the interests of a small group, or even of individual Congressional members.[44,45]

LOBBYING AND ELECTIONEERING

With the emergence of health in the policy arena, new groups have been formed, and others reinvigorated with new funds, to influence the course of events. These have come to include the largest auto, energy, drug, chemical, food processing, and insurance companies. Such interest groups have been especially active in recent years. They formed an alliance to "preserve the private market in health services" and keep their "economic interests protected."[46,47] Soft drink manufacturers funded a Calories Control Council to oppose the ban on saccharin. Candy and sweets sellers acted to thwart controls on advertising and sales to children. Dairy interests and commodity associations fought reductions in price supports, and tobacco manufacturers opposed anti-smoking initiatives.[48-54] In a not uncommon gesture of collaboration, a Congressional tobacco subcommittee chairman held hearings for the express purpose of bringing in leaders from related industries to seek their support for public policy to promote the tobacco industry.[55]

Since these trade associations are chartered as nonprofit, tax-exempt organizations—allowing their corporate members to enjoy a 50 percent tax deduction for dues payments—they became subject to the 1976 lobbying reforms.[56] This legislation, aimed at controlling lobbying excesses, was nevertheless unable to prevent a doubling of the number of paid lobbyists in the Capitol during the mid-1970s.[57,58]

Probably of greater importance to policy formulation than the influence of lobbies was the attempt in the early 1970s to correct political campaign abuses. The principal means was to limit the size of monetary contributions to candidates in national elections. As an unforeseen effect, the influence of the more powerful special interests was strengthened. At the same time, the major political parties were splintered further than before, making policy-consensus ever less likely.[59] What happened was that as a result of legislation limiting the amount of funding per candidate by a single source, Political Action Committees (PACs) on behalf of candidates proliferated. This process effectively bypassed party organizations and concomitantly lessened their power to command the loyalty of Congressional members. PACs sprang forth from a single-interest groups, including hospitals for the first time, and from labor unions and business corporations, more than quadrupling in the mid-1970s.[60] Their growth among corporations was fastest, outstripping labor PACs by more than two to one and still accelerating in the late 1970s.[61]

The strategy of the PACs is to focus on individual candidates, especially committee chairpersons and members of committees relevant to their interests. They offer attractive contributions to election campaigns, often to candidates from both major parties. As a result, spending per candidate more than doubled between the 1976 and 1978 Congressional elections. There was an emphasis on financing *incumbents,* with four to five times as much support given to those whose records show votes favoring the interest groups who financed their elections.[62-65] The well-known leader in this political strategy is the American Medical Association. The same practices hold for labor groups, agricultural associations, and other industrial producers.[66]

A DECLINING PUBLIC VOICE

This mushrooming of political activity by special interests comes at a time when there is a decline in participation by the public in the political process. Fewer people register to vote, and fewer still vote. Only 35 percent of those who were eligible voted in the 1978 Congressional elections.[67,68] Nonvoters say their vote does not matter.[69] Among those who do vote, less advantaged groups—blacks, the poor, elders, women—say they have too little influence. They are not confident that the leaders of either major party would act in their economic interests, or otherwise represent their views in policy-making.[70]

Over the last decade, many Americans have come to believe that they have ever less control over improving their incomes, their retirement security, their neighborhoods, or the adequacy of their medical care. More than

283

two-thirds think government should do more in these areas. They are willing to pay more taxes for policies that would stabilize their income and employment, and provide necessary community services.[71-74]

Judging from these surveys, it is as though disillusionment with the political process and discouragement over economic problems have engendered a sense of personal powerlessness which, paradoxically, brings many Americans to seek government leadership as a last resort. Nevertheless, two-thirds are not using the national electoral process to voice their appeal. They may be a so-called "unshaped force" which can be mobilized around ad hoc issues in volatile fashion.[75] This is perhaps part of the reason for the emergence of many small, vocal, specifically focused single-interest groups that were not identified with any political party. The success of these groups, as with most special interests whose constituencies are limited, is mainly a matter of their veto power. They are more likely to successfully stop policy changes than to initiate policies, especially ones with health-making potential.[76,77]

The diffuseness and pessimism of the general public allow greater influence in policy-making by organized and powerful special interests. The effect is that the voice of the producers and providers of goods and services is most often heard, is clearly articulated, and is well-represented in public policy-making arenas. This voice, however, excludes both a majority of consumers and of the labor force.[78-81] Since the interests of the producers lie in preserving the options which they currently enjoy, it is doubtful that they would freely give support to policy shifts to remedy health-damaging excesses and deficits for Americans.

Mass Media Mediation

Special interest groups may influence policy-making in other, less direct ways than through lobbying and electoral campaigns. They often use the communications media, which can affect policy formulation in several ways.

PRODUCER TACTICS AND PUBLIC OPINION

The most obvious use of the media by providers of goods and services is, of course, commercial advertising. Almost a fourth of all advertising is now done through the broadcast and print media. Of that, over half of the more than $10 billion spent in 1977 went for television commercials, and over a third for newspaper and magazine advertisements.[82-84] As a major source of mass media profits, commercial advertisers influence editorial views on issues such as restrictions on advertising, especially at the local level.[85]

Advertising of products does more than influence American consumption habits. It calls attention to specific options, the most profitable ones, to

284

absorb the additions to people's disposable incomes. It conveys a message of the desirable. Of about $11 billion spent annually in the early 1970s on food, alcohol, tobacco, and drug advertising, less than a fourth was for foods, and, of that, more was spent to sell soft drinks, candy, and snacks than to promote sales of bread, cereals, meat, and fish combined.[86-89] Almost 90 percent of food industry advertising is done on television, and over a third of drug promotion.

Although adult buying habits and opinions are influenced by TV commercials, children, who are not yet discriminating consumers, are much more influenced. They, in turn, attempt to persuade parents of the values extolled in some 10,000 to 14,000 food, drink, and drug commercials which they view on television each year.[90,91]

The effects of commercial advertising on public opinion go beyond its persuasiveness concerning the good life. Its subtle impact involves the impression that it conveys of offering wide varieties of choice to consumers when, in fact, the choice may be limited to packaging variations, notably among drug, tobacco, and food products.[92-94] Of greater significance is the possibility that to the extent that buying habits, and in turn personal behavior patterns, are influenced by advertising, people develop, as time passes, a rationale, a set of values or beliefs, affirming the things they do (see Chapter 5). As a result, they are likely to espouse these beliefs and views in public opinion polls, the listening posts increasingly used by both political candidates and elected officials.[95,96]

A major distinction between advertising and public information or education, health-related or otherwise, is in their principal purpose. Advertising seeks to persuade people to buy a specific item, or accept a specific slogan, and it focuses on targeted groups of people who have growing incomes and thus the means for making new choices. The *forte* of advertising is not in getting people to *change* their habits, but rather in "capturing" those segments of the population that are *ready to develop* new habits, such as youth and new entrants to the job market. In contrast, public education seeks to alter people's choices by presenting them with a broader picture of the effects of certain activities—not only the most appealing or immediate effects—sometimes by means of comparing them with alternatives. Ideally, this should foster a more critical attitude on the public's part toward what they do or what they espouse, and so promote choices that have more beneficial consequences. The limited persuasiveness of both advertising and health education, in and of themselves, was discussed in Chapters 5 and 7.

However one may conjecture about the effects of advertising on public opinion, there is no mistaking the purpose of special interests in a more direct strategy for opinion-molding through the media. The drug, sugar, cereal, and tobacco industries, among others, have in recent years attempted to impress their views on influential groups. They explicitly direct their messages to opinion leaders: health professionals and especially physicians, science writers, and broadcast news reporters. This is done by means of special "news services" or information centers; by arranging small conferences, seminars, or briefings; by publishing journals for select audiences; by setting up expert panels for television; by participating in talk shows; by placing stories in magazines; and by providing free samples, audiovisual materials, and press releases.[97-103]

INFORMATION SOURCES

The significance of this targeting strategy for public opinion becomes clear in view of the way adult Americans get their information. For health information, people turn to physicians as their most important source, and appear to have a high level of confidence in what they are told. Television and the press are second in importance, but less than a third of adults consider them to be "very reliable" for health advice.[104-106]

The most common sources of general information are the mass media, and television in particular, which is now a part of the households of 95 percent of the population. Most people buy daily papers, yet 97 percent of the towns they live in have only one daily, and almost two-thirds of all newspapers are owned by large publishing houses. Most small papers carry the syndicated views of only a few commentators, and reproduce the editorials of the large presses and two major wire services. Moreover, most communities have access to no more than three or four televised networks.[107]

This composite picture of mass communications leads to the inevitable conclusion that independent sources of information for most Americans are very few. The potential influence on the public of special interests that target their messages is therefore quite impressive. Even so, national surveys taken in 1976 reported that the public believed less than a third of what it saw on television, and far less of what it read in the newspapers.[108]

INFORMATION FRAGMENTS AND THE PUBLIC'S VIEWS

The national surveys that show a growing sense of public powerlessness and disenchantment become increasingly understandable when Americans are seen to be left holding a great deal of information that they see as unreliable and, thus, unuseable. With a base of knowledge that is so uncertain there can be little consistency of public opinion, clarity of purpose, or decisiveness on objectives and courses of action. As a result there is little foundation for people to evaluate the judgments of elected officials and other policy-makers, or to assess the competing claims of special interests.

Conflicting views reach the public in staccato fashion. When, for example, the organized agricultural commodity groups—the sugar, corn, and tobacco growers—each lobby for Federal subsidies, on what basis can Americans judge what is in the public interest? Shall there be subsidies? If so, for which commodities? Of what kind? With what effects?[109] Producers seek price supports which are passed on as higher consumer prices. They oppose subsidy payments to make up for low market prices, which can be controlled by Congressional appropriation and financed more equitably by all taxpayers.[110-115] The National Heart, Lung and Blood Institute recommends a phase-out of tobacco price supports and of tax deductions for cigarette manufacturers.[116] Producer interests oppose a uniform national cigarette tax even though the evidence shows that unequalized taxes promote smuggling, law enforcement problems, and an overall net loss of $335 million to the public purse.[117] The views of special interests are often further promoted by various administrative units within the Federal bureaucracy, with whom they have almost inevitable patron-client program relationships.[118-120]

All such conflicting views, condensed and filtered to the public through the mass media, are not likely to get, and indeed cannot be given, critical evaluation by the vast majority of the public. Furthermore, public hearings and public information from other sources, whatever the quantity, often set forth single-interest perspectives. Whether these views are competing or consonant, they are difficult, if not impossible, to evaluate in the public interest without a broader context that can suggest their implications.

This problem exists for the public and for well-intentioned officials and media people as well. There are few ready means for them to become aware, for example, of the relationship between some producer subsidies and the costs of health and illness in America, much less of the possible alternatives to current patterns. Under present policy development practices, how can the small Southern tobacco farmer react in any but a negative way to proposals to discourage cigarette smoking?

Signals of Change

CONGRESSIONAL PERSPECTIVES

As was detailed in Chapter 10, there is a growing realization in some circles of the nature of these policy development issues. In an effort to provide a more comprehensive view of national priorities and the use of national resources, the Congress instituted a biennial budget process in the mid-1970s. Its analytic arm, the Congressional Budget Office, has attempted to provide broad, accurate, and balanced studies for economic policy planning, as is its mandate.[121] A newer information-gathering arm of the Congress, the Office of Technology Assessment, has among its purposes the evaluation of current and alternative ways to enhance the national interest in such areas as national security, environmental protection, and the health of Americans. At the end of the decade, one of its priorities was to assess health promotion and disease prevention technologies, ranging from the efficacy, safety, and acceptability of biofeedback and small group behavioral techniques to the economic impact of a major reduction in smoking.[122]

Other Congressional directives went to Federal agencies in the late 1970s to develop a comprehensive environmental monitoring system, a system for continuous surveillance of Americans' nutritional status, and a system for combining data on nutrition and overall health. Congress also required the agencies concerned with environmental protection, occupational safety and health, consumer product safety, and food and drugs to coordinate their efforts through an Interagency Liaison Regulatory Group.[123] In another attempt to avoid ad hoc solutions, it authorized the Federal Trade Commission to adopt industry-wide rule-making patterns, rather than regulating advertising on an item-by-item basis.[124] The Congress has also begun to recognize, in drafting farm legislation, the interrelationships of crops and their production, supply management, and prices, and the need to balance the interests of consumers alongside producers and Federal program costs.[125,126]

Additional efforts to grasp the broad consequences of policy decisions include an increasing use of "impact" statements relating to environmental, economic, and armament issues, as well as the future of the family. As yet, however, the health impact of economic, military, energy, health care, agricultural, income, and other social policies has not been proposed as a part of public policy planning.

The end of the 1970s saw new proposals for the public financing of Congressional elections. This was an acknowledgment of the way in which policy formation is stymied by the fragmenting effect of myriad interest group influences on election campaigning. Proposals called for funds to be dispersed to candidates through party organs, rather than personal campaign committees. This would favor the future adherence of those who were elected to party discipline over loyalties to special interests.[127]

THE FEDERAL BUREAUCRACY

These Congressional signs of a somewhat more comprehensive and coherent approach to policy-making had at least potential for enhancing the interests of the public. There were also some comparable moves by Federal agencies. The Secretary of Agriculture, for example, acknowledged that farm and food supply legislation ought to be based on a national policy reflecting the nutritional needs of Americans, with compensatory means to allow everyone to obtain what they need.[128] This was similar to recommendations made six years earlier, calling for a joint health-agricultural policy, by the Department of Health, Education and Welfare, the Congress, and the National Academy of Sciences. They were ignored by the White House.[129,130]

The Food and Drug Administration moved more actively in the late 1970s to protect the safety of the national food supply. It also opened the regulation-setting process to public view.[131] The Federal Trade Commission turned to food advertising and price issues, to the health consequences to children of advertising, and to the lack of adequate options for those who do not want to eat processed foods.[132] It acted against restrictions on advertising by pharmacists, lawyers, dentists, and physicians as barriers to the "free flow of information" guaranteed under the First Amendment to both sellers and buyers.[133] The FTC view was supported by the Supreme Court in the test case over pharmacists.[134]

HEALTH PLANNING MACHINERY

The most concerted attempt to devise a mechanism for a comprehensive health policy—potentially to consolidate the purposes of some 130 Federal health laws—was written into the National Health Planning and Resources Development Act of 1974.[135] It listed as national health goals the development of accessible, efficient, and integrated personal health services, especially for primary care, and the promotion of environmental and other activities to prevent disease.[136] The expressed intent was to "extend health planning to personal health education and environmental concerns where it can be shown that planned change . . . is necessary to improve the health of the people in the community."[137] And since the planning machinery is "for a health system which serves and is paid for by the public, it should be controlled by the public. . . ."[138]

The guidelines to implement this legislation reaffirmed that these new state planning and areawide health systems agencies (HSAs) had, as the goals for the health plans that they were to develop, to both improve the health of their populations and create better health systems to serve the people. The scope for planning the health systems was defined to include, in addition to personal health services, the biophysical environment, workplaces, consumer product safety, motor vehicle accidents, nutrition, smoking, and substance abuse, among others. Priority was, however, to be given to cost containment in health services. Nevertheless, when cost containment goals were strengthened in the Act's 1979 amendments, the original intent was reiterated, concerning the "importance of disease prevention strategies for the ultimate containment of health care costs." Congress expected that "planning agencies will focus greater attention, personnel, and resources on identifying and correcting preventable diseases and conditions. In particular, such efforts should result in greater involvement in existing processes for identifying and controlling indoor and outdoor environmental contaminants and for upgrading nutritional and environmental programs."[139]

According to the Act, the authority of HSAs to carry out the broader aspects of their plans was mainly "coordinative."[140] After some years of legal challenges by the medical profession and other special interests, the law's constitutionality was finally upheld by the Supreme Court in 1978.[141]

Signs of Retrenchment

By the end of the 1970s, the prospects for carrying out the health-making intent of the national health planning legislation were looking doubtful. The organizational problems were imposing. They included the necessary dismantling of previous Federally funded planning agencies, the designation of over 200 new health systems agencies, and their release into a sea of over 12,000 other nongovernmental planning groups and another 1000 specialized governmental planning agencies. This was done in the face of two dozen lawsuits.[142,143] The vast majority of HSAs do not have boundaries coterminous with their potential collaborator planning groups. They have each been funded at less that $500,000 annually, or about half what planners say they need.[144-147]

These developmental problems were not the only reasons for the unusually slow shaping and issuance of the regulations to implement the Act. There was also the organized influence of local hospital and physician interests, in three states particularly, which successfully mounted media campaigns and gained public support for their opposing views.[148]

Under these circumstances, the HSAs at the end of the decade had avoided so central a question as the appropriate allocation of funds and other resources between the development of health services and the use of other, environmental, strategies for improving the health of those they were to serve.[149,150] At best, the Federal expectation of HSA performance in the area of illness prevention was that the agencies would continue to disseminate Federal health-promotion information into the 1980s.[151,152] However, two-thirds of HSA board members thought that they did not have sufficient authority to achieve even the health services goal of improving access to health care.[153]

Still less hopeful auguries for the capacity of HSAs to carry out their mandate were Congressional amendments to the 1974 Act, introduced in 1978 and 1979. One defined the "healthful environment" which HSAs are to plan as consisting solely of health services, health care facilities, equipment, and providers. This was in contradiction to the Act's stated goals and a direct response to an HSA that had begun to address such health-related issues as cigarette smoking, air quality, traffic safety, auto speed limits, gun control, sex education, and abortion.[154] Other amendments served to limit the influence of the consumer members of HSA governing boards, required to be a 51 to 60 percent majority, and to diminish the authority of HSAs relative to local hospitals and physicians.[155]

These efforts to narrow the scope and authority of HSAs, and to reduce the influence of public participation, call into question whether this decentralized planning machinery can be an effective means of measurably improving the health of Americans. The experience to date also illustrates the larger issue of how government and those groups, such as the health care industry, which are reimbursed by public funds can be called to account to the interests of the public, including its health and the best ways to improve it.

THE PUBLIC AND ITS HEALTH INTERESTS

Since the mid-1960s, Federal legislation has attempted to enhance public participation in programs, presumably as a means to insure accountability to the public interest or to the general interests of those consumers affected by programs. This legislated opportunity has involved people in the development of community services, the monitoring of environmental hazards, and the regulation of technology.[156-159]

There is no clear policy, however, as to what public participation is to mean. There is no consistency concerning the purposes of public involvement, the degree of influence it is to have (whether advisory or policy-making), or its place in public or private agencies. Questions as to its composition are not consistently answered, nor are the procedures to obtain and insure fair representation explained.[160]

Much emphasis has been placed on the demographic representation of the public in the governance of Federally funded health programs. By the end of the 1970s, the proposed regulations for the health systems agency boards included a broad set of requirements. These considered age, income group, language, and racial representativeness within a flexible range, and dealt also with conflicts of interest.[161,162] Women were not, nor were they required to be, proportionately represented among either consumer or provider board members.[163]

No matter how demographically balanced, representation alone cannot insure accountability for two basic reasons. First, community populations have no mechanism to call their representatives to account as to whether they have acted in their interests in making health planning decisions.[164-166]

It is for this reason that new proposals sought to have consumer representatives chosen by, and accountable to, bona fide, general purpose community groups.[167] Second, even if representatives could readily be monitored by their community constituency, they would not be able to act effectively on their behalf, under prevailing conditions of local public participation in health decision-making.

Effective Participation

The generic problem here is the vast disparity in the advantages that health professionals, as providers, have over consumers in policy and program decision-making areas. This imbalance begins with the fact that virtually all health-related planning and program funds go to provider-dominated agencies.[168] In addition, health issues involve the livelihood, and therefore, the full-time interest, of health professionals. Consumers have other full-time commitments, and usually fewer financial resources to meet them.[169,170]

Consumer training for participation in health planning has mainly focused on fiscal issues. It has almost excluded an understanding of the origins of the community's health problems, of various strategies for preventing them, and of the political issues involved in dealing with vested interests.[171,172] Professionals have informal, as well as formal, contacts within agencies at local and national levels to help them understand and foresee events. Information is expressed in their language and is prepared for them by a staff that they hire and that is accountable to them.[173-176]

None of these resources is available to consumers. Thus it is no surprise that, at best, consumer participation has in some instances increased numerically in attendance at meetings, and has fostered amicable attitudes among providers and consumers. But it has had little or no effect on the development of health plans other than ratifying the decisions of providers.[177,178] The relative cost of effective participation for consumers is far higher than for providers, and thus cannot be sustained by sheer will or concern. Those consumers who do maintain their involvement have usually been those with extra time, economic security, and higher levels of education.[179]

Shifting the Balance

LOCAL AND NATIONAL NETWORKS

In order to correct some of the imbalance between the capacities of providers and consumers to shape plans for health improvement, public-oriented proposals were put forward in the late 1970s. They called for an independent resource base for the representatives of the public on HSA boards.

This would involve the formation of a separate consumer organization with a statutory right to health-related program information and consultation, and the power to recommend and to veto the plans and management of the area health systems agency. In addition, where consumers are part of individual health care agency boards, they would form a caucus supported by a staff that they would hire, or that would be hired by their external consumer organization. Consumers would be trained more broadly concerning both the impacts of policy on health problems and the problems of impacting on policy formation. Finally, local consumer representatives and their organizations would have links to related community groups and to a national network.[180,181]

The essence of these proposals is that representatives of the public should not be totally dependent on health care provider agencies. Their understanding of health issues and of health-improvement strategies, as well as the funding and other resources that they need to sustain their participation, ought not to be controlled by providers. A degree of independence would help them to maintain a public interest perspective in health decision-making.

To finance the local-national consumer network, proposals have suggested that a small percentage of all government payments that are allocated for inpatient health care be used. In addition, the expenses individuals incurred as a result of participation, such as for attendance at meetings or reading materials, would be tax deductible just as they are for professionals.[182]

A more equitable balance of resources between consumers and providers for engaging in local health system development cannot guarantee, or even improve, the prospects for health without supportive national policy. If statutory changes were to denude the health planning machinery of its scope or authority to deal with the health-related excesses and deficits within a community, the local decisions of consumers and professionals would inevitably be constrained. Nor can the health planning structure be a health-making mechanism if national "non-health" policy (concerning the economy, energy, environmental protection, agriculture, and food) has net health-limiting or outright health-damaging impacts.

To address this issue in part, the proposed network of consumer organizations would have a national organization whose responsibility would be to serve as a technical assistance staff to the consumers who sit on the National Health Planning and Resources Development Council, dealing with broad health planning questions. This staff of professionals would provide analyses and alternatives for debate and decision. It would also conduct surveys of public views, alert consumers to timely health-important issues, arrange for expert testimony at public hearings, foster relationships among local and state consumer representatives, and support consumer training seminars.[183] In effect, it would provide nationally and locally what the professional and trade associations provide their constituencies in the process of influencing public policy.[184-186]

BUILDING SUPPORT

To put forward the health interests of the public during national debates on the broad health-important areas of public policy, such an organization might find its natural allies among the few resilient and articulate national groups that have maintained a public interest point of view.[187,188] These broad-based organizations have often provided comprehensive, systematic analyses to the public and to policy-makers, to help give perspective to the views of special interests. These special interests, in contrast, spend comparatively more of their promotion monies on media advertising, mailings, and developing personal relationships with members of Congress.[189]

By the end of the last decade, however, the potential effectiveness of public interest groups was being limited by legal judgments which denied them lawful "standing" to represent the public in court. Congressional legislation was then introduced to guarantee their legal basis.[190] The outcome of this effort will have important consequences for the influence that can be brought to bear on policy-making in the public interest.

A national consumer health-oriented organization might also forge coalitions, if not alliances, with other groups which do not purport to represent the public interest, but which support the broad interests of their members and have a record of taking actions to benefit others. These include certain general purpose farm organizations; environmental groups; labor unions; civil rights, senior citizens', and women's groups, as well as some religious, health, and other professional groups.[191-193]

PUBLIC OPINION AND ITS LIMITS

Some evidence suggests that alliances which could both interpret issues for their health-importance and advocate health-making policy might also find support among a significant portion of the public. Potential supporters include those who now refrain even from participating in elections, and those voters who feel that their views are neither heard nor represented. Support might also be found among groups that have not been able to maintain sufficient influence to get what they need, such as the poor and the unemployed.[194]

Public surveys, furthermore, show not only widespread interest in problems of health care delivery and its cost, but also support for such health-making policies as promotion of energy-efficient technologies and low auto speed limits, giving environmental protection priority over energy growth, gun control, smoking restrictions, and pricing to curb alcohol abuse. There is support in public opinion for increased governmental and consumer involvement in health care and in food policies, for the use of generic drugs, and for greater emphasis on the prevention of illness. These views are clearly contrary to those that are often held by narrow-interest trade associations and health care provider organizations.[195-210]

This is not to deny, however, that public opinion vacillates on some issues. It does not necessarily foretell what people will actually support in a specific circumstance. Public opinion can be misled when it is based on partial or inaccurate information. This last possibility may sometimes become a probability as public issues take on great complexity, such as assessing the problems of nuclear energy, food additives, and drug safety. The ongoing education, both formal and nonformal, of most Americans tends not to foster either sufficient scope or capacity for the critical consciousness that is needed to make informed judgments on public issues.[211] Moreover, when mass commercial broadcast media present such issues, giving "fair" and balanced weight to opposing views, they imply that the weight of evidence is equivocal when it may, in fact, be virtually incontestable.[212,213]

For all these reasons there may be an untapped reservoir of public readiness for a well-organized consumer health-oriented organization sufficiently financed to support its own professional staff, to consult widely, and to interpret and disseminate its findings and proposals. Its audiences would include the general public, health planning and other public interest-oriented groups, policy-makers, and media people.

When the Public Is Heard

The foregoing discussion may suggest that informed public opinion, and organized advocacy of the public interest that is founded on what is known about the health impacts of public policy, could effectively counteract the impressive influence of special interest lobbying and electioneering. That would be a misleading inference. Such a turn of political events remains no more than a possibility. However, the evidence of 40 years of national policy-making suggests that public policy development is responsive to public opinion, under certain conditions. It is most responsive when a policy change is organizationally easy to make, such as through Executive Order or in some areas of foreign policy.[214] But this is not the case for health-important policy, given its breadth and complexity, its disparate development in the Congressional and administrative bureaucracies, and its indefinite, ill-defined locus of responsibility.

Policy-making has also proved very responsive to crisis issues when they are articulated by widespread public outcries, as with the civil rights, anti-Vietnam war, and environmental movements. Health issues, as compared with the "crisis of health care costs" or other crises involving the failure of prevention, are in fact eminently undramatic, since health-making policy works in the best interests of the public when it prevents crises.

Policy-makers, moreover, are responsive to the public when special interest group opposition is least, and when changes require the least reform. They also find it easier to respond when few resources need to be reallocated from one constituency to another. Reallocations constitute a most difficult kind of politics that is made more so in times of scarce resources.

Whether elected or appointed, policy-makers in effect weigh more than the costs and benefits, tangible and otherwise, of a policy decision for the public interest. Their gains-for-costs calculations include, sometimes to the exclusion of most other considerations, the costs to the retention or enhancement of their position and power.[215] To the extent that the elective or selection process makes them debtors to special interests, any decisions they make in the public interest must come at a high cost to their future careers.[216,217]

Public opinion and organized advocacy of the public interest can sometimes countervail in this kind of situation in several ways, as recent experience has shown. Organized advocacy can bring the issue to public attention, as well as to a wider array of policy-makers. Information that describes the true costs of a problem or issue to the public, whether in dollars or health, death or degradation, and that makes explicit the losers and gainers as well as the potential of alternative courses of action, helps to articulate public opinion. This, in turn, commands the attention of policy-makers who then must listen, with the spotlight of the mass media focused on them, to a wider spectrum of views. As a result, the policy alternatives become more broadly defined. They are debated in more forums and committees, and more openly on the floor of the Congress. In the process, the issue can become somewhat redefined in terms of the public interest. Far more points of view also have to be accommodated in the final compromise language of legislation than would have been necessary without the public exposure.[218]

Street demonstrations and other dramatic gestures help to gain attention and to involve the public in an issue, at least temporarily. But solid, systematic evidence and analyses of current and future options, put forward by persistent, organized efforts, are the tools for *sustained* strengthening of public opinion and for finally resolving the policy-making issue in the public interest.[219,220]

Advocacy of the public interest, backed by public opinion, does more than move policy-makers to risk action on controversial and, therefore, politically costly issues. It has also helped to mobilize Federal agencies, state policy-makers, and political parties to act more forcefully in the interests of the public, judging by the evidence of the last two decades.[221,222]

However, merely placing consumer advocates within government agencies has not, of itself, proved an effective method for influencing policy in the public interest. These appointed individuals have often been limited by their own lack of expertise, by their lack of administrative leverage and funds, by their exclusion from policy deliberations, and by their isolation from their presumed consumer constituency.[223] At the national level, these built-in limitations are comparable to those experienced by consumer members on local health planning boards.

A further cautionary note must be made here, based on the experience of the seventies. When consumer activism is not sustained, it may be counterproductive for the public interest. When it is not adequately financed and thus is unable to command the sustained attention of the media, and when it cannot attract the aid of experts or support adequate staff, research, litigation, or necessary mobilization activities, it must become merely reactive. It then often relies on a veto strategy.

Consumer organizations, unable to match the resources that producer interests can command, have had spurts of activity which actually revitalized opposition special interest groups. Consumer advocacy impelled these special interests to close ranks and develop more effective policy-influencing tactics than previously. Moreover, when consumers draw Congressional attention to an issue, easing the entry to policy-makers' offices, special interest groups also find an open door. They have filled the void left when consumers cannot sustain long-term contacts.[224]

The Strategic Problem and Its Implications for Policy-Shaping

In order to develop health-making policy, the costs to policy-makers, themselves, of making health-damaging policy choices must be higher than the costs of making health-promoting ones. Thus the strategic political problem for making health is one of determining how the gain-for-cost calculations of elected and appointed policy-makers can be shifted in favor of policy directions that are health-making. The "gain" for policy-makers, whether as legislators or administrators, is determined by their ability to maintain or increase their power and influence over important decisions, those that determine where resources are to go, and which groups will receive more or better resources. The gamut of resources includes clear air, jobs, development funds, tax subsidies, oil drilling rights, and health services, among others.

The foregoing discussion suggests that the political problem of developing health-making policy has two facets. One is how to make direct public participation effective in health policy decisions in local communities, as illustrated in the HSAs. The larger issue is how to affect state and Federal policy-making, where the public cannot be directly involved. How can the public's health interests be adequately represented? This is today a hard, practical, health-important problem, as well as a democratic ideal.

The strategic objective is to render health-making policy choices easier, and thus less "costly," for policy-makers. Some ways to move toward this objective are suggested by American political experience as just described. The focus here is on the national scene, although its counterparts exist within state and other jurisdictions. A strategy to reshape policy in health-making directions involves the removal of organizational barriers and the lessening of organized opposition to health-making. It also includes activities that will build support for health-making. This implies that those who seek significant improvement in the health prospects of Americans, including consumer groups and health personnel, both public and private, should give attention to policy changes that may appear far removed from conventional health issues.

LOWERING BARRIERS

The costs to policy-makers of health-making will be somewhat reduced if policy changes are made organizationally easier than they are at present. One way to achieve this is by the formation of a national health board (as proposed in Chapter 4) that is responsible and accountable for improving Americans' health. Among other things, a national board would end the fragmented and independent development of policies by regulatory agencies and by health services and other bureaucracies. It would analyze the health impacts of a spectrum of policies—environmental, food, income, health care—and design more health-making policy options. Moreover, it would coordinate the administration and monitoring of these policies through their respective units.

Policy-makers would also find health-making less costly if their careers did not depend upon special interest groups. One way to ease this situation is through public financing of national elections, administered through party machinery, and not necessarily restricted to the two major parties. This would diminish the growing influence of political action committees, and more importantly, it would strengthen the parties. These changes are essential to the development and sustained support of coherent policy, passed in timely fashion and pursued over the long term. Health-making policies are by nature long-term undertakings, both in their initiation and in the benefits they bring.

BUILDING COLLECTIVE AWARENESS

Building public support for health-making policy among the electorate and among opinion leaders will also make health-promoting policy decisions easier for policy-makers. To accomplish this, better access to, and different uses of, the mass media by the public are necessary. More time and supportive technical resources are required for the discussion of public issues through the broadcast media. This follows from the fact that television is the major source of information for Americans about the world outside of their own immediately experienced environments. Partial and misleading information is relatively less harmful when people can validate or refute it through their own immediate experience. However, the nature of information about public issues is more critical simply because it cannot be personally validated. As was noted in Chapter 10, if policy issues are judged by people solely on the basis of their individual experience, then the broader and longer-term public interest may not be served.

Two facets are implicit in the development and use of information in building support for health-making. One is that more independent sources of information, more points of view, are needed.[225] This may mean new TV channels and media technologies, new radio stations and newspapers, and the public subsidies to make them possible, independent of existing communications conglomerates. New sources should include direct communications and programming from other countries. This would offer opportunities for Americans to view other ways of life and their justifications, as well as outside views of American life, rather than having all of this selected and interpreted for them by American journalists, politicians, or business interests.

Secondly, alternative definitions or interpretations of today's health problem need airing. In the mass media as elsewhere, the problem is typically defined within the context of what health services can do, in terms of numerous diseases and deaths to be dealt with. It is interpreted as a personal problem which individuals can be helped to solve, primarily through means such as personal health care or health education. This health message predominates in the newscasts, feature stories, documentaries, and dramatic presentations of the mass media.

An alternative message would interpret the health problem in broader, environmental terms, together with its reverberating consequences. It would present the problem as a public issue, requiring collective action for making environmental changes, instead of a personal problem for individuals to solve. As noted in Chapter 4, and implied throughout this book, environmental changes, both biophysical and socioeconomic, are politically costly because they mean that some resources would be controlled in the public interest, or would be transferred from those who have more of what is health-promoting to others who need more than they have.

Since people's independent sources of information are so few, and the interpretation of health-important issues is usually so narrow, organized effort is required to widen opportunities for conveying new perspectives. For it is likely that these mass media exposures to public issues will influence, in some degree, the public opinion surveys that policy-makers use. They may also affect voting patterns and, perhaps, people's consent, coopera- tion, and acceptance of the credibility of policy-makers and of producers of goods and services, both public and private.

New perspectives will not negate health information that helps individu- als to develop new personal habits. On the contrary, they will provide a context for popular support of strategies that will make the new personal choices much easier to embrace. This was illustrated in the ways that public information on cigarette smoking, and the related changes in taxa- tion and other laws restricting smoking, helped smokers to quit without re- course to special anti-smoking clinics (see Chapter 7). The relatively higher cost of cigarettes seems more recently to be deterring some adolescents from taking up the habit.[226]

Among the audiences for targeting reinterpretations of the health prob- lem and offering alternate health policies are broadcast and press journal- ists and writers, local political party and public officials, and school and university leaders. Others include potential allied groups that support health-important policies in employment, income maintenance, environ- mental protection, safe energy development, and health care. Still others include some producers of goods and services who may gain from shifts to- ward health-making policies. All of these groups are gatekeepers to larger segments of the public.

OPTIONS FOR ACTION

Through these avenues the health aspect of major public issues can be consistently brought out in the forums where the issues are discussed. Pol- icy options can be presented, in the respective policy areas, that are more health-promoting than current ways. Their costs, and how these might be equitably shared, can also be considered. Over time, the view of health- making by policy-makers and the public may assume more comprehen- sive character. This in turn may garner more support for broader and more effective health strategies. It may force more serious consideration of health- making in policy decisions.

"Health" does not require a "movement" to catch the attention of the media and of political leaders in order for health-making policy to de- velop. It does require sustained attention that is probably not achievable outside the framework of ongoing major "non-health" public policies. One of the most potentially effective ways to lessen the cost of health-making to policy-makers is to point out how health-promoting options can contribute to solving high-priority "non-health" issues, such as the fact that nonpol- luting forms of transportation will also conserve nonrenewable energy, and that the more healthful foods are less energy-intensive and potentially less inflationary.

All of these tactics require organization and stable financing of the kind proposed earlier, within government and among consumers. These organizational options for action will, in turn, allow wider segments of the public to act collectively on what they know and learn. Groups of people with diverse policy interests, who neverthless share a common concern for creating health-promoting environments, can become the nucleus of a broad, policy-shaping coalition. The potential for that coalition exists in more than a hypothetical sense. It is based on the current historical reality to which policy-makers must attend: the scarcity and rising cost of resources that have been the underpinnings of the American way of life.

SUMMARY AND CONCLUSIONS

To create a realistic possibility that the health interests of the public will be promoted by organized consumers, they must have resources that are comparable to those that are used by special interests (Fig. 11). One reasonable approach is the proposed establishment of consumer-controlled organizations, at local, state, and national levels, that would have a statutory basis and be financed by a fraction of Federal health funds. This arrangement would provide a secure foundation for the selection, training, monitoring, and staff support of consumer participants in the health planning machinery, with its 205 health systems agencies, its 50 state health coordinating councils, and its national council. In addition, overt activities to influence the electorate or individual members of Congress could be carried on by a separate organization, privately financed in accordance with laws affecting nonprofit association expenditures, much like trade and professional associations.

Mechanisms such as these could provide the stability that is necessary to sustain organized consumer contacts with other public interest groups, the mass media, and supportive professional organizations, as well as with the general public, local consumer representatives, and policy-makers. Over time, such liaisons would allow for proactive, affirmative campaigns for the development and support of policy in the health interests of the public.

Those interest groups that have a stake in the status quo may caution that efforts to affect policy priorities are fraught with potential loss to the nation. Although any policy course, whether of continuity or change, holds the possibility of unintended and adverse consequences, errors of action are more likely to affect the "haves," while errors of inaction diminish the chances for improvement among the "have-nots."

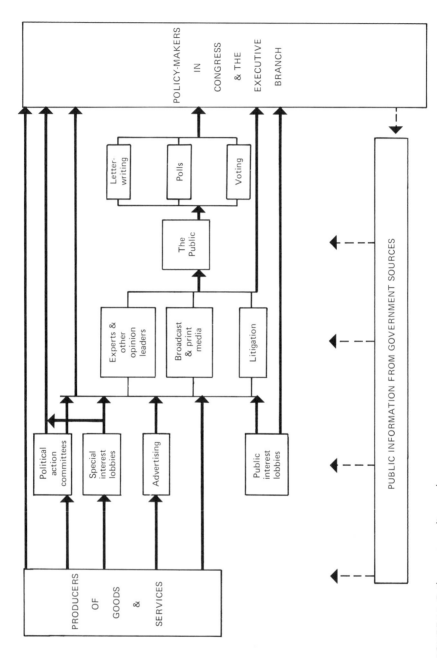

FIGURE 11. Pathways to policy-makers.

302

Whatever the prospects for effective public participation in the development of health-making policy, public involvement will best serve the prospects for the health of Americans if it is not a substitute for governmental responsibility. Health promotion will be best served if the public's action is a "goad in the flesh" to move officialdom to act in the public interest. Organized public action can challenge the health care responsibility that is vested in government to be health-oriented, to use its vast information-gathering, analytic, information translation, and dissemination capabilities in order to design health-making policy options. A broad-based consumer coalition can demand that government use its authority to control health-damaging circumstances in ways that achieve maximum gains in the health of Americans. In so doing, consumer-led health advocacy can utilize and support the signs in government of a broader perspective in policy, in its implementation, monitoring, and evaluation. This will strengthen these recent changes that are potential gains to governance in the public interest.

The prospects for health in the United States will depend on how government deals with health-important policy issues—economic, energy, environmental, and agricultural. How much more freedom from illness and disability Americans can expect throughout their lifetimes, and whether those who are now most vulnerable to illness will have reason to hope for something better, will depend on whether there is a focus within government that is made responsible for health improvement and for overseeing the health impacts of public policy. Improvements in health will also depend on whether health policy adopts, as its clear and consistent goal, the promotion of health-making habitats and habits, or whether it remains fragmented and focused on the delivery of personal health care that necessarily emphasizes the detection and control of illness.

The status quo in health policy will more easily prevail if health problems continue to be viewed as numerous diagnostic entities, or even as individual risk factors, which tempt the use of "disease by disease" and "risk factor by risk factor" solutions. If the spectrum of government's information-processing capabilities is used to reveal the more complex nature of contemporary illness and health, it will more ably meet its responsibility for the health interests of the public. If it focuses on the origins of health and illness—inextricably tied to public policy-induced environmental circumstances, corporate practices, and personal habits—it will have a basis for devising the most effective strategies for promoting health, eliminating health-damaging circumstances, and minimizing excesses and deficits in the health-important resources available to people. It will more effectively make health-damaging choices the more costly ones, and health-improving choices less costly, to both organizations and individuals. At the same time, it will be able to design the special supports that are needed by those who might incur loss during transitions in policy.

In these ways, health policy would enable individuals to be responsible for their own health, a responsibility that too many cannot now carry out because their health-promoting options are too few, or come at too high a personal cost. In so doing, health policy would allow health education to find effective expression in opportunities for healthful behavior as people face new options. It would also make the needed detection, amelioration, control, curing, and caring work of personal health services, especially of primary care, more effective and less costly.

The development of organized advocacy for the public's health may well be necessary to demand that government use its resources for health-making purposes. If so, advocacy must go far beyond the usual voicing of discontent, or of admonitions to individuals to change their ways. The message must be conveyed in ways that create widespread and informed public debate. Useable translations of the message are necessary. Explanations are needed of the complexities of the health problem, of alternate health strategies, and of their costs and gains. The true costs of *not* preventing illness must be addressed, as well as the protections that are possible for those whose livelihoods might be harmed during transitions. Workable formats for presenting the message and convenient forums for discussion are needed for the general public and for its subgroups, for the mass media and specialized professional media, for policymakers, and for scientists and methodologists. Such groundwork seems essential to effective policy-influencing action. Its ultimate strategic purpose is to make health-promoting policy decisions easier for policy-makers to choose.

Policy-makers will act, whether or not individuals are aware of these actions, and whether or not they are recognized by a majority of health professionals or approved by academic analysts. On the basis of many kinds of information that reach them in timely and convincing ways, policy-makers will continue to make the decisions that create and restrict the options from which corporations and individuals make their choices, shaping the patterns of contemporary life and health.

Those who understand this, and who seek to improve the prospects for health, will heed the lesson of human history: the largest gains in health have come from changes in people's environments that established the certainty of food and of safety. These changes were not *intended* to improve health. They were meant, rather, to improve the ease, to lower the cost, of human survival, security, and comfort. Now, at a time when history is forcing a major reshaping of policy, those concerned about, and those responsible for, the health of the American people would do well to join a larger alliance. They share a common interest with those who are designing and advocating new approaches: the expanded use of renewable and human energy, the improvement of environmental safety, and the equitable distribution of health-important resources. This kind of advocacy will provide a basis for believing that the coming policies in economics, energy, and environment, and in agriculture, food, and health care, will be health-making.

REFERENCES

1. Mushkin, S., et al.: *Cost of disease and illness in the United States in the year 2000.* Public Health Rep. (Suppl.) 93(5), 1978.
2. Gori, G., and Richter, B.: *Macroeconomics of disease prevention in the United States.* Science 200:1124–1130, 1978.
3. Office of Research and Statistics: *Medicare: utilization of home health services, 1974.* Health Insurance Statistics 79(2), 1977.
4. *Washington Post,* October 1978.
5. Milio, N.: *The team delivery of primary care: better health compared to what?* in *Policy Issues in the Team Approach to Primary Health Care Delivery.* University of Iowa Health Services Research Center, Iowa City, 1978.
6. Newhouse, J., and Friedlander, L.: *The Relationship Between Medical Resources and Measures of Health: Some Additional Evidence.* Rand Corporation, Santa Monica, Cal., 1977.
7. Ginzberg, E.: *The Limits of Health Reform: The Search for Realism.* Basic Books, New York, 1977.
8. Ginzberg, E.: *Directions for policy,* in Ginzberg, E. (ed.): *Regionalization and Health Policy.* Health Resources Administration, Washington, D.C., 1977.
9. Wildavsky, A.: *The political pathology of health policy. Doing better and feeling worse: health in the U.S.* Daedalus, Winter 1977, pp. 105–124.
10. Davis, K.: *Regionalization and national health insurance,* in Ginzberg, E. (ed.): *Regionalization and Health Policy.* Health Resources Administration, Washington, D.C., 1977.
11. Feldstein, P.: *Health Associations and the Demand for Legislation: The Political Economy of Health.* Ballinger, Cambridge, Mass., 1977.
12. Arnold, M.: *State and local health policy development.* Paper presented at the Annual Meeting of the American Public Health Association, Los Angeles, October 18, 1978.
13. Schmidt, S. M., and Kochan, T. A.: *Interorganizational relationships: patterns and motivations.* Admin. Sci. Q. 22(2):220–235, 1977.
14. Soward, E., quoted in *Doing better and feeling worse: health in the U.S.* Daedalus, Winter 1977.
15. Parsons, E. M., and Roemer, M. I.: *Ideological goals of different health insurance plans.* J. Comm. Health 1(4):241–248, 1976.
16. Fein, R.: *Supply and demand,* in Ginzberg, E. (ed.): *Regionalization and Health Policy.* Health Resources Administration, Washington, D.C., 1977.
17. Beckman, N.: *Policy analysis for the Congress.* Public Admin. Rev. 37:223–228, 1977.
18. *Federal Program Evaluations, July 1, 1975 through June 30, 1977.* Report of the Comptroller General. 1977 Congressional Sourcebook Series, Washington, D.C., 1978.

19. Ibid.
20. Bauman, P., and Banta, H. D.: *The Congress and policymaking for prevention.* Prev. Med. 6:227–241, 1977.
21. Williams, S. R., and Wysong, J. A.: *Health services research and health policy formulation: an empirical analyses and a structural solution.* J. Health Politics 2:362–387, 1977.
22. *New York Times Magazine,* March 25, 1979.
23. Wilson, R., National Center for Health Statistics: Testimony before regional forum sponsored by National Commission for Smoking and Public Policy, Philadelphia, June 16, 1977.
24. Subcommittee on Oversight and Investigations: *Cancer Causing Chemicals in Food.* Committee on Interstate and Foreign Commerce, 95th Congress, Washington, D.C., December 1978.
25. Kleinman, J., et al.: *The effects of changes in smoking habits on coronary heart disease mortality.* Paper presented at National Heart, Blood and Lung Institute Conference, October 25, 1978. (Published by the National Center for Health Statistics, Washington, D.C., 1979.)
26. Light, A. R.: *Federalism and the energy crisis: a view from the states.* J. Federalism, Winter 1976.
27. Komarovsky, M.: *Sociology and Public Policy: The Case of Presidential Commissions.* Elsevier, New York, 1975.
28. Food and Nutrition Board: *Symposium on Nutrition and Health: Role of the Federal Agencies.* Division of Biological Sciences, National Research Council, Washington, D.C., 1978.
29. Quarles, J. R.: *Existing legislation and government regulatory agencies.* Bull. N.Y. Acad. Med. 54(4):442–443, 1978.
30. Bardach, E.: *The Implementation Game: What Happens After A Bill Becomes A Law?* MIT Press, Cambridge, Mass., 1977.
31. *Final Report: Evaluation of the Impact of PHS Programs on State Health Goals and Activities.* DHEW Publication No. (HRA)77-604. U.S. Public Health Service, Washington, D.C., 1978.
32. Shonick, W., and Price, W.: *Reorganizations of health agencies by local government in American urban centers: What do they portend for 'public health'?* Milbank Mem. Fund Q. 55(2):233–271, 1977.
33. Goldberg, L. G., and Greenberg, W.: *The Health Maintenance Organization and Its Effects on Competition.* Bureau of Economics Staff Report to the Federal Trade Commission, Washington, D.C., 1977.
34. Brandon, W.: *Politics, Administration and Conflict in Neighborhood Health Centers.* J. Health Politics 2:79–99, 1977.
35. Foltz, A. M.: *Uncertainties of Federal child health policies: impact in two states.* DHEW Publication No. 78-3190. National Center for Health Statistics Research, Rockville, Md., 1978.
36. Avellone, J., and Moore, F.: *The FTC enters a new arena: health services.* N. Engl. J. Med. 299(9):478–83, 1978.
37. *State planning ruled exempt from antitrust action.* Health Law Proj. Bull. 4:132–133, 1979.
38. *PMA Newsletter* (Pharmaceutical Manufacturers Association), October 23, 1978.
39. Hornbrook, M. C.: *Market Structure and Advertising in the U.S. Pharmaceutical Industry: Some Implications for Public Policy.* National Center for Health Statistics Research, Rockville, Md., 1977.

40. Kennedy, D.: *A calm look at 'drug lag.'* J.A.M.A. 239(5):423–426, 1978.
41. Farnsworth, N.: *Prescription drugs from higher plants: sleeping giant of the industry.* J. Am. Pharm. Assoc. (in press).
42. McCalla, A. F.: *The politics of the U.S. agricultural research establishment: a short analysis.* J. Policy Studies, Summer 1978, pp. 479–484.
43. *Pressure groups.* The Economist, November 26, 1977, pp. 38–39.
44. Bacheller, J. M.: *Lobbyists and the legislative process: the impact of environmental constraints.* Am. Pol. Sci. Rev. 71:252–263, 1977.
45. *How Money Talks in Congress.* Common Cause, Washington, D.C., 1979.
46. *U.S. chamber group seeks more funds for study of national health policy.* Washington Report on Medicine and Health 32(2), January 9, 1978.
47. Weinberg, A. J.: *Washington Business Group on Health.* Washington, D.C., 1978.
48. *Washington Post,* August 13, 1978.
49. *PMA Newsletter,* January 8, 1979.
50. *How Money Talks,* op. cit.
51. *United States Tobacco Journal Newspaper* 205(45), November 10, 1977.
52. Guth, J. L.: *Consumer organizations and Federal dairy policy.* J. Policy Studies, Summer 1978, pp. 499–503.
53. Porter, L.: *Congress and agricultural policy.* J. Policy Studies, Summer 1978, pp. 472–479.
54. Hardin, C. M.: *Agricultural price policy: the political role of bureaucracy.* J. Policy Studies, Summer 1978, pp. 467–472.
55. *Economic Value of Present Tobacco Program.* Hearings before the Subcommittee on Tobacco of the House Committee on Agriculture, 95th Congress, First Session, October 6, 1977.
56. *Tobacco Institute battles restrictions on smoking.* New York Times, January 17, 1979.
57. *Tax Reform Act of 1976* (PL 94-455).
58. *Time,* August 7, 1978.
59. Broder, D.: *Campaigns, parties and the public purse.* Washington Post, April 15, 1979.
60. *Washington Post,* August 13, 1978.
61. North, J.: *The effect: the growth of the special interests.* Washington Monthly, October 1978.
62. *New York Times,* January 14, 1979.
63. *New York Times,* December 31, 1978.
64. North, op. cit.
65. *How Money Talks,* op. cit.
66. Ibid.
67. Gans, C.: *The politics of selfishness: the cause: the empty voting booths.* Washington Monthly, October 1978, pp. 27–36.
68. Hadley, J.: *Political action committees.* Washington Monthly, October 1978.
69. Ibid.
70. Miller, A., et al.: *Analysis of 1976 American national election survey.* ISR Center for Political Studies Newsletter 7(1):3, 1979.
71. Strumpel, B.: *Induced investment or induced employment—alternative visions of the American economy,* in *U.S. Economic Growth from 1976 to 1986: Prospects, Problems, and Patterns.* Vol. 8, *Capital Formation: An Alternative View.* Studies Prepared for the Joint Economic Committee of Congress, 1976.
72. Verloff, J., et al.: *Feelings of well-being survey.* ISR Newsletter 7(1):3, 1979.

307

73. Andrews, F. M., and Withey, S. B.: *Social Indicators of Well-Being: Americans' Perceptions of Life Quality.* Plenum, New York, 1976.
74. *Priority Problems, U.S.* Louis Harris Survey, September 21, 1978.
75. Hadley, op. cit.
76. North, op. cit.
77. Hardin, op. cit.
78. Navarro, V.: *Underdevelopment of health of working America.* Am. J. Public Health 66:538–47, 1976.
79. Navarro, V.: *Health and the corporate society.* Social Policy, January–February 1975, pp. 41–48.
80. *How Money Talks,* op. cit.
81. LeGrande, L.: *Women in labor organizations: their ranks are increasing.* Monthly Labor Rev., August 1978.
82. *Ad outlays double in a decade.* New York Times Magazine, January 8, 1978.
83. *Advertising of Proprietary Medicines.* Hearings before the Subcommittee on Monopoly and Anticompetitive Activities of the Senate Select Committee on Small Business, 94th and 95th Congress, First Session, Part 5, October 29–30, 1975; June 14,21, 1977.
84. Wells, A.: *Mass Communication: A World View.* National Press Books, Palo Alto, 1974.
85. Network editorial, WRAL-TV, Raleigh, N.C., April 24, 1979.
86. Senate Select Committee on Nutrition and Human Needs: *Diet Related to Killer Diseases, Part II.* February 1–2, 1977.
87. *The Smoking Digest: Progress Report on a Nation Kicking the Habit.* National Cancer Institute, Bethesda, Md., 1977.
88. *The tobacco dilemma.* Charlotte Observer, March 25, 1979.
89. Senate Select Committee on Nutrition and Human Needs: *Dietary Goals for the United States,* ed. 2. Washington, D.C., 1977.
90. *Advertising of Proprietary Medicines,* op. cit.
91. *Nutrition Education.* Hearings before the Subcommittee on Domestic Marketing, Consumer Relations and Nutrition, House Committee on Agriculture, Part I, September–November 1977.
92. Hornbrook, op. cit.
93. Kilborn, P. T.: *Tobacco: profit despite attack.* New York Times, January 25, 1979.
94. *Diet Related to Killer Diseases,* op. cit.
95. *Pressure groups,* op. cit.
96. McKinney, M. W.: *Public opinion and energy policy alternatives,* in *Energy Research.* University of North Carolina, Institute for Research in Social Science Newsletter, October 1978, pp. 19–24.
97. *PMA initiates information service for science writers.* PMA Bull., 78:3, 1978.
98. *PMA Newsletter,* May 3, 1973.
99. Rucker, T.: *Estimated expenditures by pharmaceutical manufacturers for professional persuasion-education activities.* Med. Care 14:156–165, 1976.
100. *United States Tobacco Journal Newspaper* 205(45), November 10, 1977.
101. *Tobacco interests join in their own campaign.* Wilmington Star News, July 2, 1978.
102. *Tobacco Industry Profile, 1977.* Tobacco Institute, Washington, D.C., 1977.
103. Zachar, G.: *Press swallows atom industry bait.* Critical Mass J., December 1978.
104. National Heart and Lung Institute: *The Public and High Blood Pressure: Survey Report, June 1973.* National Institutes of Health, Washington, D.C., 1974.
105. Bower, R.: *Televison and the Public.* Holt, Rinehart & Winston, New York, 1973.

106. Milio, N., et al.: *The Simplified Primary Care Data Guide,* ed. 2. National Health Planning Information Center, Washington, D.C. (in press).
107. *Pressure Groups,* op. cit.
108. Ibid.
109. *Tobacco—hazards to health and human reproduction: policy implications.* Population Reports 50(1), 1979.
110. Editorial, *New York Times,* February 26, 1979.
111. *General Farm Bill.* Hearings before the House Committee on Agriculture, 95th Congress, First Session, Part 2, March 1–4, 1977.
112. Collins, W. K., et al.: *1978 Tobacco Information.* North Carolina Agricultural Extension Service, Raleigh, N.C., 1977.
113. *Economic Value of Present Tobacco Program,* op. cit.
114. Hardin, op. cit.
115. Browne, W. P., and Wiggins, C. W.: *Resolutions and priorities: lobbying by the general farm organizations.* J. Policy Studies, Summer 1978, pp. 493–499.
116. National Heart and Lung Institute, op. cit.
117. *Miscellaneous Measures to Discourage Cigarette Smuggling.* Hearings before the Subcommittee on Miscellaneous Revenue Measures of the House Committee on Ways and Means, 95th Congress, March 21, 1978.
118. Meier, K. J.: *Client Representation in USDA Bureaus: Causes and Consequences.* J. Policy Studies, Summer 1978, pp. 484–503.
119. *Export of U.S. Agricultural Commodities.* Hearings before the Subcommittee on Oilseeds and Rice, and the Subcommittee on Livestock and Grains of the House Committee on Agriculture, 95th Congress, First Session, October 12, 1977.
120. Deaton, R.: *Agricultural trade act paves way for gains in U.S. farm exports.* Foreign Agriculture, October 30, 1978.
121. Beckman, op. cit.
122. *OTA Priorities, 1979.* Office of Technology Assessment, Washington, D.C., 1979.
123. House Committee on Science and Technology: *Summary of Activities.* Washington, D.C., 1978.
124. Sultzberger, A. O.: *One Federal agency: how it makes rules.* New York Times, January 24, 1979.
125. Porter, op. cit.
126. *General Farm Bill,* op. cit.
127. Broder, op. cit.
128. Food and Nutrition Board, op. cit.
129. Senate Select Committee on Nutrition and Human Needs: *Nutrition and Health.* Washington, D.C., 1975.
130. *Forward Plan for Health, FY 1977–81.* U.S. Department of Health, Education and Welfare, Washington, D.C., 1975.
131. *Findings and Recommendations of the Review Panel on New Drug Regulation.* U.S. Department of Health, Education and Welfare, Washington, D.C., 1978.
132. Food and Nutrition Board, op. cit.
133. Stock, F.: *Professional advertising.* Am. J. Public Health 68(12):1207–9, 1978.
134. *FTC cites AMA again.* Health Law Proj. Bull., 4, February 1979.
135. *Papers on the National Health Guidelines, Baselines for Setting Health Goals and Standards.* DHEW Publication No. (HRA) 76-640. Health Resources Administration, Washington, D.C., 1976.
136. *National Health Planning and Resources Development Act of 1974* (PL 93-641).
137. *National Health Policy, Planning and Resources Development Act of 1974:*

Report of the House Committee on Interstate and Foreign Commerce. 93rd Congress, 2nd Session, September 26, 1974.

138. Health Planning and Health Services Research and Statistics Extension Act of 1977: Report of the House Committee on Interstate and Foreign Commerce, March 26, 1977.
139. Health Planning and Resources Development Amendments of 1979: Report of the House Committee on Interstate and Foreign Commerce, May 15, 1979.
140. 1977 Program Policy Notices of the Bureau of Health Planning and Resources Development. U.S. Department of Health, Education and Welfare, Washington, D.C., 1978.
141. Federal Program Evaluations, op. cit.
142. Johnson, C.: Future role of environmental health in the Health Service Agency. Paper presented at the Annual Meeting of the American Public Health Association, Los Angeles, October 18, 1978.
143. Status of the Implementation of the National Health Planning and Resource Development Act of 1974. General Accounting Office, Washington, D.C., 1978.
144. Ibid.
145. Foley, H. A.: Presentation to the National Council on Health Planning and Development, September 8, 1978.
146. House Committee on Interstate and Foreign Commerce: Health Planning and Resources Development Amendments of 1978. Part I: Hearings, January 30–31, February 1–2, 1978.
147. Final Report: Evaluation of the Impact of PHS Programs, op. cit.
148. Zwick, D.: Initial development of national guidelines for health planning. Public Health Rep. 93(5):407, 1978.
149. Johnson, op. cit.
150. Pond, M. A.: Environmental quality as an issue in the legislative history of the National Health Planning and Resources Development Act of 1974. Am. J. Public Health 68:583–585, 1978.
151. Foley, op. cit.
152. Educating the Public About Health: A Planning Guide. U.S. Public Health Service, Washington, D.C., 1977.
153. Status of the Implementation of the National Health Planning Act, op. cit.
154. Washington Newsletter on Medicine and Health, September 8, 1978.
155. Consumer Coalition for Health, Washington, D.C., April 4, 1979.
156. Koseki, L. K., and Hayakawa, J. M.: Consumer participation and community organization practice: implications of national health legislation. Paper presented at the Annual Meeting of the American Public Health Association, Washington, D.C., November 2, 1977.
157. Biomedical Research and the Public. Prepared for the Subcommittee on Health and Scientific Research of the Senate Committee on Human Resources, May 1977.
158. Findings of the Review Panel on New Drug Regulation, op. cit.
159. Food and Nutrition Board, op. cit.
160. Koseki and Hayakawa, op. cit.
161. HEW defines policy on 'broadly representative.' Health Law Proj. Bull. 4:131–132, 1979.
162. Skyrocketing Health Care Costs: The Role of Blue Shield. Hearings before the Subcommittee on Oversight and Investigations of the House Committee on Interstate and Foreign Commerce, 95th Congress, Second Session, March 21–22, April 5–7, 1978.

163. *Board and Staff Composition of Health Planning Agencies.* Project Summary. U.S. Public Health Service, Washington, D.C., 1977.
164. Marmor, T., and Morone, J.: *HSAs and the representation of consumer interests: conceptual issues and litigation problems.* Health Law Proj. Bull. 4:117–128, 1979.
165. Matek, S. J.: *Accountability: Its Meaning and Its Relevance to the Health Care Field.* Nurse Planning Information Series 1. DHEW Publication No. (HRA) 77-72. Washington, D.C., 1977.
166. *A Working Paper on Accountability.* American Public Health Association, Washington, D.C., 1974.
167. Stoller, E. P.: *New roles for health care consumers: a study of role transformation.* J. Comm. Health 3(2):171–177, 1977.
168. Koseki and Hayakawa, op. cit.
169. Falkson, J.: *Review article: An evaluation of policy-related research of citizen participation in municipal health service systems.* Med. Care Rev. 33:156–209, 1976.
170. Greer, A. L.: *Training board members for Health Planning agencies—A review of the literature.* Public Health Rep. 91:56–61, 1976.
171. Knox, J. J.: *The functions of consumers on programs and policymaking of Health Systems Agencies and statewide Health Coordinating Councils.* Memorandum to the National Council for Health Planning and Development, May 5, 1978.
172. Diamond, E.: *Good News, Bad News.* MIT Press, Cambridge, Mass., 1978.
173. *Consumer effectiveness: now, and under NHS.* Consumer Health Perspectives 5(4), October 1978.
174. Consumer Commission on Accreditation of Health Services: *Recommendations: national quality controls.* Health Perspectives, July–August 1975.
175. Knox, op. cit.
176. Paap, W. R.: *Consumer-based boards of health centers: structural problems in achieving effective control.* Am. J. Public Health 68:578–582, 1978.
177. Ittig, K. B.: *Consumer Participation in Health Planning and Service Delivery: A Selective Review and a Proposed Research Agenda.* National Center for Health Statistics Research, Rockville, Md., 1976.
178. Douglas, C.: *Consumer influence in health planning in the urban ghetto.* Inquiry 12:157–63, 1975.
179. Cooper, T.: *The hidden price tag: participation costs and health planning.* Am. J. Public Health 69:368–374, 1979.
180. Knox, op. cit.
181. *Consumer effectiveness,* op. cit.
182. *The development of a consumer health network.* Health Perspectives 4(4,5):1–12, 1977.
183. Ibid.
184. Feldstein, P.: *Health Associations and the Demand for Legislation: The Political Economy of Health.* Ballinger, Cambridge, Mass., 1977.
185. Schmidt and Kochan, op. cit.
186. Arnold, op. cit.
187. *Pressure groups,* op. cit.
188. Tolchin, M.: *Lobbying in the 'public interest' is more effective.* New York Times, November 20, 1977.
189. Ibid.
190. Knight, J.: *Consumer issues buried in technicalities.* Washington Post, April 15, 1979.

191. Browne and Wiggins, op. cit.
192. Knight, op. cit.
193. *Action Resources.* Women's Health Action Network, Washington, D.C., 1977.
194. Piven, F. F., and Cloward, R. A.: *Poor People's Movements: Why They Succeed, How They Fail.* Pantheon Books, New York, 1977.
195. *The Harris Survey: Advance support is found for pending energy taxes.* Washington Post, December 12, 1977.
196. McKinney, op. cit.
197. *The Harris Survey: Business tax seen causing social change.* Washington Post, March 27, 1978.
198. *Washington Post,* February 1, 1979.
199. Clary, B. B.: *Prioritizing Energy Costs: A Survey Approach to Environmental Appraisal.* Department of Political Science, North Carolina State University, Raleigh, N.C., 1977.
200. *National Conference on Nonmetropolitan Community Services Research.* Prepared for the Senate Committee on Agriculture, Nutrition, and Forestry. Washington, D.C., 1977.
201. *Status of the Implementation of the National Health Planning Act,* op. cit.
202. *Adult Use of Tobacco—1975.* National Cancer Institute, Washington, D.C., 1976.
203. Whitehead, P.: *Public policy and alcohol related damage: media campaigns or social controls.* Addict. Behav. 4:83–89, 1979.
204. McComb, N. N.: *Nutrition Policy Survey: Nutrition Education* Hearings before the Subcommittee on Domestic Marketing, Consumer Relations and Nutrition of the House Committee on Agriculture, 95th Congress, First Session, September 27–28, 1977; October 6, 1977; November 7, 1977.
205. Youngsberg, G.: *The alternative agricultural movement.* J. Policy Studies, Summer 1978, pp. 524–531.
206. *Health Food Market Trends.* USDA National Food Situation Report No. NFS-161. Washington, D.C., 1977.
207. *Drug Product Selection: Staff Report to the Federal Trade Commission.* Washington, D.C., 1979.
208. Riska, E., and Taylor, J. A.: *Consumer attitudes toward health policy and knowledge about health legislation.* J. Health Politics 3:112–123, 1978.
209. Fielding, J. Successes of prevention. Milbank Mem. Fund Q. 56(3):274–302, 1978.
210. *Health Maintenance.* Pacific Mutual Life Insurance Company, 1978.
211. *Education survey.* New York Times, April 22, 1979.
212. Lekachman, R.: *Playing inflation down the middle.* Columbia Journalism Rev., March/April 1979, pp. 37–39.
213. Diamond, op. cit.
214. Monroe, op. cit.
215. Berman, L.: *OMB and the hazards of Presidential staff work.* Public Adm. Rev., November/December 1978, pp. 520–524.
216. Burstein, P., and Freudenburg, W.: *Changing public policy: the impact of public opinion, antiwar demonstrations, and war costs on Senate voting on Vietnam war motions.* Am. J. Sociol. 84(1):99–121, 1978.
217. Grabowski, H., and Vernon, J.: *Consumer product safety regulations.* Am. Econ. Rev. 68(2):284–289, 1978.
218. Bacheller, op. cit.
219. Ibid.

220. Cupps, D. S.: *Emerging problems of citizen participation.* Public Adm. Rev. 37(5):478–487, 1977.
221. Guth, J. L.: *Consumer organizations and Federal dairy policy.* J. Policy Studies, Summer 1978, pp. 499–503.
222. Hicks, A., et al.: *Class power and state policy: the case of large business corporations, labor unions and governmental redistribution in the American states.* Am. Sociol. Rev. 43:302–315, 1978.
223. Guth, op. cit.
224. Ibid.
225. Gans, H.: *Deciding What's News: A Study of CBS Evening News, NBC Nightly News, Newsweek and Time.* Pantheon, New York, 1979.
226. *Promoting Health; Preventing Disease; Objectives for the Nation* (Working Papers). Office of Smoking and Health, U.S. Department of Health, Education and Welfare, Washington, D.C., 1979.

APPENDIX

TABLE 1. A Summary of Recent Evidence: Major Circumstances and Activities Implicated in the Development of the Contemporary Health Problem and Their Interrelationships

Implicating Circumstances and Activities		Responses within the Physiologic Medium
Socioeconomic Conditions and the Biophysical, Workplace, and Home Environments	*Personal Behavior Patterns*	
National economic growth: long-term rise in per capita and disposable income	Overeating for size and activity; diet high in refined carbohydrates and/or sugar, saturated fats, cholesterol, salt; low in fiber, pectin	Cell mutations; fetal-cell carcinogenic changes
National economic downturns: short-term recession drop in purchasing power (unemployment, decline in per capita and disposable income; absolute or relative price inflation)	Physical inactivity	Development of new strains of antibiotic-resistant pathogens
	Lack of sleep (under 6–7 hours)	Activation of mouth bacteria
	Cigarette smoking	Increased absorption and production of blood lipids, cholesterol, triglycerides, and lipoprotein-bound lipids; increased load on heart, pancreas, liver, gastrointestinal tract; excessive rate of sugar absorption; colon slowdown and increase in anaerobic colon bacteria; increase in degraded cholesterol and bile acids in colon; increased blood sugar; increased blood platelet stickiness
	Paternal smoking	
Air pollution: particulates, hydrocarbons, carbon monoxide, nitrates, sulfur dioxide, sulfates, ozone, ammonium, plutonium	Use of alcohol, alcohol addiction; drinking and driving	
	Use of prescribed or over-the-counter drugs: tranquilizers, barbiturates, antidepressants, hallucinogens; oral contraceptives; estrogens, DES	
Pollution of drinking water: chloroform, nitrates, polycyclic aromatic hydrocarbons, byproducts of chlorination	Use of coffee	Replacement of oxygen with carbon monoxide in red cells; constriction of blood vessels; heart muscle tension
Contamination of food supply: antibiotics used in animal feed; pesticides in meat and dairy foods	Aggressive, time-constrained activity; persistent depressive or conflictful	Mucous membrane irritation;

316

of breast-feeding mothers; lead contamination of cow fodder and condensed milk

Worksite pollutants:
asbestos. ammonia (fertilizers); pesticides, cotton dust, sunlight, infrared, microwaves; fiber glass, smoke, soot, tar, oil; plastics, germicides, cobalt, nickel, mercury, uranium, x-rays; pathogens in hospitals
(Additionally for pregnant women: viruses, tuberculosis, venereal pathogens)

Occupational hazards:
whole-body vibration (truckers), industrial noise; alternating work shifts of 3 weeks or more often; sedentary work; increased workload (amount, intensity responsibility, conflict)

Residential conditions
lack of space for dwellers, no flush toilets; insufficient water; dilapidated

responses to unsatisfying family or work relations; responses to major changes in primary ties (divorce, separation, marriage conflict, serious illness, deaths)

Possession of handguns

Undereating, especially during childhood or pregnancy; of calories, protein, iron

During pregnancy: use of alcohol or drugs; smoking; overeating; acceptance of drug-induced labor

Parental smoking

depressed ciliary action

Depressed neutralizing function of pancreas; increased gastricacidity; irritation of gastric lining

Activation of toxic chemicals and/or procarcinogens; failure to metabolize drugs; central nervous system depression

Biodynamic strain; trauma; organ pressure changes

Desynchronization of body rhythms

Increase in free fatty acids, blood sugar; increase in catecholamines, coagulation, uric acid, pepsinogen, adrenal steroids; drop in white cell defenses; depressed immune response

Toxic effects on and insufficient oxygen and other nutrients to embryo/fetus

Excretion of substances in breast milk, including some drugs, pesticides, and viruses

TABLE 1. Continued

Types and Degrees of Human Health-Damaging Responses

"At-Risk" Health Conditions	Direct Contributory Effects	Dose-Related and Cumulative Effects
Resistance of pathogens to antibiotics	Chronic respiratory disease: sinusitis bronchitis emphysema pulmonary fibrosis Lung cancer	Dose-Related Effects: Chronic lung disease: bronchitis emphysema asthma pulmonary fibrosis Lung cancer
Weight gain for size and activity; obesity		
Hyperlipidemia: raised blood cholesterol, triglycerides, or lipoproteins: very low-density (VLDL), low-density (LDL)	Heart and vascular disease coronary heart heart attack hypertension stroke varicose veins hemorrhoids	Congestive heart failure; stroke
Hyperglycemia		Liver cirrhosis
Hyperuricemia Hyperacetaldehydemia		Dental caries
Increased blood lead	Diabetes; liver cirrhosis; genitourinary, breast, gastrointestinal, skin cancers; dermatitis, stomach ulcers, arthritis, and gout.	Acute respiratory illness: influenza bronchitis in adults and children
Reduced lung function and lung clearance capacity		Neurologic disorders
Reduced exercise capacity	Acute respiratory illness: upper respiratory infections: influenza, bronchitis, pneumonia	Among healthy persons: reduced exercise tolerance, cough, headache, eye and throat; irritation
Fatigue; lowered performance, alertness response, eye-motor		

coordination; reduced short-term memory; reduced steadiness

Increased blood pressure; increased heart rate

Precancerous vaginal adenosis in female offspring

Undernutrition:
low blood iron; vitamin deficiencies; reduced capacity to detoxify toxic substances; small size (prospective pregnant women); poor food digestive absorption; delayed healing; low birthweight; slower mental and physical development

Acute communicable diseases of childhood:
diarrhea
hepatitis
secondary tuberculosis

Acute digestive disorders:
pancreatitis
gall bladder infection

Dental caries

Strains, sprains, cuts, contusions, and fractures from industrial, auto, and home accidents

Loss of hearing

Emotional disorders:
depression
alcohol addiction
adverse drug reactions

Maternal hypertension (eclampsia); toxemia; childbirth complications; maternal deaths; immaturity of newborn; respiratory distress; hyaline membrane disease; fetal alcohol syndrome; congenital defects; sudden infant death syndrome; failure to thrive; child abuse; perinatal infant deaths

Among at-risk persons:
heart and lung disease; exacerbation, premature deaths

Retarded fetal growth, lowered birthweight; perinatal deaths

Cumulative Effects:
Chronic lung disease:
bronchitis
emphysema
asthma

Lung cancer

Heart disease; hypertension

Cancers of mouth, throat, uterus

Liver cirrhosis

Acute respiratory conditions

Malnutrition

Hearing loss

Emotional disorders

Suicide

Maternal illness and deaths

319

TABLE 1. Continued

	Types and Degrees of Human Health-Damaging Responses		
Additive Effects		Underlying Current or Prior Illness	Synergistic Effects
Socioeconomic and Environmental Conditions	Personal Behavior Patterns		
Air pollution: lead, water, dust; cigarette smoke; parental/sibling smoking; poorly ventilated rooms	Overeating for size and activity; saturated fats; cholesterol; irregular meals	Any disabling illness High blood cholesterol; glucose intolerance	With environmental conditions: low income and/or low sociocultural status in families of infants over 1 week and/or normal birthweight
Urban residence	Little physical activity; sedentary occupations; lack of vigorous exercise	Chronic illness: chronic lung conditions (in childhood or adult life) asthma allergies cardiovascular disease diabetes epilepsy osteoarthritis	Worksite exposure to carbon monoxide; asbestos; mine dust exposure
Rural isolation	Outdoor activity during heavy air pollution		
States without strict gun control	Smoking; alcohol use; youthful drinking; alcohol addiction; drug use	Low level of fitness; malnutrition	With personal behavior patterns: high-cholesterol diet smoking second birth before age 18
Prescribed drugs, x-rays	Lack of birth control for: child spacing unwanted child optimal maternal age	Acute illness: acute lung disease (history of childhood or	With current illness: chronic lung disease asthma hypertension acute respiratory
Occupational exposure to carcinogens, airway irritants, physical hazards, cotton textile dust	Decline in social network during crises, including family or primary group at		
White collar, university, professional occupations			

Work-related:
  cramped position, in-
  creased workload
Rise in disposable income;
  relative drop in travel costs
Low income:
  low wage occupations;
  underemployment;
  unemployment
Low socioeconomic status by
  education
Drop in disposable income;
  relative rise in food prices,
  interest rates
Lack of childcare services,
  education opportunities;
  frequent household crises;
  frequent job changes
Social status:
  male, black; elder, child,
  aged 45 or older;
  divorced, separated;
  single male; powerless
  female role in family
Single parent as sole worker
Pregnancy:
  under 17, 35 or older;
  single; short stature; first
  child; fifth-plus child;
  cesarean section; lack of
  prenatal or post-partum
  care

work or residence; marital
  conflict; loss of friends
Undereating for size and
  activity; low protein, low
  vitamin C; foods high in
  sugar
During pregnancy:
  use of alcohol; drugs;
  smoking after third
  month; undereating,
  overeating
Prospective and current
  fathers who smoke heavily
Insufficient use of health
  services and/or
  immunizations

adult disease)
pneumonia
acute stomach
  ulcer
Emotional disorders during
  pregnancy:
  diabetes
  hypertension
Vascular, kidney, endocrine,
  emotional disorders
Anemia, malnutrition
History of obstetric
  problems; cesarean
  section; Rh factor;
  prenatal infection;
  eclampsia, bleeding
Low birthweight; congenital
  defects
Chronic parental illness

disease
children's acute lung
  disease
diarrhea

LITERATURE REVIEW ON THE
CONTEMPORARY HEALTH PROBLEM*

IMPLICATING FACTORS IN THE BIOPHYSICAL, HOME, AND
WORKPLACE ENVIRONMENTS

The Biophysical Environment

1. Ase, J.: *Environmental causes of birth defects* Cont. Ed. Fam. Physicians 3:39–46, 1975.
2. Chapple, C.: *Developmental defects.* Birth Defects (Original Article Series) 8:1–79, 1972.
3. Dahlmann, N., et al.: *Influences of environmental conditions during infancy on final body stature.* Pediatr. Res. 11:695–700, 1977.
4. Doll, R.: *Epidemiology of cancer: current perspectives.* Am. J. Epidemiol. 104:396–404, 1976.
5. Environmental Protection Agency: *Health Consequences of Sulfur Oxides: A Report from CHESS (Community Health and Environmental Surveillance System) 1970–1971.* Research Triangle Park, N.C., 1974.
6. Environmental Protection Agency, reported in *Safe U.S. drinking is no longer a certainty.* New York Times, April 9, 1978.
7. *Exposure of patients to ionizing radiations.* WHO Chron. 20:90, 1975.
8. Federal Interagency Task Force on Air Quality Indicators: *A Recommended Air Pollution Index.* Council on Environmental Quality, Environmental Protection Agency, U.S. Department of Commerce, Washington, D.C., 1976.
9. Gofman, J.: *The plutonium controversy.* J.A.M.A. 236:284–286, 1976.
10. Hammer, D., et al.: *The Los Angeles Student Nurse Study.* Arch. Environ. Health 28:255–560, 1974.
11. Higginson, J.: *A hazardous society? Individual vs. community responsibility in cancer prevention.* Am. J. Public Health 66:359–366, 1976.
12. Kraybill, H.: *Carcinogenesis induced by trace contaminants in potable water.* Bull. N.Y. Acad. Med. 54(4):413–427, 1978.
13. Lave, L., and Seskin, E.: *Air pollution and human health.* Science 169:723–733, 1970.
14. Levy, D., et al.: *The relationship between acute respiratory illness and air pollution levels in an industrial city.* Am. Rev. Respir. Dis. 116:167–173, 1977.
15. National Institutes of Health, reported in *New York Times,* April 20, 1975.

---

*The studies which are summarized in Table 1, and form the basis for Figure 2 (p.27), represent an effort to synthesize recent published critical reviews, previous syntheses, and individual studies related to the nature of contemporary health problems. Well over 1,000 studies have been incorporated. They were drawn from the literature, primarily since 1973, concerning the impacts on health of the socioeconomic, biophysical, workplace, and home environments and of personal behavior patterns, physical activity, diet, smoking, alcohol, and other drug use. Special attention was given to the environments of the growing fetus and of young children.

16. *Oversight of Biomedical and Behavioral Research in the U.S., 1977.* Hearings before the Subcommittee on Health and Scientific Research of the Senate Committee on Human Resources, 95th Congress, Part II, June 8, 10, 1977.
17. Shy, C.: *Health consequences of alternative energy systems.* Paper presented at the Workshop on Energy and the Social Sciences, University of North Carolina, Chapel Hill, November 19, 1977.
18. Thring, M.: *Air pollution—A general survey.* Int. J. Environ. Studies 5:251–257, 1974.
19. Ury, H., and Hexter, A.: *Relating photochemical pollution to human physiological reactions under controlled conditions.* Arch. Environ. Health 18:473–480, 1969.
20. Senate Subcommittee on Agricultural Research and General Legislation: *Food Safety and Quality: Use of Antibiotics in Animal Food.* Hearings, Part II, September 21,22, 1977.
21. Williams, L., et al.: *Implications of the observed effect of air pollution on birth weight.* Social Biol. 24:1–9, 1977.
22. Wilson, J.: *Environmental effects on development—teratology,* in Assali, N. (ed.): *Pathophysiology of Gestation,* Vol. 2. Academic Press, New York, 1972, pp. 269–320.
23. Winklestein, W.: *Contemporary perspectives on prevention.* Bull. N.Y. Acad. Med. 51(1):27–38, 1975.

The Home and Workplace Environments

24. Andrew, G., et al.: *The relationships between physical, psychological, and social morbidity in a surburban community.* Am. J. Epidemiol. 105:324–329, 1977.
25. Bureau of Labor Statistics: *Occupational Injuries and Illnesses, 1976.* U.S. Department of Labor, Washington, D.C., 1977.
26. Cobb, S., and Kasl, S.: *Termination: The Consequences of Job Loss.* National Institute of Occupational Safety and Health, Cincinnati, 1977.
27. Fife, D.: *Noise and hospital stay.* Am. J. Public Health 66:680–681, 1976.
28. Gruber, G.: *Relationships Between Wholebody Vibration and Morbidity Patterns Among Interstate Truck Drivers.* National Institute of Occupational Safety and Health, Cincinnati, 1976.
29. Henriksen-Zeiner, T.: *Six-year mortality related to cardiorespiratory symptoms and environmental risk factors in a sample of the Norwegian population.* J. Chron. Dis. 29:15–33, 1976.
30. House, J.: *Occupational stress and coronary heart disease: a review and theoretical integration.* J. Health Social Behav. 15:12–27, 1974.
31. Jonsson, A., and Hansson, L.: *Prolonged exposure to a stressful stimulus (noise) as a cause of raised blood pressure in man.* Lancet, January 8, 1977, pp. 86–87.
32. Key, M., et al.: *Occupational Diseases: A Guide to Their Recognition.* National Institute of Occupational Safety and Health, Cincinnati, 1977.
33. Lebowitz, M.: *Occupational exposures in relation to symptomatology and lung function in a community population.* Environ. Res. 14:59–67, 1977.
34. Loring, W., and Hinkle, L.: *The Effect of the Man-Made Environment on Health and Behavior.* Center for Disease Control, Atlanta, 1977.

35. Pell, S.: *The identification of risk factors in employed populations.* Trans. N.Y. Acad. Sci. 36(4):341–356, 1974, Series II.
36. Stellman, J., and Dawn, S.: *Work Is Dangerous to Your Health: A Handbook of Health Hazards in the Workplace and What You Can Do About It.* Random House/Vintage, New York, 1973.
37. Theorell, T., and Floderus-Myrhed, B.: *'Workload' and risk of myocardial infarction—A prospective psychosocial analysis.* Int. J. Epidemiol. 6:17–21, 1977.
38. Wingel, C. M., Hughes, L., and LaDou, J.: *Physiological effects of rotational work shifting: A review.* J. Occup. Med. 20(3):204–210, 1978.

IMPLICATING FACTORS DERIVED FROM SOCIOECONOMIC STATUS

The National Economy

39. Brenner, M. H.: *Fetal, infant, and maternal mortality during periods of economic instability.* Int. J. Health Serv. 3(2):145–155, 1973.
40. Brenner, M. H.: *Health costs and benefits of economic policy.* Int. J. Health Serv. 7:581–623, 1977.
41. Brenner, M. H.: *Trends in alcohol consumption and associated illnesses.* Am. J. Public Health 65(12):1279–1292, 1975.
42. *Estimating the Social Costs of National Economic Policy: Implications for Mental and Physical Health and Criminal Aggression.* Joint Economic Committee Print, 94th Congress, October 1976.
43. Eyer, J.: *Does unemployment cause the death rate peak in each business cycle? A multifactor model of death rate change.* Int. J. Health Serv. 7:625–663, 1977.
44. Eyer, J.: *Hypertension as a disease of modern society.* Int. J. Health Serv. 5:539–558, 1975.
45. Eyer, J.: *Prosperity as a cause of death.* Int. J. Health Serv. 7(1):125–150, 1977.
46. Karlberg, P., et al.: *Clinical analyses of causes of death with emphasis on perinatal mortality.* Monogr. Paediat. 9:86–120, 1977.
47. Kitagawa, E., and Hauser, P.: *Differential Mortality in the U.S.: A Study in Socioeconomic Epidemiology.* Harvard University Press, Cambridge, Mass., 1973.
48. *Leading causes of death in Africa, Asia, and Latin America.* WHO Chron. 29, 1975.
49. *Leading causes of death in North America, Europe, and Oceania.* WHO Chron. 29:106–107, 1975.
50. National Center for Health Statistics: *Mortality Trends in Czechoslovakia (1930–67).* U.S. Public Health Service, Washington, D.C., 1969.
51. Puffer, R. R., and Serrano, C. V.: *Patterns of Childhood Mortality: Inter-American Investigation of Mortality in Childhood.* Pan American Health Organization, Washington, D.C., 1973.

52. Thompson, R.: *The mortality of Swedish and U.S. white males: a comparison of experience, 1969–1971.* Am. J. Public Health 66:968–974, 1976.
53. Senate Committee on Labor and Public Welfare: *Full Employment and Balanced Growth Act of 1976.* Hearings, May 15, 17–19, 1976.
54. Select Committee on Nutrition and Human Needs: *Food Price Changes, 1973–74, and Nutritional Status.* Washington, D.C., 1974.
55. Stein, Z., et al.: *Famine and Human Development: The Dutch Hunger Winter of 1944/45.* Oxford University Press, New York, 1975.
56. Vallin, J.: *World trends in infant mortality since 1950.* World Health Stat. Rep. 29:646–674, 1976.

Age, Sex, Income, and Race

57. Antonovsky, A., and Bernstein, J.: *Social class and infant mortality.* Soc. Sci. Med. 11:453–470, 1977.
58. Berg, J., et al.: *Economic status and survival of cancer patients.* Cancer 39:467–477, 1977.
59. Brooks, L.: *The decomposition of effects of sociodemographic variables on area infant mortality rates: a path-analytic solution.* Paper presented before the Statistics Section, American Public Health Association, 105th Annual Meeting, Washington, D.C., October 31, 1977.
60. Brown, R.: *Interaction of nutrition and infection in clinical practice.* Pediatr. Clin. North Am. 24:241–251, 1977.
61. Chase, H. C.: *Infant mortality and its concomitants, 1960–1972.* Med. Care 15(8):662–674, 1977.
62. Clarke, M., et al.: *Peptic ulceration in men: epidemiology and medical care.* Br. J. Prev. Soc. Med. 30:115–122, 1976.
63. *Clinical and Subclinical Malnutrition, Their Influence on the Capacity To Do Work.* Final Progress Report, 1971/75. Milwaukee Medical College of Wisconsin and Research Service, 1975.
64. Coser, R. L.: *Why Bother? Is research on issues of women's health worthwhile?* in *Women and Their Health Research Implications for a New Era.* National Center for Health Statistics Research, Rockville, Md., 1975.
65. Eisner, V., et al.: *Improvement in infant and perinatal mortality in the United States, 1965–1973, Priorities for intervention.* Am. J. Public Health 68(4):359–366, 1978.
66. Freeman, H., et al.: *Relations between nutrition and cognition in rural Guatemala.* Am. J. Public Health 67:233–239, 1977.
67. Gove, W. R., and Tudor, J. F.: *Sex roles and mental illness.* Am. J. Sociol. 78:812–835, 1973.
68. International Union of Nutritional Sciences: *Report: Guidelines on the at-risk concept and the health and nutrition of young children.* Am. J. Clin. Nutrition 30:242–254, 1977.
69. Keil, J. E., et al.: *Hypertension: effects of social class and racial admixture: the results of a cohort study in the black population of Charleston, S.C.* Am. J. Public Health 67:634–639, 1977.
70. Lerner, M., and Stutz, R. N.: *Have we narrowed the gaps between the poor and*

325

the non-poor? Part II. Narrowing the gaps, 1959–1961 to 1969–1971: mortality. Med. Care 15(8):620, 1977.

71. Lewis, C. E., and Lewis, M. A.: *The potential impact of sexual equality on health.* N. Engl. J. Med. 297:863–869, 1977.

72. Morris, J., and Heady, J.: *Social and biological factors in infant mortality.* Lancet 268:346, 1955.

73. Naeye, R., et al.: *Relation of poverty and race to birth weight and organ and cell structure in the newborn.* Pediatr. Res. 5:17–22, 1971.

74. Nathanson, C. A.: *Sex roles as variables in preventive health behavior.* J. Comm. Health 3(2):142–155, 1977.

75. Nathanson, C. A.: *Sex, illness and medical care.* Soc. Sci. Med. 11:13–25, 1977.

76. *Differentials in Health Characteristics by Marital Status, U.S.: 1971–72* Series 10, No. 104. National Center for Health Statistics, Rockville, Md., 1976.

77. *Infant Mortality Rates: Socioeconomic Factors, U.S.* National Center for Health Statistics, Rockville, Md., 1972.

78. *Trends in "Prematurity," U.S.: 1950–67.* National Center for Health Statistics, Rockville, Md., 1972.

79. *Nutrition survey shows dietary deficiencies.* Health Resources News, March 1974.

80. Owen, G.: *Comment.* Am. J. Public Health 67:229–230, 1977.

81. Pollack, E. S.: *Mental health demographic profile for health services planning.* Statistical Notes for Health Planners. 4:1–9, 1977.

82. Rethersford, R.: *The Changing Sex Differential in Mortality.* Greenwood, Westport, Conn., 1975.

83. Rosen, G.: *Preventive Medicine in the U.S. in Historical Perspective.* Task Force Report, National Conference on Preventive Medicine, Washington, D.C., June 9–11, 1975.

84. Rush, D., et al.: *The rationale for and design of a randomized controlled trial of nutritional supplementation in pregnancy.* Nutrition Rep. Int. 7:547–553, 1973.

85. Scrimshaw, N. S.: *Nutrition and the health of nations,* in *Occasional Papers* (Series I-911). Institute of Nutrition, University of North Carolina, Chapel Hill, 1978.

86. Silverman, C.: *The epidemiology of depression—A review.* Am. J. Psychol. 124:883–891, 1978.

87. Sinclair, J., and Saigal, S.: *Nutritional influences in industrial societies.* Am. J. Dis. Child. 129:549–553, 1975.

88. Verbrugge, L. M.: *Females and illness: recent trends in sex differences in the United States.* J. Health Social Behav. 17:387–403, 1976.

89. Waldron, I., and Eyer, J.: *Socioeconomic causes of the recent rise in death rates for 15–24 year olds.* Soc. Sci. Med. 9:383–396, 1975.

90. Waldron, I.: *Why do women live longer than men?* Soc. Sci. Med. 10:349–362, 1976.

91. Weaver, J. L.: *Policy responses to complex issues: the case of black infant mortality.* J. Health Politics 1(4):433–443, 1977.

92. *Women's utilization of mental health services studied.* Evaluation 3(1–2):30–31, 1976.

93. Yeracaris, C. A., and Kim, J. H.: *Socioeconomic differentials in selected causes of death.* Am. J. Public Health 68:342–351, 1978.

Women, Children, and Income

94. Ackerman, B. D.: *Prevention of hyaline membrane disease.* Pediatr. Ann. 7(3):95–104, 1978.
95. Arms, S.: *Immaculate Deception.* Houghton-Mifflin, Boston, 1975.
96. Garbarino, J.: *A preliminary study of some ecological correlates of child abuse: the impact of socioeconomic stress on mothers.* Child Dev. 47:178–185, 1976.
97. Gersten, J.: *An evaluation of the etiologic role of stressful life-change events in psychological disorders.* J. Health Social Behav. 18:228–244, 1977.
98. Gordon, M., and O'Sullivan, M. H.: *The early identification of high-risk pregnancies.* Pediatr. Ann. 7(3):36–63, 1978.
99. Higgins, A.: *Nutrition status and the outcome of pregnancy.* J. Can. Diet Assoc. 37(1):17–35, 1976.
100. Hunt, V.: *Occupational Health Problems of Pregnant Women. Report and Recommendations for the Office of the Secretary.* U.S. Department of Health, Education and Welfare, Washington, D.C., 1975.
101. Hunter, R., et al.: *Antecedents of child abuse and neglect in premature infants: a prospective study in a newborn intensive care unit.* Pediatrics 61:629–635, 1978.
102. Low, J. A., et al.: *Intrauterine growth retardation: a preliminary report of long-term morbidity.* Am. J. Obstet. Gynecol. 130:534–543, 1978.
103. Muller, C.: *Methodological issues in health economics research relevant to women.* Women and Health 1:1, 1976.
104. Newberger, E., et al.: *Child health in America: toward a rational public policy.* Milbank Mem. Fund Q., Summer 1976, pp. 249–298.
105. Newberger, E., et al.: *Pediatric social illness: toward an etiologic classification.* Pediatrics 60:178–185, 1977.
106. Owen, G., and Lippman, G.: *Nutritional status of infants and young children: U.S.A.* Pediatr. Clin. North Am. 24:211–227, 1977.
107. Slocumb, J., and Junitz, S.: *Factors affecting maternal mortality among American Indians.* Public Health Rep. 92:349–356, 1977.
108. Senate Select Committee on Nutrition and Human Needs: *Maternal, Fetal and Infant Nutrition.* Hearings, June 5, 6, 1973. 93rd Congress, Part I.

Women, Children, and Personal Behavior Patterns

109. Clarren, S., and Smith, D.: *The fetal alcohol syndrome.* N. Engl. J. Med. 298(19):1063–1067, 1978.
110. Holsclaw, D. S., and Topham, A. L.: *The effects of smoking on fetal, neonatal and childhood development.* Pediatr. Ann. 7(3):105–136, 1978.
111. Jain, A.: *Mortality risk associated with the use of oral contraceptives.* Studies Fam. Planning 8(3):50–54, 1977.
112. Jick, H., Dian, B., and Rothman, K. J.: *Noncontraceptive estrogens and nonfatal myocardial infarction.* J.A.M.A. 239(14):1407–1408, 1978.
113. Jick, H., et al.: *Oral contraceptives and nonfatal myocardial infarction.* J.A.M.A. 239(14):1403–1406, 1978.

114. Kaminski, M., and Schwartz, D.: *Alcohol consumption in pregnant women and the outcome of pregnancy.* Alcoholism Clin. Exp. Res. 2(2):155–163, 1978.
115. Little, R.: *Moderate alcohol use during pregnancy and decreased infant birthweight.* Am. J. Public Health 67(12):1154–1156, 1977.
116. *Oral contraceptives and heart risk.* Fam. Planning Persp. 7:145–147, 1975.
117. Sartwell, P.: *Oral contraceptives—another look.* Am. J. Public Health 68(4):323–326, 1978.

IMPLICATING FACTORS LINKED TO PERSONAL BEHAVIOR PATTERNS

Physical Activity

118. Belloc, N.: *The relationship of health practices and mortality.* Prev. Med. 2:67–81, 1973.
119. *GAO report recommends new law to control guns.* Nation's Health, April 1, 1978, p. 3.
120. Gyntelberg, F., and Meyer, J.: *Relationship between blood pressure and physical fitness, smoking and alcohol consumption.* Acta Med. Scand. 195(5):375–380, 1974.
121. Morris, J.: *Primary prevention of heart attack.* Bull. N.Y. Acad. Med. 51(1):62–74, 1975.

Diet

122. Cleave, T.: *Over-consumption.* Public Health 91(3):121–127, 1977.
123. Gordon, T., and Kannel, W.: *Effects of overweight on cardiovascular diseases.* Gerontology 28:80–88, 1973.
124. Holtzman, N.: *The goal of preventing early death,* in *Papers on the National Health Guidelines. Conditions for Change in the Health Care System.* Health Resources Administration, Washington, D.C., 1977.
125. Hood, L. F., et al.: *Carbohydrates and Health.* AVI Publishing Company, Westport, Conn., 1976.
126. Howell, M.: *Diet as an etiological factor in the development of cancers of colon and rectum.* J. Chron. Dis. 28:67–80, 1975.
127. Joossens, J.: *Pattern of food and mortality in Belgium.* Lancet 50:1069–1072, 1977.
128. Kneese, A., and Schulze, W.: *Environmental problems: environment, health, and economics—the case of cancer.* Am. Econ. Rev. 67(1):326–332, 1977.
129. Kuller, L.: *Epidemiology of cardiovascular diseases: current perspectives.* Am. J. Epidemiol. 104:425–456, 1976.
130. Logan, R., et al.: *Risk factors for ischemic heart disease in normal men aged 40—Edinburgh-Stockholm Study.* Lancet, May 6, 1978, pp. 949–954.
131. Olefsky, J., et al.: *Effects of weight reduction on obesity.* Clin. Invest. 53:64–67, 1974.

132. *Prevalance and natural history of obesity in the United Kingdom,* in *Research on Obesity.* H.M. Department of Health and Social Security, London, 1976.
133. Schettler, G.: *Risk factors of coronary heart disease: West German data.* Prev. Med. 5:216–225, 1976.
134. Smith, W.: *Epidemiology of hypertension. Med. Clin. North Am.* 61(3):467–486, 1977.
135. Stamler, J., et al.: *Risk factors and the etiopathogenesis of atherosclerotic diseases.* Am. Assoc. Pathol. Bacteriol. 62(2):100–152, 1971.
136. Senate Select Committee on Nutrition and Human Needs: *Diet Related to Killer Diseases: Obesity.* Hearings, February 1,2, 1977.
137. Select Committee on Nutrition and Human Needs: *Dietary Goals for the U.S.,* January 1977.
138. Senate Select Committee on Nutrition and Human Needs: *Nutrition and Diseases, 1973. Part II.* Hearings, April 30–May 2, 1973.
139. Wilhelmsen, L., et al.: *Primary risk factors in patients with myocardial infarction.* Am. Heart J. 91:412–419, 1976.
140. Wolf, P., et al.: *Epidemiology of stroke.* Adv. Neurol. 16:5–19, 1977.

Smoking

141. *Health Consequences of Smoking, 1975.* Center for Disease Control, Atlanta, 1975.
142. *The Health Consequences of Smoking—A Reference Edition: Selected Chapters from 1971 through 1975; Reports with Cumulative Index for All Reports, 1964–1975.* Center for Disease Control, Atlanta, 1976.
143. Cohen, B. H., et al.: *Risk factors in chronic obstructive pulmonary disease (COPD).* Am. J. Epidemiol. 105:223–232, 1977.
144. *The effects of smoking on health.* Morbid. Mortal. Weekly Rep. 26(18), 1977.
145. Huhti, E., et al.: *Chronic respiratory disease, smoking and prognosis for life—an epidemiological study.* Scand. J. Respir. Dis. 58(3):170–180, 1977.
146. Lebowitz, M.: *Smoking habits and changes in smoking habits as they relate to chronic conditions and respiratory symptoms.* Am. J. Epidemiol. 105:534–543, 1977.
147. Leeder, S., et al.: *Change in respiratory symptom prevalence in adults who alter their smoking habits.* Am. J. Epidemiol. 105:522–529, 1977.
148. *Respiratory Diseases. Task Force Report on Prevention, Control, and Education.* National Heart, Lung and Blood Institute, Washington, D.C., 1977.
149. Wald, N.: *Mortality for lung cancer and coronary heart disease in relation to changes in smoking habits.* Lancet, January 17, 1976, pp. 136–138.

Alcohol Use

150. *Alcohol: a growing danger.* WHO Chron. 29:102–105, 1975.
151. *Alcohol and Health, June 1974.* Alcohol, Drug Abuse and Mental Health Administration, Washington, D.C., 1974.
152. Baker, S. P., and Fisher, R. S.: *Alcohol and motorcycle fatalities.* Am. J. Public Health 67:246–249, 1977.

153. Bell, R., and Thomas, D.: *Mortality experience of alcoholics and drug addicts under SSI, January 1974–April 1975.* Research and Statistics Notes, No. 1, February 4, 1977.
154. Burch, G. E., and Giles, T. D.: *Alcoholic cardiomyopathy,* in Kissin, B., and Begleiter, H. (eds.): *Biology of Alcoholism.* Plenum, New York, 1974, pp. 435–460.
155. Cowan, D. H.: *The platelet defect in alcoholism.* Ann. N.Y. Acad. Sci. 252:328–341, 1975.
156. DeLint, J., and Schmidt, W.: *Alcoholism and Mortality.* Addiction Research Foundation, Toronto, 1974.
157. Fisher, E., et al.: *Alcoholism and other concomitants of mitochondrial inclusions in skeletal muscle.* Am. J. Med. Sci. 261(2):85–99, 1971.
158. Hinderer, H.: *On the task of combating alcoholism according to the law of the German-Democratic Republic.* Br. J. Addiction 66(1):9–17, 1971.
159. Leszcynski, B.: *The problem of alcoholism in the light of research on accidents among textile workers at work in Poland.* Humanizm Pracy (Warsaw) 9(1):70–74, 1971.
160. Lieber, C. S.: *The metabolic basis of alcohol's toxicity.* Hosp. Prac., February 1977, pp. 73–80.
161. *Summary Proceedings, Tripartite Conference on Prevention.* Alcohol, Drug Abuse, and Mental Health Administration, Washington, D.C., 1977.
162. Turner, T., et al.: *Measurement of alcohol-related effects in man: chronic effects in relation to levels of alcohol consumption.* Johns Hopkins Med. J. 141:239, 1977.
163. Virkkunen, M., and Alha, A.: *On suicides committed under the influence of alcohol in Finland in 1967.* Br. J. Addiction 65(4):317–323, 1971.
164. Wapnick, S., and Jones, J. J.: *Alcohol and glucose tolerance.* Lancet 11(7769):180, 1972.
165. Zylman, R.: *A critical evaluation of the literature on 'alcohol involvement' in highway deaths.* Accident Anal. Prev. 6:163–204, 1974.

Other Drug Use

166. Abelson, H., and Fishburne, P.: *Non-Medical Use of Psychoactive Substances: 1975/76. Part I.* Response Analysis Corporation, Princeton, 1976.
167. Austin, G. A., et al.: *Drug Users and Driving Behaviors.* National Institute on Drug Abuse, Rockville, Md., 1977.
168. Basu, T.: *Interaction of drugs and nutrition.* J. Hum. Nutrition 31:449–458, 1977.
169. Christakis, G.: *Diets, drugs, and their interrelationships.* J. Am. Diet. Assoc. 52:21–24, 1968.
170. Louria, D.: *The epidemiology of drug abuse and drug abuse rehabilitation,* in Glatt, M. (ed.): *Drug Dependence.* MTI Press, Baltimore, 1977.
171. Pradhan, S. N.: *Drug Abuse: Clinical and Basic Aspects.* C. V. Mosby, St. Louis, 1977, pp. 11–83.
172. Sharma, S.: *Barbiturates and driving.* Accident Anal. Prev. 8:27–31, 1976.

173. Smart, R. G.: *The Problems of Drugs and Driving: An Overview of Current Research and Future Needs.* Addiction Research Foundation of Ontario, Toronto, 1975.
174. Sterling-Smith, R. S.: *Alcohol, marihuana and other drug patterns among operators involved in fatal motor vehicle accidents,* in Israelstam, S., and Lambert, S. (eds.): *Alcohol, Drugs, and Traffic Safety. Proceedings of the Sixth International Conference on Alcohol, Drugs and Traffic Safety. Toronto, September 8–13, 1974.* Addiction Research Foundation of Ontario, Toronto, 1975, pp. 93–105.
175. Weathersbee, P. S., and Lodge, J. R.: *Caffeine: its direct and indirect influence on reproduction.* J. Reprod. Med. 19(2):55–63, 1977.
176. Weiss, K.: *Vaginal cancer: an iatrogenic disease?* Int. J. Health Serv. 5:235–251 (1975).

TABLE 2. Statistical Basis for Figure 4: Differences in Illness, Disability, and Death Between Low- and High-Income Groups*

Frequency of Acute and Chronic Conditions and Their
Percentage Distribution for the U.S. Population and Selected Income Groups

Conditions	All Income Groups		Low-Income Population		High-Income Population	
	Frequency†	Percent of all Conditions	Frequency†	Percent of all Conditions	Frequency†	Percent of all Conditions
Total	3015.0[a]	100.0	2670.6	100.0	2454.1	100.0
Acute Conditions	1960.0	65.1	1642.0[b]	61.5	1837.0[b]	75.0
Respiratory	1057.0	35.1				
Injuries	343.0	11.4				
Infections, other	202.0	6.7				
Digestive	90.0	3.0				
Maternity	17.0	0.6				
Other acute	251.0	8.3				
Chronic Conditions	1055.0	34.9	1028.6[c]	38.5	617.1[c]	25.0
Respiratory	269.0	8.9	248.0	9.2	234.9[d]	9.6
Circulatory	216.5	7.2	333.5	12.5	158.8	6.5
Endocrine, metabolic, other	157.0	5.2	65.2	2.4	35.8	1.5
Musculoskeletal	145.7	4.8	185.7	7.0	71.9[d]	2.9
Skin	146.4	4.8	96.5	3.6	67.3	2.6
Digestive	106.9	3.5	99.7	3.7	44.4[d]	1.8

*To obtain the death rates shown in Figure 4 (p.45), "other races" and "white" were used as proxies for low-income and high-income groups respectively since death rates by income group are not available. The restricted activity day rates shown in Figure 4 were obtained by adding the products of the income-specific prevalence and the number of restricted activity days per condition for each chronic condition (except for exclusions noted in footnote c). (Source of data in addition to those cited for Tables 7 and 8: *Minority Health Chart Book*, American Public Health Association, Washington, D.C., 1974.)

†Incidence and prevalence adjusted as rate per 1000 population in specified groups.

ªSee Tables 7 and 8 for listing of conditions, methods, and sources. Total acute and chronic conditions for "All Income Groups" include all the conditions used by the National Center for Health Statistics Health Interview Survey plus cancer.

ᵇTotal acute conditions for "low" (family income under $5000) and "high" income (family income $15,000 or more) populations are based on data collected by the National Center for Health Statistics in 1973, a year earlier than the acute illness incidence for "All Income Groups." Incidence for "All Income Groups," 1973, was 1720 per 1000 population.

ᶜTotal chronic conditions for "low" and "high" income populations do not include mental illness, alcohol or drug addiction, and some less common muscle bone, skin, and digestive conditions.

ᵈIncludes both "middle" and "high" income rates, (i.e., $5000 and above) for tuberculosis, arthritis, and four digestive conditions.

TABLE 3. Health-Promoting and Health-Damaging Conditions: Examples of Excesses and Deficits and the Social Groups Most Likely to be Affected

Health-Damaging Conditions	Health-Promoting Conditions	
	Excess	Deficit
Excess	*Conditions:* high food availability, animal protein; processed foods; pollution from high use of nonrenewable forms of energy	*Conditions:* inadequate supply of food, amount or variety; high levels of pollution
	Social Group: the affluent in urban areas	*Social Group:* the poor in urban poor areas
Deficit	*Conditions:* high food availability, animal protein; processed foods; low levels of pollution	*Conditions:* inadequate supply of food, amount or variety; low levels of pollution
	Social Group: the affluent in non-urban areas	*Social group:* the poor in non-urban areas

TABLE 4. When New Information Through Health Education Can Best Be Health-Promoting

		Individual's Knowledge of Options	
		Aware	Not Aware
Range of Options	Narrow	Resources required	Knowledge and resources required
	Wide	Assistance unnecessary	Knowledge helpful
Absolute or Relative Cost of Options	High-cost	Resources required	Knowledge and resources required
	Low-cost	Assistance unnecessary	Knowledge helpful

TABLE 5. When Reinterpretation of Circumstances by Social Support Can Best Be Health-Promoting

		Individual's Perception of Circumstances	
		Perceived as hazardous	*Not perceived as hazardous*
Observable Circumstances	Unequivocally hazardous	Reinterpretation not necessary	Reinterpretation necessary: Consciousness-raising
	Interpretably hazardous	Reinterpretation potentially most useful	Reinterpretation not necessary

TABLE 6. Health Policy Alternatives in a Prevention-Oriented Ecological Framework

		Alternatives for Setting Options for Populations		
		Change Number of Options	*Change Relative Cost of Options*	*Change Both Number and Relative Cost*
Current Population Options	Health-promoting circumstances and activities	increase($\uparrow$)	decrease ($\downarrow$)	increase number and decrease relative cost
	Health-damaging circumstances and activities	decrease ($\downarrow$)	increase ($\uparrow$)	decrease number and increase relative cost

335

TABLE 7. Estimated Percentages of All Americans and Those in Special Groups Who Are At Risk for Modern Illness

	Living in Health-Damaging Circumstances*		Doing Health-Damaging Things*		
	Percentage of Special Groups	Special Group as Percentage of All Persons	Personal Habits and Coping Practices	Percentage of Special Groups	Special Groups as Percentage of All Persons
Socioeconomic Group					
poverty level	(29) blacks	12	car driving[7]	(70) drivers	91
	(17) children	[4]	nonuser, auto seat belt	(51) aged 20 or older	43
	(15) elders	[5]	no regular exercise	(73) aged 20 or older	34
		[2]	lack of vigorous exercise[8]		47
family income under $5000	(12) families	11	sedentary paid work[9]	(44) employed	20
family income under $7000	(29) families	25	underweight[10]	(9-29) aged 2,4,6	7
low paid jobs[1]	(20) work force	8		(8) aged 17 and older	
unemployed over 6 months	(18) work force	0.6		(6) women 17-44 years‡	2
separated or divorced	(6) adults	4	retarded height[11]	aged 2,4,6	3
living alone	(30) elders	3	obese[11]	(16) adolescents	
				(12) adults	13
Biophysical, workplace, and home environments			excess dietary calories[12]	(16) obese adolescents	27
polluted air[2]	all in metropolitan central cities	30		(40) adults	
infectious drinking water[3]		19	excess dietary fat, cholesterol sugar[13]	(37) aged 17 and older	53–80
unfluoridated community water[4]		51	smokers	(43) pregnant women‡	26
					0.6

inadequate housing[5]	(23) children aged 5–13	4
	(6) households	6
hazardous jobs[6]	(37) employed persons	14
Environment of unborn (women)‡		
hazardous jobs and worksites	(16) working women	3
	(30) pregnant women	0.4
poverty	(30) women household heads and individuals	15
overworked	(11) pregnant women	2
ill	(12) pregnant women	0.2
anemic	(24) pregnant women	0.3

alcohol beverage users	drinkers:	
	(42) adults	31
	(32) adolescents	
	potential problem drinkers:	
	(17) adults	12
	problem drinkers:	
	(7) adults	5
	(15) adults	14
	(11) adolescents	
	(6) pregnant women‡	0.1
nonmedical drug users	(30) married women 15–44 yrs or their spouses	25
no (or late) prenatal care	(24) infants born to women under 20 or 35 and older‡	4
nonusers, birth control	(21) unintended infants born to married women[15]	0.3
inadequate immunizations for one or more of six communicable diseases[16]	(25–38) children 1–4 yrs	
	(20–84) children 5–12 yrs	5 to 14

337

TABLE 7. Continued

Responding in Physiologically Health-Damaging Ways*			Result: The Profile of Modern Illness* [19]	
Physiologic Responses	*Percentage of Special Groups*	*Special Groups as Percentage of All Persons*	*Conditions*	*Percentage of All Annual Illness†*
trouble hearing	(4) aged 6–11	11	*Acute*	65
	(15) adults		respiratory	35
trouble reading	(4) aged 6–11	0.5	colds, upper	17
edentulous	(11) adults	8	respiratory	
decayed or missing teeth	(0.6–11) per person aged 6 and older	7§	influenza	16
			pneumonia	0.3
elevated serum cholesterol[17]			bronchitis	0.7
			other	0.6
moderate	(25) adults	18	injuries	11
high	(16) adults	11	infections	7
high blood pressure[18]	(18) adults	12	common	
untreated	(10) adults	7	childhood	0.8
blood pressure			virus	3
above borderline hypertension	(5) adults		venereal	0.2
untreated hypertension	(2) adults		other	3
			digestive	3
			dental caries	0.8
			other	2.2
			maternity	0.6
			other acute	8.3
			Chronic	35
			respiratory	9
			sinusitis	3
			asthma/hay fever	3
			bronchitis	1
			emphysema	0.2

338

Condition		
other	2	7
circulatory		
heart	1.7	
hypertension	2	
cerebrovascular disease	0.2	
varicosities and hemorrhoids	4	
endocrine, metabolic, nervous, genitourinary, and other		5
diabetes only	0.7	
musculoskeletal		5
arthritis	3	
impairments, not paralysis	2	
other	0.2	
skin		5
digestive (including ulcer and liver conditions)		4
cancer		0.5
breast, uterus, cervix	0.2	
other	0.3	

*Percentages are rounded to the nearest whole, except those under 1 percent.
†Total rate is 3015 conditions per 1000 persons per year.
‡Increases the risk of having low-birth-weight or congenitally malformed babies.
§Number per person.

NOTES AND SOURCES FOR TABLE 7

Most of the data presented in Table 7 are from national surveys of the National Center for Health Statistics and the Bureau of the Census. The figures have been adjusted to the 1976 population, using primarily 1975–76 data; nutritional data are for 1971–74; housing, 1970; vision, hearing and teeth, 1963–65, the latest available. Children are those under 18 years; adults, those aged 18 and older; and elders, those 65 and older, unless noted. Cut-off points for at-risk and non-risk levels are based on epidemiologic and clinical studies cited below and in Table 8.

Notes

1. Laborers and farmworkers; service and paid household workers.
2. Persons in central cities of metropolitan areas.
3. Does not include exposure to chemicals or other toxic substances.
4. Some additional persons have access to fluoridated school drinking water.
5. Assuming one household per inadequate housing unit.
6. Industries which have above average rates of occupational illness and injury.
7. A total of 130 million cars, assuming 1.5 persons per auto.
8. Those who do not bicycle, jog, or swim, assuming these activities are mutually exclusive.
9. White collar workers.
10. Self-judged by adults.
11. Measured by thickness of skinfold over triceps muscles.
12. Self-judged as overweight by adults; men tend to underestimate their overweight; women overestimate their overweight.
13. Excludes those who are underweight, those who exercise vigorously, and those who are not white collar workers; assuming each group is mutually exclusive. (The larger figure is from the Health and Nutrition Examination Survey, May 1979.)
14. Excludes marijuana used by 22 percent of adolescents; hallucinogens, by 5 percent of adolescents; and opiates, by 3 to 6 percent of adolescents.
15. A total of 273,000 unintended infants were born to women aged 15 to 20 out of 595,000 children born to women in that age group; many were unmarried and therefore are not included in the National Center for Health Statistics survey, which includes only married women.
16. Rubella, measles, diphtheria, pertussis, tetanus, polio.
17. Moderate serum cholesterol is 220–259 mg %; high is 260 or more mg %.
18. High blood pressure is 160 (or more) systolic pressure, or 95 (or more) diastolic pressure; above borderline is 105 diastolic or higher.
19. The Profile of Modern Illness is based on the latest available data for each illness, collected by the National Center for Health Statistics between 1968 and 1976. Each set of findings was linked to the International Classification of Diseases, adapted for the U.S. in 1965, under the Eighth Revision, to avoid duplication. Rates of all reported acute and chronic conditions, adjusted per 1000 persons per year, were added, with cancer (based on the prevalence of persons in 1971 with a history of cancer) which is not included in National Cen-

ter for Health Statistics survey, to give the total number of health problems, 3015 per 1000 persons per year. This was then assumed to equal 100 percent of annual illness.

Infections of childhood included only chickenpox, measles, mumps, pertussis, and rubella; venereal diseases consisted of syphilis and gonorrhea only; "other" infections included intestinal diarrhea, hepatitis, polio, and tetanus.

Mental problems and alcohol and drug dependency have not been included in National Center for Health Statistics survey data. The following estimates, derived from various sources, should be considered only suggestive of the problems. An estimated lifetime incidence of schizophrenia is 1 percent of the population (Ban). The incidence of schizophrenia is estimated between 0.5 and 2.5 per 1000 population, and the prevalence is at least 4 per thousand (Eisenstein).

The incidence for neuroses is estimated between 2 and 3 per 1000 population, and less than 1 per thousand for psychoses (Silverman). About 24 percent of adults aged 18 to 64 have emotional problems that are "substantial" or "severe." Of these about one-fourth are limited in their work activities, while somewhat fewer (1 in 7) need help with their daily living (Nagi).

There are an estimated 5.5 million alcoholics in the U.S. (5.2 percent of persons aged 15 and older, or 26 per 1000 among all age groups), plus an equal number of "problem drinkers" (Brody). However, other estimates are 295,000 alcohol- and drug-dependent persons aged 20 to 64, or about 1.5 per 1000 among all age groups (Krute).

Mental retardation exists at 3.2 per 1000 among persons aged 20 to 64 years; this rate would be higher for the total population if retarded children were included (Krute).

If these health problems (schizophrenia, neuroses, alcoholism, and drug dependency) were added to the prevalence of chronic illnesses, the total for chronic conditions would be 1091 per 1000 persons, bringing the overall frequency for acute and chronic illnesses to 3051 per 1000 persons in the U.S.

Sources

Living in Health-Damaging Circumstances

Bureau of the Census: *Population characteristics.* Current Population Reports, Series P-20, No. 307, U.S. Department of Commerce, Washington, D.C., April 1977, Tables 6, 10, 19, 22, 25, and 26.

Bureau of the Census: *Population characteristics.* Current Population Reports, Series P-20, No. 313, U.S. Department of Commerce, Washington, D.C., September 1977, Table 4.

Report to the Congress on Early Childhood and Family Development Programs to Improve the Quality of Life for Low-Income Families. Office of the Comptroller General, General Accounting Office, February 1979.

Social Security Administration: *Social Security Bulletin, Annual Statistical Supplement, 1975.* Publication No. (SSA) 77-11700, Table 10.

U.S. Departments of Labor and Health, Education and Welfare: *Employment and Training Report of the President.* Washington, D.C., 1977, Tables A-1 and A-4.

Craun, G. F., and McCabe, L. J.: *Review of the causes of waterborne disease outbreaks.* J. Am. Water Works Assoc. 65(1):74–84, 1973.

National Center for Health Statistics: *Statistics Needed for Determining the Effects of the Environment on Health.* Serial 4, No. 20, (HRA) 77-1457. Rockville, Md., 1977.

1970 Census of Housing. Vol. 50, Part 1, U.S. Summary. Bureau of the Census, Washington, D.C., 1972.

Health. United States, 1976–1977. Health Resources Administration, Washington, D.C., 1978.

Social Indicators of Equality for Minorities and Women. Report of the U.S. Civil Rights Commission Washington, D.C., August 1978.

Hunt, V.: *Occupational Health Problems of Pregnant Women. Report and Recommendations for the Office of the Secretary.* U.S. Department of Health, Education and Welfare, Washington, D.C., 1975.

Hemminki, E., and Starfield, B.: *Prevention of low-birth-weight and pre-term birth: literature review and suggestions for research policy.* Milbank Mem. Fund Q. 56(3):339–361, 1978.

Doing Health-Damaging Things

Bureau of the Census: *Statistical Abstract of the U.S., 1976.* ed. 97. U.S. Department of Commerce, Washington, D.C., 1976.

National Center for Health Statistics: *Exercise and participation in sports among persons 20 years of age and over: United States, 1975. Advancedata,* No. 19, March 15, 1978.

U.S. Departments of Labor and Health, Education and Welfare: *Employment and Training Report of the President.* Washington, D.C., 1977, Tables A-1 and A-4.

National Center for Health Statistics: *Dietary intake of persons 1–74 years, U.S. Advancedata,* No. 6, March 30, 1977.

National Center for Health Statistics: *Height and Weight of Children: Socioeconomic Status, U.S.* Rockville, Md. 1972.

National Center for Health Statistics: *Height and Weight of Children, U.S.A.* Rockville, Md., 1970.

National Center for Health Statistics: *Selected Body Measurements of Children 6–11 Years, U.S.* (1963–65 data) Rockville, Md., 1973.

Brown, E., and Knittle, J.: *Prevention of Disease Through Optimal Nutrition: A Symposium.* Mt. Sinai Medical Center, New York, 1976.

Health. United States, 1976–1977. Health Resources Administration, Washington, D.C., 1978.

National Center for Health Statistics: *Pregnant workers in U.S. Advancedata,* No. 11, September 15, 1977.

National Center for Health Statistics: *Height and weight of adults 18–74 yrs, U.S. Advancedata,* No. 3, November 19, 1976.

Metropolitan Life Insurance Company: *Statistical Bulletin.* Vol. 39–42, 1958–61.

Proceedings of the Conference of the Decline in Coronary Heart Disease Mortality. National Institutes of Health, Washington, D.C., May 1979.

Highlights of the Surgeon General's Report on Smoking and Health. Morbid. Mortal Weekly Rep. 28(1), January 12, 1979.

Third Special Report to the U.S. Congress on Alcohol and Health from the Secretary of Health, Education and Welfare. Washington, D.C., 1978.

Drugs, Society and Human Behavior. National Institute on Drug Abuse, Washington, D.C., 1972.

Morbid. Mortal. Weekly Rep., April 6, 1978.

Center for Disease Control: *Unintended teenage childbearing—U.S., 1974.* Morbid. Mortal. Weekly Rep. 27(16):131, 1978.

National Center for Health Statistics, December 30, 1976.

Responding in Physiologically Health-Damaging Ways

National Center for Health Statistics: *Hearing Levels of Children by Demographic and Socioeconomic Characteristics, U.S.* Rockville, Md., 1972.

National Center for Health Statistics: *Examination and Health History Findings Among Children and Youths, 6–17 Years, U.S.* (1963–65 data) Rockville, Md., 1973.

National Center for Health Statistics: *Binocular Visual Acuity of Children, U.S.* Rockville, Md., 1972.

National Center for Health Statistics: *Hearing and Related Medical Findings Among Children, U.S.* Rockville, Md., 1972.

National Center for Health Statistics: *A comparison of levels of serum cholesterol of adults 18–74 years, U.S., 1960–62 and 1971–74.* Advancedata, No. 5, February 22, 1977.

National Center for Health Statistics: *Blood pressure of persons 6–74 years, U.S.* Advancedata, No. 1, October 18, 1976.

Result: The Profile of Modern Illness

National Center for Health Statistics: *Acute Conditions, Incidence and Associated Disability, U.S., July 1974–June 1975.* Series 10, No. 114, DHEW Publication No. (HRA) 77-1541.

Center for Disease Control: *Reported morbidity and mortality in the United States, 1976.* Morbid. Mortal. Weekly Rep. 25(53), August 1977, Table 1(B).

National Center for Health Statistics: *Prevalence of Selected Chronic Respiratory Conditions, U.S., 1970.* Series 10, No. 84, DHEW Publication No. (HRA) 74-1511, September 1973, Tables A, 1,2,3,5,9, and 14.

National Center for Health Statistics: *Prevalence of Chronic Circulatory Conditions, U.S., 1972.* Series 10, No. 94, DHEW Publication No. (HRA) 75-1521, September 1974, Tables A,1,3,4,8,9,11, and 12.

National Center for Health Statistics: *Prevalence of Chronic Conditions of the Genitourinary, Nervous, Endocrine, Metabolic, and Blood and Blood-Forming Systems and of Other Selected Chronic Conditions, U.S., 1973.* Series 10, No. 109, DHEW Publication No. (HRA) 77-1536, March 1977, Tables A, 5, and 13.

Ban, T. A., and Lehman, H. E.: *Myths, theories and treatment of schizophrenia.* Dis. Nerv. Syst. 38:665–671, 1977.

Alcohol, Drug Abuse and Mental Health Administration: *Summary Proceedings of the Tripartite Conference on Prevention.* DHEW Publication No. (ADM) 77-484, 1977.

Brody, J. A.: *Medical surveillance program of the new epidemiological and special studies branch of NIAAA: an approach to an epidemiologic program on alcohol abuse and alcoholism.* Alcoholism 1(4):349–354, 1977.

National Center for Health Statistics: *Prevalence of Chronic Skin and Musculo-skeletal Conditions, U.S., 1969.* Series 10, No. 92, DHEW Publication No. (HRA) 75-1519, August 1974, Tables A,3,6,11, and 12.

National Center for Health Statistics: *Prevalence of Selected Chronic Digestive Conditions, U.S., July–December 1968.* Series 10, No. 83, DHEW Publication No. (HRA) 74-1510, September 1973, Tables A,2,3,8, and 10.

National Cancer Institute: *Third National Cancer Survey: Incidence Data.* Monograph No. 41, DHEW Publication No. (NIH) 75-787, March 1975, Table 6.

Center for Disease Control: *Abortion surveillance, U.S., 1975.* Morbid. Mortal. Weekly Rep. 26(30):1977.

National Center for Health Statistics: *Advance report, final natality statistics, 1975.* Monthly Vital Stat. Rep. 25(10):Suppl., 1976, Table 1.

Levin, D., et al.: *Cancer Rates and Risks, ed. 2.* National Institutes of Health, Washington, D.C., 1974, Table 2.

Slocumb, J., and Kunitz, S.: *Factors affecting maternal morbidity and mortality among American Indians.* Public Health Rep. 92:349–356, 1977.

Eisenberg, L.: *Primary prevention and early detection in mental illness.* Bull. N.Y. Acad. Med. 51(1):118–129, 1975.

Silverman, C.: *The epidemiology of depression: a review.* Am. J. Psychiatry 124:883–91, 1978.

Nagi, S.: *An epidemiology of disability among adults in the United States.* Milbank Mem. Fund Q., Fall 1976, pp. 439–465.

Krute, A., and Burdette, M. E.: *1972 Survey of Disabled and Nondisabled Adults: chronic disease, injury and work disability.* Soc. Sec. Bull. 41:3–17, 1978, Table 1.

TABLE 8. Selected Risk Factors and Estimates of Their Contribution to All Annual Deaths, Illness, and Associated Days of Disability*

Deaths	Percentage of All Deaths‡	Cigarette Smoking	Air Pollution	Dietary Excess (calories, fat, cholesterol)	Dietary Deficits (calories, iron, protein)
	Annual Deaths, Illness, and Associated Days of Disability		_Percentage Contribution of Each Selected Risk Factor to Major Causes of Death and Illness_		
Cardiovascular	51	30	1–5	30	†
Cancer	19	30		30	†
Accidents	5				
Diabetes	2			30	
Respiratory	4	30	5–10		†
All other	18				†

Illness and Disability	Illness‡	Disability Days‡	Cigarette Smoking	Air Pollution	Dietary Excess (calories, fat, cholesterol)	Dietary Deficits (calories, iron, protein)
	Percentage of all					
Acute:	65	53				
respiratory	35	23	15			†
injuries	11	13	10			
infections	7	5				†
digestive	3	3			40	†
maternity	0.6	1	30			55-60
low birthweight only						
other acute	8	8				†
Chronic:	35	47				
respiratory	9	12	60			†
circulatory	7	9	25		50	†
endocrine, nervous (including hearing and vision, diabetes)	5	7				
diabetes only	(0.7)	(0.9)			80	†
musculoskeletal	5	7				
digestive	4	5				
cancer	0.5	0.6	20	0.2–2	35	†
other chronic	5	7				†

345

TABLE 8. Continued

Deaths	Percentage Contribution of Each Selected Risk Factor to Major Causes of Death and Illness				
	Hazardous Jobs and Worksites	Alcoholic Drinking or Abuse	Non-medical Drugs	Hypertension	Percentage of Deaths Attributable to Combined Risk Factors
Cardiovascular	1–5	5–10	1–5	13	50
Cancer	5–10	5–10			50
Accidents	30	30	20		45
Diabetes				13	37
Respiratory	20	5–10			35
All other		8			8

Illness and Disability	Hazardous Jobs and Worksites	Alcoholic Drinking or Abuse	Non-medical Drugs	Hypertension	Percentage of Combined Risk Factors Contributing to Illness and Days of Disability	
Acute:						
respiratory					36	33
injuries	15	40	†		20	20
infections					50	50
digestive					15	15
maternity					40	40
low birth-weight only					—	60
other acute					15	15

346

Chronic:					
respiratory	10			65	65
circulatory	5–10			62	62
endocrine, nervous	+	17	(-)1	33	33
(including hearing and vision, diabetes)					
diabetes only				14	14
musculoskeletal	+	+	+	10	10
digestive		5–10			
cancer	15–25	1–5		50	
other chronic				15	15

*Percentages are rounded to the nearest whole, except those under 1 percent.
†Contributory to an unknown extent.
‡Yearly rates per 1000 persons are: 8.9 deaths; 3015 acute and chronic conditions; and 18,200 associated days of disability, exclusive of disability of persons in long-term institutions, who add an additional 11 percent of days to the total.

NOTES AND SOURCES FOR TABLE 8

Days of disability, as treated in Table 8, are based on the conditions surveyed by the National Center for Health Statistics (NCHS). These are reported as days of restricted activity (including days lost from work or school and days in bed) for each type of acute condition per 100 persons per year and per chronic condition per year. All rates were adjusted to 1000 persons. For chronic conditions, the number of restricted activity days for each condition was multiplied by the prevalence rate for each condition. These products were totaled, giving 9520 days per 1000 persons, assuming no person was restricted by more than one chronic condition on the same day. This was added to 9730 days of restricted activity from acute conditions per 1000 persons, giving 19,250 days per 1000 persons, as shown in Figure 1 (p. 11). These estimates are based on national NCHS surveys done between 1968 and 1975, the latest available for specific chronic conditions.

The percentage distribution of days of disability in Table 8 is based on summary survey data from NCHS *Current Estimates from the Health Interview Survey* for 1976, and includes the likelihood that some people suffer from *more than* one chronic illness on a *single* day of disability. The total days of restricted activity from both acute and chronic illness are thus reported as 18,200 per 1000 persons. Days of disability were then allocated for each illness according to the prevalence of those conditions in the U.S.

Estimates of contributions of individual risk factors are taken directly from studies listed in the secondary sources below, or computed from primary sources also listed, and were developed as follows:

The percentage of deaths from cardiovascular disease due to hypertension is estimated as 50 percent of stroke deaths, all deaths from hypertension and hypertensive heart disease, plus 6 percent of deaths from ischemic heart disease (Gori; Winkelstein).

The percentage of all deaths attributable to combined risk factors allows for conservative assumptions based on the sources listed below. For cardiovascular and cancer deaths it is assumed, based on national data, that half of all people who smoke are overweight *(Health, U.S.)*; for accidents, half of all people in hazardous jobs take alcoholic drinks or use drugs; 55 percent of diabetics who are hypertensive are also overweight, and 17 percent of those who die with cardiovascular disease have hypertension *(Report of the National Commission on Diabetes)*; alcoholism contributes to almost 90 percent of deaths from liver cirrhosis and to one-third of suicides, and half of homicides (included in "all other") *(Alcohol and Health)*.

For estimating combined risks as a percentage of illness, major assumptions were: for infections, other acute conditions, and other chronic conditions, 15 percent were due to undereating, assuming that at least that proportion of illness was among those 15 percent of Americans who are eligible for, but not receiving, food stamps, and therefore undernourished, i.e., about 30 to 65 million persons (Schrimper); for circulatory disease and cancer, it is assumed that one-third of overweight persons also smoke *(Health, U.S.)*; accidents from all causes produce 27 percent of chronic musculoskeletal conditions, 13 percent of deafness and hearing impairments, 10 percent of blindness and vision impairments in persons aged 20 to 64 years (Krute); 80 percent of new diabetics are overweight *(Report of the National Commission)*; alcohol abuse is responsible for liver cirrhosis, half of vehicular and industrial accidents, and 60 percent of all other accidents by adults *(Alcohol and Health)*.

Contributions of combined risks to disability days assume a constant ratio between the proportion of illness for a given type of condition and the proportion of days of disability experienced because of that type of condition.

Sources

Alcohol and Health. Third Special Report to the U.S. Congress. National Institute on Alcohol Abuse and Alcoholism, Washington, D.C., June 1978.

Biomedical Research and Research Training Amendments of 1978. Hearings before the Subcommittee on Health and the Environment of the House Committee on Interstate and Foreign Commerce, 95th Congress, Second Session (H.R. 10908, H.R. 10062, and H.R. 10190), March 1–3, 1978.

Boden, L. I.: *The economic impact of environmental disease on health care delivery.* J. Occup. Med. 18(7):467–472, 1976.

Dick, T., and Stone, M.: *Prevalence of three major risk factors in a random sample of men and women and in patients with ischemic heart disease.* Br. Heart J. 40:617–626, 1978.

Frame, P., and Carlson, S.: *A critical review of periodic health screening.* J. Fam. Practice 2(1,2,3,4), 1975.

Franz, M.: *Nutritional management in diabetes.* Minn. Med., January 1979, pp. 41–46.

Gori, G., and Richter, B.: *Macroeconomics of disease prevention in the United States.* Science 200:1124–1130, 1978.

Health. United States, 1976–1977. Health Resources Administration, Washington, D.C., 1978.

Hemminki, E., and Starfield, B.: *Prevention of low birthweight and preterm birth: literature review and suggestions for research policy.* Milbank Mem. Fund Q. 56(3):339–361, 1978.

Krute, A., and Burdette, M. E.: *1972 Survey of Disabled and Nondisabled Adults: chronic disease, injury and work disability.* Soc. Sec. Bull. 41:3–17, 1978, Table 1.

Louria, D.: *The epidemiology of drug abuse and drug abuse rehabilitation,* in Glatt, M. (ed.): *Drug Dependence.* MTI Press, Baltimore, 1977.

National Center for Health Statistics: *Acute Conditions, Incidence and Associated*

349

Disability, U.S., July 1974–June 1975. Series 10, No. 114, DHEW Publication No. (HRA) 77-1541, February 1977, Table 1.

National Center for Health Statistics: *Advance report, final mortality statistics, 1975*. Monthly Vital Stat. Rep. 25(11, Suppl.), February 11, 1977, Table 8.

National Center for Health Statistics: *Current Estimates from the Health Interview Survey, U.S., 1976*. Rockville, Md., November 1977.

National Center for Health Statistics: *Disability Components for an Index of Health*. Serial 2, No. 42. Rockville, Md., July 1971.

National Center for Health Statistics: *Advance report, final natality statistics, 1975*. Monthly Vital Stat. Rep. 25(10, Suppl.), December 30, 1976, Table 1.

National Center for Health Statistics: *Prevalence of Chronic Circulatory Conditions, U.S., 1972*. Series 10, No. 93. DHEW Publication No. (HRA) 75-1521, September 1974, Tables A, 1,3,4,8,9,11, and 12.

National Center for Health Statistics: *Prevalence of Chronic Conditions of the Genitourinary, Nervous, Endocrine, Metabolic, and Blood and Blood-Forming Systems and of Other Selected Chronic Conditions, U.S., 1973*. Series 10, No. 109. DHEW Publication No. (HRA) 77-1536, March 1977, Tables A, 5, and 13.

National Center for Health Statistics: *Prevalence of Chronic Skin and Musculoskeletal Conditions, U.S., 1969*. Series 10, No. 92. DHEW Publication No. (HRA) 75-1519, August 1974, Tables A,3,6,11, and 12.

National Center for Health Statistics: *Prevalence of Selected Chronic Digestive Conditions, U.S., July–December 1968*. Series 10, No. 83. DHEW Publication No. (HRA) 74-1510, September 1973, Tables A,2,3,8, and 10.

National Center for Health Statistics: *Prevalence of Selected Chronic Respiratory Conditions, U.S., 1970*. Series 10, No. 84. DHEW Publication No. (HRA) 74-1511, September 1973, Tables A, 1,2,3,5,9, and 14.

National Heart, Lung and Blood Institute: *Respiratory Diseases—Task Force Report on Prevention, Control, Education*. DHEW Publication No. (NIH) 77-1248, March 1977.

Nuttal, F.: *Obesity and diabetes mellitus*. Minn. Med., January 1979, pp. 19–21.

Report of the National Commission on Diabetes to the Congress. Vol. III. DHEW Publication No. (NIH) 76-1024, December 1975.

Schrimper, R.: *Food programs and the retail price of food*. Paper presented at the Fourth Food Policy Seminar, U.S. Department of Agriculture, Washington, D.C., February 14, 1978.

Winkelstein, W.: *Contemporary perspectives on prevention*. Bull. N.Y. Acad. Med. 51(1):27–38, 1975.

INDEX

nonrenewable energy controls in, 171
summary of, 182
job stability and, 124
oil price controls in, 123
renewable resource emphasis measures in, 167-168
speed limit legislation in, 124
tax incentives in, 123
England, employment policy in, 173
Environmental policy
automobile safety provisions of, 122
compliance with, 119-120
components of, 118
economic effects of, 120, 126
health effects of
direct, 119-120
indirect, 120-121
summary of, 123
housing provisions of, 121-122
hypothetical design of. See Health policy, design of, socioenvironmental.
reshaping of, rationale for, 166
social implications of, 118-119

FARM policy. See also Food policy.
aim of, principal, 147
beef production and, 151
commodity distributions and, 150-151
commodity priorities in, health implications of, 154
concentration-consolidation tendencies and, 148
consumption patterns shaped by
health implications of, 150, 156
historical perspective of, 155-156
prices in relation to, 152-153
energy considerations in, 149
feed-grain pricing in, 151-152
health implications of, summary of, 159-160
hypothetical design for. See Health policy, design of, socioenvironmental.
international implications of, 149
land set-aside measures in, 154
macroeconomic effects of, 143-144
milk production and, 151-152
postwar history of, 147
price determination in, 155

price supports in
energy costs of, 153-154
inflationary impact of, 154
of dairy products, 151-152
of feed grains, 151
of livestock, 151
of peanuts, 153
of soybeans, 153
of tobacco, 158
reform of
crop substitutes in, 177
crop usage shifts in, 177-178
energy conservation measures in, 176-177
Scandinavain approach to, 180
socioenvironmental approach to. See Health policy, design of, socioenvironmental.
storage subsidies in, 154
unintended effects of, 148
"Fast food," health implications of, 156
Federal Trade Commission (FTC), advertising regulation by, 288, 289
"Flight-fight" response, 47-48
Food and Drug Administration (FDA)
recent reform enactments of, 289
regulations of
cost factors in, 146-147
risk factors in, 146
Food policy. See also Farm policy.
Consumer Price Index and, 150
European approach to, 179-180
health implications of, summary of, 159-160
hypothetical design for. See Health policy, design of, socioenvironmental.
income-specific effects of, 143, 144
provisions of
food stamp program in. See Food stamp program.
safety regulations in, 146-147
school feeding programs in, 144-145
supplemental food program in. See WIC (Food Supplement Program for Women, Infants, and Children).
reform of
health implications of, 178-179
nutrient balance shifts in, 178
product usage shifts in, 177-178

353

health education in, 79-80
integration of, 83-84
national organizational coordination in, 84
personal health services in, 82-83
present shortcomings of, 207
social support methods in, 80-81
comprehensive reform of
consumer networks in, proposals for, 292-294
deferral of, consequences of, 279-281
economic ramifications of, 202-203
environmental considerations in, 203-204
financing plans for, 198-200
general implications of, 207-208
goal clarification in, 201-202
independent information sources in, 299-300
planning legislation in. *See* National Health Planning and Resources Development Act of 1974.
public interest coalitions in, 294
potential of, 301
reorganization plans for, 200-201
socioenvironmental approach to, *See* Health policy, design of, socioenvironmental.
strategic problem in, 297
tactical responses to, 298-301
cost-effectiveness of
assessment of, simplified method for, 245-248
demographic considerations in, 244-245
dimensions of, 244-245
guidelines for determining, 243-244
iatrogenic factors in, 244
patient compliance in, 245
design of
choice in
economic instability and, 73-74
limits on, 73
mechanism of, 76
personal income and, 74-75
consumer participation in
local-national networks for, 292-294
prospects for, 303-305
public support for, 294-295

option-setting in, 76-77
schematic representation of, 78
rationale for, 69-70
research studies in, 84
socioenvironmental
components of, 253-254
foreign trade considerations in, 259-260
health impact estimation in, 254-256
personal care approach compared with, 260-263
program costs in, 256-257
rationale for, 252-253
social costs in, 257-258
summary of, 260
transitional costs in, 258-259
strategic principle in, 76
ecological framework for, 77, 79
environmental-energy-economic interface with, rationale for, 117-118
environmental impact of, 3-5. *See also* Environmental policy.
expenditures in
containment of, 192
distribution of, 190
Federal allocations of, 191-192
hospital-related, 190-191
financing in
expanded governmental approach to, 198-200
methods of, 192-193
minimal governmental approach to, 198-199
general functions of, 3
goals of
controversy over, 189
identification of, 70-73
national, 189
strategic, 298
inflationary tendencies of
economic ramifications of, 195
reform of
certification of need in, 196
professional standards review organizations (PSROs) in, 196-197
sources of, 192-194
personnel specialization and, 193-194
planning machinery for. *See* National Health Planning and Resources

355

Health systems agencies (HSAs)
  authority of, 290
    restrictions on, 290-291
  Congressional limitations on, 290-291
  consumer participation in, 292-293
  funding of, 290
  goals of, 289
  hospital care and, 196
Hospital care
  certification of need and, 196
  cost-effectiveness of, 191
  energy management programs and, 197
  environmental risks in, 203-204
  expenditures for, 190-191
  financing of, 192-193
  health systems agencies and, 196
  inflationary nature of, 194-195
    economic ramifications of, 195
    inequities caused by, 196
  personnel specialization and, 193-194
  professional standards review organizations and, 196-197

ILLNESS
  cumulative risks of, 19-20
  incremental
    biophysical factors in, 20
    personal behavior patterns in, 22-24
    socioeconomic factors in, 21-22
    underlying conditions in, 24-25
  life-threatening, physiological processes in, 56, 58
  mutual-causal factors in
    relationships among, 25-26
    schematic illustration of, 27
    socioeconomic implications of, 26, 28
  origins of
    behavioral
      nutrition and, 16-17
      personal habits and, 17-18
    dose-related, 19
    environmental, 14-16
    holistic approach to, 60-61
    relationships between, 13-14
    summary of, 18-19
  primary vs. secondary prevention of, comparative evaluation of, 217-219
  quantification of
    annual incidence in, 9-10

income variation in, 44, 45
  overall profile in, 13
  policy implications of, 13
  severity in, 10, 12-13
  social definition of, 3
Income, health options in relation to, 74-75
Income maintenance
  European approaches to, 172-173
  socioeconomic assessment of, 175-176
  U.S. reform proposals for, 174-175
Income tax policy
  current effects of, 128-129
  health implications of, 129-130
  health insurance deductions in, 194
  job creation in relation to, 130
  progressive consumption-based alternative to, 168
  regressive approach to, 129-130
  subsidy approach to, 129
Inflation
  containment of, ad hoc measures for, 196-197
  health impact of, 21
  hospital care and, 194-196
  personal health services and, 192-195
Interagency Liaison Regulatory Group, health-related functions of, 288
Interpersonal-physiological interface, societal implications of, 58-60

LEAD paint control, recent developments in, 122
Lobbying
  legislation in response to, 282-283
  political action committees in, 283
  public interest advocacy in response to, 295-296
    adverse effects of, 297
  trade associations in, 282

MASS media, policy influence of. See Advertising.
Medicare-Medicaid
  initiation of, 192
  reimbursement arrangements under, 193
  screening/treatment effectiveness of, 245
  spending increases for, 195
    containment of, 196

357

358